The 1972 Detroit Tigers

The 1972 Detroit Tigers

Billy Martin and the Half-Game Champs

TODD MASTERS

McFarland & Company, Inc., Publishers
Jefferson, North Carolina, and London

Library of Congress Cataloguing-in-Publication Data

Masters, Todd.
The 1972 Detroit Tigers : Billy Martin and the half-game champs / Todd Masters.
p. cm.
Includes bibliographical references and index.

ISBN 978-0-7864-4820-3
softcover : 50# alkaline paper ♾

1. Detroit Tigers (Baseball team)—History. 2. World Series (Baseball) (1968) 3. Martin, Billy, 1928–
4. Baseball managers—United States—Biography. I. Title.
GV875.D6M38 2010
796.357'640977434—dc22 2010001573

British Library cataloguing data are available

On the cover: Manager Billy Martin restrained by umpires John Rice (left) and Larry Barnett (UPI)

Manufactured in the United States of America

McFarland & Company, Inc., Publishers
Box 611, Jefferson, North Carolina 28640
www.mcfarlandpub.com

Table of Contents

Acknowledgments

I would like to thank the many people who contributed to this effort along the way. Many thanks to the fine writers of the period for the *Detroit Free Press* without whom this work would not be possible. The writing of the late Joe Falls, Jim Hawkins, Curt Sylvester, Charlie Vincent and others was as informative and entertaining in doing the research for this book as it was the day it was delivered to our door steps. The same can be said for the writers of *The Sporting News*, and *Street & Smith*'s *Baseball Annual*, publications that were invaluable in reconstructing that period in baseball history. Thanks also to the friendly and helpful staff at the Michigan State University Library, where I spent an untold number of hours combing through microfilm.

Special thanks go to Ernie Harwell, Jim Northrup, Larry Osterman, and Dick Tracewski, all of whom were very gracious with their time and in sharing insights and behind the scenes views of that Tiger team. Thanks to Rick Thompson, director of media relations for the Detroit Tigers Baseball Club, for his help as well. Much gratitude goes out to Mathew Lutts at the Associated Press and to Jenny Ambrose at the National Baseball Hall of Fame for helping me put together the great photos from the 1972 season. Thanks to Doug Feldmann for all of his great works that served as a model and inspiration, and for taking me under his wing and helping me along the way.

My greatest thanks go out to all of my friends and family who listened to my idea, helped me develop it further, and then encouraged me along the way. Special appreciation goes to my wife, Diane, and sons, Nicholas and Peyton, who were always there for me.

Preface

When Brandon Inge struck out against St. Louis Cardinal relief pitcher Adam Wainwright to end the 2006 World Series, a rare chapter was concluded in the history of the Detroit Tigers. That unexpected playoff run resulted in the first pennant for the Tigers in 22 years and represented their first post-season appearance of any kind in 19 years. Unfortunately for Detroit fans, dry streaks have been all too common in the 109-year history of the franchise through 2009. Despite being a charter member of the American League and one of the more tradition-steeped and storied clubs in major league baseball, the Tigers have reached post-season play only twelve times in more than a century of play. Seven of those appearances came during the first half of the twentieth century, with the Ty Cobb–led run of pennants from 1907 to 1909, followed nearly three decades later by back-to-back World Series appearances in 1934–35 by the Gehringer, Greenberg, Goslin gang, and then with a pennant and world championship sandwiched around World War II in 1940 and 1945.

Seven pennants over the first fifty years of American League play would have to be viewed as a moderately successful period, especially when compared with the other seven teams that comprised the league during that time. It was nowhere near the total achieved by the New York Yankees, who had won 17 pennants by 1950; otherwise, Detroit trailed only the Philadelphia Athletics franchise (nine), and had won the same number as the Boston Red Sox.

Over the next 60-plus years, however, post-season baseball became a rare event in the Motor City. Nearly a quarter of a century would pass between 1945 and the Tigers' next appearance, when they reached the Fall Classic in 1968 and won the World Series in dramatic fashion. Sixteen years after that, they reached the summit again with a dominant 1984 regular season and World Series win. Those two treasured seasons marked the only two pennants (and world championships) the team would win between the end of World War II and the close of the twentieth century. Perhaps because the championship seasons have been so rare, and their spacing was such that entire generations of Tiger fans identified with them as their own, most of Detroit's other seasons, good and bad, have been overshadowed.

Lost between those venerated '68 and '84 squads is the often-overlooked 1972 Detroit Tigers team. Unlike those other two more well-acclaimed seasons from Tiger lore, the 1972 club did not jump out in front of the American League standings in dominant fashion and then coast home in a blaze of glory. Instead, their year was a struggle from start to finish. It was a journey down the uncertain road of a team inflicted with an aging roster, thin pitching staff, injuries, batting slumps, and a league-wide despise of their outspoken and combative manager. Yet despite the obstacles and hardships, the team fought and scrapped its way to a level of success enjoyed by few teams in Detroit Tiger history. Fueled by a team made up of familiar heroes and the excitement of one of the tightest races in baseball history, more than two million fans poured through the turnstiles at Tiger Stadium before the final out was recorded that season.

I was 11 years old in the summer of 1972. Too young to fully appreciate the glory of the near-legendary Tiger team from four years earlier, the '72 season instead became my first encounter as a devoted fan living through the daily passion involved with a tight pennant race. In a time that doesn't seem that long ago, yet already differs so much from today, the trials and tribulations of a long season were experienced in a very different way. There were no cable broadcasts that allowed you to watch every game. ESPN and its nightly highlights didn't exist. The proliferation of sports-talk radio was still a decade away. Online stories, blogging, or chatting with baseball junkies on Internet message boards would have seemed more believable as part of George Jetson's world. Instead, following the Detroit baseball team from a small town in mid–Michigan consisted of listening to Ernie Harwell and Ray Lane on a small transistor radio tucked beside the pillow, or reading game accounts and looking at box scores in the daily newspaper spread out on the kitchen table or family room floor. If you were lucky, there might be a grainy black-and-white photo in the paper that provided a visual image to something you heard via the static-filled airwaves the previous evening. A real treat was provided on those 35 evenings or Saturday afternoons, when George Kell and Larry Osterman beamed a game into your living room on the Tigers' television network. The family trip each summer to see a game in Tiger Stadium was simply the highlight of the year.

I've never forgotten the excitement or the crushing disappointment I felt while following baseball that summer and fall. Those emotions came together on October 12, 1972, when barely a month into the fifth grade, I was bowled over. My classroom teacher pulled me and another boy from class and took us to the teachers' lounge where we sat and watched the fifth and deciding game of the American League playoffs. That sense of happy wonderment, sitting and watching baseball in a locale foreign to even the most curious of students, was replaced later by a gnawing despair as my beloved Tigers fell behind and struggled to prolong their season. That innocent adulation I felt about the team that day was replaced in later years by a more mature understanding of what had occurred. When an aging team was broken up soon thereafter, and the pains of the rebuilding project that became Detroit's baseball club of the middle 1970s set in, I realized I had experienced the end of a special era in the franchise's history. As the years passed by and that season receded further into the annals of dusty old archives, I often thought that 1972 had been a very special, but overlooked summer among Tiger fans and a tale worth revisiting again. This book is the story of the 1972 Detroit Tigers.

As I began my research and looked back at that season, it also became apparent to me that 1972 had been a watershed year in the game's history. It was caught between the tranquil sport that had remained largely unchanged for decades, thanks to the controlling interest of a group of tight-fisted businessmen, and the sport it would evolve into by the end of the 1970s, with loud personalities, exploding scoreboards, million-dollar contracts, and increased media attention; both good and bad. That season, tensions came to a head that would eventually change the game drastically. Transitions were also taking place on the field, where many of the old standouts from the 1960s were still around, but their impact on the game was diminishing. Players like Aparicio, Killebrew, Powell, Robinson, Howard, and McLain in the American League, as well as Aaron, Mays, Williams, Clemente, Gibson, and Torre in the National League, were being overtaken in stature by names like Jackson, Hunter, Blue, Murcer, Fisk, Ryan, Mayberry, Carew, Carlton, Bench, and others. The way the game was being played was also under attack that summer. Changes would come immediately after the season that would forever alter the pace and tactics that had been in place for nearly three-quarters of a century, but not before that one final season had been played in 1972 under the old format.

One of the most prevalent figures in the story is Tiger manager Billy Martin. His impact on the team that season is undeniable, just as was the case throughout the other eight stops he made in his managerial career. Much has been documented elsewhere about the flaws, mostly off-field and often involving character, which were the cause of many of Martin's short-lived regimes as a manager. While many of those same traits undoubtedly existed during his stay in Detroit, and some close to the team during that period didn't always have a glowing regard for the man, the goal of this work was neither to glorify nor vilify Martin, but instead to show the combative nature and personality he brought to the ball club.

I will attempt to delve into the game as it existed then, both on and off the field, and the forces that were at work that season. The primary focus, however, will be the day-to-day happenings within the 1972 season for the Detroit Tigers as well as their competition in the American League. I've detailed the journey, starting from before spring training and continuing through post-season play, in an effort to capture the feel of a season-long divisional race over the marathon that is otherwise known as a major league baseball season. It is written from the viewpoint of a Tiger follower at the time, intertwined with the local and global events of that summer. But mostly it is the story of a team for which nothing came easy, and each and every run and victory was a battle.

Introduction: A Summer to Remember

It was a summer to remember. The turbulent 1960s, with their social and political strife, were over. The page had been turned to a new decade, one that promised greater tranquility, fewer demonstrations of civil unrest, both collectively and individually, and one free of the political chaos that had dominated the latter half of the previous decade. By 1972 it was time for the "silent majority" to once again reassert itself as the voice of reason for the country. Certainly, the 1970s were by no means turning into an idyllic period. As the year 1972 commenced, the war in Vietnam was still raging, but removal of U.S. ground troops was underway and the government had extended overtures for peace talks to the North Vietnamese, giving many Americans hope that the long, largely unwanted war was drawing to a conclusion. A February trip by President Nixon to Red China was historic in its significance and viewed as a potential small step towards warming relations in the Cold War. Two more trips were planned for an Apollo program that was making trips to the moon seem routine. It was an election year, the first since the explosive campaign in 1968 that had been filled with violent protest and even assassination. However, with an incumbent president enjoying a 60 percent approval rating, few expected a repeat of the hysterics from four years earlier.[1]

As the weather warmed heading into the summer of 1972, it appeared that Father Time reached back once more to the decade just passed, clinging to the anarchy that so dominated that period. The peace talks with the North Vietnamese that sounded so promising just weeks earlier broke off in early spring and instead brought about the U.S. increasing its bombing to unprecedented levels, triggering renewed energy to anti-war protests across America.[2] In May the country was horrified once again when a prominent Southern governor was struck down by a would-be assassin's bullet while campaigning for president on the Democratic primary trail. A month later a strange story surfaced about a break-in at the Democratic National Committee's headquarters in Washington, D.C., and throughout the summer and early fall, revelations began to emerge that left much of the country feeling uneasy about the role their chief executive had in the act and its subsequent cover-up. The presidential campaign was marred by fractions in the Democratic Party over the ticket's top man and questions over his vice presidential nominee. There was civil unrest over the rights of African Americans and women. And if those events over the summer hadn't dislodged any sense of calm the country might have enjoyed, the news coming from Munich, Germany, that first week of September certainly left the country aghast. Palestinian terrorists killed eleven Israeli athletes who had been competing at the Summer Olympic Games, with much of the drama and horror playing out in living rooms via ABC television.

In the city of Detroit people reacted to these events in the same way as most others across the country. The world was a much bigger place at that time, or at least it seemed like it. Outside of those who had family members in the military serving in Southeast Asia, the happenings halfway around the world were of little consequence to the daily routines of most people. Almost any news outside of the immediate vicinity was regulated to tiny snippets through limited mediums. There were no 24-hour news networks, bombarding each household with the "latest" on that day's story, and continual analysis by the pundits. Most people received their news from newspapers, usually of the local variety, and the content in those was oftentimes much more dated than today's newspapers. Television news came via one of the three major networks, in half-hour segments each evening via one of the revered, stately anchors of that time, with limited reporting from the actual newsworthy location. Radio had similar limitations, and the proliferation of talk radio had not yet settled in. The events of the world, and even the national stage, seemed much further away.

People in Detroit and across the state of Michigan did look forward to a baseball season that at least allowed for cautious optimism. The Detroit Tigers were still the most popular sporting diversion in town, and despite three years having passed since that magical summer in 1968 that saw their heroes run away with an American League pennant before capturing a dramatic come-from-behind, seven-game triumph in the World Series over the St. Louis Cardinals, a love affair still existed between the fans and the team. It was a bond of familiarity, built over nearly a decade of good times and bad. The Tigers were a veteran team in 1972. The core was made up of players in their 30s who had been in a Detroit uniform their entire careers. Al Kaline had signed fresh out of high school in 1953 and was entering his 20th season with the Tigers. Norm Cash had played briefly with the Chicago White Sox, before coming over to Detroit in 1960, and was entering his 13th season with the team. Mickey Lolich, Bill Freehan, Dick McAuliffe, Jim Northrup, Willie Horton, Mickey Stanley, and Gates Brown had all signed their initial professional contracts with the Tigers, and had been playing in the major leagues together since at least 1964. For those born after World War II, these players *were* the Detroit Tigers, and they defined an era.

In the 109-year history of the Detroit franchise, there have been perhaps four collections of players that crystallized an era of baseball. The first occurred shortly after the formation of the American League with the Ty Cobb–led consecutive pennant winners of 1907–09. Those teams featured the greatest player of his era in Cobb, who was augmented by the underrated and fellow Hall of Fame member Sam Crawford, and pitchers George Mullin and Wild Bill Donovan. In the mid–1930s, Mickey Cochrane, Charlie Gehringer, Hank Greenberg, Billy Rogell, and Marv Owen made up one of baseball's greatest infields ever. Together with outfielders Goose Goslin, Pete Fox, and JoJo White, as well as pitchers Tommie Bridges and Schoolboy Rowe, Detroit enjoyed consecutive A.L. pennants in 1934–35, and even topped the one million mark in home attendance in 1935, a remarkable accomplishment at the depths of the Great Depression. Nearly 50 years later, another talented collection of players captured the imagination of Tiger fans. Jack Morris, Lance Parrish, Alan Trammell, Lou Whitaker, Kirk Gibson, and Chet Lemon were the foundation for baseball's winningest team of the 1980s, with the 1984 world championship serving as the culmination for that wildly popular group.

However, as great as each of those teams were and as popular as they might have been with the fans of their particular era, long-time observers of Detroit baseball generally side with the teams made up of the likes of Kaline, Cash, Lolich, Freehan, Horton, etc., as the most popular of all time. Those teams defined Tiger baseball for more than a decade, and within that span some of the most endearing personalities, controversial figures, and memorable moments in the franchise's history took place. They formulated during the closing stages of the Mickey Mantle–led portion of the New York Yankee dynasty. They survived the tragic death of two managers at a fragile time in their development and learned to win through painful lessons gained during a 1967 campaign that saw them let a pennant slip through their fingers. People in Detroit looked upon them as a saving grace in 1968 when they galvanized a riot-torn city and provided a common cause for citizens of all races to root for the pennant-bound team. The championship season in 1968 saw them draw a home attendance of more than two million fans, an almost unheard of total at that time and one never previously reached. That level of popularity was sustained over the next three years as the Tigers topped attendance figures of 1.5 million each season (totals surpassed only six times in the franchise's previous 68 seasons).[3]

By the spring of 1972, however, the shine had been removed from the championship trophy they had gained 3½ earlier. The Baltimore Orioles had dominated them since the inception of divisional play, and the feeling among baseball insiders was that Detroit's core was getting long in the tooth and maybe a bit complacent. The Tigers' window of opportunity for another championship run was closing quickly. In 1971 a new manager had been hired in the person of Billy Martin, and his fiery manner proved wildly popular with the fans in Detroit and breathed new life into the ball club. Such new additions as Eddie Brinkman, Aurelio Rodriguez, and Joe Coleman had fit in with the old favorites and proved likeable themselves. Now heading into a new season, the feeling within the organization was the Tigers were ready again to compete with the seemingly invincible Baltimore club.

This is the story of that 1972 season for the Detroit Tigers. It would be perhaps the final chance to restore the glory they had attained four years earlier, yet they would have to overcome age, injury, batting slumps, lack of pitching depth, and a tight four-team divisional race in order to do it. There would be close contests, bitter disputes, on-field fights, and an unexpected players strike along the way. It was an exciting summer to be a baseball fan in Detroit and across the state of Michigan, with the season being played against the backdrop of one of the most violent, eventful, and history-making years of the twentieth century.

I

Ascending to the Mountaintop ... and Tumbling Back Down

It began with a trade. A remarkable decade that would see the Detroit Tigers franchise survive tragedy, civil unrest, heartbreak, and controversy, all while steadily building towards arguably the most memorable and beloved team in its long history, began with a trade. It was a trade of epic proportions; the type of high-profile transaction that is commonly debated among fans, but rarely executed. On April 17, 1960, the Tigers and Cleveland Indians hooked up in a straight-up deal of veteran outfielders. Detroit traded the reigning batting champion of the American League, Harvey Kuenn, coming off of a .353 batting average in 1959, for outfielder Rocky Colavito, the muscular A.L. home run champion from that same season. It was a trade unlike any seen previously or since, and invited the type of scrutiny and opinion that any follower of the game was bound to reveal.

While the trade did not immediately improve the fortunes of either team on the field, it did bring attention back to a Detroit baseball team that was looking to resurrect itself in the American League. The 1950s had been a lost decade for baseball in the Motor City. After capturing a pair of pennants in the mid–1930s, another in 1940, and a world championship in 1945, the Tigers had fallen on hard times. There had been a series of near-misses in the ultra-competitive A.L. immediately after World War II, with the last coming in 1950 when the team won 95 games but finished three games back of the pennant-winning New York Yankees. After that, the bottom fell out for a proud franchise and charter member of the junior circuit. Detroit finished as a second-division club in eight of the next ten seasons, winning more games than it lost only three times during that stretch.

The bright spot during that otherwise dark decade was the play of a young outfielder named Al Kaline. Kaline had been picked up off the sandlots of Baltimore in 1953, signing for the princely sum of $35,000 with legendary scout Ed Katalinas.[1] Although lacking in strength as a gangly 18-year-old, Kaline possessed tremendous athletic ability and uncommon baseball skills. He bypassed the minor leagues entirely and made his debut in Detroit that summer, just days after his high school graduation. The next summer he played 135 games in the Tiger outfield, trying to hold his own while competing against men much older than he was. In 1955, however, he exploded, becoming the youngest player in history to win a batting championship, hitting .340 at age 20, while bashing 27 home runs. Throughout the rest of the decade he established himself as one of the great young talents in all of baseball. He became the cornerstone of the franchise, never hitting lower than .295, while displaying power, driving in runs, and playing the outfield as well as anybody in the game.

As the 1960s dawned, the Detroit team appeared to be on the upswing. Ownership of the franchise had been garnered by John E. Fetzer, who by 1961 had bought out shares from ten other partners to become the sole proprietor of the Tigers. Fetzer was a radio and television mogul who had been part of the consortium that had purchased the franchise in 1956. While in his twenties, he had built and operated a radio station at a small missionary college in southern Michigan, which he eventually purchased and moved to Kalamazoo, Michigan. After World War II, Fetzer continued to build a radio empire, featuring stations all across the Midwest, before delving also into television just as that medium was taking off. He was a life-long baseball fan and jumped at the opportunity to be involved in the game as an owner when the family of Walter Briggs put the team up for sale as part of the settlement of the late owner's estate. Among Fetzer's first actions as the sole owner of the Detroit team was to rename the ballpark Tiger Stadium, replacing the family surname from the previous ownership, which had been used for the team's home for more than twenty years.

On the playing field, better days were on the way, as well. Trades for Colavito and a promising left-handed-hitting first baseman named Norman Cash provided additional muscle around Kaline in the Tiger lineup. A talented group of young arms led by Jim Bunning, Frank Lary, and Paul Foytack was joined by veteran Cleveland starter Don Mossi to form a quality rotation of starting pitchers. Although they fell back slightly record-wise in 1960, the team was accumulating talent and looked to move up in the standings the next season, as the American League expanded from eight to ten teams.

In 1961 the Tigers assembled arguably the most powerful lineup in its history with Kaline (.324 average, 19 home runs, 82 RBIs), Cash (.361-41-132), and Colavito (.290-45-140) creating a formidable trio in the middle of the batting order. The team led the major leagues in runs scored that season, plating more runs than even the famous New York Yankees, which were led by Roger Maris' record-setting 61 home runs and Mickey Mantle's 54. The season rejuvenated interest in Detroit, where fans hadn't enjoyed a finish any higher than fourth place in the American League since 1950. Approximately 1.6 million fans passed through the turnstiles at Briggs Stadium, cheering on the Tigers as they battled the Yankees deep into September for the league lead. At season's end, the Tigers had won 101 games, but still finished eight games behind the powerful New York squad. The anomaly of winning 100+ games without winning a pennant (100 wins in a season has only been achieved five times in Detroit's 109-year history) only added to the sting of coming up short to what was generally considered at the time as the second-greatest Yankee team ever.

The on-field renaissance didn't last, however. In 1962 the Tigers finished fourth with 85 wins, eleven games behind the pennant-winning Yankees. In 1963 they dropped even further, to sixth place in the ten-team league, with a 79–83 record. Attendance dropped with the team's record as only a little more than 821,000 made up the home attendance in 1963, barely half the 1961 total. Many of the players who contributed to the great '61 season couldn't sustain the level of production they had enjoyed that summer. Cash, Colavito, Lary, Mossi, Foytack, Jake Wood, Dick Brown, and Steve Boros were among the players whose performance fell off considerably over the next two seasons.

Away from the glare of the major league spotlight, however, the Detroit organization was putting together the pieces for a team that could compete over the long term and be in the thick of the American League race on a yearly basis. Fetzer had turned the running of the organization over to "baseball men," the primary one being Jim Campbell, who had been named the general manager in 1962. Campbell had been with the organization since 1949, working his way up through various jobs in the minor league system before finding a home on the business side of the franchise in Detroit. He was from Ohio, and had played baseball at Ohio State University. Campbell shared many of the same conservative midwestern values as his boss and understood what it took to turn a profit while operating the team.[2] He believed in building a club through the farm system and player development rather than via flashy trades. By the time he had assumed the general manager's role, the seeds had been planted for an eventual harvest of players who would not only make up the Tiger teams for more than a decade, but also become icons for the franchise for years to come.

A left-handed, 18-year-old pitcher from Portland, Oregon, named Michael Stephen (Mickey) Lolich had signed with the Detroit organization in 1959 and was in the process of working his way up through the Tigers' minor league system through stops in Knoxville, Denver, and Portland. While the big league team was running neck and neck with New York for most of that summer of 1961, 18-year-old Mitchell Jack Stanley, 19-year-old William Ashley Freehan, and 21-year-old James Thomas Northrup shared their inaugural seasons in professional baseball with the Duluth-Superior Dukes, a low-level minors (Class C) team in the Northern League. A year later, a powerful young 19-year-old from Detroit named Willie Horton made his professional entrance in that same remote upper-midwestern town. They climbed the minor league ladder, joining along the way the likes of Joe Sparma, John Hiller, Don Wert, Ray Oyler, Ike Brown, Tom Matchick, Tom Timmerman, and a brash young pitcher by the name of Dennis Dale McLain, who the Tigers had claimed in the first-year waiver draft from the White Sox organization in the spring of 1963. Many of them would meet up on the 1964 and 1965 Triple-A Syracuse teams, clubs that were loaded with future major league talent that would eventually make its way to Detroit.[3]

As the parent team struggled to middle-of-the-pack finishes from 1962 to 1965, some of the young talent that had been stocked in the Tigers system was already being infused into the Detroit lineup. Bill Freehan fast-tracked his way to the big league team in 1963 and quickly assumed the role of full-time catcher after spending barely a year in the minor leagues. Lolich joined him that same season as a promising, hard-throwing left-handed pitcher. A small, feisty infielder by the name of Dick McAuliffe was already on the Detroit club, having made his debut in 1960, and quickly assumed the starting job at shortstop. He had started with the Tiger organization in 1957, signing as a 17-year-old, and had served as a rookie utility infielder with the '61 team. By 1965 they had been joined in Detroit by Northrup, Stanley, Horton, Wert, McLain, Sparma, Gates Brown, and John Hiller, each of whom was being slated for a major role on the big league team.

The young Tigers made steady improvement as the players gained experience at the big league level. They ascended to a third-place finish in 1966, their best showing in five years, while winning 88 games. However, the season proved to be tragic and tumultuous season for the young team. Manager Charlie Dressen suffered a serious heart attack a month into the season. The former skipper of the great Brooklyn Dodger teams of the early 1950s had taken over the Detroit job in 1963 and was considered adept at developing young players. The heart attack was his second in a little more than a year, and he died in a Detroit hospital several weeks later of complications. Dressen's position was filled by one of his coaches, the former long-time Tiger back-up catcher from the post–World War II period, Bob Swift. Tragically, Swift fell ill in July with ailments that were later diagnosed as cancer and was replaced by another coach, Frank Skaff, who guided the team through the rest of the season. Swift died shortly after the conclusion of the season of lung cancer.

The cruel blow of having two leaders stuck down in a season made the next managerial hire more crucial than usual.[4] Not only was the shock of losing two managers to unexpected deaths an element that the Tiger brass needed to factor into the fragile needs of their young team, but from owner John Fetzer and general manager Jim Campbell on down, there was a sentiment that the team was ready to start winning. A void had been created in the American League since the Yankees had won their last pennant in 1964. Mantle, Maris, Yogi Berra, Whitey Ford, Elston Howard, Bill Skowron, Bobby Richardson and others who had once been part of New York's star-studded lineup were either no longer the players they once had been or were gone from New York entirely. With the likes of Kansas City and Washington no longer supplying the Yankees with gifts through lopsided trades, and the implementation of a common amateur draft throughout all of the major league teams, the talent pool had dried up considerably in New York and on their half-century stranglehold on World Series appearances. A pair of relative newcomers jumped into the void, with Minnesota winning the pennant in 1965 and Baltimore following in 1966.

The feeling within the Detroit organization was that the Tigers were ready to join the party—if not to start dominating the league. Their talent was the equal of any and better than most. Bill Freehan was the best young catcher in baseball. Norm Cash, although never able duplicate his great 1961 season, remained a formidable force in the middle of the Detroit lineup. McAuliffe had shifted from shortstop to second base, where he became one of the better players in the game at that position. Don Wert was a steady hitter and fine defensive third baseman. The outfield of Al Kaline, Willie Horton, Jim Northrup, Mickey Stanley, and Gates Brown was easily the deepest in the league, and provided a mixture of hitting prowess with defensive excellence. Kaline remained the heart and soul of the franchise. An amazingly steady player, he hit for average and power, ran the bases well, and manned right field as well as anybody in baseball not named Roberto Clemente. Horton had blossomed into a feared power hitter, capable of hot streaks that frightened opposing pitchers and managers. Northrup and Stanley were talented all-around performers who were entering their prime. The pitching staff with Lolich, McLain, and Sparma, along with another solid starter that had been picked up from Boston in Earl Wilson, had developed to the point that the rotation was as young and talented as any in the game.

The choice for manager turned out to be a curious one.[5] Mayo Smith, a 52-year-old veteran with an ordinary track record in previous managerial stints nearly a decade earlier in the National League with Philadelphia and

Cincinnati, was the choice as the Tigers prepared for what looked to be a wide-open 1967 American League race. When the defending champion Orioles got off to a poor start and battled injuries, effectively taking them out of the race, Detroit's new manager found himself part of a four-team fight for the pennant with Minnesota, Chicago, and a surprising Boston Red Sox team that had finished in ninth place the previous season. The Tigers appeared to be the strongest of the contenders, holding advantages in talent and depth over their competitors. However, as the summer wound down, consistency proved difficult for Detroit to harness. Smith's team developed a penchant for choking away too many winnable games, particularly in the late innings when leads too often slipped away and turned into losses.

A charged social and political climate in Detroit during that summer of 1967 provided the backdrop to the Tigers participation in the closest pennant race in league history. The burned out shells of buildings in downtown Detroit, leftover from one of the worst wave of rioting in American history that summer, marred a race that went into its final week with four teams still in contention. The feeling among local followers was that the Tigers had done everything in their power to give the pennant away.[6] Spotty starting pitching, an inconsistent bullpen, inopportune batting slumps — particularly the one by Cash — and fluke injuries down the stretch to such key players as Kaline and McLain had exhausted the patience of even the most optimistic Tiger fans.

Yet, the prize was still there for the taking as the team played a pair of season-ending doubleheaders with the fifth-place California Angels at Tiger Stadium. Winning three of four games over the two days would guarantee at least a tie for the pennant, and possibly even allow the Tigers to win the title outright. However, while the upstart Red Sox were sweeping a pair of games from what had been the first-place Minnesota Twins, the Tigers could manage only a pair of splits in the weekend doubleheaders. Included was a devastating 8–6 loss in the second game on Saturday, courtesy of a blown 6–2 eighth-inning lead when it appeared the team was on the verge of a crucial doubleheader sweep on the first day. Detroit won the first game on Sunday and then jumped out to an early 3–1 lead in game two to retain hope. McLain couldn't protect the lead, however, and lasted only into the third inning before giving way to a slew of Tiger relievers who had no better results as the Angels pounded a desperate Detroit team, 8–5. The pennant went to Boston. Detroit finished a game back.

The utter disappointment from that '67 season forged a fierce determination in the team in 1968. After losing the season opener at home to the Red Sox, the Tigers reeled off nine straight wins, took over first place for good by the second week of May, and eventually ran away with the American League pennant. They won 103 games, the most in club history. The civil strife within the city of Detroit had cooled down from the previous year, and despite a summer filled with some of the most tumultuous events in American history, the city managed to subsist in relative calm. Within that atmosphere of an uneasy serenity, Detroit and the entire state of Michigan got behind their baseball team like no other summer in franchise history. Attendance at Tiger Stadium topped more than two million fans for the first time, and Tiger fans forged a love affair with their heroes that would last a lifetime.

Horton, Northrup, Freehan, Cash, McAuliffe, and Kaline paced a Tiger attack that led the major leagues with 185 homers, a figure that dwarfed the next-highest team total by more than fifty. Horton hit .285 and smashed 36 homers, which was the second-highest individual total in all of baseball. Northrup hit 21 homers, including four grand slams, during the regular season and added another in the World Series while leading the team in RBIs with 90. Freehan hit 25 home runs, drove in 84, and won his fourth straight Gold Glove award as the best defensive catcher in the American League. Freehan also finished second in the voting for the league's MVP, and was considered by many to be the unofficial team leader. After a slow start, Cash came on strong and finished with 25 homers while holding down first base. McAuliffe was the catalyst in the lineup as the leadoff man, pacing the league with 95 runs scored. Kaline, despite being injured for large portions of the year, still managed to contribute with a .287 average and 10 homeruns. When the Tigers weren't mauling the opposition with their firepower, they often found ways to rally in the late innings and steal wins in close games. Their trademark became the come-from-behind victory, fueled by rallies in the seventh inning or later (40 times), with 30 of those coming in their last turn at bat.[7]

The late rallies and close wins were in stark contrast to 1967 when Detroit was too often on the losing end of such games. The bullpen had been largely retooled with an emphasis on putting young hard throwers at Mayo Smith's disposal in the late innings. Mickey Lolich rebounded from a sub-par year and went 17–9 mostly as a starter. Earl Wilson and Joe Sparma were solid contributors in the rotation, as were John Hiller and Pat Dobson, who provided quality starts when they had the opportunity. But the ace of the staff, and the undisputed star of that year in Detroit and across the entire major leagues, was Denny McLain.

McLain exploded into baseball superstardom in 1968, putting together one of the great statistical seasons in major league history. He won 31 games, becoming the major's first 30-game winner in 37 years, lost only six, and put up a sparkling 1.96 ERA while raking in both the Cy Young and MVP awards. The on-field accomplishments provided the platform for McLain's equally meteoric rise to celebrity status. He had always been brash and cocky, never lacking in bravado, but his larger-than-life personality emerged as his great season developed. McLain played the Hammond organ in nightclubs as part of a combo, and had even recorded a record. He said that he considered himself a musician who happened to play baseball, rather than the other way around. He could be a loose cannon with the press, capable of saying almost anything in any situation, which made him a magnet for the writers. As his 1968 season rolled along and the wins kept building, his celebrity transcended the sports pages. He made television appearances with the likes of Ed Sullivan, Glen Campbell, and the Smothers Brothers, all superstars within that medium at the time, and was the subject of a feature story in *Life Magazine*, among others. In just a few short months he became the biggest name in the game.

The World Series that fall was a seven-game classic. In the last matchup of true pennant winners, ahead of the introduction of intra-league playoffs, Detroit rallied from a three games-to-one deficit to defeat the defending world champion St. Louis Cardinals. Many of the heroics in that World Series came from less likely sources, at least based on regular-season performances. Mickey Stanley moved from center field to shortstop for the Series in an uncharacteristic and shocking gamble by Mayo Smith. The move was made not only to lend an additional bat to the Tiger lineup (shortstop had been an Achilles heel offensively all season), it also opened an outfield spot for Kaline, who because of injuries and the great years put together by Horton and Northrup had been rotated in and out of the lineup during most of the campaign. The gamble paid off as Stanley played his new position competently, making only two harmless errors while playing under intense scrutiny. Kaline had a superb series, batting .379, which was second on the team to Cash, and tied Northrup with eight runs batted in over the seven games. McLain struggled and lost two games when matched against Cardinal ace Bob Gibson, but did manage to win a do-or-die sixth game in St. Louis' Busch Stadium as part of the Tigers' improbable Series comeback. The biggest Tiger hero of the Series, however, was Mickey Lolich, who won complete-game victories in Games 2 and 5 (both coming off of Detroit losses), and then showed remarkable composure in beating Gibson in a classic Game 7 showdown. The big hit of the Series was provided by Northrup, whose two-out seventh-inning triple into deep left-center field scored Cash and Horton, breaking up what had been a scoreless game to that point.

The 4–1 Game 7 win over the most intimidating pitcher in baseball in Gibson triggered a celebration in Detroit equaled only by the end of World War II a generation before. Thousands poured into the streets in downtown Detroit at the conclusion of the game, which was being televised back to Michigan and across the nation that afternoon. Detroit's Metro Airport was overrun by mobs of fans wanting to greet the team's flight, forcing the landing to be redirected to the more inconspicuous Willow Run Airport, a half-hour drive away. With the Series win and the magical season in the books, the names of McLain, Lolich, Kaline, Freehan, Horton, Northrup, Stanley, McAuliffe and others were forever embedded in the hearts of Detroit Tiger fans everywhere. The franchise had reached the pinnacle of the baseball world, and with a talented core of seasoned veterans, many of whom were in or nearing their prime, the future remained extremely bright as well.

Any attempt to defend their championship, however, was quickly doused. The Tigers had no sooner received their championship rings on Opening Day in 1969 before they were fighting an uphill battle. The Baltimore Orioles quickly jumped out to a lead in the newly formed American League Eastern Division and never let up. Major league baseball had expanded that winter, placing new franchises in Kansas City and Seattle in the A.L., and Montreal and San Diego in the N.L. With the new additions, the two leagues were subdivided into East and West divisions. Detroit found itself in the newly founded American League East with the '67 pennant-winning Red Sox and the '66 winning Orioles, along with the Yankees, Cleveland Indians, and Washington Senators. In the inaugural season of divisional play, Baltimore led Detroit by six games by the end of May, increased that to 13½ games by the end of June, and stretched it even further to fifteen full games by July 31.[8]

The Orioles were in the early stages of one of the greatest three-year runs in baseball history. Dave McNally, Mike Cuellar, and Jim Palmer headed one of the strongest pitching rotations in modern annals. Frank Robinson, Boog Powell, Brooks Robinson, Don Buford, Paul Blair, and Dave Johnson headed a dangerous and balanced attack. Earl Weaver, their small in stature but large in fiery temperament manager, kept umpires on their toes and his team playing air-tight, mistake-free baseball. In his first full season as the team's manager, Baltimore was winning games at a .700 clip well into August.

Detroit played respectably for much of the season, but couldn't maintain the torrid pace being set ahead of them. Individually, McLain went 24–9 in a successful encore to his Superman deeds from a year earlier while still making many of his outings look ridiculously easy. He won the Cy Young award for the second straight season (tied with Baltimore's Cuellar), started flying his own plane, and generally alienated himself from his teammates as his celebrity status and star treatment continued to grow. Lolich went 19–11 and finished second in the league in strikeouts. Kaline, Northrup, and Horton had excellent years at the plate again. However, the team lacked the fervor that had existed a summer earlier. The late rallies, the big hits at key moments, the great defensive plays came with less regularity in 1969. Mayo Smith's low-key demeanor was ill suited to light a fire under a team that been to the mountaintop the year before but now found itself being lapped by the front-running Orioles. Baltimore would finish with a whopping 109–53 record, nineteen games ahead of the 90–72 Tigers.

Things got even worse in 1970. Just as spring training camps were preparing to open for pitchers and catchers that February, baseball commissioner Bowie Kuhn suspended McLain indefinitely for his involvement in bookmaking. The announcement came just days before a *Sports Illustrated* story was published detailing McLain's involvement in a bookmaking operation, as well as his placing of bets on college basketball games via the clubhouse pay phone in Lakeland.[9] Around the same time, McLain's attorneys were filing for bankruptcy protection on his behalf. The surfacing of these stories gave outsiders a glimpse of the problems besetting a baseball giant whose star was quickly tarnishing.

Without its ace pitcher, Detroit managed to stay in the race through the first half of the season, running second most of the way behind the front-running Orioles, with the Red Sox, Yankees, and Indians nipping behind them. While the everyday lineup remained mostly the same as in previous years (with the exception of Cesar Gutierrez taking over as the starting shortstop), the pitching staff had undergone a largely necessitated re-tooling. Sparma and Wilson had fallen out of favor as regulars in the rotation and been replaced by new faces like Mike Kilkenny, journeyman Joe Niekro, and a 22-year-old left-hander named Les Cain, who had been predicted for stardom.

Kuhn lifted McLain's suspension on July 1, and the winner of 55 games over the previous two seasons made his much-anticipated season debut that same evening. A huge crowd of 53,863 turned out that night at Tiger Stadium to welcome Denny back while also hoping his return would provide the impetus for a rally over the second half of the season so the Tigers could overtake those hated Orioles. Instead, McLain's presence seemed to serve as a distraction to the rest of the team. He failed to win any of his first five starts, and it quickly became apparent the layoff had taken a toll. The impact of pitching 51 complete games and 661 innings over the previous two seasons was also being felt, with treatment for chronic shoulder pain part of his regular routine. By late August the team was fading badly, and McLain struggled to a 3–5 win-loss record with a ballooned 4.65 ERA in fourteen starts. On August 28 he inexplicably dumped buckets of water over two Detroit newspaper writers in the Tiger clubhouse. General manager Jim Campbell immediately suspended McLain for his actions. Before that suspension had ended, he was suspended again by Commissioner Kuhn. This suspension was for carrying a handgun on a Detroit road trip earlier that summer. Denny McLain's season was finished.

The ball club that had been 57–45, in second place and only 6½ games behind Baltimore on August 1 finished 22–38 over the last sixty games. The Tigers ended up in fourth place in the American League East, 29½ games behind the first-place Orioles. "We quit like dogs," summarized Northrup at the time of the dreadful finish.[10] He had actually been one of the few Tigers who could at least claim a decent year statistically, with numbers of .262-24-80. Horton hit .305 in an injury-plagued season, but otherwise there were few highlights. Freehan's season-long back problems deteriorated to the point that he would need off-season surgery. However, the biggest drop-off had come with a pitching staff that had accumulated a team ERA of 4.09, one of the worst in baseball. Mickey Lolich, less than two years removed from his World Series hero status, led the American League with nineteen losses and had an ERA above the league average of 3.72. Kilkenny, Niekro, and Cain were unable to make up the slack from Detroit's erstwhile aces, combining to go 32–26 with an ERA over 4.00. The bullpen, outside of second-year man Tom Timmerman's 27 saves, was a weakness once again.

The glow was gone from the '68 world championship and the team was booed vigorously at Tiger Stadium as the '70 season spiraled downward. The fall guy would be manager Mayo Smith, who was released after the season's last game. General manager Jim Campbell wasn't ready to tear his ball club apart, but wanted new leadership in the dugout. He had met late in the summer with Billy Martin, the exiled former manager of the Minnesota Twins. Talks progressed as the season wound down, and shortly after the last game of the 1970 season had been played, Campbell acted on what had been the worst-kept secret in town and hired Martin as his next manager on October 2.

Billy Martin (right) argues with umpire John Rice during the 1972 season. The fiery Martin re-energized a Detroit club that had gone stale in its last seasons under Mayo Smith (AP/Wide World Photos).

In Alfred Manuel Martin, the Tigers were acquiring a 42-year-old keg of dynamite as their next field general. He had been out of baseball in 1970 after managing the Minnesota Twins to a division title in 1969, but was a hot commodity while considering other offers at the time he settled on Detroit. He had a bold, brash style and wasn't afraid to step on toes if he needed to. "I believe in being aggressive," he said at his introductory press conference, a comment that applied both on and off the field. "I believe in forcing the opposition into making mistakes."[11] Despite the on-field success in his single season as the Twins' manager, the Minnesota brass had decided that Martin was not worth the baggage their combustible field general brought with him. That made him a risky pick as well.

Martin had been born into the broken marriage of a Portuguese musician father and an Italian mother. The name "Billy" had come from "Bellizz," an Italian diminutive meaning "most beautiful" which was the nickname he had been given by a relative when he was young.[12] His mother raised him with little money in a tough, multi-ethnic neighborhood in West Berkeley, California. His small physical stature was offset by a rough-and-tumble nature. His teenage years were filled with fisticuffs and minor scrapes with the law. He was an intelligent but unmotivated student, staying in school during the war years of the 1940s, primarily so he could remain eligible to play sports. The Oakland Oaks of the Pacific Coast League saw enough in the scrawny teenager to sign Martin out of high school in 1946. Playing for the local professional team, Martin soon became a favorite of the Oaks' manager, Casey Stengel, who influenced the New York Yankees to sign him and bring him to New York soon after Stengel became the manager of the franchise in 1949.

Working around a pair of short stints of military duty, Martin became a semi-regular second baseman for the New York Yankees during their dynastic run of pennants in the early and mid–1950s. He had a feisty and combative playing style, was involved in a number of on-field and off-field fights, and gained a reputation for making plays in big moments. He made a clutch catch in Game 7 of the 1952 World Series against the Brooklyn Dodgers and batted .500 and was named MVP of the 1953 Series, also against Brooklyn. Off the field he ran with Mickey Mantle and Whitey Ford. Their often alcohol-fueled antics were not viewed favorably by the Yankee management, which saw Martin as a bad influence on their star players.[13] A well-publicized barroom brawl at the famous Copacabana in early 1957 involving several members of the Yankee team turned out to be Martin's undoing in New York. He was traded to bottom-feeder Kansas City shortly thereafter, a move that broke his baseball heart. He spent the rest of his career bouncing from team to team, battling injuries along with everything and everyone else, including one season (1958) in Detroit, where he played with Al Kaline.

When his playing career ended, he went into scouting but was soon back in uniform as the third-base coach for the Minnesota Twins. In 1968 he was asked to take over as manager of the Twins' floundering Triple-A team in Denver of the Pacific Coast League and led them to an impressive 65–50 record. With only that one partial season as manager of a minor league club under his belt, he was named to the same position for the big league club in 1969 and took the reins of a talented but underachieving Twins team playing in the newly formed American League West. It was against his nature to sit back and wait for the long ball off the bats of Twins sluggers like Harmon Killebrew, Bob Allison, and Tony Oliva.[14] Instead, Martin forged the Minnesota team into his own image: aggressive on the bases and well versed in the subtleties of base stealing, the hit and run, and the suicide squeeze. Players like Cesar Tovar, Rod Carew, and Leo Cardenas thrived under his tutelage, and the team became daring and unpredictable. Carew, his young second baseman and future Hall of Famer, stole home an astonishing seven times that year, including twice in the same game against Detroit and Mickey Lolich, exemplifying the style of play Martin preferred. They led the American League in runs scored and ran away with the division title, winning 97 games a year after they finished below .500 and in seventh place in the old ten-team format.

Unfortunately, Martin's off-field demeanor was often as aggressive as his on-field personality. He was very demanding in his ways and compromise did not come easy with him. He feuded constantly with Twins owner Calvin Griffith and assorted underlings in the Minnesota front office over matters ranging from personnel to the handling of his post-game clubhouse. His most volatile off-field incident that season occurred when he beat up one of his pitchers, Dave Boswell, outside of the Lindell AC, an infamous bar in downtown Detroit and frequent hangout for ballplayers. Boswell had purportedly made a threatening remark towards one of Martin's coaches before threatening Martin himself.[15] The challenge was more than the combative young manager could resist, and he pummeled Boswell outside the bar. The incident was consistent with Martin's reputation for being involved in altercations throughout his playing and coaching career. Most of the inci-

Detroit executive vice president and general manager Jim Campbell masterminded the McLain trade with Washington, which turned out to be one of the most lopsided deals in major league history. In the trade the Tigers netted key ingredients for their 1972 pennant run (National Baseball Hall of Fame Library, Cooperstown, New York).

dents involved alcohol, and the locale was usually some watering hole dotting the lonely trail of a journeyman ballplayer's life. The Boswell incident, along with an earlier confrontation that resulted in punches between Martin and the Twins' traveling secretary, proved to be more than the conservative Minnesota organization wanted to put up with. He was released shortly after their playoff series with Baltimore (a three-game sweep by the Orioles) concluded.

While the Detroit organization was still as conservative as any in baseball, general manager Jim Campbell and owner John Fetzer decided to roll the dice with the hiring of Martin. His personality was in stark contrast to that of the more placid Mayo Smith, a point that was not lost when the decision was made on the new manager. "This has been a tough club to handle," team vice president Rick Ferrell was quoted as saying at the introductory news conference.[16] The hope was that Martin could light a fire beneath an underachieving team that still had a nucleus of talent that approached any in the game. In his 1980 autobiography, *Number 1*, Martin described the challenge presented to him when he was hired as Tiger manager:

> Jim Campbell had told me that there were cliques on the club and that I had to be tough on them. He told me to do what I thought I had to do to turn the club around and he'd back me. The team had finished fourth in '70, and being a team of older veterans they were set in their ways. They had won a pennant in 1968, and they were still thinking they were world champions, and they refused to admit to themselves that '68 had come and gone. There was no speed on the club, and they didn't want to bunt or hit-and-run. All they wanted to do was go up there and swing the bat, the way they had played under Mayo Smith when he managed them to the pennant in '68.[17]

The comment about Detroit being a team of older veterans was not unique. New blood hadn't been added to the regular lineup from the Tiger farm system since Northrup and Stanley had come up from Syracuse in 1966. Upon his dismissal, the departing Mayo Smith quipped, "This club has got a little age on it," undoubtedly referring to the fact that the team's elder statesmen, Kaline and Cash, were 36 years old, McAuliffe, Northrup, Lolich, and Brown were in their early thirties, while a slew of other key players were nearing the milestone age of 30.[18] In an age when strength and conditioning programs and year-around training was neither sophisticated nor commonly followed, many players were considered on the decline by their early thirties. A pair of superstar-caliber players of the era, such as Mickey Mantle and Eddie Mathews, had recently retired at what would now be considered the relatively premature age of 36.

Besides the age that was creeping upwards with the team, another common perception was that the Tigers had been a poor defensive club since their championship season. Defensive shortcomings had betrayed an inconsistent pitching staff and could often be attributed as a direct cause in tight games that turned into losses. Shortstop and third base had turned into black holes for Detroit, and a constant revolving door seemed to accompany each of those positions in recent seasons. Steady glovemen like Ray Oyler, Dick Tracewski, and Don Wert hadn't hit well enough to maintain a regular spot in the lineup, while those that swung a more dangerous bat couldn't provide the defensive stability required at those positions, either.

Less than a week after the daring hiring of their new manager, the Tigers made an even bolder move in an attempt to remedy their apparent shortcomings. With the nation's sports media gathered on the eve of the World Series opener in Cincinnati, baseball commissioner Bowie Kuhn called a 3:00 P.M. press conference for Friday, October 9, 1970. Rumors had Kuhn announcing the re-instatement of McLain from the suspension that had ended his season.[19] Instead, the Tigers rocked the baseball world with a trade that overshadowed the start of the Fall Classic and dwarfed even the Kuenn-for-Colavito deal a decade earlier. With Jim Campbell standing next to Kuhn and Washington Senators owner Bob Short, the announcement was made that Detroit had traded their troubled pitching ace, McLain, to the Senators with infielder Don Wert for infielders Aurelio Rodriguez and Ed Brinkman and pitcher Joe Coleman as part of what would ultimately be an eight-player deal. The trade of one of baseball's biggest stars had been finalized during a charter flight between Minneapolis and Cincinnati, as baseball executives left the site of the A.L. playoffs and headed to the Queen City for the start of baseball's biggest event.

Denny McLain at a press conference announcing his trade to the Washington Senators in October 1970. By the end of that season, the Tigers had tired of the former 30-game winner's antics and dumped him on the lowly Senators, reaping a mint in return (AP/Wide World Photos).

For Washington the trade was a desperate attempt to breathe life into a franchise that was on baseball life support. Short was looking for the drawing card that would guarantee a regular box-office attraction every four days. "I had to get a player who will put people in the stadium and McLain is the most colorful ballplayer in the game today. He will put people in my ball park." Short's manager, the all-time great Ted Williams, who had been lured into managing by Short in 1969 as his first attempt at creating a box-office draw, recognized immediately the heist that his team had been on the short end of. "The price was too high," he grumbled to reporters when asked about the trade.[20] Williams' disgust was evident in his failure to appear as part of the trade announcement.

For Detroit the move was viewed as a well-calculated gamble. McLain had worn out his welcome in Detroit. Management and teammates alike had tired of his antics and the constant drama that surrounded him. Suspicions were growing that the troubles he encountered on and off the field in 1970 were probably only the beginning, and that his best pitching years were likely behind him.

The key from Detroit's perspective was the acquisition of Rodriguez. The Tigers viewed him as a future star at third base, a spectacular fielder, only 22 years old, who also was developing as a productive hitter. Williams had tried to keep him out of the trade talks, but Campbell and Martin insisted on his inclusion. Brinkman was the veteran shortstop the team had been seeking for several years. The 29-year-old Brinkman was a quality defensive shortstop, possessing one of the finest throwing arms in the game at his position. He had been a hands-on project under Williams with the bat, and had made significant progress at the plate over the past two seasons. In Rodriguez and Brinkman, Detroit had addressed with one daring stroke two trouble areas dating to their championship season.

The bonus in the deal was Coleman, a quality, hard throwing right-handed starting pitcher. Only 23 years old, he was already a veteran of four full seasons in the majors and had won 40 games with a perennial second-division club. Tiger hitters had maintained a high regard for Coleman since he had defeated them three different times in 1968. He was envisioned as the new number two starter, behind Lolich, who would be inheriting the top spot with McLain's departure.

The restructured team with the new manager felt its way along during the first half of 1971. Baltimore, as had become customary since the inception of divisional play, jumped out in front in the pennant race. Detroit, meanwhile, struggled to keep its head above .500 for the first two-thirds of the season. Among the highlights of the season's first half were the initial encounters with McLain. On May 14 in RFK Stadium in Washington, D.C., McLain beat his former teammates in a complete-game 3–2 victory. The tables were turned a little over a week later in Tiger Stadium, however, as 53,337 fans crammed in to watch McLain return to Detroit and face his former pitching rival, Lolich. The two had feuded at times over their careers together, with the spats often spilling over into the press. The pitching matchup had an irresistible quality to it. This time Cash and Kaline reached McLain for two-run homers and Lolich twirled a four-hit, 10-strikeout blanking of the Senators in a 5–0 Tiger win.

As the campaign played out into late summer, it appeared little was changing from recent seasons. On July 25, Detroit was 51–49 and ten games back of the Orioles. However, three weeks later they had climbed to ten games over .500 and had shaved 1½ games off that lead. The team continued to trail Baltimore by a similar margin before a hot steak by Detroit in early September, culminating in five straight wins over the Orioles at mid-month, reduced the lead to 6½ games. Faint hopes surfaced for Detroit fans who were eager to break up the Baltimore stranglehold on the division. However, Baltimore cut short all such talk as they ran off an eleven-game winning steak to end the season while the Tigers inevitably cooled off. The Orioles ended up at 101–57, twelve games ahead of Detroit.

Despite the second-place finish, the season was deemed successful. The Tigers finished with a 91–71 record, their best since the 1968 championship season, and bettered the marks of all but three (Baltimore, Oakland, Pittsburgh) of the 24 major league clubs that year. The pitching was much improved, with the team ERA decreasing by nearly half a run per game. Lolich especially seemed to thrive under the new manager. Entrusted with the top spot in the rotation, the portly left-hander had a Cy Young Award–caliber season, going 25–14 while pitching an astonishing 376 innings. Cash and Freehan enjoyed big comeback seasons at the plate, and the offense clicked such that the team finished second in the league in runs scored. The blockbuster trade with Washington had turned out to be a heist of Louisiana Purchase proportions. Rodriguez and Brinkman solidified the left side of the Detroit infield and sealed leaks where routine outs had been hemorrhaging away in previous years. Coleman, despite being knocked cold by a line drive off of the bat of the Cardinals' Ted Simmons in his final spring training appearance, proved to be a consistent starter in the Detroit rotation and was rewarded with his 20th victory in the next-to-last game.

The biggest development of 1971, however, came in the fire that returned to the team. The tenacity of Billy Martin rubbed off on his new team, and by the campaign's second half they were indoctrinated in his style of play. The late-season surge fueled a sense of optimism for the next season. By taking ten of the eighteen meetings between the two clubs, including the five straight in September, the Tigers took a cue from their confrontational manager and set their sights on dethroning the big, bad Baltimore Orioles in 1972.

"The Orioles are a great ballclub," said Martin at season's end. "They're better than I thought they were. But we'll give them a battle next year if we get the pitcher we need. We can beat Baltimore, and Baltimore knows it."[21]

Even the usually reserved Kaline chimed in about Detroit's chances against their recent nemesis. "The way we finished up will give the Orioles something to think about in the winter months."[22]

For Kaline and a nucleus of players that had been together for the better part of a decade in Detroit, the sand was filling quickly at the bottom of their career hourglass. The 1968 season was more than three years removed and remained the lone gold star on a team resume that seemed capable of holding so much more. Sweeping changes had been made in the McLain deal, and the team had improved greatly yet still finished well back of Baltimore. Some observers were starting to suggest the team needed to make even bigger changes and that a youth movement needed to begin. That would have to wait, however. The nucleus was again in place to make a run at another World Series appearance. Coming off a solid season and with a renewed determination, the Tigers organization would look forward to a chance to add another championship to that resume before their dwindling window of opportunity closed forever.

II

Dark Clouds Gather Over Sunny Skies

Optimism reigned as the Tigers gathered for spring training in Lakeland, Florida, the third week of February in 1972. Billy Martin had been rewarded for the solid finish the previous season with a raise and an additional year tacked onto the original two-year deal he had signed in 1970. Armed with his new contract and a better feel for what his club was capable of heading into his second season at the helm, Martin continued his verbal charges against his primary competitor for the upcoming season.

"We can beat Baltimore, and Baltimore knows it," he said at a dinner appearance in Detroit shortly before heading down to Lakeland.[1] Martin's confidence had been buoyed by a curious off-season move made by the Orioles, when they traded their star right fielder, Frank Robinson, to the Los Angeles Dodgers for four young prospects. Robinson was the same age as Al Kaline, and like the Tiger star remained a formidable presence in the middle of the Oriole lineup. Admittedly, Robinson had advanced to an age where he needed the occasional day off, but he remained with Boston's Carl Yastrzemski the best clutch hitter in the league. He also gave the Orioles a measure of competitiveness, a hard edge, as their unquestioned leader, which would surely be missed.

Despite having undergone knee surgery in January, Martin was in good spirits. He went to Florida early to recuperate, do some fishing, and think about what had been accomplished during his first season in Detroit, and what was possible in 1972. "What last year did for these guys is make them realize that they can beat Baltimore," he said in February. "They know they can beat 'em now. It's just a question of putting everything together. The players feel and I feel if we start healthy—without any injuries—we can beat them."[2] Martin's only frustration stemmed from the Tigers' failure to pick up an additional starting pitcher ... or two.

Baltimore's controversial trade of Frank Robinson stripped the dynastic Orioles of their spiritual leader and took away a big bat from their lineup. Many, including Tiger manager Billy Martin, felt the departure of Robinson from the Baltimore lineup opened the door for Detroit to win the A.L. East in 1972 (National Baseball Hall of Fame Library, Cooperstown, New York).

Martin was already in the process of establishing a reputation that would remain with him throughout the remainder of his managerial career. When it came to handling a pitching staff, he had a propensity for riding his big horses. In Mickey Lolich, Martin found the horse he would ride the hardest. Lolich's 1971 performance was nothing short of amazing — every bit the equal to or perhaps even greater than Denny McLain's 31–6 season. Lolich rebounded from a 14–19 record in 1970 to a 25–14 mark in his first season under Martin. He also had an unheard of total of 376 innings pitched, the most in baseball since Grover Cleveland Alexander had logged 383 in the Dead Ball era season of 1917. Lolich thrived under the increased workload given to him by Martin and pitching coach Art Fowler. He led the American League with a franchise-record 308 strikeouts and a career-low ERA of 2.92. More importantly, he proved to be the stopper that Martin insisted he could be. Fifteen times that season he won a start that followed a Tiger loss. Teamed with Joe

Coleman (20–9, 3.15 ERA), Detroit could boast a 1–2 punch at the top of its pitching rotation that was as good as any in baseball.

The problem was that there was very little established behind them. Les Cain, still only 24 years old, continued to be a promising left-hander. His short career, however, had been marked by a series of shoulder problems, which limited his starts and made him hard to rely on. Behind Cain, neither Joe Niekro nor Mike Kilkenny had become reliable starters for a team envisioning itself as a pennant contender. There had been talk at the baseball winter meetings in December that Detroit was in trade negotiations for Ken Holtzman of the Chicago Cubs or Sam McDowell of the Cleveland Indians, but both players ended up going elsewhere. Jim Northrup and Willie Horton were the two names most frequently rumored as being offered in trade, although some close to the Detroit situation questioned how hard Jim Campbell pushed in such negotiations.

"I felt we could get a top starter if we could trade Northrup," reflected Martin years later. "But Campbell for many years had been the farm director for the Tigers, and these were all the kids who had won the pennant for the team in '68, and though some of them might have been going downhill, he wouldn't listen to me because they were his babies, and he didn't feel he could get rid of them."[3]

With nothing significant having happened on the trade front, the biggest Tiger news of the offseason came at the annual winter press party, where owner John Fetzer announced he had signed a forty-year lease on a 52,000-seat domed stadium that was scheduled to be built on the Detroit riverfront and ready for opening in 1975.[4] The $85 million multi-purpose facility was to be designed with all of the modern amenities of the day, greatly departing from the franchise's tradition-rich home since 1900, venerable Tiger Stadium. The mid–January press party was typically a social occasion where media members who covered the team on a regular basis were treated by the team at the Sheraton Cadillac Hotel. The social aspect was upstaged on that night, however, when Fetzer began the evening with the announcement, sending the media members scurrying to report the story back through their news services.

As the team gathered in Lakeland under warm, sunny skies, they took note of the new $180,000 lighting system that had been installed at Joker Marchant Stadium. The light fixtures, standing beyond the outfield fences and extending high into the sky more than 400 feet from home plate at Detroit's spring training stadium, provided a challenging target for slugger Willie Horton as he settled in for his rounds of early batting practice. Kaline, feeling as good as he had in years, banged one over the left field wall on his first swing of the spring.

Martin added his own twists to the usual array of mundane spring training drills. One such routine saw his pitchers wearing shin guards while coaches hit line drives at them with fungo bats, in an attempt to sharpen their fielding skills. But mostly he recognized he had a contending team made up of veteran players, with few jobs openings on the line. He believed in working his players hard in the spring, but without over-exerting them for excessive hours under the Florida sun.[5] By better organizing practices and drills and keeping players constantly moving, he believed with coaches Joe Schultz, Dick Tracewski, Art Fowler, and Charlie Silvera that they could avoid unnecessary wear and tear on the players ahead of the grueling 162-game regular season. Outside of an early ankle injury to Norm Cash, which hampered the Tiger first baseman for a couple of weeks, and a nine-day contract holdout by Lolich, the early days of camp passed smoothly as the Grapefruit League games began. There was idle talk of a potential strike that was being threatened by the players association over pension fund issues with the owners, but few, if any, believed anything would come of it.

Lolich's holdout presented a dilemma to the Detroit management, which had lobbied for the candidacy of their ace over Oakland's Vida Blue for the Cy Young Award the previous season. Blue had been the media darling of 1971 and appeared to be a legitimate threat for 30 wins prior to cooling off in the second half of the season. Blue's 24–8 record, 1.92 ERA (more than a full run better than Lolich's), and 301 strikeouts certainly justified his selection as the award winner, despite the fact he won one fewer game than the Detroit ace. Lolich, looking to capitalize on his big season, was reportedly asking for a salary in the neighborhood of $80,000–$95,000 per season, a considerable increase from the estimated $58,000 he made in 1971. The big sticking point in the negotiations, however, was his demand for a groundbreaking three-year contract, a term almost unheard of in 1972, especially with Detroit.

"We've offered Mickey a substantial raise — in fact, we're willing to make him the second highest paid player on our ball club," said Campbell at one point during the holdout. "But as far as any multi-year contracts or other gimmick contract clauses which are strictly illegal, the answer is no."[6]

Lolich would eventually settle on a one-year deal for $81,300 for 1972, agreeing on the same day Atlanta's Henry Aaron inked a three-year, $600,000 contract, making him the highest-paid player in the game. The Tiger ace unexpectedly arrived in camp and signed the contract a day before the March 1 deadline for all players to report. Campbell typified the organization's conservative fiscal approach after the signing by saying, "Mickey is the best pitcher in the league. I didn't say the highest paid, just the best."[7]

A salary breakthrough had taken place that winter when Al Kaline signed a one-year contract for $100,000, becoming the first Tiger player ever to reach that lofty plateau. For several years, his salary had represented an unofficial cap for Detroit players, as Jim Campbell used Kaline's status as "Mr. Tiger" to create a ceiling, and then slotted players in the salary hierarchy behind him. Coming off a season in which he had hit .294 in 133 games, the star veteran was still looked upon as an integral piece in the lineup. However, Martin's plans heading into the new season were for Kaline to be a semi-regular in right field, no longer looked upon to play everyday, with the hope to keep him fresh and available for the right situations. Kaline could also see time at first base when Martin wanted to sit down Cash against a tough left-hander. His versatility as a hitter was important to Martin, who liked the way the career .300 hitter could handle the bat in any situation.

"He's a super player who fits in anywhere," said Martin. "I like to send him to the plate in the number two spot. He's the best there is at moving up the runner. He can also hit it out of the park."[8]

The rest of the outfield was to be manned by the same faces that had been familiar to Tiger fans for nearly a decade. Willie Horton had battled injuries for the past couple of seasons but still managed to hit .289 with 22 home runs and 72 runs batted in during only 119 games in 1971. The muscular left fielder was still considered a formidable power source and, when hot, could break up games with regularity. He had a public spat with Martin the year before, after the Tiger manager yanked him out of a game for failing to run out a ball, causing Horton to demand to be traded at one point. But that had seemingly been patched up, and big things were expected from the 28-year-old Detroit strong man in 1972.

Horton's backup in left field was expected to be Gates Brown. The 33-year-old Brown had spent most of the six years prior to Martin's arrival as a pinch-hitter deluxe, and had only been used in the outfield in emergency situations. Brown's thick, 5'11", 225-pound physique presented a picture more conducive to being a powerful presence at the plate than a ground-covering outfielder in left. His throwing arm had always been considered suspect, as well. However, with Horton battling injuries during much of 1971, Martin had given Brown more playing time than he had had since 1965. "The Gator" responded with a sparkling .338 average and eleven home runs, and could expect a bigger role in the upcoming season.

Center field would be shared by Mickey Stanley and Jim Northrup. Northrup, 32, was considered the better hitter of the two, and would typically play center on days that Kaline was in the lineup and a right-hander was on the mound. He had hit .270-16-71 the year before, and had promised Martin bigger numbers in '72. He was competent defensively in right, center, or left and provided his manager with flexibility late in games. Stanley,

30, was a superb defensive center fielder, having been awarded three Gold Glove awards in his career. He was also one of the better base runners on the team, presenting Martin with one of his few pieces with any kind of speed. However, Stanley's hitting throughout his career had been up and down (even though he hit a career-high .292 in 1971), and when the other regular outfielders were available, it was difficult to keep their bats out of the lineup. Many of Stanley's appearances could be expected as a late-inning defensive replacement, usually with Northrup sliding over to left, replacing Horton or Brown.

Like the outfield, the infield would also be made up of a familiar cast. Norm Cash was entering his 13th season in Detroit, and had been the A.L.'s Comeback Player of the Year in '71 after being rejuvenated under Martin. He was coming off of a 32-home run, 91-RBI season while hitting .283, his highest batting average since his 1961 batting title. He would remain the everyday first baseman against most pitching, even at the advanced age of 37. Second base belonged to a steady platoon of veterans Dick McAuliffe, 32, and Tony Taylor, 36. The left-handed hitting McAuliffe had struggled to a .208 mark in '71, but still retained some sock, having bashed 18 home runs. He was a steady fielder and a smart base runner, ideal in his accustomed leadoff spot against right-handed pitching. Taylor had been a mid-season pickup the previous year. A long-time National Leaguer, Taylor was the prototypical 1960s middle infielder, a decent defender and a slap hitter who could move runners along or execute a bunt. Even though he was not particularly fleet of foot, Taylor did have excellent base running skills, and was one of the few Tigers capable of stealing an occasional base. He would typically be penciled into the one or two slot in the batting order against left-handers.

The left side of the infield belonged exclusively to Eddie Brinkman and Aurelio Rodriguez. They had appeared in 159 and 154 games, respectively, in their first season in Detroit, and could plan on being in the lineup for a similar numbers of games again. Brinkman had a slim, angular body at 6' and 170 pounds, and wore long sideburns and distinctive aviator-style glasses. At age 30, he may not have had the greatest range of any shortstop of that era, but he knew how to position himself well, and fielded cleanly nearly every ball he reached. He had a very strong and accurate throwing arm, making him especially effective on balls fielded in the hole, as well as on cutoff and relay plays.[9] He went 56 straight errorless games in one stretch of '71, and provided the stability to the infield the Tigers had been lacking in recent seasons at the shortstop position. The only downside to his game was at the plate, where he slid to a .228 average with only one home run, after being in the .260 range the previous two seasons while under the tutelage of Ted Williams.

Rodriguez at age 24 was the baby of Detroit's everyday lineup. His first year with the club impressed the Tiger brass that traded for him. Only the great Brooks Robinson of Baltimore could rival his flair for the spectacular play at third base. He possessed arguably the best arm in the game at that position, and fans enjoyed reacting to the bullets he zinged across the infield with regularity. His ability to suck up ground balls that other third sackers weren't capable of, combined with the great arm, made him an asset despite his relatively high error total (23) that most were convinced would be reduced with another year of experience. At the plate, Rodriguez hit .253 with fifteen home runs in his first year with the Tigers. With his closed right-handed stance, there were thoughts of Rodriguez becoming a proficient number-two hitter, capable of shooting balls into right field through the infield gap when a runner occupied first base. That notion seemed to be in conflict, however, with the occasional power displayed, resulting in an abundance of ground balls coming from his propensity for trying to pull pitches on the outside half of the plate.

The utility infield role looked like it would be handled again by four-year veteran Ike Brown. The solidly built right-handed hitter provided more value with a bat than a glove. He showed flexibility to play almost anywhere, and was capable of showing up at first base, second base, third base, or in the outfield. Cesar Gutierrez was the only other true shortstop on the roster heading into spring training, but he was quickly sold to Montreal, leaving Rodriguez and McAuliffe as the emergency backups to Brinkman.

Tiger catcher Bill Freehan during spring training at Lakeland, Florida, in 1972. The 30-year-old Freehan was a key figure in the Detroit lineup, both offensively and defensively, and was generally acknowledged as the team's on-field leader (AP/Wide World Photos).

Bill Freehan was entering his tenth season with the club, and would once again man the catcher's job while being looked upon as one of the team leaders. After suffering through injury-plagued seasons in both

1969 and 1970, the big catcher had undergone spinal fusion surgery in September 1970 and rebounded nicely, playing in 148 games in his first season under Martin. Offensively, he put up impressive totals of .277-21-71 in 1971 while re-establishing his place as the best catcher in the American League. In an attempt to ease the workload on Freehan, who had caught a major league-leading 144 games the previous season, the Tigers purchased the contract of National League veteran Tom Haller from the Dodgers in an off-season deal. The Tigers hoped the left-handed bat of the 35-year-old Haller would be a threat to find the inviting right field stands at Tiger Stadium. Martin also planned on bringing north a third catcher that spring, with youngsters Tim Hosely, Gene Lamont, and converted outfielder Paul Jata battling for that final roster spot. Hosely, who had been a bit of a slugger at Triple-A Toledo in 1971, hitting 23 home runs plus two more in a late season call-up to Detroit, was considered the odds-on favorite for that third-string job.

The biggest question marks regarding Detroit's chances of overtaking Baltimore in the division centered on a pitching staff that was woefully thin beyond Lolich and Coleman. Between the two, they had started 83 of the 162 contests the year before, completing 45 of those starts. The rest of the staff combined had managed only eight complete-game outings. While Cain was presumed to be the third starter in the rotation, his history of chronic shoulder problems and general lack of reliability left him as a far-from-certain commodity as well. Lolich, in a light-hearted attempt at answering a reporter's question about the candidates for the fourth spot in the rotation, quipped, "Have we found the third one yet?"[10]

The Tigers continued to be in the market for an established starter as the Grapefruit League schedule commenced, hoping one would emerge on the trade market at a reasonable price. There were even rumors that Denny McLain's name had surfaced and was of interest to the team again. The Washington franchise had relocated to Arlington, Texas, that winter, and McLain, coming off of an embarrassing 10–22 win-loss mark in '71, was no longer viewed as the hopeful franchise savior as he had been in the Senators' last season in the nation's capital. Jim Campbell, still looking like the cat that swallowed the canary over the original deal, quickly squashed any notion of McLain returning.

"Les Cain is my third starter," Martin said as convincingly as he could early that spring. "Tom Timmerman and Mike Kilkenny will get a shot at the fourth slot."[11]

Cain buoyed the optimism that permeated camp that spring by reporting on the first day nearly 35 pounds lighter than he had been the previous season while telling everyone who would listen that he felt great. One person who believed in the potential of his young left-hander was Campbell.

"Look what Cain did last year. He won ten games for us and I can't remember a time when he wasn't hurt or his arm wasn't aching. If he can win ten games under those conditions, think what he can do healthy."[12]

Besides the physical issues, however, Cain was a nibbler, often trying to get batters to chase pitches rather than challenging them with his more-than-ample stuff. Largely because of this timid approach, Cain averaged nearly six walks per nine innings pitched, an alarmingly high rate for a starting pitcher who was being relied upon to win between 15 and 20 games. Kilkenny was much the same way, even after spending the better part of three seasons in Detroit.[13] Kilkenny averaged well over four walks per nine innings, which partly explained an unsightly 5.02 ERA in 1971.

"Les Cain has got to cut the mustard," explained Martin. "His arm feels good and we think he can win. Mike Kilkenny has been straight with me and I believe he now has the confidence to do the job as a starter."[14]

Timmerman was the polar opposite to Cain and Kilkenny. The 32-year-old veteran of 9½ seasons in the Tiger minor league system had made 144 appearances in Detroit since making his big league debut in 1969, relying largely on guts and tenacity rather than overpowering stuff. Included was an impressive 27-save season during the free-fall 1970 season. The bespectacled Timmerman took to the mound with a bulldog mentality. He wasn't afraid to back hitters off the plate and pitch inside, nor did he avoid challenging them when the situation called for it. His willingness to take the ball when called upon and his approach on the mound endeared him to Martin. "I judge pitchers on heart, stomach, and arm."[15]

Another player who figured in part of the discussion for a possible starting role that spring was journeyman Joe Niekro. Niekro possessed average tools at best as a conventional pitcher, but was experimenting with the knuckleball in an attempt to duplicate the success of his more famous brother Phil, who was the ace of the Atlanta Braves staff. The younger brother's 6–7 record and 4.50 ERA in 1971 suggested that he hadn't perfected the pitch. Although he would ultimately find that success nearly a decade later, in 1972 he was still a player struggling to establish himself as anything more than a marginal major league pitcher.

The back of the bullpen appeared to be a team strength. Left-hander Fred Scherman emerged as a workhorse among Martin's relief corps during his first season in Detroit. Scherman appeared in a team-record 69 games, compiling eleven wins and twenty saves. Help was expected in the coming season from Ron Perranoski, who had been the ace reliever in Minnesota during Martin's lone season as manager by saving 31 games in 1969. He had been a mid-season pickup by Detroit in 1971, and the presumption was that the 36-year-old veteran screwball artist could still contribute in pressure situations.

Timmerman could also factor into the late innings stopper role, depending on how much he was used as a starter.

Outside of Coleman, who got the start over Lolich, Northrup, who filled in at first base while Cash was taking it easy with his gimpy ankle, and Haller, who got the start behind the plate, the Tigers opened exhibition play on March 5 with their expected regular lineup intact. They dropped the first two games to Minnesota before knocking off the defending world champion Pittsburgh Pirates, 3–0, in Lakeland for their first win. Timmerman was the early pitching star with two scoreless innings in the starting assignment. Despite getting off to a 1–5 start in exhibition play, the early signs remained encouraging for Detroit. Rodriguez was off to a sizzling start, batting .455 after that first week, following an offseason in which he had greatly curtailed the number of games he played in winter ball, gotten married, and added ten much-needed pounds to his slim frame. Kaline hit the ball hard in his first games, while Horton and Northrup looked to be in great physical shape following rigorous training regimens in the offseason and early spring.

The biggest surprise over the first half of the spring had been the number of young pitchers that warranted long looks from Martin and pitching coach Art Fowler. Chuck Seelbach, Phil Meeler, Bob Ware, Lerrin LaGrow, Dan Fife, Jack Whillock, Bill Gilbreth, Bob Strampe, Bill Slayback, and Fred Holdsworth were among those that stood out during the early going. The soon-to-be 24-year-old Seelbach quickly established himself as a contender to make the team in the bullpen, while Holdsworth was a 19-year-old Northville, Michigan, native only two years removed from high school who threatened to crack the starting rotation.

"This is the best group of young arms we've had in camp since Denny McLain and Joe Sparma and Mickey Lolich and that group broke in seven or eight years ago," commented Campbell on the sudden and surprising surplus of talented young arms that were in camp, fresh out of his prized farm system. "I'm not saying that just to blow smoke either. We've got some kids in this camp who can pitch."[16]

While Martin and Campbell sorted through the young pitchers at their disposal, they allowed their staff ace to work himself slowly into shape for the regular season. Lolich was mostly regulated to work in minor league intra-squad games throughout the first half of the exhibition schedule, with orders to work on a slow curveball and save his precious left arm.

"Billy has told me to take it easy down here this spring because of all the innings I pitched last year — and because I'm going to be pitching a lot this year," Lolich said shortly after reporting to camp. "I just want to get ready for opening day."[17]

Breaking up the monotony of six weeks of camp and a month-long pre-season schedule of games was an unexpected visit to the team from former player-turned-journalist Jim Bouton. The ex-pitcher, known mostly from his playing days as a starter with the Yankees in the early and mid–1960s, had written a tell-all book titled *Ball Four,* which documented his experiences as a member of the Seattle Pilots and Houston Astros during the 1969 season. The controversial book had painted a less-than-flattering picture of some teammates, coaches, and managers from that season, enlightening readers with tales often involving vulgarity or poor taste by the major leaguers. A prominent subject in the book had been his manager with the expansion Seattle team, Joe Schultz, who now served as the third base coach for Martin. Bouton was now working for an ABC affiliate in New York and showed up in Bradenton midway through the spring, as the Tigers prepared for a game with the Pirates. As Bouton approached his former manager for the first time since the 1970 release of the book, an enraged Schultz and Martin unloaded a profanity-laden tirade his way and chased him off the field. Martin later described the former player as "a Benedict Arnold."[18]

As the Florida weather heated up, so did the Tigers' bats. The hitting started to come around after a slow start, and combined with the continued strong pitching, the team began to win with regularity and soon evened its record at 7–7. With the regular-season opener in Boston drawing nearer, the veteran team began to hit its stride. The only thing hampering the waves of optimism from camp was the ever-growing threat of a strike that might jeopardize the beginning of the season. On March 15, union chief Marvin Miller met with the team to discuss the possibility. At stake was the size of the owners' contribution to the players' retirement and health care plan. Afterwards the players voted unanimously in favor of supporting a walkout while giving Miller the power to call one on their behalf should negotiations fail to progress. For the first time, the possibility of a stoppage of major league baseball was becoming more real.

As one sized up the competition in the A.L. East that spring, the Orioles were not the only team Detroit had to concern themselves with. Boston and New York had made moves to improve and were positioning themselves to take care of any vulnerability that Baltimore might show. The Orioles, though, were the team to beat, even with the trade of Frank Robinson. They had finished 1971 with an unheard of four twenty-game winners in their rotation. Joining perennial stalwarts Dave McNally, Mike Cuellar, and Jim Palmer had been former Tiger reliever Pat Dobson, who had gone 20–8. The starting quartet was coming off an unbelievable 81–31 combined record and was expected to be equally strong in '72. Boog Powell, Dave Johnson, Mark Belanger, and Brooks Robinson would again make up their regular infield. Don Buford and Paul Blair would occupy their usual left and center field positions, respectively. Merv Rettenmund, who had been considered the best fourth outfielder in the majors for a couple of years, was ready to take over right field for Robinson. Rettenmund was coming off .322 and .318 seasons, and had driven in 75 runs in 1971 as a backup player. Supplementing the Oriole cause was the graduation to Baltimore of infielder Bobby Grich and outfielder Don Baylor, the 1970 and 1971 Minor League Player of the Year winners.

The Red Sox had finished 85–77 the previous season and had pulled off a 10-player trade with the Milwaukee Brewers in an off-season attempt to shore up their pitching staff. Gone were George Scott and Jim Lonborg, both key players in the 1967 improbable pennant for Boston. In return the Red Sox acquired Marty Pattin, a quality starter who had been buried on bad teams since the inception of expansion, and Lew Krausse, a veteran swingman who could fill many roles on a pitching staff. They also received Tommy Harper, a quality hitter who could play in either the outfield or infield and provide base-stealing ability at the top of the Boston lineup. Pitching would remain the big question mark for a team that still boasted a batting order that included the likes of veteran shortstop Luis Aparicio, third baseman Rico Petrocelli (28 homers in '71), outfielder Reggie Smith (30 home runs), and the great Carl Yastrzemski. Yaz in particular could be expected for a bounce-back season after having a rather ordinary 1971.

New York had made major strides in 1970, finishing second with more than 90 wins, before falling back to fourth place in '71 (82–80). Optimism was justified in the Bronx, however, as the Yankees boasted some of the best young talent in the league. Bobby Murcer (.331, 25 home runs), Ron Bloomberg (.322), and Thurman Munson (.251–10) were all 25 years old or younger. They joined steady veterans like Roy White, Horace Clarke, Gene Michael, and Felipe Alou in a dangerous lineup that combined hitting and speed. The pitching staff was still led by ace Mel Stottlemyre, with Fritz Peterson, Steve Kline, and Mike Kekich expected to round out the rotation. Their big addition would come late in spring training with the acquisition of reliever Sparky Lyle from Boston in exchange for first baseman Danny Cater. Lyle was a true stopper or "closer" as late-inning relievers would be known as in later years, though still rare in 1972. New York had struggled to fill that role, finishing with a major league-low 12 saves in 1971.

Cleveland and Milwaukee rounded out the division, though neither figured to be a factor in the divisional race. The Indians had lost 102 games the year before and had traded their ace pitcher, Sam McDowell, who still possessed one of the most feared fastballs in the game. Milwaukee had shifted over from the American League West, replacing Washington, which had relocated to become the newly named Texas Rangers. The Brewers were in only their fourth year of existence, having originated as the ill-fated Seattle Pilots in 1969, and still retained a roster suggestive of an expansion team.

The odds makers listed Baltimore as a prohibitive 1-to-4 favorite to take the division. Detroit had the second-highest odds at 4-to-1. Boston and New York were both listed at 6-to-1. *The Sporting News* in their baseball preview edition said about the Orioles: "Balance, depth, and pitching should mean repeat. But don't forget F. Robby's gone."[19]

Elsewhere, the Oakland A's were favored to win the American League West again. The Swinging A's, as they were beginning to be called, had arguably the best young talent in baseball. Even with reigning A.L. MVP and Cy Young award winner Vida Blue holding out in a contract dispute, the Athletics' pitching staff nearly rivaled in depth and quality that of Baltimore. Their lineup mixed speed and power as well as any with the likes of Campy Campaneris, Sal Bando, Joe Rudi, Dave Duncan, Mike Epstein, and a young 26-year-old superstar outfielder by the name of Reggie Jackson.

The Chicago White Sox, Minnesota Twins, and Kansas City Royals were expected to battle it out for second place in the A.L. West. Chicago had made an off-season splash with their trade for the talented but enigmatic Dick Allen. Minnesota had slipped since their 1969–70 division championship teams but still had Harmon Killebrew, Rod Carew, and defending A.L. batting champ Tony Oliva in its lineup. Kansas City had young talent but hadn't harnessed consistency. All three teams clubs were considered long shots at making a serious run at Oakland. California and Texas figured to round out the bottom of the division.

In the National League, the East Division was expected to be ruled again by the world champion Pittsburgh Pirates. They had upset the Orioles in seven games in a classic World Series the previous fall. Their lineup with Manny Sanguillen, Dave Cash, Al Oliver, Richie Hebner, Bob Robertson, Willie Stargell, and the great Roberto Clemente was the most dangerous in the major leagues. The Chicago Cubs, New York Mets, and St. Louis Cardinals were considered outside threats, capable of putting together great seasons, although each had its weaknesses. Chicago had a great everyday lineup and strong starting pitching but was considered, like Detroit, a bit long in the tooth. New York had the great starting pitching led by Tom Seaver, but its everyday lineup was suspect in many areas. The Cardinals still had veteran superstars like Bob Gibson, Lou Brock, and 1971 N.L. MVP Joe Torre, but not enough talent around them. Philadelphia and Montreal were weak sisters in the division and would battle to stay out of the division's cellar.

The Los Angeles Dodgers were the sexy pick to win the N.L. West title. It was presumed that the addition of Frank Robinson would lend toughness to an otherwise talented team that had seen three different rivals win the division since 1969. The Cincinnati Reds, the 1970 pennant winners, and the San Francisco Giants, defending division champions, were also considered strong contenders. Atlanta and Houston were both thought to be talented and dangerous clubs, but probably didn't have enough to win the most competitive division in baseball. San Diego, in its fourth year of existence, was still a perennial 100-loss team.

As the Grapefruit League season wound down, Detroit looked primed for the start of the regular season. After a slow start, the team won 15 of its last 19 spring training games and finished 16–9 overall, its best pre-season record in more than 20 years. Martin, mindful of not over-working his teams too early ahead of the long regular season, appeared to have brought his veteran team along perfectly through the month of March. Rodriguez hit .391 to lead the team in Grapefruit action. Northrup hit .373, Kaline .358, Cash .326, and even Brinkman batted .308. Freehan led the team with 15 RBIs. Horton knocked in seven runs in one game against Boston. Lolich, looking like he was ready to pick up where he left off from his spectacular 1971 season, went 4–0 with a 2.12 ERA in limited work. Coleman was 3–1 with an ERA of 1.64. The overall team ERA was 3.19, and many of the young pitchers looked like they could be contributors at some point during the season.[20]

The hope was that the momentum could carry into the regular season. A fast start would be beneficial, as the first three weeks would be played against divisional rivals. The Tigers were set to open in Fenway Park against the Red Sox on Thursday, April 6, and would follow that three-game series with home series against New York and Boston, before going on the road to Baltimore and Milwaukee.

Dark clouds began to appear, however, over what looked to be a sunny ending to the Tigers' time in Lakeland. In the final week of March, more talk surfaced publicly concerning a possible player strike due to failed negotiations with owners over pension funding. The players' association was threatening a March 31 deadline. What were thought to be veiled threats turned more solemn in tone as negotiations stalled. On March 29, a players-only meeting was held in the Detroit clubhouse concerning preparations for a strike that was appearing more imminent. Afterwards a tight-lipped Haller, who had been elected Detroit's players representative to the union, presented a less-than-optimistic tone when asked what was discussed: "I'd rather not say what our feelings are. What we have to say is really irrelevant. We'll go along with whatever the majority wants."[21]

Tiger management countered with moves of their own. No advances were given to players on their 1972 salaries, shutting off a courtesy that had been common in years past. Campbell ordered traveling secretary Vince Desmond to only dole out per diems (meal money) on a daily basis, rather than in advance for extended days. The club also decided to make its final roster cuts early in order to send some of their young talent to the minors before a walkout occurred. Heading over to Tiger Town for their minor league assignments were pitchers Holdsworth, Strampe, and Ware, catcher Gene Lamont, and outfielders Ike Blessit and Bob Molinaro. That left pitchers Phil Meeler and Chuck Seelbach, along with outfielder/infielder/catcher Paul Jata, as the only rookies to make the team.

On March 31, as the Tigers prepared to play the Red Sox in a rare spring training night game in Lakeland, utilizing the new lighting system that had been put in place that winter, the players' association authorized a walkout effective at midnight unless an agreement was reached. Ed Brinkman's home run off Sonny Siebert capped the 6–2 Detroit victory in Florida, some two hours before the unthinkable happened. For the first time in history, a work stoppage was underway in the major leagues. Baseball had struck out.

III

Strike One!

On Friday, April 1, 1972, a day observed as both Good Friday and April Fool's Day, the players of the Detroit Tigers and the rest of the teams across both leagues ventured into uncharted waters. Never in the history of the game had major league players walked out and caused a work stoppage. With exhibition games on the schedule for that day, owners opened the parks in Florida and Arizona so that the stoppage could not be deemed a lockout. Many of the players milled about the various spring training towns, not quite sure of what to do next. The traveling secretaries for most clubs distributed one-way travel fares so that players could return to their off-season residences, but otherwise the clubs locked up the training facilities after that first day, leaving players without professional-grade fields to gather at or train on.

The action taken was by far the most aggressive to date for the players union, which could be characterized as being in its toddler stage, if not still in its infancy. There had been previous attempts throughout the history of baseball of players unifying to gain bargaining power with ownership, but never with any substantial gains. Things began to change, however, when the Major League Baseball Players Association was formed, and in 1966 hired Marvin Miller, a renowned economist for the United Steel Workers Association, as its executive director. Under Miller's leadership the union had been able to make small advances in their basic agreements with the owners — marking the first progress in decades in some instances — in areas such as minimum salary, post-season shares, expense money, grievance handling, and even a structure for arbitration hearings for contract disputes.

The point of contention in the early spring of 1972 centered on additional funding for the players' pension fund. Historically, the only modest funding had come from gate receipts from the annual All-Star game and World Series games. Later, a portion of radio and television rights fees that were collected for those games was added to the pension's funding as well. Baseball's exclusive rights deal with NBC-TV in 1967 for a national game of the week, as well as an exclusive rights deals for the All-Star and post-season games, had provided owners with a much more lucrative source of broadcast income. After Miller's hiring by the MLBPA, the players gained a bigger cut of that annual revenue in the 1969 Basic Agreement, which was also earmarked for the players' pension fund.

What the union discovered some three years later, however, was that cost-of-living expenses had increased 17 percent since 1969. They wanted an additional $1.5 million contribution from the owners to the pension fund over the $5.45 million that was being invested annually to help offset that loss in spending power. The owners, who had largely gone along with the unification attempt by the players and the minimal gains achieved in recent years thanks to the negotiation tactics by their annoying union head, decided to take a hard stand on the pension increase issue.

Very few people among owners, media, fans, and probably even the players thought the talk of a strike over the pension funding issue had any real possibility of coming to fruition. However, Miller and the union's legal counsel, Dick Moss, visited each of the 24 teams at their camps during the month of March. At those meetings, the players for each club took a vote on whether to authorize strike action should the negotiations falter. After Miller and Moss met with all of the teams, the players had given their approval by a league-wide vote of 663 to 10 authorizing strike measures.[1] As negotiations between Miller and the owners lagged during spring training, the player reps for each team were called to Dallas on March 31 for an emergency meeting.

As the player reps and Marvin Miller met at a hotel at Dallas' Love Field Airport (which nearly a decade earlier had served as part of the backdrop to one of the most infamous days in American history[2]), most outsiders expected the outcome to be nothing more than a routine update on the status of negotiations. After four hours, the media began to sense that something bigger was happening. When the player reps emerged, many were flush and choked for words, scrambling to make hasty exits back to their spring camps and the teams they represented. Miller then made the shocking announcement that a strike would be effective at midnight that evening unless an "appropriate settlement is reached with the owners" or "if the owners agree to submit the dispute to binding arbitration."[3]

The announcement rocked the sports world, coming only days before the opening of the 1972 season. Nobody knew what to expect next. Many hoped that it was only posturing by the players and that the union would quickly come to their senses, while others thought the season and maybe even the sport itself was in jeopardy. For the owners and others who represented the establishment within the game, the action by the players appeared to be a form of betrayal, and the sentiment was that they needed to be punished.

Tiger GM Jim Campbell, who was as fiscally conservative as any power broker in baseball, lashed out at his players and deemed them "damn greedy."

"I'm disgusted with the whole lot of them," he said at the time. "This game has been pretty good to them. And I think baseball deserves something better. We've been more than fair. They've got a helluva lot better pension program and medical coverage than the scouts and other people in baseball, who made their jobs possible. And then they do something like this."[4]

"We negotiated and negotiated until there was nothing else for us to do but strike," said Tigers union rep Tom Haller. "And we felt that the longer we waited, the more the owners would feel that we didn't mean exactly what we said. I don't think the owners really believe we were in favor of a strike."[5]

Within the Tiger clubhouse at Joker Marchant Stadium that evening, a mixture of disbelief, confusion, and anger permeated the charged atmosphere. Some players talked of loyalty to the union, while others seemed eager for the team reps, Haller and Niekro, to return from Dallas with more information. A few of the team leaders, namely Freehan and Kaline, were trying to organize informal workouts for the club, while others talked about leaving Lakeland and going home. Their obviously enraged manager made his feelings clear as he sounded loudly, "No curfew tonight. Have fun, you pot lickers," while he strode through the clubhouse.[6]

Billy Martin's view of the situation was decidedly self-serving. After turning around a talented but floundering franchise the previous season, only to come up short to the seemingly invincible Orioles, his team's strong spring only made him believe even more that the pieces were in place for Detroit to overtake Baltimore for the top spot in the A.L. East in 1972. The walkout by the players served as a cruel blow to those ambitions.

"This really hurts," he said before leaving that night. "We were in excellent shape ... we were ready to go. This is going to hurt us more than it hurts anybody else because we're ready right now and we've got a lot of older guys who have to play every day to stay in shape."[7]

On Saturday the reality of the situation set in even further. "You know, this is like a bad dream," said Martin. "I keep thinking if I roll over and wake up, none of it will have happened. I'm a manager without a team."[8]

The reality set in for the players as well on that first day of the strike. As management was forced to cancel the exhibition games scheduled for that day, teams also cut off the amenities given to players as part of spring training accommodations. Meal money, which had been distributed to the players on a daily basis while the strike deadline loomed, was terminated completely. The Lakeland Holiday Inn, which was the spring training home for the Tiger organization that housed many of the players, all on the club's tab, began distributing room bills to the players starting with that Saturday morning. Fourteen Tigers decided to get out of Lakeland that first day and picked up their one-way plane tickets to off-season residences scattered around the country. Most of the rest were either uncertain of where to go or what to do, and only Kaline, Freehan, Lolich, Northrup, and Niekro showed up at a local high school field in Lakeland to work out.

With the Tiger team largely a veteran group, many of the players had families in Florida with them, and were staying in rental properties with leases that had not expired. The contentiousness between ownership and players even showed up in petty displays, such as the edict from management that no personal or family belongings of the players could be stowed on the equipment trucks headed back to Detroit. For families like the Freehans, Northrups, and Stanleys, this created quite an inconvenience, as between them they had brought 17 bicycles down to Lakeland, courtesy of the team equipment trucks.[9]

Disruption in the lives of the players met with little sympathy. Public sentiment was decidedly on the side of the establishment. Most fans and media didn't really understand the issues at hand. The players were portrayed as greedy money mongers who had turned their back on the game and its fans. In retrospect, that portrayal is curious, considering the enormous leverage the owners still had over players at that time. In 1972 professional players at the major league level were nowhere near the mega-millionaires of today's game with their agents, lawyers, media consultants, personal trainers, and other various handlers looking out for their best interests on all fronts. An established player was well paid for the times, but not on the level of earning lifetime financial security for themselves and their heirs, as is often the case today. The average MLB salary in 1972 was $32,500. The minimum salary was $13,500, roughly the same as the average household income in the United States at that time.[10]

That salary structure was the product of nearly 100 years of ownership holding the upper hand on salary and benefit levels over the players. The reserve clause within the basic contract tied a player to the club who owned his rights for eternity. Free agency was still a pipedream. Without the players' leverage of being able to play out a contract and putting one's value on the open market, the clubs could keep salary levels at an owner-friendly structure, with sharp increases unlikely to occur from year to year over the life of a player's career. A player such as Al Kaline, who had by almost any measure been among the top five percent of players during his career, was only reaching a salary level of $100,000 in what was his twentieth season in a Detroit uniform. Ownership kept that status quo by discouraging any kind of formal representation on the player's behalf when it came to contract negotiations. Attorneys or early versions of player agents who showed up with a player to discuss contact negotiations were often ignored or even asked to leave the premises. Players were forced to bargain with management without the benefit of any tangible knowledge of salary structures within the team or across the leagues. The strike was the first real display of unity from the players used to gain leverage in hard negotiations.

Marvin Miller sensed that the MLB ownership's hard stance on the additional funding for the pension fund was about more than just dollars. They "are out to break the association," he commented to the press shortly after the walkout began.[11] Much of that belief came from management's cool response to a last-ditch attempt on his part to save the start of the season. On April 4 as a compromise to the original $1.5 million demand for additional funds from the owners, he proposed a much smaller shell-out of $255,000 from management, with $817,000 of the difference being funded from a reserve fund that had been held in escrow. The reserve had been built up through investments of earlier contributions to the pension fund, over funding of expected retirement payouts, and an overestimation of the cost of disability benefits. The money belonged to the players association, but the owners held veto power as to its distribution.

As the traditional Opening Day in Cincinnati became the first regular-season game sacrificed to the work stoppage, ownership held its hard line on negotiations. Through chief negotiator John Gaherin, they questioned the wisdom of shifting money from that account as well as the actual amount of the reserve fund. They delayed a response to Miller's proposal by asking that an independent actuary of their choosing conduct a study as to the fund's actual value.

Miller, who undoubtedly was the target of much of the anger from baseball management as well as fans, held firm in his assessment of ownership's ploys. "What the owners have done perhaps is to make me a symbol of the contempt they hold for the players," he said. "They talk as if the players are a bunch of stupid jerks. In reality players of today are in every way different regarding awareness than the players of 25 years ago. But the owners are the same people who were running the game then."[12]

There was a sentiment among observers that ownership and management were digging in their heels, not only on the pension funding issue immediately at hand, but also to set the tone for the next round of negotiations with the Players Association for the next Basic Agreement contract. The current agreement was set to expire at the end of the year and both sides were gearing up for a war that was sure to include a battle over the reserve clause. A dominant group of owners led by Cardinals owner Gussie Busch, a camp that Detroit's Jim Campbell was squarely part of, was openly hostile towards the negotiations with Miller and the players.

"No question about it," commented an unnamed owner to a press member during the negotiations. "One big reason for our firm stand now is what effect it will have on negotiations on the basic agreement when it comes up. That could bring on another strike that could put the kibosh on baseball for a long time."[13]

When the strike passed the one-week mark and season openers had been canceled across both leagues, frustration built on all fronts. For the fans, Opening Day in major league baseball still represented a holiday of sorts — the unofficial start of spring, especially in traditional baseball cities in northern climates like Detroit, Boston, New York, Chicago, Cincinnati, and Philadelphia. With the proliferation of color television sets among Americans in the 1960s and early '70s, the National Football League had grown immensely in popularity and had taken some of the spotlight away from baseball. However, baseball was still the sport for the masses. The common man could more closely relate to the game, its skill set and the nuances and strategies of the sport than he could with football. It is the game they had grown up with, and their fathers and grandfathers had as well. In no other professional sports league did the fans celebrate the opening of the season like they did for baseball. President Nixon even appealed to both management and the players to find "resolution to the strike."[14]

The build-up of fan interest throughout spring training, only to have the start of the season postponed abruptly, fueled a backlash from those eager for baseball. The "national pastime," as it had been called for generations, was part of a higher standard that Americans looked to. The players and their leader, Marvin Miller, were generally viewed as the villains in the situation. Letters to the editor in newspapers across the country and in *The Sporting News* were overwhelmingly against the Players Association. "They are well paid to play a game" was a common sentiment expressed through the editorial responses. "Many young men would play the game for nothing" was another frequently expressed thought.[15]

Getting paid became a point of contention among players as their regular-season salaries started to be missed. Players on both ends of the salary spectrum felt the sting of missing a paycheck. A rookie or player with little experience at the major league level making the minimum salary was losing his much-needed $75 per day during the strike. At the other end, an established star player, like Kaline making $100,000 on his contract, was losing out on $556 per day. Henry Aaron of the Atlanta Braves, who was reportedly the highest-paid player in baseball for 1972, was losing more than $1000 each day of the walkout. Many players were poorly versed on the issues, and communication between the union and their members was sometimes poor, especially after the players had dispersed from their spring camps. Some players publicly advocated ending the walkout if the owners would commit to further negotiation. Others questioned whether gains in pension funds for retired players was worth potentially sacrificing their own careers. As the days passed and the resolve of the players was tested, the strength of the players' union was at stake.

In an attempt to break the stalemate, Miller suggested that the dispute be taken to arbitration. The owners refused. "We're just trying to make a sensible business arrangement, which is critical to our costs," Gaherin said on behalf of the owners. "I'm confident solutions can be reached and the problem solved while the players are playing, but we don't want to submit this to a third party who'll have no responsibility in living with the results."[16]

Dick Moss responded for the players by filing charges of unfair labor practices with the National Labor Review Board. The basis of the charges was twofold. Refusal by the owners to bargain and negotiate in good faith was the obvious charge. However, the more alarming claim was that "pressure was put on players in an attempt to undermine the association."[17] The assertion was that actions had been taken against certain players because of their activities on behalf of the players association. The most obvious example being cited was the outright release during the strike by the Chicago White Sox of their player representative, veteran relief pitcher Joel Horlen. A few other player reps were left feeling uncertain about their roster spots due to their union activity, although Detroit's Tom Haller, despite being a newcomer to the team, was not one of them.

Despite the strong-armed tactics by the owners, the players' resolve remained firm. As the strike passed the one-week mark, it was the owners who started to feel the financial pinch of no revenue stream. With payments coming due for spring training costs, overhead for front office members, organizational employees, and stadium costs, as well as costs for players and facilities for minor league seasons that were just getting underway, the loss of regular season gates was taking its toll. NBC's cancellation of the first *Saturday Game of the Week* broadcast (which incidentally was scheduled to be Detroit at Boston) cost the owners a $200,000 payment. Three teams — the San Diego Padres, Chicago White Sox, and the recently relocated Texas Rangers — were all rumored to be in serious financial trouble and unable to hold out much longer. To cut costs, the White Sox and California Angels each released upwards of twenty players from their minor league systems.

By April 10 the owners showed signs of compromise, although the gesture only opened the next major point of contention between the two parties. The owners offered to make concessions on the pension funding but insisted that the players would not be paid for the games they missed due to the walkout. On the surface this seemed like a logical demand as explained by the owners' chief negotiator, Gaherin. "The players will not be paid for the days they have not played so far this season. Further that the clubs will try to make up most of the cancelled games so as to complete a 162-game schedule, and the players will be expected to participate in that schedule within the framework of the basic agreement."[18]

Marvin Miller immediately rejected any notion that the players would be denied pay for the days missed, while the previously canceled games would then be made up later in the schedule. He compared it to slavery. Player salaries were paid during the regular season twice monthly, regardless of the number of games played during the pay period. Miller insisted that if the owners planned on rescheduling the games canceled during the strike as either parts of doubleheaders or on what had been originally been open dates, the players would be paid their full 1972 salaries. Some players openly discussed forfeiting their pay over the strike dates as a means to ending the walkout and perhaps partnering with the owners to give free tickets for fans or charity donations as goodwill gestures. Miller remained steadfast and pressed for full pay for the players.

By the next day, both sides seemed ready to settle. A compromise was tentatively agreed upon for the pension funding increase. A players meeting late in the evening of April 11 was set to vote on the proposed deal. At 1:00 A.M. on Tuesday, April 12, the players accepted the proposal. Formal acceptance by the owners came less than 48 hours later, when they approved the settlement in a meeting in Chicago on Thursday, April 13.

Ultimately the two sides settled on a $500,000 payment to the pension fund for 1972, most coming from the reserve fund that had been held in escrow. The deal would only be in effect for the one season and then would expire with the rest of the Basic Agreement between the players association and the owners on December 31. It was sure to be a point of negotiation for the next agreement.

Neither side budged on the debate over whether players would be paid for games made up due to the walkout. The compromise was to cancel those games. They would not be made up, and the players would not be paid for the games lost. The season would start on Saturday, April 15, with the games already scheduled for that date. As a result, teams would play schedules of uneven length. Detroit, Cleveland and Milwaukee were scheduled to play 156 games. Boston, New York, California, and Oakland were slated to play 155 games; Baltimore, Chicago, Kansas City, Minnesota, and Texas would have 154. Additionally, the balance between home and road games for each team was upset. Teams that were scheduled to open with homestands during that first week and a half lost those home games. The Minnesota Twins were the most severely impacted, missing out on seven games at Metropolitan Stadium.

Most pundits figured the imbalance in the schedule would be a greater factor in the National League, particularly the N.L. West, which looked like a potential five-team dogfight. However, since the advent of divisional play three years earlier in the American League, the smallest margin of victory for a division winner had been nine full games. The Orioles and A's remained prohibitive favorites again, coming off of ten- and fifteen-game margins, respectively, in 1971.

As the players scrambled to get to the destination of their opening games, they could not have realized the magnitude of their ten-day strike. Despite the modest gains in pension funding, the walk away by both sides over pay for the strike time, and the backlash of public sentiment towards the players, major inroads had been made in the owner-player relationship that had remained largely static through the first 100 years of the game's history. Through solidarity stemming from the biggest stars of the game all the way down to the rookie utility infielder barely hanging on to a roster spot, the players had leveraged their way into concessions from ownership.

Jack Aker, a veteran relief pitcher for the New York Yankees that spring, put it succinctly: "We felt strongly that we were being tested, that the owners refused to make any concessions because they didn't believe we could stick together and strike."[19]

IV

The Race Begins

Opening Day in Detroit is always special for both the baseball traditionalist as well as the casual fan. The date on the calendar may say early April, but in Detroit and the state of Michigan Opening Day has for many years been the unofficial first day of spring. In 1972, however, the day came as an afterthought. The high hopes from the promising spring showing by the Tigers had been doused by the strike. The initial outrage by fans over the striking players was followed by a measure of indifference by many as the delayed opening to the season dawned. The local media had kept the team on the front burner through coverage of the strike developments and the comings and goings of the players during their unplanned absence. The Detroit papers even went ahead with their pre-season analysis of the team and made predictions for the season. Jim Hawkins, beat writer for the *Detroit Free Press*, picked the Tigers to win the A.L. East, if and when the season eventually resumed.

The originally scheduled opening three-game series in Fenway Park with the Red Sox had been canceled, as had a two-game series with the Yankees in Detroit, including the traditional Opening Day at Tiger Stadium. When the settlement was finalized on Thursday, April 13, the decision was made to start the season as quickly as possible. A series-opening Friday home game with Boston would be the final casualty to the ten-day strike. The season opener was now slated for Saturday afternoon with Boston.

"I hope we can still win," said Martin the day before the game, still bitter over the interruption that had damaged his carefully planned preparations for the season. "I can't have the same feeling that I had before the strike. Ten days ago we were on the brink ... we were ready to open the season in our prime. Now I'm going to have to work twice as hard as I would have before."[1]

The prevailing thought among baseball people was that the nearly two-week layoff would most affect hitters, whose timing would be off. Ted Williams, the Texas Rangers manager who was still being considered in most circles as the best all-around hitter of the twentieth century and the paramount authority on all things concerned with hitting a baseball, said it would take weeks for hitters to catch up. Others, like Baltimore manager Earl Weaver, believed that the careful build-up of pitchers arms during spring training would now be jeopardized. Almost all agreed that injuries, particularly pulled muscles and hamstrings, would be hard to avoid. It was assumed that players would have lost their edge in conditioning, a problem that was likely to be compounded by so many early-season games being played in cold-weather cities. Many thought that an aging team like the Tigers would be especially susceptible.

With only one day to prepare after the strike had ended, Martin held a Friday workout at Tiger Stadium. Players meandered in throughout the three-hour practice on a cold and breezy day. Roughly half the squad had scrambled to catch flights into Detroit from their off-season homes. Many of those that had migrated back to the Detroit area during the strike had been practicing together during informal sessions at the University of Michigan's Yost Fieldhouse. Mickey Lolich tried to keep his arm in shape by throwing batting practice for the Romeo (Michigan) High School baseball team. Even so, Martin had only modest expectations for his pitching ace, who would be taking the ball in the opener.

"I had a long talk with Lolich and all I expect him to do is go five innings," said Martin. "After the Friday practice he commented on his pitching strategy in the early going. The win is the important thing right now. I'm going to be switching pitchers a lot sooner than I normally would. I'll wait until I know they're right before I let them go all the way."[2]

Martin's theory would be tested in that first game against the Red Sox. Before a Tiger Stadium crowd of 31,510, the smallest Opening Day attendance in more than a decade, Lolich bounced the opening pitch to Boston leadoff man Tommy Harper. That first pitch appeared to be an omen, as Harper later singled in that same at-bat. The following two hitters, Luis Aparicio and Carl Yastrzemski, also singled to load the bases with no outs. After a strikeout of outfielder Reggie Smith, Rico Petrocelli singled to left, scoring Harper. Yastrzemski, seeing the ball coming in from the outfield towards home plate, headed to third while thinking that Aparicio was also attempting to score on the hit. As he reached third base, he found his teammate already standing contently on the bag. Yastrzemski was tagged for the second out, while Lolich worked himself out of a potentially disastrous first inning, giving up only one run.

In the bottom of the second inning, Bill Freehan managed a two-out double to right field off Red Sox starter Marty Pattin. Shortstop Eddie Brinkman then lifted a fly ball that dropped barely over the screen at the 365-

foot mark in left field for a two-run homer, giving Detroit a 2–1 lead. Boston managed to tie the game before the Tigers put together three straight singles in the bottom of the seventh inning to score the eventual game-winning run. Freehan's sharp single with Norm Cash on second base didn't appear deep enough to score the Tiger first baseman. However, Cash, who was never known for his speed on the base paths, challenged Yastrzemski's throw from left field, which got away from catcher Duane Josephson as he reached to make the tag.

But the story of the game was Lolich who, after allowing a scratch hit to Bosox second baseman Doug Griffin in the fourth inning, retired the last 17 batters in a complete-game, 3–2 victory. It was a remarkable performance by the rubber-armed Detroit workhorse, who got stronger as the game progressed despite not having pitched to major league hitters for more than two weeks. Red Sox manager Eddie Kasko was frustrated at his team's inability to get to Lolich in the early going, especially that first-inning rally that netted only one run.

"We had him and we let him get away," he said. "You don't do that with a guy like Lolich. He wasn't throwing well at the start, but he got stronger as he went along."[3]

Ironically, the first date on the resumed schedule was April 15, a payday for major league players, who were paid on the first and 15th of every month once the regular season started. Each player received a pro-rated check for 1/182 of his salary, or one day's pay from the 182 calendar days that comprised the original schedule of the 1972 season.

After the Sunday game was postponed due to wet, cold weather (a day that had a couple of remarkable accomplishments in the National League — Chicago Cubs rookie pitcher Burt Hooton tossed a no-hitter against Philadelphia and San Francisco's tall, angular slugger Dave Kingman hit for the cycle and drove in six runs in a 10–6 win over Houston), the Tigers prepared to hit the road for an eight-game road trip with visits to Baltimore, Milwaukee, and Texas. The games with the Orioles were the focus as the team worked out on an off day on Monday at Tiger Stadium. The sunny skies and warmer temperatures that fell upon the Detroit area that day seemed to heat up the optimism for a team easing its way into the season. Talk of beating the Orioles head-to-head in the coming series and creating a fast start permeated the team before the players headed to the airport.

"I'll match our team against their team anytime, as long as both sides are in good shape," said Martin with more enthusiasm than he had shown since the strike. "That's the only thing that bothers me about this series, the fact that we had the long layoff. But a sweep is possible ... it could happen."[4]

Nothing in that first road game in Baltimore on April 18 did anything to dampen the optimism. The team sported newly styled road uniforms, breaking from the traditional grays that had been worn for years. The new look featured double-knit pullover jerseys with dark blue (almost black) and orange stripes at the bottom of the sleeves and collar, as well as orange trip outlining the dark blue "DETROIT" across the chest. The pants were similarly styled with striped waistbands and sock stirrups, jazzing up a road look that dated to the early century with the traditional all gray. In that first game of the series, Joe Coleman struck out eight of the first sixteen Baltimore batters on his way to a strong 7⅓-inning effort. Norm Cash hit a solo home run and Aurelio Rodriguez stroked a two-run single off Jim Palmer. Fred Scherman finished the game on the mound, and despite Martin getting ejected for arguing balls and strikes with the umpires, the Tigers won, 5–3.

Despite being only the second game of a revised 156-game season, the win was unusually savored by a Detroit team sick of inhaling the exhaust fumes of a Baltimore team that had sped away from the Tigers in each of the past three years. "Usually they beat me with a late home run," Coleman said after winning against a team that had been a personal nemesis.[5]

"I know it doesn't mean that much being so early in the year and everything, but when you beat this team it feels good," said Al Kaline, hoping to contend again before his long career concluded.[6]

Tigers veteran catcher Bill Freehan saw the early-season victory as an opportunity to reverse the roles of the two teams, breaking a trend that had existed since the world championship season of 1968. "These games mean a lot to us. Maybe we can get the jump on them for a change. Maybe we can tell them 'you look at our backs for a change.'"[7]

In the other clubhouse, Earl Weaver held court with the media, well aware that Detroit had his team squarely in its sights in 1972. He continued to dismiss the loss of Frank Robinson and instead played up the wealth of talent his team had added with the trade, as well as from the plentiful Oriole farm system. His team was trying to become the first club in history to win 100 games four years in a row.

> We should be so much bleeping better this year.... In right field we've got the guy who led our club in hitting the last two years (Merv Rettenmund) ... in left field we've got the guy who led the league in runs scored last season and he missed 40 games (Don Buford). And in center field we've got a guy who's going to have the greatest year of his career (Paul Blair). If any of those guys gets into a slump, I've got Don Baylor who only hit .320 or better in every league he's ever played in.[8]

The Sunday rainout and the off day preceding the trip to Baltimore allowed Martin to come back with Lolich in game two of the series. The Orioles, however, came up with three runs in the bottom of the eighth inning, breaking a 2–2 tie, and dealt Detroit its first loss, 5–2. After the game Martin got into a scuffle with an unruly fan outside the team bus as it prepared to leave Memorial Stadium. No real damage seemed to come out of the incident, which was quickly dismissed other than the Tiger manager complaining to beat writers about the scuffmarks on his new $150 pair of Italian-made boots.

The rubber game of the series proved to be as frustrating to Martin as the blemishes on his boots. Tom Timmerman got the first crack at the number-three spot in the rotation and went seven strong innings, giving up only two hits, in what was only his fourth career start. Unfortunately, one hit was a home run to Blair in the fourth inning, and former Tiger Pat Dobson held the Tigers in check, tossing a three-hitter in a 1–0 Baltimore win.

Detroit next traveled back into the cold, wet spring weather that had afflicted the Midwest. Milwaukee was scheduled to open its home slate with the Tigers, but the rain mixed with snow caused another postponement. Elsewhere there was baseball on that date, and among the highlights were the Texas Rangers playing their first home game in Arlington, Texas. A disappointing crowd of just over 20,000 showed up for their first view of the newly located franchise (the erstwhile Washington Senators). The fans that did show up that night were not disappointed, as Frank Howard, the hulking, veteran slugger, bombed a tape-measure home run in his first plate appearance and the Rangers defeated the California Angels, 7–6. Within the division, Baltimore won again as Dave McNally twirled a three-hitter while beating Cleveland, 6–0. The win gave the Orioles a 5–1 record, putting them two games up on Detroit as the first week of league play wrapped up.

On Saturday the weather improved enough for the Brewers and Tigers to play, and Coleman ran his record to 2–0 with an impressive two-hitter over seven innings of work. Milwaukee's first hit didn't come until the seventh inning when John Briggs beat out a grounder in the hole at short. Unfortunately, the next batter broke up the shutout, too, as left-handed-hitting outfielder Joe Lahoud homered. In the meantime, the Tiger bats were breaking out with their loudest effort of the season, scoring eight runs on 13 hits. The hitting stars on the day were Dick McAuliffe and Gates Brown with three hits each, while Cash had two hits and knocked in three runs in the 8–2 win.

It was a different story the next day, as the Tigers hit into three double plays and stranded at least one runner in every inning (twelve for the game) against second-year pitcher Jim Slaton. On the other side, Martin had countered with his number-four starter, Les Cain, for the first time. The enigmatic Cain continued to baffle and frustrate his manager and the Tiger brass. Predicted for stardom at an early age, the young pitcher (still only 24 years old) had battled injuries and inconsistency since winning twelve games in

1970. In this game he gave up five hits and four walks over the first six innings, working out of trouble in every frame but the fourth, when he walked Ron Theobald and John Briggs before giving up a double to George Scott that scored both runners. Scott, who had come over to the Brewers with Lonborg in the blockbuster off-season deal with Boston, had been hitting only .058 coming into the game. The final score was a 3–0 win for the Brewers, and the loss again had Martin wondering about the makeup of his starting rotation after Lolich and Coleman.

"He was behind on every hitter," complained Martin about Cain. "It had nothing to do with the layoff. He's had that same problem ever since I've known him. He's got to learn to get ahead of the hitters."[9]

Even though his team had won the game, third-year Milwaukee manager Dave Bristol was impressed with the deep Detroit lineup. "Just look at the guys they've got sitting on the bench," he said after the second game of the series. "They've got guys like Al Kaline, and Mickey Stanley, Dalton Jones, and Tom Haller who aren't even in the game. And you look down their lineup and there isn't a weak spot."[10]

The Monday following the Brewers series was supposed to be an off day for Detroit, but it did not come without controversy. Instead of flying out of Milwaukee on Sunday evening and spending their day off in the warmer climate of Arlington, Texas, the Tigers were forced to remain in town since the Brewers had scheduled the makeup game for Friday's postponement for that open date. Customarily an early-season cancellation would not be scheduled for the same series, but rather for later in the schedule when the weather would likely be more favorable. That would have seemed to be especially true when forecasts called for more cold weather and even snow flurries. When Monday's game was called because of the conditions, the Tigers, and especially Martin, were furious. The third postponement in the first ten days of the season was more than Detroit had experienced in all of 1971. Instead of working out under sunny skies in Texas, the team spent most of the day waiting around the hotel and in the airport as Vince Desmond, the team's traveling secretary, scrambled to get them on a flight out of Milwaukee as quickly as possible.

"We wind up wasting an off day is what we do," sputtered Martin as he fumed over the decision of Milwaukee GM Frank Lane to schedule the makeup game for that day.[11] Some in the Tigers' organization felt that the Brewer brass was getting back at Detroit for not giving the go ahead to move Friday's game to an afternoon contest. Because of the strike, the date had turned into Milwaukee's home opener, and the Brewers had wanted to play it in daylight instead of as a night game. Detroit had refused, however, since the Tigers were playing the previous night in Baltimore and would be arriving in the early A.M. in Milwaukee.

The team's disposition improved greatly, however, after they had played the franchise's first American League games in the state of Texas. The Tigers took both games of a short series from the newly located Rangers. In the opener, second baseman Tony Taylor's first hit of the season was good for a two-run triple, and Lolich tossed a four-hit complete game in a 4–1 victory. The next night Coleman was even better with a three-hitter to go 3–0 on the season and Detroit won again, 8–1. Detroit had trailed 1–0 in the top of the fifth before sending ten men to the plate and exploding for five runs. Cash homered in the game, but the most impressive statistic of the night may have been Coleman's three sacrifice bunts.

Upon returning to Detroit, the Tigers welcomed the red-hot Chicago White Sox. The new-look Sox were riding a seven-game winning streak as they headed into Tiger Stadium for the weekend series. Their biggest change from the previous season was the addition of former National League star Richie Allen to the middle of their lineup. The enigmatic Allen was playing on his fourth different team in four seasons, all while averaging 30 home runs, 93 RBIs, and a .288 average over the previous three campaigns. Still only 29 years old, Allen, who now insisted on being called "Dick" instead of "Richie," was off to a sizzling start with the White Sox, hitting .410 with three homers. Hitting behind speedsters like Pat Kelly and Walt Williams, and with another quality hitter in Carlos May hitting either directly in front of or behind him, Allen had made the White Sox an extremely dangerous team.

Friday, April 28, marked the first night game of the year at Tiger Stadium. Behind the hot bats of Cash, who had three more hits, including another home run and four RBIs, and Eddie Brinkman, who also had three hits and four RBIs, Detroit won a laugher, 12–0, over Chicago. Timmerman gave up only three hits and made further strides towards establishing himself as the third starter in the rotation.

NBC beamed the Saturday afternoon game all over the country as their game of the week, and the Tigers won convincingly again, this time 6–1. Lolich bested the White Sox workhorse knuckleballer Wilbur Wood. Wood had entered the game with a 2–1 record and had pitched extremely well, as his miniscule 0.25 ERA suggested. However, Freehan, Stanley, and Horton marked the occasion by blasting their first home runs of the season as the offense rolled for the fourth straight game.

"We're beginning to get it all back together, I think," said Freehan. "I've never seen this team play as well as we did during the last few games of spring training and I think we're getting it together again."[12]

On Sunday Detroit's four-game winning streak ended when Sox catcher Ed Hermann hit an eighth-inning grand slam off Coleman to give Chicago a 6–3 victory. The loss, however, did not cost the team its position in the standings as the Tigers finished the month of April in first place with a 7–4 record. Baltimore ended the day one game back at 7–6, and Cleveland was slightly behind them at 6–6.

May started with big news coming out of Boston, although not for the hometown Red Sox. Vida Blue, the Oakland A's pitching phenom, most valuable player and Cy Young Award winner from the previous season, ended his holdout and signed a contract for 1972 as the team prepared to open its series in Boston. The news of the signing spurred more than just curious interest among those associated with the game, as Blue had demanded from A's owner Charles O. Finley a contract worth $115,000 after his tremendous 1971 campaign. That was a salary commensurable with the top established stars of the game, and not one easily given to a player who had pitched in only eighteen career major league games prior to his breakthrough season. After missing all of spring training and the first two weeks of the regular season, Blue ended his holdout by signing for a reported $63,000, well below the lofty figure he had been seeking. Despite being one of the brightest young stars in the game and a top gate attraction, the lanky left-handed flamethrower had no real leverage left by extending his holdout. The A's were one of the most talented teams in all of baseball and figured to contend with or without their star pitcher. What's more, the team held his rights indefinitely.

Detroit opened the month with a home split of a two-game series against the Kansas City Royals. Timmerman pitched another strong game in the opener until he threw the ball away on an infield chopper, scoring one Royals run and setting up another. The error decided the outcome, breaking up a 3–3 tie in the eighth inning. The second game was all Tigers as they cruised to a 6–1 victory behind the complete-game pitching of Lolich. Freehan had two hits and two RBIs, while Horton crushed a pitch into the upper deck in left field for his second round-tripper of the season. Kaline, who had struggled at the plate throughout the month of April, rang up a pair of triples in the win.

After an off day, Texas came to town for a weekend series and the Tigers took two out of three from the Rangers. In the opener, Joe Coleman lost a tough-luck 2–1 decision, his first loss to his former franchise. On Saturday, Timmerman came back with a strong outing in a 4–1 win that evened his win-loss record at 2–2. After the game many on the team celebrated by watching on the clubhouse television as Riva Ridge took to the winner's circle at the Kentucky Derby. On Sunday another champion in the sports world was crowned as Wilt Chamberlain scored 24 points and pulled down 29 rebounds in a 114–100 win over the New York Knickerbockers. The win gave the Lakers a 4–1 decision over the Knicks in the NBA championship series. Meanwhile, back in Detroit, Lolich improved his record to 5–1 in a workmanlike 7–4 win over the Rangers. Gates Brown hit his first home run in the victory.

As the Tigers moved on to Chicago to start a five-game road trip, they made a personnel move by trading little-used left-handed pitcher Mike Kilkenny to the Oakland A's for minor league first baseman Reggie Sanders. Kilkenny had once been a promising pitcher for Detroit, starting a total of 36 games for manager Mayo Smith in 1969–70. With Martin's arrival as manager, Kilkenny's place in the rotation faded away. He went 4–5 with a 5.02 ERA in eleven starts in 1971, but like left-handed counterpart Les Cain, Kilkenny struggled to throw strikes consistently enough to suit the new skipper. At the point he was traded, Kilkenny had fallen so far into Martin's doghouse that he had seen action in only one game in 1972. Things wouldn't get much better for Kilkenny, however, as he lasted only one game in Oakland before moving on to Cleveland and then San Diego before the season ended.

With a roster spot available, the Tigers recalled pitcher Bob Strampe from Toledo. The twenty-two-year-old right-hander joined a bullpen that mostly consisted of Fred Scherman on the left side and rookie Chuck Seelbach slowly gaining trust as a right-handed reliever. The rest of the staff, including Joe Niekro, Ron Perranoski, and rookie Phil Meeler, had seen little duty through the first three weeks of the season.

As Detroit moved into Chicago's Comiskey Park, the Tigers dealt White Sox ace Wilbur Wood a loss for the second time of the young season. Coleman snapped a personal two-game losing streak and picked up his fourth win in a 4–2 Tiger victory. The next night, Timmerman tore a nail in the early innings and drew blood, and Martin was forced to call on his long relievers for one of the few times thus far in 1972. The result was not pretty as Meeler and Strampe got roughed up while making their major league debuts in a 7–0 drubbing by Chicago. Tom Bradley crafted the shutout for the White Sox.

Thursday, May 11, was an off day for Detroit, but the baseball world was stunned by news that the San Francisco Giants had traded legendary Willie Mays to the New York Mets. The trade had been rumored for several days, although the shock of seeing Mays in anything other than a Giants uniform was the equivalent of the sun not rising in the east. The forty-one-year-old was no longer the mega-superstar he had been for the past two decades; an icon for the game itself, Mays hoped to be rejuvenated by going back to the city where his career had begun with the New York Giants.

Elsewhere that day, another icon of his sport, Bobby Orr, led the Boston Bruins to a Stanley Cup championship. The 3–0 win over the New York Rangers that night gave the Bruins their second title in three seasons. Orr was named winner of the Conn Smythe Trophy as the most outstanding player of the Stanley Cup playoffs.

On Friday in Kansas City, the Tigers' game with the Royals was rained out, marking their fourth postponement of the young season. Between weather cancellations and scheduled off days, Detroit had played on only 18 of 28 dates since starting the season on April 15. The fact that they hadn't played more than three straight days at any point certainly could have contributed to the inconsistency the team had shown, especially when coming off the two-week layoff because of the player walkout.

When play resumed on Saturday, Lolich improved his record to 6–1 with a 3–1 win over the Royals. Freehan contributed two hits, including his second home run, and knocked in three runs, giving him 17 RBIs on the season to rank second in the league. His sizzling start saw him hitting .343 a month into the season, and when combined with the hot start of Cash gave Detroit a formidable middle of the batting lineup. Cash's start was even more impressive as he was leading the American League in batting at .371, and ranked second in the league in home runs. Martin was filling out his lineup card with Freehan in the fourth spot, with the power-hitting Cash right behind him. For Freehan, who typically had hit lower in the lineup throughout his career, the chance to hit cleanup in the Tiger lineup was a welcome challenge.

"I don't think there's a player in the league who wouldn't like to hit fourth if he had the chance," he said. "When you've got a guy like Cash coming up behind you, you're going to get better pitches to hit."[13]

Freehan's strong start was a positive sign for a Detroit team that had come to rely on its long-time catcher as one of the pillars for the entire organization. He was a Detroit native, although he played most of his prep career in Florida after his family moved to Tampa. He returned to attend the University of Michigan, where he started as a sophomore on both the baseball and football teams. He set a Big Ten record by hitting .585 in 1961, and then turned professional later that summer after signing for a $100,000 bonus with the Tigers. By 1963 he had assumed the bulk of the catching duties in Detroit, and a year later garnered all-star recognition. In 1965 he won the first of five straight Gold Glove awards while also being one of the most productive at his position at the plate. Between 1967 and 1971, he never hit fewer than 16 home runs in a season nor failed to drive in fewer than 52 runs. Back and arm injuries, which hampered Freehan's effectiveness in both 1969 and 1970, were thought to be some of the reasons for the team's fall-off after its World Series season. His value to the Tiger team was reflected through the American League's annual MVP voting, where he received votes in five of the nine full seasons he had been in a Detroit uniform.

On Sunday the Tigers and Royals played a makeup doubleheader, splitting the twin bill. Coleman won his fifth game in the opener, a 3–2 decision, but rookie Chuck Seelbach, coming out of the bullpen to make his first start, wasn't able to complete the sweep as the Tigers lost, 8–4. The split gave Detroit an overall record of 13–8, good for second place in the A.L.

East, a half-game behind the Cleveland Indians, who had surged to the top spot.

Over in the National League in New York on that Sunday in mid–May, Willie Mays rose to the occasion once again in his legendary career. In his first game as a Met, and against his former team nonetheless, Mays smacked a home run to break a 4–4 tie and provided the margin of victory in a 5–4 win over the Giants.

Baltimore provided the opposition when the Tigers returned to Detroit to open a key ten-game homestand. Even though the date was only May 15, Tiger Stadium would be the setting for an interesting homestand that began with three games against the team acknowledged as Detroit's primary rival for the division crown. That series would be followed by a single makeup game with Boston, three games against Cleveland, and then winding up with three games against Milwaukee. The Orioles had struggled since that early series against the Tigers. They came into this series in third place with an 11–11 record, 2½ games behind Detroit and three games behind the Indians. The early-season series provided a golden opportunity for the Tigers to open some distance between the two teams.

The first Monday Family Night crowd of the year at Tiger Stadium settled in to watch a promising start as Gates Brown and Horton hit solo home runs off Jim Palmer in the first two innings. However, the Tigers could muster only two more hits thereafter, and the Orioles pulled out a hard-fought 3–2 victory. Afterwards, Weaver dismissed any generalizations about his team's slow start by comparing their position to the previous season. "Hey, we were four games behind the Boston Red Sox after 35 games last season and we were only seven games over .500 after 45 games."[14] He also took the opportunity to slide a jab in at a Tiger team and its manager that Weaver felt was making too much out of the early-season series. "I don't know if they had the magic number counted or not."[15]

The game had been played despite the shock and disbelief of many Americans, as news disseminated of that day's developments in Laurel, Maryland, where George Wallace had been shot four times and was listed in critical condition. With a presidential election scheduled for November, the former Alabama governor had been campaigning for the Democratic Party nomination when the shooting occurred in a rally at a shopping center parking lot. With civil unrest already at an alarmingly high rate and protests over the United States' war in Vietnam common, people feared that the summer campaign season would prove to be as tumultuous as the previous presidential election year of 1968. That year had seen the unexpected decision of President Johnson to not run for re-election, the assassinations of Martin Luther King, Jr., and Robert F. Kennedy, and the chaos in the streets in cities across the country, including outside the Democratic convention in Chicago. Wallace survived the shooting but would live with paralysis that left him unable to walk for the remainder of his life. For the country, the assassination attempt was yet another dark episode in a period of American history that left many shaken over the violence that had invaded the ideal of a democratic government.

May 16 was Billy Martin's 44th birthday, but it was the Orioles who had the party, knocking around Detroit pitchers for fourteen hits as Baltimore cruised to an 8–3 whipping of the Tigers. Timmerman was the first of four ineffective hurlers and took the loss, which left Detroit in danger of being surpassed by Baltimore in the standings after losing the first two games of the series. In the first of the many turning-point games that arise during the course of a long major league baseball season, the Tigers turned to their ace left-hander to stop the slide. Mickey Lolich did the job and became the first seven-game winner in either league with a convincing 6–1 victory, allowing Detroit to salvage one game in the series. Lolich's fast start, coming on the heels of his remarkable 1971 season, must have seemed satisfying to the Tiger organization, especially when compared to the fate of former ace Denny McLain. After making five appearances for the Oakland A's, McLain had been relegated to the minor leagues that week, his once-shiny star diminishing quickly behind the repeated beatings he was taking from hitters now eager to tee off on his mediocre stuff.

Mickey Lolich delivering a pitch at Tiger Stadium in May 1972. Lolich picked up where he left off on his superb 1971 season, going 22–14 in 1972 while pitching a whopping 327 innings (AP/Wide World Photos).

The batting hero in the series finale with Baltimore had been an unlikely star in Tom Haller. Haller had been acquired in the offseason as an upgrade as the backup catcher, a role previously held by Jim Price, and to provide an alternative left-handed bat to the lineup on days that Martin wanted to rest Freehan. Haller was now 35 years old, a veteran of many years on both sides of the San Francisco Giants–Los Angeles Dodgers rivalry, but was expected to have enough left to help the team in 1972. Unfortunately, between his duties as the team player representative with the union and having a miserable spring on the field, his time with Detroit had not gone well. In this game, Haller broke an 0-for-9 start at the plate by crashing a game-breaking, three-run homer off Dave Leonard and ended up with four RBIs on the day.

Boston then came to town to make up the game that had been postponed during the first weekend of the season. Coleman came through for his sixth win (6–2) on a three-hitter, and Cash and Haller again provided the heroics on offense. Cash hit his seventh round-tripper of the season, while the suddenly hot Haller had two hits, including a double, two runs scored, and two RBIs off Red Sox pitcher Lew Krausse. The Tigers' two straight wins set up an unlikely early-season showdown with the first-place Cleveland Indians, who came to town sitting a half-game ahead of the Tigers in the standings.

The Indians were the American League's surprise team through the early portion of the 1972 season. Losers of 102 games the previous season, Cleveland had managed to grab the division lead after five weeks of play with much of the same roster. Ray Fosse was still the catcher, and the player most often mentioned with Freehan when conversations turned to the A.L.'s best at that position. Chris Chambliss and Graig Nettles were fine looking young players at first and third base, respectively, just a few years before they would gain greater fame as key cogs in the mid-to-late '70s New York Yankees pennant-winning and world championship teams. The rest of the Cleveland lineup was made up with non-descript players, such as Jack Brohamer, Frank Duffy, Eddie Leon, and Del Unser. There was a talented rookie outfielder who would soon establish himself as an all-star third baseman for nearly a decade named Buddy Bell, and a new manager in Ken Aspromonte, but the biggest change in the makeup of the Indians came through the addition of veteran pitcher Gaylord Perry.

Perry had been acquired in an off-season trade for Cleveland's long-time flamethrower Sam McDowell, much to the chagrin of Tiger GM Jim Campbell, who had been rumored to be among the suitors for McDowell. In Perry, the Indians thought they were adding a solid starting pitcher who had typically won sixteen to eighteen games a season for San Francisco, and had toiled throughout his ten-year career in the shadow of the Giants' flamboyant pitching ace, Juan Marichal. Now 33 years old, Perry had taken the American

League by storm with a 6–2 early-season record and a microscopic ERA. Maybe even more importantly for him, he had gotten into the heads of hitters all across the league, including those that hadn't seen him yet. Word traveled fast that Perry was "loading up" the balls between pitches, and from his exaggerated antics on the mound, as well as his lack of denials off the field, he did nothing to discourage talk about his diving spitball.

Martin was determined to catch Perry in the act when the new Indian ace opened the three-game weekend series. When the Tiger manager thought he detected unusual movement in the Cleveland right-hander's pitches early on, he challenged the umpires to inspect. In the first inning, home plate umpire Lou Dimuro came out to the mound and looked over Perry's glove, hat, sleeves, and any other place that Perry might be loading up with a foreign substance, but to no avail. Meanwhile, Perry tantalized the Detroit bench by continuing between pitches to run the fingertips of his right hand across different parts of his uniform and through the graying hair just above his right ear, never giving up the illusion that he was picking up a substance.

Perry's team staked him to an early lead when a first-inning infield tapper was thrown into the right field bullpen by Tiger starter Les Cain, sending Tom McCraw all the way to third base prior to scoring. The giveaway run proved to be too much for Detroit to overcome on this night as Perry, despite being inspected at Martin's request three other times by the umpires, tossed a five-hitter, including retiring the last fifteen Tiger batters in order, in a 2–1 Cleveland victory.

"He's a one-pitch pitcher," complained Martin afterwards to the media. "A spitter ... Vaseline ball, whatever it is. If he didn't have it, he wouldn't get my guys out. We've handled every other kind of pitch. He doesn't have a curve and he doesn't throw hard. My guys come back to the dugout and tell me what the ball does — at the last second it just dips real bad."[16]

If the Friday loss was a disappointment, the Saturday game was even worse. Aurelio Rodriguez committed a two-out error in the first inning that allowed Indian left fielder Alex Johnson to reach base. Graig Nettles followed the mistake with a drive into the right field stands off of Timmerman, giving the Tribe an early 2–0 lead. From there the Tiger right-hander shut down the Tribe the rest of the way, overcoming three other Detroit errors. Still, the Tigers' frustrations at the plate continued. They left eight men on base in scoring position, and twelve overall. Martin used eighteen players in the game, including six pinch-hitters, in an attempt to jump-start an offensive attack that had suddenly gone stale. It was not enough, however, as they lost for the second straight time by a score of 2–1.

The next day, a Bat Day crowd of 52,150 filed into Tiger Stadium hoping that Lolich could pitch the hometown team to a win in the final game of the series. For the second time in four days, the popular left-hander came through, boosting his record to 8–1 with a 5–0 shutout. The win did not come without tribulation as Horton, while trying to beat the relay on a double-play grounder, badly pulled a thigh muscle and collapsed just past first base before leaving the game on a stretcher. He would be placed on the 15-day disabled list immediately after the game. His replacement in left field, Gates Brown, also suffered a muscle pull in his leg after attempting to steal second base and had to be removed. The key hit for the day was registered by Stanley, who came in to replace Brown, and tripled in two runs. The three-bagger by Stanley, who was the third player to bat in the cleanup position that day, boosted his batting average to .350 for the season.

"I don't ever remember hitting cleanup in my life," said Stanley after the game. "And it wouldn't have happened today if Gates hadn't got hurt."[17]

After an off day, Milwaukee came into Detroit while sitting in last place in the division. It was the former Red Sox ace, Jim Lonborg, however, who threw a four-hit shutout in game one of the series, besting Coleman, 3–0. Detroit scratched out a 5–3 win in the second game as Seelbach captured his first career victory. Seelbach entered the game in relief of starter Les Cain, who was pulled after 5⅓ innings despite not allowing a hit. Cain issued five walks in those five-plus innings, including loading the bases with free passes in the sixth, before being pulled from the game by Martin. The key hit was provided by Rodriguez, who broke a tie by lining a single that accounted for two runs. The Tiger third baseman had been struggling at the plate and had even been replaced in the starting lineup that night by Taylor. Rodriguez entered the game as a pinch-hitter for McAuliffe, and after hitting into a double play in the sixth inning, delivered the clutch game-winning hit in the eighth.

The Tiger hitting woes returned in the final game of the series, however, as Milwaukee won, 2–0. It was Skip Lockwood tossing a six-hit complete-game shutout for the Brewers, besting Lolich, who saw his personal seven-game win streak snapped. Lolich only gave up a two-run homer to Brewer catcher Ellie Rodriguez, but struggled in his six innings of work while giving up four hits and six walks. The only real excitement for the Tiger Stadium fans that day came in the ninth inning when reliever Phil Meeler fielded a ball dribbled down the first base line by Milwaukee's Billy Conigliaro. When Meeler tagged the Brewer outfielder near his face, Conigliaro took exception to the act, and a brief shoving match ensued between the two, causing both dugouts to empty. Martin, who never saw a brawl he didn't like, led the charge from Detroit's dugout, located on the third base side of the infield. "I wanted the guy who tried to punch my pitcher," he said afterwards.[18]

Martin's actions might have been with the intent to put some fire into a Detroit team whose bats had turned cold over the previous two weeks as much as to serve retribution towards a journeyman outfielder who took a swipe at a rookie pitcher. The homestand had proved disappointing, with the team finishing with a substandard 4–6 mark over the eleven days in Detroit. "We're just not hitting," said Martin after the Milwaukee series. "And when you're not hitting, anybody can come in and beat you two out of three."[19]

Martin's words certainly held true as all the hot bats from spring training down in Lakeland faded into a distant memory. The two hottest hitting regulars during the early weeks of the season were now cooling off as the calendar headed towards June. Cash's batting average had dropped nearly 100 points in two weeks, and despite being tied with Oakland's Dave Duncan for the A.L. lead in home runs with eight, he had only 19 RBIs. Six of Cash's eight round-trippers to that point had been solo shots. Likewise, Freehan watched his average drop to .292 before he was forced to miss a little more than a week of action with an injured thumb, yet he still remained tied with Cash for the team lead in RBIs.

The rest of the hitters were struggling mightily and Martin mixed and matched his lineups each night to try to find some semblance of an offensive attack. McAuliffe and Taylor were being platooned religiously at second base, but neither was off to a good start. McAuliffe was hitting .203, although his 22 walks placed him among the league leaders in that category and allowed him to get on base regularly enough to stay in the lineup as the leadoff man against right-handed pitching. Taylor was sitting at .222 in limited at-bats against left-handers. Brinkman's average had dipped below .250, to .248, after being well above .300 for most of April, and despite playing every game he had knocked in only two runs for the month of May. Rodriguez had no home runs and only ten RBIs in a team-leading 125 at-bats while hitting a very pedestrian .240.

The big guns in the outfield were off to slow starts as well. Kaline, Horton, and Jim Northrup had been the primary run producers in the Tiger outfield for the better part of a decade. Each was struggling to find his stroke, as spring was turning to summer in 1972. Kaline got off to a very slow start, and despite heating up some in more recent weeks, was still hitting only .250 with no home runs and only six RBIs. Martin had resorted to using the veteran star off the bench as a pinch-hitter in a number of early contests. Horton, who was starting to heat up before he was injured, was still well behind his usual pace, having only four homers and nine RBIs. Northrup was perhaps the biggest disappointment of the early weeks, not so much for his dismal .234 batting average, but for paltry power numbers that included no homers and five RBIs in 94 at-bats and a miserly .266 slugging percentage. In an attempt to get Northrup kick-started, Martin had even used him in the unfamiliar role of leadoff hitter for a number of games but with limited success.

As six weeks of the season went into the books, the leading hitters on the team were a pair of part-time outfielders in Stanley and Gates Brown, each sporting a .327 mark at the plate. Stanley had appeared in 25 games, mostly while coming in during the late innings to play center field. Brown had been seeing some action in left field against right-handed pitchers, but had still registered eight appearances in the role he would always be best known for—as a pinch-hitter. Between the injuries that seemed to regularly afflict Horton and Kaline and the ineffective hitting of Northrup, both Stanley and Brown were getting plenty of at-bats as Billy Martin juggled playing time for his five outfielders.

Detroit looked to rebound from the sub-par homestand as the Tigers hit the road for an unusual five-game series over the Memorial Day weekend in New York. The Yankees had struggled in the early weeks of the season and came into the series in fourth place in the A.L. East, two games under .500 yet only four games out of first place. In the first game the Tiger bats broke out of their slumber in an 8–2 win. The first two hitters in Martin's lineup did their job as Taylor and Rodriguez accounted for five hits and scored five runs. Little-used utility men Ike Brown and rookie Paul Jata started at first base and in the outfield in order to get additional right-handed hitters in the lineup against Yankee lefty Mike Kekich. Timmerman won his third game of the season and Fred Scherman pitched 3⅔ innings in relief for the save. In the second game the Tigers managed a tight 2–1 victory but not without a cost as the number of players with physical ailments increased. Coleman gained his seventh victory, but was forced to leave the game early with stiffness in his right shoulder. Scherman came on for the second straight day and pitched another 2⅓ innings for his sixth save. Kaline pulled a calf muscle and left the game in the first inning, joining Horton (disabled list), Gates Brown (pulled muscle), and Freehan (fractured thumb) among the walking wounded for Detroit.

The injury situation didn't improve in game three when Cain felt tenderness in his shoulder while warming up before the game and then lasted only five pitches before having to come out in the bottom of the first inning. Although it wasn't known at the time, those would be the last pitches he would ever throw in a major league game. Despite the early setback, the Tigers still managed their third straight win in Yankee Stadium as Seelbach went 6⅔ innings of effective long relief, Stanley knocked in three runs, and Freehan returned to the lineup without missing a beat and contributed two hits while playing first base.

The big story in the 5–4 victory was the rookie Seelbach, who had gained the trust of Martin in the early season and had already surpassed more experienced bullpen options like Ron Perranoski and Joe Niekro in the staff pecking order. Seelbach had come on strong in the Detroit organization by winning ten straight games at Toledo in 1971. He had been the team's number one draft pick in 1970, drafted twelfth overall out of Dartmouth, where he had been a pitching star on the same staff as fellow future major leaguer Pete Broberg as well as an accomplished swimmer. Seelbach had won a job in the Tiger bullpen for 1972, but now with Cain back on the DL and the need for a fourth starter becoming more pressing, Seelbach had made a case for the job. "If I start Seelbach, that means I lose him in the bullpen for four days and right now he's my number one right-handed relief pitcher too," mused Martin as he mulled over his options after the New York game.[20]

If it seemed that Detroit had been fortunate to escape each of the first three games of the Yankee series with wins, that luck changed in the Memorial Day doubleheader to wrap up the series. A light-hitting (.206 coming into the day) backup outfielder named Rusty Torres delivered a key pinch-hit two-run single in each game that led to Yankee victories. In the first game, Lolich was largely ineffective and suffered his second straight loss, while getting little help from the bullpen work of Strampe, Meeler, Scherman, and Perronoski. In the second game the injury jinx continued, as New York pitcher Fritz Peterson lined a Joe Niekro pitch back off the Tiger hurler's knee, ending his outing in the third inning. The new Yankee relief ace, Sparky Lyle, closed out both games for his eighth and ninth saves of the young season, souring what began as a promising launch to Detroit's road trip.

On the last day of May, Detroit pulled out a wild back-and-forth victory in Cleveland against the slumping Indians. Cleveland was coming off of a weekend where the Indians had been swept four straight games by the visiting Orioles and had lost the momentum they had carried into Detroit just twelve days earlier. Trailing 2–1 in the eighth inning, the Tigers exploded for three runs on a pair of home runs — a solo blast by Cash and then a two-run shot by Stanley. The home runs were the first by a Detroit hitter in nine days. Seelbach could not hold the lead, and the Indians came back to tie it at four, but Brinkman lifted a sacrifice fly in the tenth inning to give Detroit the 5–4 lead. Scherman held off Cleveland in the bottom half of the tenth to preserve the win.

Cleveland returned the favor in the second game as Gaylord Perry baffled the Tigers again in a 1–0 shutout victory. Perry allowed only one Detroit runner to advance past first base while gaining his league-leading ninth win against only three losses. Coleman lost his fourth game and dropped to 7–4.

Despite the loss to Perry and the Indians, Detroit left Cleveland in first place in the division as the first day of June ended. The initial two months of the Tiger season had been marked by cold, wet weather, numerous cancellations, and inconsistent play on the field. The offensive attack, hampered more by the 10-day layoff than any other phase of the team, struggled to regain its spring form. The pitching, which had been a question mark heading into the season, had been surprisingly good, however. The heavy frequency of scheduled days off mixed with weather postponements had allowed Martin to maximize the number of starts his two workhorse pitchers, Lolich and Coleman, were able to make over the first quarter of the season. Timmerman had proved to be a nice surprise as an effective third starter in the rotation. The bullpen, manned primarily by Scherman and Seelbach, had been solid for the most part, although its depth figured to get tested as the long season wore on.

What the first two months had provided was the positioning Detroit needed as it plunged into the summer months. They had shaken off the ill effects of the two-week strike well enough to sit atop the standings at the one-quarter mark of the season, and one sensed that they hadn't played their best baseball yet. That contrasted sharply with the past three seasons when Baltimore had run away and hid from the rest of the division, and Detroit had never really contended deep into the season. Although still only one-half game behind the Tigers in the standings, the Orioles were off to a very inconsistent start themselves, especially at the plate, and seemed much more vulnerable than in past seasons. The rest of the division was a study in either parity or mediocrity, depending on the point of view. Cleveland had surprised with an early surge but didn't appear strong enough to contend over the entire season. Boston and New York had gotten off to disappointing starts and each was looking up at .500, although they had managed to stay within sight of the teams ahead of them. Five teams were bunched within five games of first place, and even the last-place Brewers were only 6½ games out. It hadn't been pretty, but the Tigers were where they needed to be seven weeks into the season. For baseball fans in Detroit and across the state of Michigan, the summer of 1972 promised to be very interesting.

American League East Standings through June 1, 1972

	W	*L*	*Pct.*	*GB*
Detroit Tigers	21	17	.553	—
Baltimore Orioles	20	17	.541	½
Cleveland Indians	19	17	.528	1
Boston Red Sox	16	19	.457	3½
New York Yankees	17	21	.447	4
Milwaukee Brewers	13	22	.371	6½

V

Measuring Up to the Competition

As spring turned to summer, a couple of trends were becoming clear for the 1972 season. A noticeable decline in hitting, particularly in the American League, was being greeted by a parallel drop in fan attendance figures. With the first two months of the baseball calendar now torn off, those trends were met with concern by ownership and league officials as blame for the hitting woes aimed at the two-week player walkout turned stale and rationalization for indifferent fan interest, such as unusually cold, wet spring weather, melted away with the summer sun.

The first week of June found American League hitters with an overall batting average of .232 and teams averaging just 3.3 runs per game.[1] Both numbers rivaled figures from 1968, which outside of Detroit, where that magic year was relished, the season was unflatteringly known as the "year of the pitcher." The league-wide .232 mark was an alarming fifteen points lower than the .247 league average over the full 1971 season. So far in 1972, the Kansas City Royals were the only team that had even matched the overall mark from the previous season (hitting exactly .247 at the time). Among the worst offenders were the Texas Rangers, hitting a woeful .204 as a team, and the Milwaukee Brewers, who were averaging a paltry 2.6 runs per game. Through the first seven weeks of 1972, Oakland was leading the league in home runs (just under one per game) and runs scored (4.1), while at the other end of the spectrum Cleveland had only twelve homers in 36 games played. Detroit was at .243 and averaging 3.6 runs per contest; however, their 24 homers in 38 games was well behind the pace they had set the previous season when they led the majors with 179 home runs. Only four A.L. teams were on pace to hit 100 homers in 1972 (based on a 162-game schedule), after eight of the twelve teams had hit that figure a year earlier.

Individually, Chicago's Pat Kelly was leading the American League in hitting at .327. Oakland left fielder Joe Rudi was next at .324, and KC outfielder Lou Piniella was at .320. Norm Cash of the Tigers was ninth in the league at .289. The A's Dave Duncan and Reggie Jackson were tied for the league lead in homers, each with ten. Chicago's Dick Allen led in RBIs with 32, with Jackson at 26, and Minnesota's Bobby Darwin and Oakland's Duncan at 25.

The beneficiaries of the weak hitting were the league pitchers. To date, 49 shutouts had been thrown, with Baltimore's Dave McNally already owning four, and four other pitchers around the league had three each. Six pitchers (with enough innings to qualify) had ERAs under 2.00. Eight of the twelve clubs had team ERAs under 3.00.

Attendance likewise lagged around the American League. One million fans was the gold standard in paid home attendance for individual clubs in 1972. Franchises that regularly reached that figure typically separated themselves as those that would operate on a solid financial base from those that would struggle. The American League was in a period where it was fighting the image of being the inferior league, both in quality of play and in star power, and at least half of its teams would be challenged to reach the magic attendance figure that season. The unprecedented strike by the players had not helped an already tenuous situation for many clubs, and soured many casual fans whose indifference was made known by the scores of empty seats in ballparks all over the circuit.

The Washington franchise had been relocated that season to Arlington, Texas, by owner Bob Short in an effort to alleviate the attendance woes his team had endured in the nation's capital. His new Ranger team was greeted with disappointing crowds in its new home city, leaving many to wonder why the team had been relocated at all. The tough, blue-collar fans in Baltimore had been particularly tough on the players following their return. Long-time third baseman great Brooks Robinson, who also happened to serve as the team's player representative, had been booed regularly in the early season, as much for his role in the player walkout as for his slow start at the plate. The Orioles' early-season three-game home series with the Tigers had drawn a measly 18,000 fans, an embarrassing figure considering the games were between the two prime contenders for the division crown. Their falloff in attendance for home games followed similar declines in New York, Milwaukee, Cleveland, Oakland, Minnesota, and other cities around the league.

The biggest surprise on the positive side had come in Chicago, where the new-look White Sox were running nearly 150,000 fans ahead of their 1971 attendance figure heading into the first week of June. Their new slugger, Dick Allen, had captured the imagination of Sox fans in the Windy City where the Comiskey Park organist belted out the theme song from "Jesus Christ Superstar" every time he came to bat. Never had the fans' new-found faith been more rewarded than in that weekend's Sunday doubleheader against the Yankees, when after winning the opener White Sox manager Chuck Tanner decided to give his new star a rest in the nightcap. Trailing by two runs in the bottom of the ninth inning, Tanner sent up Allen in a pinch-hitting role with two men on base. Allen delivered a game-winning (walk-off was not part of the baseball vernacular in 1972) three-run homer to win the contest, sending 51,904 Chicago fans into hysteria.

Detroit was also one of the few towns where attendance seemingly hadn't been impacted by the strike. The Tigers were still a statewide draw, and the familiarity among fans with the long-time favorites like Kaline, Cash, Freehan, Horton, Lolich and so many others still endured. The fact that Detroit was in a divisional race and had taken on many of the combative traits of its fiery manager gave fans even more reason to come down to Tiger Stadium that summer. Attendance at Tiger Stadium was running even and at times ahead of its 1971 pace.

The first weekend in June found the Tigers welcoming the Minnesota Twins, who were coming to town for a series that would signify the start of three straight weeks of games against the other division. Minnesota had just recently been bypassed for the top spot in the American League West by Oakland and sat a game and a half behind the A's, yet owned the best run differential of any team in the A.L. The Twins were in a bit of a transformation, relying more on pitching and defense to win games than they had in the recent past, but still had many of the old familiar names in their lineup. The muscular slugging first baseman, Harmon Killebrew, was having his last big season at the plate. Rod Carew was a young veteran at second base, having hit over .300 for three consecutive seasons. Cesar Tovar still patrolled the outfield and batted leadoff most days. Danny Thompson was a better hitter than shortstop. Missing from their lineup, however, was the defending batting champion, Tony Oliva, who was recovering from floating bone chips in his left knee, ill effects from his knee surgery the previous September. Minnesota's big bat so far that season had been a 29-year-old rookie outfielder named Bobby Darwin, who had ranked among the league leaders in home runs and runs batted in all season.

The biggest transformation for Minnesota had come from its pitching staff, which had been one of the league's poorest in 1971. Veteran left-hander Jim Kaat entered the opener on Friday night with a 6–1 win-loss mark, but even more impressive was his 1.11 ERA. Those numbers meant little to the Tigers who barraged the Zeeland, Michigan, native with six hits and four earned runs in his first 1⅔ innings. The game wasn't decided until the bottom of the eleventh inning, however, when Gates Brown doubled off the left field wall, scoring Mickey Stanley with the winning run.

The next afternoon it was Brown striking again as he hit a two-run homer in the first inning, McAuliffe bombed a three-run homer in the second, and Joe Niekro pitched a workman-like eight innings to gain his first decision in a 5–3 Tiger victory. Brown's heroics might not have matched those of Cincinnati Reds catcher Johnny Bench, who was completing a streak that day where he had homered seven times in a five-game span, but were impressive nonetheless.

"I've been saying for years I can do the job," Brown said after the game. "I am just glad Billy is giving me the chance to play. It makes it a lot easier when you know you are going to play. Yes sir. It is suddenly fun again."[2]

With injuries to Willie Horton, who was still on the disabled list, and Al Kaline, who was seeing limited duty with muscle pulls behind his left knee, Brown was playing regularly against right-handed pitching while manning left field. After spending most of his years under Mayo Smith as one of baseball's premier pinch-hitters, the Gator was relishing his chance to play more under Billy Martin, but was realistic about his role.

"When Willie gets better and Al starts playing more, I know I won't be in there that much. It would have really bothered me a few years ago. No more. Now I know the circumstances.... Heck, I don't care as long as we win. I need the money."

On Sunday, June 4, Tom Timmerman pitched a masterpiece of a complete-game four-hit effort. However, he had been matched up against the Twins' 21-year-old right-hander, Bert Blyleven, who had shut out the Tigers through six innings before plunking Jim Northrup with a pitch in the bottom of the seventh. Mickey Stanley made Blyleven pay for that mistake by lofting a drive over the left-center field scoreboard for a two-run homer that proved to be the winning blow in an eventual 3–0 shutout victory.

Stanley was another Tiger outfielder who was seeing regular playing time with the injuries to the other outfielders. He had started less than half the games he had appeared in so far that season, with most of his appearances coming as a defensive replacement in center field, where he was one of the game's best players. With his long, loping strides, the 6'1" Stanley was supremely adept at getting a jump on the ball as it left an opponent's bat and tearing across the outfield grass until he arrived at the point where the ball came down into his waiting glove. His range was particularly valuable in Tiger Stadium with its vast center field, which included the deepest outfield fence in the majors at 440 feet.

It was at the plate that Stanley was regarded as being less of a threat than the perceived outfield regulars Horton, Northrup, and Kaline. Despite hitting a career-high .292 in his first season under Martin, Stanley had registered his lowest number of at-bats in four seasons. He had started 1972 as a platoon player in center field, but with the injuries to Horton, Northrup's slow start, and age and injuries seemingly catching up with Kaline, Stanley's hot start at the plate provided an attractive option for Martin to put on his lineup card each day.

"Mickey's coming through with the RBIs now and that's what he wasn't doing last year," said Martin after the sweep of the Twins. "And you should have seen him in batting practice. He must have hit five in a row into the stands. I think we're finally starting to jell."[3]

Detroit's sweep of Minnesota coincided with Oakland's sweep of the Orioles in Baltimore and put the Tigers a season-high three games out in front in the division race. Two nights later they made it four straight wins with an 8–6 victory over the visiting California Angels in the first game of a Shrine Night doubleheader. Mickey Lolich won his first game in two-and-a-half weeks despite giving up three home runs in a less-than-stellar performance. The win was Lolich's ninth of the season and the 150th of his career.

In the nightcap, Clyde Wright shut down the Tiger bats on only four hits in a listless 4–0 loss. The good news came on the scoreboard, where both Baltimore and slumping Cleveland lost, increasing Detroit's lead to four full games in the division. The series finale was not as successful, however, as the Angels took the rubber game, 5–1. In that game the Tigers got their first look at California's big off-season acquisition, the flame-throwing right-hander, Nolan Ryan. Although he limited Detroit to only three hits in a complete-game effort, Ryan downplayed the showing by saying afterwards that he "didn't have my overpowering stuff" and complained of a "tired arm."[4]

After an off day, Detroit awaited the arrival of the Oakland A's for a big three-game weekend series. The match-up would be between the two current division leaders and promised to be an early feeling out of the balance of power in the American League. The first game started strongly for the Tigers on a cold, windy June 9 evening. McAuliffe and Cash both homered off of the A's staff ace, Jim "Catfish" Hunter, giving them an early 4–0 lead. Timmerman couldn't make that lead hold up, however, and neither Seelbach nor Scherman could stop the bleeding as Oakland knocked out fifteen hits, including home runs by Sal Bando, Ollie Brown, and Gene Tenace, in a 10–5 A's victory.

Oakland's roughing up of Timmerman only increased the speculation that Detroit was heavily in the trade market for another starting pitcher. With the June 15 trade deadline less than a week away, rumors swirled that a deal with Minnesota for Jim Perry involving Horton or Northrup was on the table. Detroit general manager Jim Campbell tried to downplay the rumors, yet didn't deny that his team was looking for another pitcher.

"We are actively looking for another starting pitcher, sure. But it seems that's what everyone else is looking for too."[5]

On Saturday, the A's bats were hot again as they jumped on Lolich with early homers from Bando and Joe Rudi on their way to a 5–2 win. The homers were the fifth and sixth the Detroit ace had given up in the past fifteen innings he had pitched, well above the success rate that A.L. batters were used to having against Lolich.

"This is something that runs in streaks," said Lolich, trying to find an explanation for his recent ineffectiveness. "I had an off-day. I wasn't throwing very hard. These days come and go. Every pitcher has them, it's just bad when you get them at the same time the team is going bad. It's starting to get me down a little bit. I'm supposed to carry this club. I know I'm supposed to win. And things just haven't been going too good for me lately."[6]

Meanwhile, Oakland's rookie left-hander Bob Hamilton was shutting down the Tigers for 7⅓ innings with only two runs allowed. The A's victory was their eighth in a row, part of a stretch that would see them win 18 of 21 games, including going 11–2 up to that point, on a fourteen-game road trip. Despite the hot streak Oakland was on, Tiger manager Billy Martin refused to give credit, instead insisting that "we're just not playing good ball." Later he grudgingly gave credit to the team with the best record in the league.

"Don't get me wrong, Oakland is the best hitting club we've seen this year. I think we'd beat 'em head to head if we had it all together, but right now they're hitting and doing everything right."

Before he left the subject, Martin again lamented his team's inconsistency and placed blame indirectly on the strike. "If we were playing the way we played this spring, we'd be 10 games in front easy! We were all sharp and swinging the bat then."[7]

A series of potentially ugly developments during the game sowed seeds for future fireworks between two teams that had clashed in the past and admittedly didn't like each other. Perhaps coincidentally, Detroit pitchers managed to plunk three Oakland batters with pitches during the second of back-to-back beatings by the A's. Included among the hit batsmen were two of Oakland's offensive catalysts, leadoff hitter Bert Campaneris and slugging outfielder Reggie Jackson. Jackson had gestured towards the mound after he had been hit, but umpires were able to calm the situation before things turned violent. Although the A's batters who had been hit during the game were obvious targets for a manager who liked to send messages to the other team, Martin denied the pitches were deliberate.

"We weren't throwing at Reggie and we weren't throwing at their pitcher either. I'd stake my life on it, that's how sure I am. Of course they won't believe that. And I really don't care whether they do or not."[8]

Away from the flared tempers between the A.L. division leaders, a major milestone was reached in major league baseball that Saturday. In Philadelphia,

Atlanta's Henry Aaron hit a sixth-inning grand slam off Wayne Twitchell as part of a 15–3 Braves rout of the Phillies. The home run was Aaron's tenth of the season, but of more significance, it was the 649th of his career, putting him ahead of the Mets' Willie Mays for second place on the all-time home run list. To those that had been tracking it closely, the passing of Mays by Aaron had been inevitable. At age 38, the Atlanta right fielder/first baseman was three years younger than the more-celebrated Mays. More importantly, however, while Mays had been slowing down at an alarming rate in recent years, Aaron was in the midst of a power surge that was as strong as any period in his 18-year career. He had hit 129 round-trippers over the previous three seasons, including a career-high 47 in 1971. His strong start again in 1972 convinced most that Aaron was a legitimate threat to the immortal Babe Ruth's epic total of 714.

Back in Detroit more than 40,000 fans poured into Tiger Stadium for the Sunday finale with the A's, hoping the Tigers could salvage one game from the series. The weekend would draw a total just under 98,000 fans, proving baseball was strong and healthy in Detroit. The game had been tied through eight innings, with Joe Coleman and Oakland lefty Ken Holtzman dueling. With two outs in the top of the ninth inning, the A's had put the potential lead run in Ollie Brown at second base. However, Bill Freehan saved the day by lulling the Oakland runner, who had wondered too far off the base on the pitch, into a false sense of security. As Brown sauntered slowly back towards the bag, the Detroit catcher bolted through the grass on the left side of the mound until a spooked Brown broke back towards second base. Freehan's flip to shortstop Eddie Brinkman picked the runner off for the third out. Cementing his status as the hero of the day, Freehan led off the bottom of the inning and hit Holtzman's first pitch for a game-winning home run, allowing the Tigers to take one game of the series from their cross-division rival.

"It's just natural reaction to be fired up after you make a play like that," said Freehan in the Detroit clubhouse after the game, talking about the chasing down of the Oakland runner just prior to his dramatic game-winning hit. "I wasn't thinking about a home run. I wasn't thinking about anything. I was just looking for a strike. That was the same pitch I had been popping up all afternoon."[9]

The homer was only the fourth hit allowed by Holtzman, who had been Oakland's best pitcher through the first two months of the season. The big left-hander had been acquired during the offseason from the Cubs after also being pursued by the Tigers at the winter meetings.

It was a tough-luck day for Coleman, who didn't get the win despite throttling the Oakland batters with an assortment of hard fastballs and his baffling forkball, limiting them to just two hits in eight innings. Seelbach got the win despite being in trouble during his one inning of work. Coleman dismissed the importance of adding to his statistical record over the much-needed win by the team. "We needed to win this game more than I needed a win."[10]

After going 5–4 during the nine-game homestand, Detroit hit the road for its longest trip of the season, a fourteen-day, twelve-game journey that included visits to both coasts and games against three of the best teams in the league. First they headed to Minnesota for a three-game series with the Twins. In the opener that happened to be the *NBC Monday Night Baseball* debut for 1972, the Tigers managed to scratch out a 2–1 victory behind solo home runs from Norm Cash and Mickey Stanley. Despite giving up nine hits in only six innings pitched, Joe Niekro was able to scatter enough of them to hold the Twins to just one run. Fred Scherman took over from there, slamming the door shut over the final three innings in relief.

On Tuesday, the Twins evened the series with a 3–1 win in a rain-shortened game that lasted only six innings. The loss was Detroit's fifth in its last seven decisions, and coupled with an Oriole hot streak, left the two teams tied at the top of the division. The four-game lead the Tigers enjoyed only a week earlier had eroded. Detroit took the series, however, by pulling out a 3–2 victory in the rubber game Wednesday night. A Rodriguez squeeze bunt scored Brinkman with the winning run, while Lolich went the distance for his tenth win, equaling the league-leading totals of Wilbur Wood and Gaylord Perry. The complete-game effort was Lolich's first in six attempts, and despite feeling sick that night, he limited Minnesota's scoring to a two-run homer by Killebrew. The 36-year-old first baseman's home run was the 522nd of his career, which moved him past Ted Williams into sixth place on the all-time list.

Thursday, June 15, was an off day, most of which was spent in Minneapolis as the team prepared to fly to the West Coast to face the California Angels. The date was significant because the trade deadline had arrived. Deals after the midnight deadline would require a player to clear waivers prior to being traded, prohibiting almost any substantial move. Detroit's ability to stay in the divisional race while riding two starting pitchers—Lolich and Coleman primarily, with Timmerman slowly gaining trust as a third starter—was certain to be tested as the schedule became less forgiving. Off days and weather postponements would almost certainly become fewer and farther between as the summer weather set in and the makeup doubleheaders mounted. The need for another reliable starter would become more critical, especially as the team tried to keep pace with Baltimore and its imposing four-man staff of McNally, Cuellar, Palmer, and Dobson.

Fueling rumors that a trade was imminent was the sighting of Texas owner Bob Short in Minneapolis during the Tigers series. Short had already been fleeced once by Campbell in the McLain trade with Washington 20 months earlier but was again in discussions with the Detroit general manager. The subject this time centered on Dick Bosman, a quality right-handed starter who had suffered for years on bad Washington and now Texas teams. Despite the talks, Campbell seemed frustrated when asked by the press about his efforts to land a starting pitcher for his contending team.

"I can't trade Bill Freehan ... I can't trade Aurelio Rodriguez ... I can't trade Ed Brinkman. Those are some of the names that keep coming up when we start talking about top-notch pitchers. We could afford to trade one of our outfielders if we got the right pitcher in return. But we're not going to take just anybody, just to be able to say 'Whee, we made a trade.' A lot of people are interested in the pitchers we already have."[11]

As the Tiger contingent boarded a plane and flew west to Anaheim, the trade deadline passed quietly on the East Coast for Detroit. There was rumor of a Horton-for-New York's Mel Stottlemyre offer that apparently was turned down by the Yankees, and an inquiry into the availability of Milwaukee's Jim Lonborg, but nothing materialized. For the second time in less than a year, including the winter meetings that past December, Campbell had failed to deliver the starting pitcher that Billy Martin so desperately wanted.

More bad news of the off-the-field variety came the next day. An appeal against a court decision preventing the sale of bonds to finance the $126 million domed stadium intended to be the future home of the Tigers was overruled, effectively ending any momentum towards public financing for such a structure. The decision was based on sentiment to not use public money for construction of a stadium used mostly for the benefit of a private business, namely the Detroit Baseball Club. Tigers owner John Fetzer accepted the decision evenly and seemingly closed the door to further court battles over the outcome. Instead, he acknowledged that Tiger Stadium would continue to be the franchise's home as it had been under various names since 1912.

"There's not going to be any renegotiation of our lease. We have been very happy operating in Tiger Stadium. We can use that stadium for years more."[12]

As play began on June 16, Detroit and Baltimore stood tied at the top of the A.L. East standings with identical 28–22 records. The two teams were starting to separate somewhat from the rest of the pack, as Cleveland was now four games back in third place and fading after its fast start. Detroit started play in Anaheim that night already knowing that Baltimore was a winner for the eighth straight time back in Minnesota. The Tigers kept pace behind a two-run homer from McAuliffe and a solo shot by Stanley to back Coleman's three-hit, 10-strikeout masterpiece in a 3–0 Detroit victory over the Angels.

The next night began in similar fashion. Baltimore kept the pressure on with a 4–1 win over Minnesota for its ninth straight win. Then Detroit went out and was blown away for most of its game by Angel left-hander Rudy May, who struck out twelve batters over the first seven innings. The Tigers had managed to scratch out a couple of runs, however, and when May got lifted for a pinch-hitter in the bottom of the seventh in a 2–2 tie, they had their opportunity. Stanley, who had struck out three times against May, led off the ninth inning with a single off California reliever Lloyd Allen. Gates Brown followed with a hit, and then Tony Taylor singled in Stanley with what proved to be the winning run. Timmerman pitched eight strong innings, which was just long enough to be the benefactor of the ninth-inning rally for his fifth win (5–5), while Seelbach polished off California in the Angels' half of the ninth for the save.

On Sunday afternoon, Lolich came through with his best performance in weeks in a 2–0 shutout victory over the light-hitting Angels, besting Nolan Ryan. The game had been a scoreless duel between two of the premier strikeout pitchers in the league that season until Jim Northrup crushed a ball into the Angels' bullpen in the seventh inning. The home run was Northrup's long-overdue first of the season, coming in his 142nd at-bat. Cash added an insurance run with a solo shot in the ninth inning, his twelfth, to complete the three-game sweep in Anaheim.

Elsewhere in the league that day, Oakland's Vida Blue, the reigning Cy Young and MVP awards winner, gained his first victory of the season with a four-hit shutout of the Indians. Blue had struggled to find that elusive first win since coming off his lengthy spring holdout and now found himself with a 1–3 record since his return. The bigger news to Detroit, however, was that Baltimore had finally been cooled off, losing 4–3 at Minnesota. The Twins' victory had ended the Orioles' nine-game winning streak and moved the Tigers back into sole possession of first place, a mark not lost on Martin as he continued his war of words with his chief competitor in the division race.

> This has got to have an effect on them, no matter what Weaver says. They win nine in a row, then they lose once and they drop one game out of first place. I'm glad this happened. Now they know they've got a race on their hands, and that could make a difference with that ball club. One writer just asked me how it felt to be back in front of Baltimore again. Hell, we've been in first place more than they have this year. That question should be the other way around. And we haven't busted loose yet. If we can keep going in Oakland, we'll have Baltimore with their backs against the wall when we go in there next weekend.[13]

On Monday, June 19, 1972, people might have taken note of a strange front-page article in their morning newspaper that invited mild curiosity. The *Detroit Free Press* placed the story at the bottom left of the page, well below the front section's primary news of a 24-hour strike by the nation's airline pilots that was set to take effect that day. What readers had no way of knowing was the story headlined "GOP Election Aide Held in Snoop-in" would dominate the nation's attention for the next 27 months.[14] Details in the article told of arrests made in association with an odd break-in over the weekend in Washington, D.C. The target was the Democratic Party's headquarters, and among the six people arrested as part of the attempted burglary was James W. McCord, a security worker for the Commission for the Reelection of the President. No one knew that the primary name of the office complex which housed the Democratic headquarters, Watergate, would become synonymous with a scandal that would bring down a president within two years and impact how the office itself was viewed by the media, the people of the country and the world, and by the office holder themselves through the rest of the twentieth century and beyond.

Of larger significance within the world of baseball was a Supreme Court ruling handed down that same day. By a 5–3 vote, the court upheld the exemption of anti-trust laws in the governing of major league baseball and repealed the challenge of the reserve clause by former player Curt Flood. Flood, who was best known to Tiger fans as the St. Louis Cardinal center fielder who slipped on the Busch Stadium turf and watched Jim Northrup's drive sail over his head for the decisive two-run triple in Game 7 of the 1968 World Series, had been traded by the Cardinals following the 1969 season and took to court the long-standing reserve clause that forever bound a player to a franchise regardless of his contract status or length of service. The clause had effectively curtailed any notion of a player being able to determine a "market value" of his services, and suppressed any type of free movement by the players.

"I think the decision is constructive in its recognition that baseball has developed its present structure in reliance on past court decisions," said the commissioner of baseball, Bowie Kuhn, after hearing the decision. "The decision opens the way for renewed collective bargaining on the reserve system after the 1972 season."[15]

For the players the news was clearly a setback. But as the recently concluded strike had proved, major changes in the leverage of the players with the owners was possible through collective bargaining, and the reserve clause was a major target to be chipped away in future negotiations.

"We will continue in our efforts to remedy the inequities in baseball's present reserve system through collective bargaining" said Marvin Miller, executive director of the Major League Baseball Players Association.[16]

That evening in Oakland, A's first baseman Mike Epstein hit a three-run homer off Niekro to give his team the early lead. Detroit got two runs back on a Cash home run, and then scratched across a run in the eighth inning to tie the game. The Tigers missed a golden opportunity in that inning, however, as Horton, back off the disabled list, grounded into a bases-loaded, inning-ending double play. The missed opportunity came back to haunt them in the bottom of the inning when Oakland took advantage of some poor relief pitching. Seelbach gave up three straight singles to start the inning before Scherman came in and walked Epstein and Dave Duncan to force in two runs. Before the inning had ended, Phil Meeler allowed a run to score on a wild pitch and another on a sacrifice fly, as the A's broke open the tight game for a 7–4 win.

On Tuesday, Detroit's frustrations against Oakland continued when Joe Rudi led off the bottom of the eleventh inning with a homer off Seelbach to win the game, 3–2. The Tigers were able to muster only solo homers from Kaline and Cash off Catfish Hunter, who went all eleven innings for the A's. Kaline's home run, like Northrup's earlier on the West Coast swing, was his first of the season. The lack of offensive punch wasted another fine start by Coleman, who went eight innings, giving up only five hits and one earned run. Down the coast in Anaheim, the Orioles pulled out a 4–1 victory over the Angels, moving into a tie again with the Tigers.

Detroit managed to salvage the final game of the series with Oakland, just as the Tigers had eleven days earlier. Bill Freehan, who doubled in three runs, provided the big hit in the 5–2 victory. The three RBIs gave the Tiger catcher a team-leading 27 for the season. The win also pushed Detroit back into first place as Baltimore dropped a 6–3 game against California that evening.

With only a game separating the two teams in the standings, both Baltimore and Detroit flew cross-country to play a three-game weekend series, opening on Friday at the Orioles' home park, Memorial Stadium. With more than a third of the season having already been played, it appeared the division was settling into a two-team race. The two teams would play seven games against each other over the next eleven days, meaning every game was an opportunity for one of the teams to gain ground directly on the other. They would not meet again until September, a fact not lost on either side as the significance of the upcoming series came into focus.

For Baltimore the season to that point had been a struggle, particularly at the plate. Outside of their starting pitching, which remained strong, nothing about the 1972 edition of the Orioles resembled the teams that had averaged 106 wins a year over the past three seasons. Only the recent nine-game win streak had kept the team's head above water and from falling well behind in the standings. Their team batting average was .219, one of the lowest marks in the American League. Earl Weaver had juggled his lineup continuously, trying to find a combination that could produce the few runs his club needed most games. The shuffling of an everyday lineup that had been one of the most consistent in baseball history over recent seasons resulted in inconsistency in the field as well as at the plate.

Among the biggest fall-offs from previous seasons were such former stalwarts as leadoff man Don Buford, who was hitting .207 with one home run, and Paul Blair, who was hitting .254 with three home runs. Both had been key table-setters in Weaver's great lineups between 1969 and 1971. Second baseman Dave Johnson was hitting .242 after being in the .280s the previous two seasons. Catcher Andy Etchebarren and shortstop Mark Belanger, neither of whom was known as a great hitter, were nonetheless sinking to new lows, batting .175 and .168, respectively, as regulars in the Orioles lineup. Merv Rettenmund, who had hit .322 and .318 in a part-time role over the past two years, prompting Baltimore to trade Frank Robinson to make room for him, checked in with a woefully unproductive .254 average with three homers and only nine RBIs. Even old pro Brooks Robinson was suffering through a sub-par start with only two home runs and 18 RBIs while trying to make up for the "other" Robinson.

"Sure, I've felt it. You could feel it right from the start of spring training," said the Oriole third baseman about the loss of his namesake in Baltimore's attack. "Frank meant a lot to us. You just don't lose a player like that and not feel it. I guess I've been trying to make up for it myself."[17]

Weaver was asked incessantly about the trade, especially with the team not playing up to its recent standards and struggling at the plate. When asked again near midseason about the loss of Robinson, the Orioles manager quipped, "Hell, we've missed Boog a lot more."[18]

His comment referred to the biggest disappointment of all for Oriole followers, the anemic hitting from their all-star first baseman, John "Boog" Powell. The muscular left-handed hitting slugger with the blonde brush cut was less than two years removed from being the MVP of the American League when he put up numbers that included a .297 average, 35 home runs, and 114 RBIs. Heading into the important series with Detroit, he was hitting a putrid .168, with only four home runs and 18 RBIs. There was talk of poor eyesight and a possible need for glasses, but whatever the cause, his fall-off at the plate most exemplified the sudden helplessness of the Baltimore attack.

As the teams readied for their series in Baltimore, Weaver tried to downplay the lack of prowess his hitters had shown thus far in the season. "I'm not worried. We've never led the league in hitting yet. Powell has got some glasses coming and maybe they'll help, and Brooks has been getting the big hits for us. We'll be all right."[19]

The Orioles' best players so far had been a pair of rookies in infielder

Bobby Grich and outfielder Don Baylor. Both had been minor league stars for Baltimore's Triple-A Rochester team in recent years and were more than ready for their big league promotions. Grich gave Weaver tremendous flexibility in the lineup, playing well at every position in the infield. He also showed pop in his bat, as his .279 average and potential for power attested. Baylor was a big, rangy outfielder, fast and powerful, who was leading the team in home runs with seven and stolen bases with nine.

Baltimore veteran left-handed starter Dave McNally may have summed up his team's position best when he stated during that stretch of games with Detroit, "The biggest surprise to me is that we have played this poorly and we are still only two games out. But nobody is running away with this anyway. If some other team had caught fire earlier in the season, we'd be in trouble. We're not going to collapse, though. We feel this is a two-team race—just a matter of who starts hitting."[20]

Weather delayed the start of the three-game series. Hurricane Agnes dumped nearly 20 inches of rain in the Baltimore area, causing as many as 12 deaths in Maryland that week, and the Friday night game was postponed. With a make-up doubleheader scheduled for Saturday, Detroit manager Billy Martin decided to fire both barrels of his pitching shotgun at the Orioles, starting his two workhorses, Lolich and Coleman, in the twin-bill. In the first game the home run bug bit Lolich again. He pitched well but gave up long balls to Etchebarren and Blair, while Detroit could do nothing against McNally and reliever Roric Harrison. McNally, in fact, hurt his back in the second inning but continued to pitch with an assortment of off-speed pitches that kept the Tiger hitters in check.

"I didn't have a thing after the second inning—nothing," he said after the game. "I just threw the ball to the plate and hoped they wouldn't hit it."[21]

Following the 3–1 loss in the opener, Coleman came out and pitched brilliantly in the second game. The Tigers held a 1–0 lead in the bottom of the ninth, and Coleman was one out away from the victory when he walked Rettenmund. Terry Crowley then blooped a double that scored Rettenmund from first base and sent the game into extra innings. The game remained tied until the top of the twelfth inning, when Cash led off with a single off Oriole pitcher Doyle Alexander and eventually came around to score on a Stanley sacrifice fly. Coleman finally gave up the ball at that point to Chuck Seelbach, but only after going eleven innings while allowing four hits and striking out eleven Baltimore hitters in a dominant performance. Seelbach then closed out the much-needed victory with a save.

On Sunday afternoon the great pitching continued for the Tigers as Tom Timmerman struck out nine hitters through six innings. However, other than a Gates Brown solo homer in the first inning off Jim Palmer, Detroit could do nothing against the tall 26-year-old right-hander. When Brooks Robinson singled in the lead run in the sixth inning, the Orioles had all the runs they would need in a tight 2–1 win in the rubber game of the series. The two victories-to-one advantage in the series by Baltimore tied the two teams once again for the top spot in the A.L. East, with both teams sporting identical 33–26 records.

As the team returned home to open a short two-game series with the Yankees, Detroit optioned rookie pitcher Phil Meeler to Toledo and purchased the contract of pitcher Bill Slayback, with the intentions of immediately giving him a start in the Tiger rotation. Coming off three games in two days and having burned his only three reliable starters, Martin was looking for someone to fill a starting spot. The 24-year-old Slayback was a 6' 4", 185-pound Californian who had gone 7–4 at Triple-A Toledo while averaging more than a strikeout per inning. On Monday, June 26, Slayback gave the Detroit manager more than he could have dreamed of by no-hitting New York through the first seven innings. After Yankee outfielder John Callison singled to right to open the eighth, the air started to leak out of the balloon for the rookie right-hander. However, as Slayback walked off the mound after 8⅓ innings in his major league debut, the Tiger Stadium crowd of 30,961 gave him a standing ovation. Slayback was on his way to a 4–3 victory in an unexpected strong start. After the game, Martin announced that his rookie pitcher would immediately become the new fourth starter, taking the place of Niekro, who was being shoved to long relief.[22] Detroit swept the short series the next night with a 5–2 decision. The outcome was decided in the first inning when Rodriguez, Kaline, and Horton homered in succession off journeyman pitcher Wade Blasingame. Lolich, working on two days rest, earned the win while fanning nine in an otherwise workmanlike effort.

The Tigers next visited Boston for the first time all season. Coleman was battered around in the opener, giving up eight hits in 4⅔ innings pitched. The 5–3 Boston win was avenged the next night when Detroit staged a dramatic win. Red Sox rookie pitcher Lynn McGlothen shut the Tigers out through eight innings, and the visitors trailed, 4–0, heading into their last at bat in the top of the ninth inning. When Bill Freehan's ground ball was bobbled by the usually sure-handed Doug Griffin at second base, it didn't appear that any real damage would be done. However, after Cash fouled out, Kaline walked and Northrup singled, scoring Freehan. Paul Jata singled in Kaline, and then McAuliffe doubled to score two runs and tie the game. After the next three Detroit batters also managed to reach base, Freehan, batting for the second time in the inning, lofted a drive over the Green Monster in left field for a grand slam and an unlikely come-from-behind victory. Coupled with Baltimore's loss to New York, the Tigers moved two games ahead of the

Orioles as the rivals returned to Detroit for part two of their seven games in an eleven-day stretch.

Back in Detroit, pennant fever was starting to grip a city that hadn't tasted first place this late in the season since the world championship season of 1968. With the team seemingly starting to roll, up two games on its chief rival and now getting ready to host the Orioles in its own ballpark, Tiger fans gobbled up tickets to the four-game holiday weekend series. On Friday, June 30, 48,662 filled Tiger Stadium only to watch Grich lace a two-out first-inning single, which was followed by a Powell fly to left that eluded Willie Horton, who fell down on the play. The two runners then scored on a Brooks Robinson double, and the Tigers were down early, 2–0. The tone continued in the bottom of the inning when the first two Detroit batters reached base, only to have Northrup ground into a rally-killing double play. In the fifth, Don Buford reached base on Freehan's passed ball following a called third strike. The mistake was costly, as Buford came around to score what proved to be the winning run in a 3–2 Oriole victory. Pat Dobson, the ex-Tiger reliever from the Mayo Smith days, went the distance in the ever-important series opener and a personally satisfying win.

"I wanted to win this game more than any other game I've ever pitched," said Dobson after the game. The dig was directed not as much towards his former team, but rather towards comments attributed to Billy Martin and a jibe he had made about "hear(ing) the home runs ringing in the upper deck" whenever Dobson pitched in that stadium.[23]

On Saturday afternoon NBC was in town to televise the national game of the week, featuring a classic pitching duel between Lolich and McNally, winner of twenty games in each of the past four seasons. The matchup held to form into the sixth inning, when Kaline broke up the scoreless deadlock by driving a McNally pitch into the lower deck of the left field grandstand for a home run. Detroit added another run in the eighth and led 2–0 going into the top of the ninth inning. Lolich, meanwhile, shut down the Orioles on seven singles, and no Baltimore runner advanced past first base. But with one out and a runner on first, Baltimore second baseman Dave Johnson, who was suffering through a miserable season at the plate, smacked a drive deep into left field that looked like it had home run written all over it.

As Tiger left fielder Jim Northrup went back to the fence near the 365-foot mark, it appeared that the drive off Johnson's bat would sail into the lower deck beyond the portion of fence known as the auxiliary scoreboard and tie the game. As the ball came down on its steady descent, however, Northrup braced himself at the base of the fence, grabbed the screen portion with his right hand, and leaped as high as he could with his glove hand outstretched. Timing his jump beautifully, the ball settled into Northrup's glove just above the nine-foot-high screen, robbing the Baltimore batter of a home run. He came down in a crumple at the base of the fence, but jumped up quickly and fired the ball into Eddie Brinkman, who relayed the ball back to first baseman Paul Jata. The play doubled off Oriole runner Tom Shopay, who tried to scramble back from the shortstop side of second base. The result was a game-ending double play.

"I got there just before the ball did," said Northrup after the game. "I couldn't go back any further. It was jump then or never jump."[24]

The play became one of the season's signature moments, etched in the memory of anyone who followed the Tigers that year. For Northrup the play served as a bit of redemption, both from the game the previous evening and for his overall slow start with the bat. He entered the game as a pinch-runner for Horton, and then stayed in as a defensive replacement in left field. There he became the focus of boo-birds and hecklers out in the left field seating areas prior to the game-saving catch. "I had a bad night Friday, so they were ready for me today."

The thirty-two-year-old outfielder with the silver hair was likely to show up at any of the outfield spots on a given day or night. His natural position was right field, which he played capably. But the presence of future Hall of Famer and multiple Gold Glove winner Kaline prevented that position from being Northrup's on a full-time basis. Only the ever-increasing number of games that Al missed due to age and injury allowed Northrup to play as regularly as he did at his most natural position. Instead, he saw primary duty in center field against right-handed starting pitchers, where Martin was willing to sacrifice Mickey Stanley's tremendous defensive ability in order to get Northrup's left-handed bat in the lineup. On days when Kaline was manning right field and Detroit held a lead late in the game, Martin often inserted Stanley into center field as a defensive replacement and then shifted Northrup over to left, where he was better than either Horton or Gates Brown as a fielder. Out of the 127 games Northrup would play in the field that season, he manned multiple outfield positions within the same game on 35 occasions.

It was at the plate, however, where the fans' frustrations with Northrup mounted most. He had been both a baseball and football star at Alma College in Michigan, and had moved quickly through the Tiger system after turning professional. He hit sixteen home runs in his second season in the majors in 1966, and had been a semi-regular in the Detroit outfield ever since. His breakout season came in 1968 when he hit five grand slams, including one in the World Series. Yet despite a string of very fine seasons, it always seemed he was capable of more. He had a sweet lefty swing and could propel balls into the deepest reaches of the right field bleachers in stadiums throughout the league. He hit .295 in 1969 with 25 home runs, statistics that seemed like they should be the norm for a player of Northrup's ability. But with the 1972 season more than forty percent complete, he was scuffling along with only two home runs and nine RBIs, less than half of what the perennially light-hitting Brinkman had produced. Martin shared the fans' exasperation over the streakiness, the weak swings at times against left-handed pitchers, and the inconsistency. It was no secret that Northrup and Martin feuded constantly. But with the injury-prone Horton and Kaline in and out of the lineup so often, it was doubtful the team could win a pennant without a big second half from the player known to his teammates as "the Fox."

Whatever momentum that might have been gained from the dramatic victory on Saturday disappeared quickly on Sunday. Sporting new glasses at the plate, Powell delivered a first-inning, three-run homer off Coleman that set the tone for Baltimore in an eventual 7–2 victory over the Tigers. The Orioles' Mike Cuellar held Detroit off the scoreboard until Freehan hit a meaningless ninth-inning two-run homer off the facing of the upper deck in left field. Things got even worse the next night as the two teams played their final game against each other until September. With 50,835 fans in the stadium and a national TV audience watching, Northrup socked an early homer, giving Detroit a 2–0 lead against Baltimore's top starter, Jim Palmer. The lead wouldn't last, however. The Orioles sent ten batters to the plate in the sixth inning, scoring six runs on six hits and two Tiger errors. Two innings later, they sent twelve batters to the plate and scored seven more runs. Before it was over, the previously weak-hitting Baltimore team had knocked around six Tiger pitchers for 21 hits, including three home runs, in a 15–3 romp. Palmer's complete-game victory (his record was 11–4) gave Baltimore the three games-to-one edge in the series, and tied the two teams once again for the division lead.

"We go into Chicago next, and we've got to win there too," said Weaver, taking in stride the series win as well as the 9–4 record his team had in head-to-head games against Detroit, versus the scores of Tiger backers who were jumping ship and now expected to see their team get bypassed by the high-flying Orioles. "In order for us to win the pennant, or for Detroit to win it for that matter, we've got to beat the bleep out of everybody day in and day out."[25]

For Detroit it was time to regroup. The team licked its wounds as the Tigers moved into Kansas City for a Fourth of July matchup with the Royals. As Baltimore continued its hot streak with a 2–1 win in Chicago, the Tigers looked helpless in a listless 1–0 loss in the heat and humidity of midsummer in Missouri. Kansas City's Roger Nelson completed the game for his first win as a starter in the majors since 1969, holding Detroit to only four hits.

The loss dropped Detroit's record to 37–31, and the Tigers fell out of first place for the first time in 57 days. The off-season question marks about the team began to creep back into the minds of fans and media, and observers both close to the team and from afar began to whisper about the age of the team and the lack of depth on the pitching staff. Doubts concerning those weaknesses and Detroit's ability to hold up through the heat of the long summer left many expecting the Tigers to begin falling back in the race, and for the Orioles to take control as they had for the past three seasons.

The Fourth of July is a traditional marker in the long baseball season, a point where keen baseball observers note not only the positioning of the teams at that holiday date but also the direction they are headed. Weaknesses that had been covered through the spring months get exposed as the games run together and the grind of the season takes its toll. Teams built to win, with talent and depth, experience and poise, begin to assert themselves. For a Detroit team that had managed a solid start and had sat at the top of its division for most of the first three months, the past two weeks had been a blown opportunity to take control. Worse yet, they had allowed their chief competitor to grab the top spot away from them in head-to-head action. As July 4, 1972, came and went, there was little doubt that the next few weeks would be a crucial juncture in the season for the Detroit Tigers.

American League East Standings through July 4, 1972

	W	*L*	*Pct.*	*GB*
Baltimore Orioles	38	30	.559	—
Detroit Tigers	37	31	.541	1
Boston Red Sox	32	34	.485	5
New York Yankees	31	35	.470	6
Cleveland Indians	28	39	.418	9½
Milwaukee Brewers	27	40	.403	10½

VI

Hitting Their Stride

The biggest story in baseball on July 4, 1972, centered on the checkered career of ex-Tiger Denny McLain. After starting the season with a forgettable stint with the A's, McLain had been banished to Oakland's Birmingham, Alabama, Double-A affiliate until he was traded in late June to the pitching-starved Atlanta Braves. The Braves viewed McLain as both a desperation-worthy pitching candidate for their rotation and a player whose off-field persona still made him one of baseball's few true drawing cards. More than fifty thousand fans turned out in Atlanta to watch McLain's National League debut on the evening of the nation's 196th birthday, and their new pitcher drew a standing ovation as he headed to the mound to start the game. McLain's effort was nondescript in what turned into an anticlimactic 3–3 washout after rain ended the game with the Chicago Cubs in the eighth inning. McLain's return to the big leagues overshadowed a brilliant performance that day by future Hall of Famer Tom Seaver, who lost a no-hit bid in the ninth inning in his 2–0, one-hit shutout of the San Diego Padres.

The races in the National League were starting to take shape much as predicted. The senior circuit's surprise team in the early season had been the New York Mets. Besides their riveting acquisition of future Hall of Famer Willie Mays, the Mets had strung together seven- and eleven-game winning streaks during the first five weeks while winning games at a .700 clip into early June. Injuries, as well as the team settling to a level of play more commensurate with their talent level brought New York back to the quickening paces of the hard-hitting and defending world champion Pittsburgh Pirates. As the country paused to observe the Fourth of July holiday, the Pirates found themselves leading the N.L. East by a game over the Mets and 6½ games over both the Cubs and the St. Louis Cardinals. Over in the N.L. West, the Cincinnati Reds had raced past the early leaders of their division, the Los Angeles Dodgers, and now led the Houston Astros by ½ game and the Dodgers by a staggering 7½.

Back in the American League, the Western Division was becoming the exclusive domain of the Oakland A's, who sported the best record in baseball at 46–24. Their lead was a full five games ahead of the Chicago White Sox and 9½ over the Minnesota Twins. Gaining on the rest of the division were the Kansas City Royals, winners of 22 of their past 31 games, making them the hottest team in the A.L.

An expansion team in 1969, the Royals had quickly sown the seeds for a club that would blossom by the mid-seventies into one of the best in baseball, and one that would make an extended run of excellence, lasting nearly 15 years. Kansas City finished a remarkable 85–76 in only its third year of existence in 1971, and despite getting off to a slow start in 1972, had a lineup filled with exciting young players. They boasted five of the top seven hitters in the league, with outfielders Richie Scheinblum (.333, 1st), Lou Piniella (.314, 2nd), and Amos Otis (.300, 5th), infielders John Mayberry (.297, 6th) and Cookie Rojas (.294, 7th), and catcher Ed Kirkpatrick (.293, but not enough at-bats to qualify for league-leader status) leading the way as part of KC's A.L.-leading .265 average. Mayberry, a Detroit native who had been obtained from the Houston organization in the offseason, had been the big addition to the Royals' attack in 1972. He provided a much-needed power threat to the middle of the Kansas City lineup, and already had nine home runs and 45 RBIs (2nd in the league). The Royals could beat teams with their legs as well, as shortstop Fred Patek (17 stolen bases) and Otis (13) were among the leaders in that category.[1]

In the second game of their series with the Tigers, the Royals battered around Mickey Lolich for ten hits and six earned runs in only 5⅓ innings on their way to an 8–2 win. It was Detroit's fourth straight loss, and dropped the Tigers two full games behind Baltimore, which had just beaten Chicago, 1–0. The Tigers managed only three measly singles in the game (giving them a total of seven hits in the series thus far), including a two-run single by Tony Taylor, who accounted for two of the three hits.

Taylor was one of the few Detroit hitters finding success on a regular basis as midseason approached. His .336 average, albeit in a platoon role against predominantly left-handed pitching, was by far the best on the squad. In fact, Freehan (.282 and a team-leading 36 RBIs), Northrup (.253), and Cash (.251) were the only Tiger regulars who were over the .250 mark entering the Kansas City series. More typical of the batting marks Billy Martin had to consider each day as he filled out his lineup card were the plummeting numbers held by such regulars as Horton (.234 and only 12 RBIs), Rodriguez (.235), McAuliffe (.225), Stanley (.224), and his everyday shortstop, Brinkman (.197).[2]

The final game of the series was a milestone of sorts. The Tigers were completing their second and last trip of the season into Kansas City, and with it were playing their final game ever in KC's Municipal Stadium. Work was being completed that summer on the Royals' shiny new stadium, complete with artificial turf and a waterfall over the center field fence, as part of the Harry S Truman Sports Complex that would be ready for the opening of the 1973 season. Municipal Stadium had been a home to professional baseball for nearly fifty years, and with the exception of the 1968 season, had hosted major league baseball since 1954, when the Athletics migrated from Philadelphia. The steel girder stadium was reminiscent of Tiger Stadium, except that its double-decked grandstands only extended down both lines from the infield, leaving only a small bleacher area in the outfield, which limited its capacity at just over 35,000. The stadium was probably best remembered for the intense heat that baked the field during the humid Missouri summers, and for the wide expanses in the outfield that saw power alleys of 409 and 382 feet at the left-center and right-center field fence, respectively.[3]

The Tigers celebrated their last game in the old stadium by exploding for their second-highest hit total of the season (13) in a 7–0 romp over the Royals. Coleman earned the complete-game shutout victory to push his record to 10–7, but the real story was the awakened bats of several Detroit hitters. Rodriguez, who was suffering through an 0-for-22 stretch, laced a first-inning double that represented the team's first extra-base hit in 22 innings. Brinkman broke out of a 1-for-31 slump with a single and two RBIs. Horton and Stanley each got hits to break out of 1-for-18 steaks, Freehan contributed two hits and three RBIs, while Taylor banged out three more hits on the night. The win allowed Detroit to keep pace with Baltimore, which rode Mike Cuellar's five-hitter and lead-producing hit in the eighth inning in a 2–1 win over Chicago for the Orioles' fifth straight victory.

The next night it was the Tigers' turn to play in Chicago, and the hits rang off the Detroit bats again. They knocked out twelve more hits, including home runs by Kaline and Ike Brown, but it took a well-placed hit by the red-hot Taylor to deliver the victory. With the score tied at two in the top of the eighth inning, Paul Jata was on base with no outs and the White Sox expecting a bunt from Taylor. With the corner infielders charging, Taylor slammed a ball over the head of Dick Allen at first base and into the right field corner. The resulting triple put the Tigers ahead to stay, as Chuck Seelbach got the decision in relief of Tom Timmerman in the 6–4 Detroit win.

Before the game the Tigers made a roster move, releasing the often-injured Les Cain from the major league roster and assigning him to Toledo. The move effectively ended any chance of Cain ever pitching in Detroit again, but with his squad in a pennant race and in need of game-ready arms, manager Billy Martin couldn't afford to wait any longer for a pitcher who had not regained his form since being injured earlier in the season. "He's thrown on the sidelines four times since then, and hasn't thrown hard at all," said Martin. "Right now I don't think I could take a chance on putting him out there."[4]

Added to the roster was left-handed pitcher John Hiller. The story of Hiller's improbable return began back in the mid-sixties when he had forged a role as a swingman capable of pitching in almost any role. During the championship season in 1968, he served out of the bullpen for half the season before manager Mayo Smith turned to Hiller as his fourth starter for most of the last two months. His one-hit shutout over Chicago was one of the memorable pitching gems of that magical season. Consistency was something that Hiller was never able to harness over the next couple of seasons, however, and he was in jeopardy of losing his spot on the team when he suffered a heart attack during the winter of 1970–71, at age 26.

Before the heart attack, Hiller had grown to the point that he resembled the body type of Lolich, and admittedly had not lived the life of a finely tuned athlete. The setback seemed to change his outlook towards his health, as well as igniting a determination to pitch again for Detroit. Following intestinal bypass surgery, Hiller spent a year's recovery on his own in his hometown of Duluth, Minnesota. The 28-year-old professional athlete started physical rehabilitation with the most basic of exercise routines while also working a full-time job to make ends meet. After months of tortuous therapy, he worked his way back into shape. When the doctors gave him clearance to play again, Hiller wanted to make a comeback with the Tigers.

The Detroit organization was not quite as enthusiastic about the apparent fairy-tale comeback attempt. Heart surgery in 1972 was not nearly as common a procedure as it is today, and it was almost unthinkable to believe that someone would recover from such an ordeal and compete again in professional sports. An event from the previous fall was still fresh in Detroiters minds as well, which contributed to the trepidation. The Detroit Lions' Chuck Hughes suffered a massive heart attack and died while on the field at Tiger Stadium in November of 1971. Hiller's comeback attempt was largely viewed as tempting fate and going against good sense. Instead, the Detroit organization offered Hiller in the spring of 1972 a job as a spring training batting practice pitcher and minor league pitching coach.

After the big league team headed north to start the season, Hiller stayed with the minor league affiliate in Lakeland and continued to work himself back into game shape. By July of 1972, with Detroit desperate for pitching help, the organization was finally ready to take a chance on their former left-hander. He had lost a lot of weight and appeared trim, even skinny, to many who remembered the more rotund Hiller from only a couple of years back. It was his left arm, however, that people in the organization would soon be speaking about. His fastball was better than ever. Combined with a sharp breaking ball and an excellent change-up, Hiller definitely looked like a player that could help the team the rest of the way.

In typical Martin fashion, he put Hiller and Cain together in a competitive bullpen session to determine who would be added to the staff. By all accounts, it was no contest. Hiller blew away Cain in the head-to-head matchup and was added to the roster. Years later in *The Tigers of '68*, Hiller described the resolve he had in that bullpen session: "I don't want to be irreverent or anything, but they could have put Jesus Christ on the mound next to me, and I'd have out-thrown him. After what I'd been through, no way I wouldn't get that job."[5]

On Saturday, July 8, Hiller appeared in a major league game for the first time since the regular-season finale in 1970. Thrown into a long relief role that day, he pitched a credible three innings, giving up only four hits, with the only real damage coming from a mammoth home run off the bat of Allen, the league's leader in homers and RBIs.

"I was more relaxed than I thought, I'd be," he said after the game. "I've been more nervous than this on the first day of spring training. I threw more strikes than I thought I would too. But then I've been through a lot the last two years, and this is what I want. I really want it."[6]

Unfortunately for Detroit, the game had already gotten away from the Tigers by the time Hiller entered the contest. The White Sox scored three runs in the second inning, courtesy of a couple of defensive gaffes by the normally solid Tiger defense. Norm Cash was eaten up by a ground ball for an error, and then Northrup misjudged a fly ball that dropped into center field, undoing an otherwise solid effort by the rookie Billy Slayback, as Chicago prevailed, 5–2.

On Sunday the two teams split a doubleheader. Chicago took the first game, 5–4, scoring the winning run in the bottom of the ninth inning. In the nightcap, Lolich struck out ten White Sox, but it took a Tom Haller two-run homer in the top of the ninth inning, his third hit of the game, for Detroit to pull out the 4–2 victory. The win was Lolich's 14th of the season. Despite managing only a split in the doubleheader as well as in the series, Detroit gained ground and moved back into a tie with Baltimore. Amazingly, the Orioles had been swept at home in a four-game series by the A.L. West's last-place team, the Texas Rangers.

On Monday, July 10, as those same Texas Rangers came into Detroit to open a series, the nation focused much of its attention on the Democratic National Convention, which opened that day in Miami. While roving bands of protestors tore down fences and clashed with police and state troopers armed with night sticks and mace, the first night of the convention was highlighted by the party's decision to award all of the delegate votes from the state of California's recent primary to Democratic front-runner George S. McGovern. The decision, which went against the wishes of such Democratic powerbrokers as Ted Kennedy, Hubert Humphrey, and Jimmy Carter, assured the senator from South Dakota of the delegate total to win the nomination.

At Tiger Stadium that evening, Detroit jumped all over the visitors from the Lone Star State. The Tigers scored two runs in the bottom of the first inning, led 7–0 after three innings, and cruised to an 8–3 victory. The offensive stars were Cash, who belted two home runs, and Northrup, who crashed a two-run job, lending plenty of support to Coleman, who won his 11th game against seven losses. The victory also propelled the Tigers back into sole possession of first place, as Baltimore was stunned by Kansas City in the ninth inning of a 3–2 loss. Leading 2–1 with two outs in the ninth inning, KC's Richie Scheinblum blooped a single off Mike Cuellar and then scored ahead of Lou Piniella on a two-run homer that won the game.

As news of the Orioles' collapse filtered down to the respective clubhouses in Tiger Stadium, ever-opinionated Rangers manager Ted Williams took the opportunity to comment on the Baltimore team he had just played the previous series and the apparent shift of balance taking place in the American League. "They're not getting the hitting that they have in the last three years, there is no question," he said, referring to Baltimore. "But you look in the book and they're also three years older. They're trying to inject youth into their team and it's helping, but the older players are just not doing what they have in the past.

"Two or three years ago it was true that the Eastern Division was much tougher than the West, when Baltimore was so strong. But it's possible that now the best clubs are in the West. Oakland and Chicago have given us a much harder time and shown more strength than either Detroit or Baltimore."[7]

Whether Williams' words provided additional motivation or not is unclear, but the Tigers continued their domination of the Rangers the next evening. On a date in which Boris Spassky of the Soviet Union and U.S. grand master Bobby Fischer opened play in a $250,000 series of chess matches for the championship of the planet, Detroit managed a 6–5 win on a hot, muggy evening. The victory did not come easy as Texas leadoff man Dave Nelson hit a first-inning home run and the situation deteriorated quickly from there for Tiger starter Tom Timmerman, who lasted only one-third of an inning. However, behind some lively hitting, as well as five strong innings of long relief from Fred Scherman, the Tigers managed to tie the game at five by the sixth inning. The tie was broken when Mickey Stanley crushed his ninth home run, which also gave him 30 RBIs, putting him among the team leaders in both categories despite hitting only a miniscule .229. Chuck Seelbach, who pitched the final 3⅔ innings, picked up the win in the 6–5 Detroit victory. Detroit completed the sweep the next night with a 3–1 victory behind the complete-game effort of Slayback. The series sweep was doubly rewarding when Kansas City exploded for seven runs in the top of the tenth inning in Baltimore, giving the Royals an 11–4 victory. The big hit was a grand slam by KC second baseman Cookie Rojas. That increased Detroit's lead to two games again in the A.L. East.

Kansas City came to Detroit next, and the Tigers greeted the Royals with five runs in the bottom of the first inning in the first game of the series. That was more than enough for Lolich, who seemed back on track while holding the Royals without a run into the eighth inning. Brinkman was the leading hitter in the game with a two-run single to cap the first-inning rally, and he later scored Ike Brown on a suicide squeeze in the third. The 6–4 Tiger win gave Lolich an overall mark of 15–6, the best record among pitchers in either league.

The Tigers' five-game winning streak came to an end the next day as the Royals' Bruce Dal Canton beat them, 1–0. Coleman again was the recipient of a tough-luck decision, as he combined with Seelbach on a three-hitter in the loss. The only run of the game came in the fourth inning, when Mayberry lined a two-out single that scored Amos Otis. The most noteworthy footnote about the Friday evening affair may have come when Martin put Tom Haller's name in his lineup at catcher. That same evening, the umpire crew's Bill Haller, Tom's older brother, took his regular turn as the home plate umpire, marking the first occasion in major league history when a brother combination had been behind the plate as catcher-umpire in the same game.

That same night, Cleveland's Gaylord Perry put together an amazing pitching performance against the Texas Rangers. Perry pitched shutout ball against Texas for the first 13 innings of a scoreless tie. Luckily, after being lifted for a pinch-hitter in the top of the fourteenth inning, the Tribe scratched across a couple of runs and Perry was able to gain his fifteenth win against only seven losses. The battle for the winningest pitcher in the majors continued between Perry, Lolich, and Chicago's Wilbur Wood.

As the four-game series with Kansas City moved into the weekend, the calendar reached mid–July. With it, the sports world sleepily welcomed the beginning of another professional sports season as NFL training camps opened up around the country. The big story locally as the Detroit Lions opened camp at the Cranbrook prep school was the contract holdout by quarterback Bill Munson. Elsewhere around the NFL, the storylines focused on enigmatic superstar running back Duane Thomas, who had left the Dallas Cowboys' camp under mysterious conditions, as well as the holdout by the biggest name in the game, Joe Namath, who was asking for the staggering figure of $250,000 per year to quarterback the New York Jets.

While the NFL season was just beginning, major league baseball was in midseason. The Tigers nipped any chance of a losing streak by winning on Saturday, 5–3, against the Royals. The game started in wearisome fashion as the Tigers left the bases loaded in the first inning without scoring, and then loaded the bases again in the second, this time with nobody out. However, after a strikeout and a pop-up, the runners were still standing at their respective bases, but now with two outs. Coming off the 1–0 loss the night before, in a game in which Detroit had managed only four hits, and with the team's maddening inability to string together any consistency at the plate, it appeared another frustrating day might be at hand, especially when Northrup grounded a ball straight at the KC shortstop, Fred Patek. But as the ball bounded off the grass and onto the dirt portion of the infield, it bounced over the head of Patek, who at 5'4" was the shortest player in the game. Two runs scored on the bad-hop single and the Tigers were on their way to a 5–3 win. The winning pitcher was Timmerman, who lasted six innings, his longest effort in his past five outings. The victory and solid outing turned in by Timmerman helped cool the speculation in the media that the outing was paramount to his remaining in the rotation.

"Billy showed nothing but confidence in me," he said after the game about the tenuous position of his starting spot. "I didn't feel today was a do or die day. Not at all."[8]

The solid pitching efforts continued the next day as Slayback hurled his best game yet, whitewashing the team with the highest team batting average in the league, 2–0. Cash and Aurelio Rodriguez provided the runs, courtesy of solo home runs, but it was the rookie right-hander who sent the 38,514 fans home happy from Tiger Stadium. Slayback evened his record at 3–3 with a five-hit, seven-strikeout effort, but more indicative of his efforts was the 1.64 ERA he sported, which reflected the quality starts he had given Detroit since his call-up from Triple-A.

A little bit farther down I-75 another great pitching performance occurred. Joe Niekro, who had just been optioned to Toledo to make room for rookie pitcher Fred Holdsworth, twirled a perfect game for the Mud Hens against Tidewater. Niekro had been selective with his comments to the media concerning his demotion, even though he was obviously upset about the lack of faith the organization had shown in him and the uneven work Martin had given him during the first half of the season. What the 1,258 fans at the Lucas County Recreation Center in Toledo couldn't realize that day is that they were watching a pitcher who would continue to struggle for another half a decade and change leagues and teams two more times before finding the success with the knuckleball that his older brother, Phil, had already achieved with the Atlanta Braves. By the early 1980s, Joe Niekro would be a multi-year 20-game winner while becoming one of the top pitchers in the National League during that period.

Chicago next came into town to close out the ten-game homestand for the Tigers. Lolich was strong again, striking out eleven White Sox batters while pitching his way to his 16th win in a 3–1 Detroit victory. Northrup hit his fifth home run of the year, a tape-measure shot off the facing of the third deck that sat over the right field stands at Tiger Stadium. All five of Northrup's round-trippers had come in less than a month's span, and his .419 batting streak during that period had raised his season average by 76 points, putting him among the team leaders in batting.

The attendance for the series opener with Chicago was 41,900. The big crowd for the Family Night promotion offered for each Monday evening game during the season pushed the attendance total for the season at Tiger Stadium past the one million mark. The milestone was reached at its earliest date in Detroit history, and mid-season forecasts had the projected season attendance nearing the highest in team history, totals achieved during the 1968 (2.0 million) and 1950 (1.95 million) seasons.

The fact that the strong attendance figures were being accumulated in a season that started with a public relations black eye like the player walkout and during a period where fan interest in baseball in general—and particularly in the American League—had waned considerably in recent years made it even more impressive. In 1972 Tiger Stadium was not revered as a cathedral of baseball as purists and romantics would later view it. Throughout its long history, the stadium was always considered a bastion for hitters with its excellent background, favorable distances in the power alleys, and that inviting right field upper-deck overhang. But like many of the older, traditional stadiums of the time, such as Yankee Stadium, Fenway Park, and Wrigley Field, it was viewed by many as outdated, dirty, and without the many amenities that most thought were needed to keep a younger generation coming to the game. The "cookie cutter" or "multi-purpose" stadiums that popped up throughout much of the National League in the late '60s and early '70s, with their artificial turf and crowd-engaging scoreboards, were considered to be the best direction for cities that wanted to progress with a modern sports facility. The thought that those modern stadiums lacked identity or did not hold the charm of the older stadiums was not yet in vogue.

Although later generations would remember Tiger Stadium with its bright blue and orange plastic seats, the interior of Tiger Stadium in the early '70s was a sea of drab park-bench-green, with wooden seats throughout the stadium except in deep center field, where there were dozens of rows of

Detroit's Tiger Stadium, one of the most hitter-friendly parks in all of baseball. Including playoff games, the Tigers drew more than 2 million fans in 1972, only the second time in their long history they reached that milestone figure (National Baseball Hall of Fame Library, Cooperstown, New York).

bleacher seats. The scoreboards were strictly functional — score, batter, count, number of outs — and not for entertainment purposes. The giant scoreboard behind the center field bleachers provided the out-of-town scores and pitching match-ups. The only music was provided via bouncy tunes played by the stadium organist. The concourse area was narrow, dark, and crowded. The concrete floors were sticky and smelled of stale beer. Bathrooms were visited only when absolutely necessary.

What fans did have as they settled into their seats in the double-decked stands surrounding the playing field were some of the best vantage points in the sport to watch a baseball game. The ground in foul territory was small, leaving fans close to the action. The upper deck was suspended immediately over the lower seating areas, giving fans in the upper reaches the illusion that they could reach out and touch the action. Smells of grilled hot dogs, roasted peanuts, and cigar smoke wafted through the air. The field was an eye-catching, bright shade of green, and carefully manicured — one of the best playing surfaces in baseball. The cries of uniformed vendors plying their trade barked over the steady buzz of the crowd. Hot dogs cost fifty cents. A soda cost thirty cents. Beer was seventy cents.[9]

While the ballpark slowly changed over the years, so did the fans that filled it. In 1972, it would have been rare to find a fan wearing apparel indicative of their love of the local team, as would become customary in later years. Some might be wearing a Tiger cap, but that would likely be the only visual indicator as to the loyalty of the home crowd. Men were typically dressed in slacks and a buttoned-down shirt. Ties would not be out of the ordinary; shorts and t-shirts would be. For women, the attire was usually slacks and a blouse, or maybe even a dress. Many fans wrote out the lineups and kept score in their 35-cent scorebook, probably with a 10-cent pencil picked up from a vendor.

Ticket prices were set at a tidy $4 for box seats, $3 for reserved seats, $2 for general admission lower deck seats, and $1 to sit in the upper-deck bleachers that extended from the upper left-center field area all the way over to right-center.[10] Besides the Family Nights on Monday evening games, Ladies and Retirees Days were held each Saturday afternoon. Shrine Night, Polish American Night, and Knights of Columbus Night were annual events that catered to sects of the fan base. Free bat, ball, and cap days were huge draws for families with youngsters.[11]

But most of all the fans that summer were attracted to a team full of familiar names that was contending once again. The old heroes from '68 — Kaline, Cash, Lolich, Freehan, McAuliffe, Horton, Stanley, Northrup, Gates Brown — were still playing major roles. Rodriguez and Brinkman had become favorites with their everyday presence and wizardry in the field. Down in the dugout, Martin had become a favorite with the blue-collar, working-class fans of the auto capital of the world. His fiery demeanor and aggressive brand of baseball enthralled him with fans that had become disenchanted with Mayo Smith's "wait and see" approach. The strong finish in 1971 and the interesting race that was developing in 1972 had reignited interest in the Tigers throughout Detroit and all of Michigan, and fans showed that by coming out in numbers that had the Tiger franchise leading the A.L. in attendance by a wide margin. By the All-Star break their attendance total would be more than 250,000 fans greater than the next closest team in the league (Chicago), and only the Mets and Dodgers in the National League had greater attendance totals at that point.

As the Chicago series resumed on Tuesday night, Norm Cash tripled in two runs in the third inning, but it took a Stanley triple off the right field fence followed by a Brinkman sacrifice fly in the 11th inning to finally win the game, 4–3, over the White Sox. Seelbach came out of the pen again and retired all eleven Chicago batters he faced to gain the victory. Chicago took the last game of the series, 3–2, when former Angel outfielder Rick Reichardt hit a pair of homers to back the effort of Wilbur Wood, who matched Lolich with his 15th win of the season. The left-handed knuckleball pitcher for the White Sox allowed Detroit only five hits on the evening.

The big news of the day came before the game when word passed through the Detroit clubhouse that Baltimore manager Earl Weaver had selected Lolich and Cash as reserves to the American League All-Star squad. They would join Freehan, who had been elected through the fan balloting. The honors came with controversy. Martin poked jabs through the press at his managerial rival for selecting three of his own Baltimore starting pitchers to the team (Palmer, McNally, and Dobson), even though Martin doubted that he'd use them.

"He picked 'em, but is he going to use them?" asked Martin, who was already looking for signs of Weaver using the mid-summer classic as a means for gaining a competitive edge on Detroit. "I'll bet you Lolich pitches before they do."[12]

Before the focus could turn to the mid-summer classic, the Tigers had to close out the pre–All-Star game portion of their schedule with a trip to Texas to face the Rangers in a four-game series. The series started on a positive note when Bill Slayback turned in an overpowering performance, fanning thirteen Texas batters in an easy 5–1 Detroit victory. The rookie right-hander was quickly establishing himself as the number-three starter, surpassing the struggling Tom Timmerman in Martin's rotation. "He pitched another great game," said the Detroit manager after the game. "The kid ought to be 7–0, but we just haven't gotten many runs for him."[13]

On Friday, the Rangers drew their largest crowd since moving to Arlington from Washington, D.C. More than 24,200 fans showed up at Arlington Stadium (still less than Detroit's average home attendance per game), a crowd that more than doubled their average gate of just over 10,000 per home date. Moved by owner Bob Short during the previous offseason, the Rangers were actually drawing less fans as a first-year franchise in the Dallas–Fort Worth area than the lame-duck Senators had the year before in the nation's capital. The record crowd didn't have much to cheer for, however. After allowing a run in the bottom of the first inning, Lolich handcuffed the Rangers the rest of the way for his 17th win of the season in a 3–1 Tiger victory. McAuliffe and Cash each homered to provide the bulk of Detroit's offense. Things were even easier the next night, as Detroit cruised to a 6–2 victory. Coleman benefited from the plentiful run support and went the distance for his twelfth win against eight losses.

On Sunday, July 23, the final day before the All-Star break, the series finale was scheduled at 5:30 P.M. local time in Arlington. Whether it was the highly unusual start time, fatigue, or maybe the lure of a three-day break that was just hours away for most of the team and coaches, the Tigers came out listless in a 3–1 loss to the last-place Rangers. Timmerman didn't make it out of the first inning, getting pulled after giving up three first-inning runs while recording only two outs. With the three-day break pending, Martin had the luxury of using nearly everyone on his pitching staff if needed. He wouldn't have to, however. Slayback was called into the game and gave a heroic effort, pitching seven shutout innings while giving his team an opportunity for the comeback that never happened. For only the second time in twelve tries all season, Texas held on to beat Detroit.

While Freehan, Cash, Lolich, and Hiller headed for Atlanta to participate in All-Star game festivities (Hiller as a specially appointed non-roster invitee in recognition of his extraordinary comeback effort), the rest of the team either headed back to Detroit or dispersed elsewhere for three days of relaxation away from baseball. The break came on the heels of Detroit's best stretch thus far in the season. Since falling two games back of Baltimore on July 5, the team had gone on a 14–5 run that left the Tigers holding a one-game lead on the Orioles and a five-game lead on the surging Red Sox. The significance of the hot streak was magnified by the fact that while Detroit was winning at a .700 clip for that three-week span, Baltimore was more than holding its own by playing .600 ball during that same period.

"It did us a lot of good to stay ahead of Baltimore by winning 12 of 15 games before All-Star time," noted Freehan, as he prepared to move on to Atlanta as the starting catcher for the American League. "The Orioles were in a hot streak and they weren't able to take over because of the way we were playing."[14]

The way Detroit was playing and winning was not exactly what had been scripted before the season started. Most pundits expected the Tigers to be among the more potent clubs offensively, certainly in the American League and possibly throughout baseball. They had led the majors in home runs in 1971 and had finished fifth in the majors in runs scored. Their everyday lineup was filled with veterans with proven track records, and much of the same was expected in 1972. Instead, the team had struggled offensively through much of the season's first half. They were in the middle of the pack in the A.L. in runs scored, averaging a modest 3.5 runs per game. With the exception of Cash, there really hadn't been a consistent home run threat, and only Cash, Freehan, and Stanley had produced runs at a rate that most expected. Compounding the diminished power numbers were the paltry batting averages that led to an overall team mark of .230. On days when the ball wasn't flying out of the ballpark a time or two, stringing together enough singles and doubles to put runs on the board was proving to be a challenge.

Making the batting affliction even more difficult to overcome was the negligible contribution Detroit received from its pitchers at the plate. There had been talk within the game for a number of years about eliminating the pitcher in the batting lineup and replacing him with a "designated pinch hitter." The concept had been experimented with at different times in a few spring training games but without a general consensus on how or when to implement it. In 1972 the pitcher still took his regular turn at the plate in both leagues, and Tiger pitchers were among the most inept in all of baseball. Lolich, who had by far the most at-bats on the team among Detroit's hurlers, was hitting .085, hadn't knocked in a run, and had scored only two. Coleman was hitting .118 with two RBIs and two runs scored. Timmerman was at .103 with two runs scored. Seelbach, Scherman, Niekro, Slayback, and Cain had combined for 10 hits and only three runs scored. The lack of offensive contributions Detroit received was best exemplified when compared against the offensive exploits of the Oakland A's, leaders of the Western Division at the break. Their top two starters, Catfish Hunter and Ken Holtzman, had combined for 24 hits and nine RBIs, while carrying a commendable .200 batting average. The two had also helped their cause by chipping in with 15 sacrifice bunts.[15]

"When our offense comes around, we'll really be tough to handle," said Freehan of the facet of the Tigers' game that had never fulfilled the promise it had shown in spring training. "I'm thinking of quite a few who can improve the job they are doing with the bat."[16]

Martin was already countering the sub-par seasons that seemed to be plaguing so many of his big guns. Never one that liked to sit back and wait for the late-inning, three-run homer to win the game, Martin always preached aggressive baseball, and started to use that philosophy more often with his team in Detroit. Batters were hitting behind runners, laying down sacrifice bunts, utilizing the hit and run while also employing his favorite tactic, the suicide squeeze. Martin would use any means he could to move a runner up a base, and the team took on that personality as well. Although they lacked team speed, the Tigers began running the bases more aggressively, taking unexpected chances, knocking down middle infielders on double-play chances, anything to prevent an out or score a run. That type of approach was becoming more common as they grasped for ways to offset the diminished power numbers of players like Horton, Kaline, and Northrup. It also gave added value to players who could handle a bat in any situation, like Taylor, McAuliffe, and Brinkman. Finding ways to scratch out the two or three runs it took to win each day became the norm rather than waiting for those home runs that weren't coming with their old consistency.

It was pitching that was supposed to be the Achilles' heel for Detroit and its big disadvantage in the head-to-head duel with Baltimore. However, what they lacking in pitching depth they were managing to make up in quality. Martin was relying heavily on his workhorses, Lolich and Coleman, in the starting rotation, while Scherman and Seelbach were seeing the vast majority of meaningful relief work. Lolich was having another outstanding year, 17–6 with a 2.39 ERA. His win total topped the majors, and there was even talk about him being a legitimate 30-win candidate. He was tied for the league lead in complete games (17, tied with Perry), strikeouts (156, tied with California's Nolan Ryan), and was third in innings pitched (199, behind Wood and Perry). Coleman was 12–8 with a 2.20 ERA, and was third in the league in strikeouts with 139. Scherman and Seelbach had combined for nine wins and 16 saves. Overall, the staff's 2.74 ERA was third in the American League behind Baltimore (2.34) and Oakland 2.69), while having the most strikeouts (540) and allowing the second-fewest hits of any staff (632).

Supporting the pitching staff was arguably the best defensive team in baseball. Their .985 team fielding percentage was the best in the A.L., as was their league-low 46 total errors, eight fewer than the next-lowest total (Baltimore) and nearly half of the worst offenders in the A.L. (Texas and Minnesota).[17] Among the defensive stalwarts was Freehan, who despite being in his ninth season as the full-time catcher for the Tigers, was still among the best at his position. What he may have lost in arm strength and throwing out would-be base runners he was making up in his calling of games while guiding the pitchers. Stanley in center field was as good a defensive player at the position as any in the league, and had by that point in the season established himself as the regular middle outfielder most days in Martin's lineup. Kaline, when he was in the lineup, was still a quality right fielder, and Northrup was more than adequate in any position he played in the outfield. In the infield Cash was a solid defensive first baseman, and the duo of McAuliffe and Taylor more than held their own at second base.

The defensive stars, though, were the two imports from Washington who arrived the previous season. In Aurelio Rodriguez at third base and Ed Brinkman at shortstop, Detroit owned the best left side of an infield in baseball. For all the frustration Rodriguez caused at the plate with his high strikeout frequency and maddening habit of trying to pull outside pitches, he remained a magician with a glove at the hot corner. He was matching the best fielding third baseman in most expert's minds, Brooks Robinson, in total chances (well ahead of any other A.L. third basemen) and had committed only eight errors on the season (slightly less than Robinson). His ability to snag hard grounders with the backhand as he went towards the foul line or charge topped balls inside the bag and then gun out the runner at first with his rifle arm made him a fan favorite.

It was Brinkman, however, who was the glue to the infield, and perhaps even for the entire team. Playing nearly every inning of every game (he would be the only Tiger to play in every game that season), "Steady Eddie" provided the backbone for a team that relied on veteran knowledge and the minimization of mistakes to eke out victories by the slightest of margins most nights. Brinkman was born in Cincinnati, Ohio, and was a teammate of Pete Rose while playing at the city's Western Hills High School. Ironically, it was Brinkman, not Rose, who was the prep team's star. He batted .460 his senior season and won fifteen games as a pitcher. When asked about Rose by a professional scout, his high school coach made the comment that Rose was "a good ball player, (though) not a Brinkman."[18] He signed for what was then considered a whopping bonus of $75,000 with the Washington Senators and quickly reached the big leagues. There he became the epitome of a good-field, no-hit infielder.

Shortstop Ed Brinkman was the glue to the best defensive team in the majors in 1972. The smooth-fielding Brinkman went 72 consecutive games without an error that season. Despite hitting only .203, he was later named as the "Tiger of the Year" by the local chapter of the Baseball Writers Association of America (National Baseball Hall of Fame Library, Cooperstown, New York).

He was, however, the textbook perfect example for playing shortstop. Neither fleet of foot nor overly athletic, Brinkman relied on positioning and smarts to put himself in position to make plays. Once he got himself into position, he rarely made mistakes. Through the 88 games Detroit had played prior to the All-Star break, Brinkman had committed only *three* errors. Every other shortstop who had played a comparable number of games and handled a similar number of chances that season was already well into double digits in errors. Brinkman had already broken the record for the longest streak of consecutive games without an error at shortstop and was adding to it with every errorless game. His consistency in the field and the stability he gave the entire team made him the most irreplaceable player on the field for Billy Martin. At the plate Brinkman's average hovered around the .200 mark, but the man who may have looked like Barney Fife with sideburns and a baseball uniform was an intense competitor and a tough out in the clutch who had knocked in a lot of key runs that season.

The team felt good about itself as the majority dispersed for three days of golf, barbecues, beaches, and cottages. The Tigers had played their best baseball by far over the preceding two weeks, and the team was now fourteen games over .500 and seemed to be rising. They knew that August would be a daunting month, as the debt incurred by the early-season weather cancellations would be paid in full through a month chock-full of doubleheaders. They also knew that Baltimore would be right there with them to the end. But with ten weeks to play, they had to like where they stood. The two expected contenders in the division seemed to be separating from the rest of the pack. Boston had managed a hot streak throughout July and now had a winning record overall but was considered young at too many key spots to be a real contender. New York had been horribly inconsistent thus far, was struggling to keep its head above .500, and wasn't expected to mount much of a threat. Cleveland, after its surprisingly fast early-season start, had plummeted sharply and was now only a game ahead of the last-place Milwaukee Brewers.

With the All-Star break at hand, Freehan may have best summed up the team's outlook for the rest of the season. "We know what we have to do to win our division. If we keep pushing day after day, we'll be right where we want to be in October."[19]

American League East Standings through July 23, 1972 (All-Star break)

	W	*L*	*Pct.*	*GB*
Detroit Tigers	51	37	.580	—
Baltimore Orioles	50	38	.568	1
Boston Red Sox	45	41	.523	5
New York Yankees	42	43	.494	7½
Cleveland Indians	36	51	.414	14½
Milwaukee Brewers	35	52	.402	15½

VII

Out of a Hat and into the Lineup

Following two of the more compelling All-Star games in baseball history, the affair played on July 25, 1972, in Atlanta was rather nondescript. The game did go into extra innings, where San Diego's Nate Colbert scored the winning run courtesy of a Joe Morgan single in the tenth, giving the National League a 4–3 victory. The biggest moment in the game came when the Braves' "Hammerin'" Henry Aaron delivered a sixth-inning, two-run homer in front of an adoring home crowd.

Mickey Lolich played the most prominent role of Detroit's contingent on the American League squad. Following A.L. starter Jim Palmer, Lolich pitched the fourth and fifth innings, setting down six of the seven National League batters he faced. During that stretch he went against four straight future Hall of Famers in Willie Mays, Aaron, Pittsburgh Pirate slugger Willie Stargell, and Cincinnati's Johnny Bench, allowing only a harmless single to Bench. His battery mate was Bill Freehan, who caught the first five innings for the A.L. Freehan went 0-for-1 at the plate, although he drew a walk and scored the A.L.'s first run in the third inning. Norm Cash was the third Tiger representative. He replaced starting first baseman Dick Allen and went 0-for-1.

Following three days of rest for the remainder of the club, the Tigers resumed American League play on Thursday, July 27, with a makeup doubleheader in Milwaukee. The Tigers picked up from where they left off prior to the break by taking a pair of dramatic victories against the Brewers. The nightcap of the doubleheader saw the major league debut for Fred Holdsworth. The recently turned 20-year-old pitcher had been an early sensation in spring training, but showed nervousness while allowing four first inning runs. He helped the Tigers start digging out of their hole, however, when he singled to start the third inning, keying a four-run rally by the Tigers that pulled them back into the game. The big hit in the inning was utility man Ike Brown's two-run single. Heading into the eighth, they still trailed 5–4 before exploding for another four runs and romping to an 8–5 victory. Eddie Brinkman's two-run single provided the go-ahead tally for the Tigers.

As exciting as the nightcap had been, the win in the opener was even more improbable. Milwaukee starting pitcher Bill Parsons limited Detroit to one hit through the first eight innings, out-pitching Lolich, who had gone the first seven for the Tigers. With Detroit trailing 2–0 and down to its final two outs in the ninth inning, Aurelio Rodriguez reached base on a Brewer error. Willie Horton then singled for only Detroit's second hit of the day. That brought up Cash, who was already 0-for-3 against Parsons in the game. The Detroit first baseman proceeded to drive a Parsons pitch into the right field bleachers in Milwaukee's County Stadium for his 19th home run of the season, giving the Tigers a shocking 3–2 lead. Chuck Seelbach slammed the door on Milwaukee in the bottom of the ninth inning for his seventh win, and Detroit had stolen the dramatic victory.

The win was emblematic of the type of magic that existed with the 1968 team, and it wasn't lost on anyone, including the perennial team comic, Cash. "It was a big hit. I'll admit it myself," he said when the day was over. "We were getting the bleep kicked out of us. If we had lost that game, the way we were going we could have been in trouble this whole series."[1]

For Cash, the game-winning homer may have been his biggest hit of the season. Even though he was second in the league in home runs and had provided Detroit with its only consistent power source throughout the season, his critics could note that of his nineteen round-trippers to date, twelve had been solo shots. Criticism was nothing new for Cash, however. The 37-year-old Texan had been a mark for fans and local media ever since his Ruth-like 1961 season, when he hit .361 with 41 homers and 132 RBIs. The batting title proved to be an aberration in a career where Cash would finish most other seasons with a batting average closer to .260 than .360. It was "the dumbest thing I ever did" he quipped many times in subsequent years.

He was from Garza County, Texas, and had played both football and baseball at San Angelo Junior College. He was drafted by the NFL's Chicago Bears as a running back, but signed to play baseball with the Chicago White Sox instead. After being a little-used player with Chicago, Cash ended up in Detroit and blossomed. Although he never came close again to a .361 batting average, he remained a dangerous home run threat in the Detroit lineup, especially in Tiger Stadium. There, his propensity for pulling the ball was conducive to reaching the inviting right-field overhang, 325 feet down the line, or the power alley with its right-field fence looming only 370 feet away from home plate. "Stormin' Norman" hit 30 or more homers four different times between 1961 and 1966, while never knocking in fewer than 79 runs a season during that period. For the remainder of the decade, however, his

Key cogs in the Detroit attack in 1972 were (left to right) Al Kaline, Jim Northrup, and Norm Cash. Kaline and Northrup both recovered from slow starts to provide the Tigers with solid hitting down the stretch run of the divisional race. Cash led the team with 22 home runs and 61 RBIs (AP/Wide World Photos).

career appeared to be on the decline. Under the guidance of Mayo Smith, Cash was often held out of the lineup against certain left-handed pitchers, and frequently found himself being platooned with ad hoc first basemen, such as Freehan, Mickey Stanley, or Al Kaline. While Cash's playing time diminished slightly, his production remained steady. In the world championship season he hit 25 homers despite playing in the second fewest games in his career (127). In Smith's final season (1970), Cash registered only 370 official at-bats and saw his home run total drop to fifteen, while many fans and media began to surmise that a new first baseman was needed in Detroit.

Instead, the hiring of Billy Martin as Detroit manager invigorated Cash's career and catapulted him into an entirely different regard with Tiger fans. Responding well to the new manager's approach, Cash slammed 32 home runs in 1971 and drove home 91, winning the Comeback Player of the Year award for the second time in his career. He narrowly missed the A.L. home run title, losing to White Sox third baseman Bill Melton in the final days of the '71 campaign. The comeback season helped endear him with Detroit fans as he never had been before, and elevated Cash into being one of the favorites of a team made up of familiar players. His comical on-field gestures and antics with umpires, opponents, and fans made him a league-wide favorite, as did the lesser-known nightlife he enjoyed along the trail of taverns and saloons that populated every stop in the A.L. circuit. Earlier in the season, Cash had even premiered with his own television show on local TV in Detroit. The short-lived program was an attempt to capture some of the humor and popularity that the thirteen-year Tiger possessed with a talk show format that featured guests, including teammates and visiting players from around the league.

As Detroit celebrated its doubleheader sweep over Milwaukee, things got even better when news arrived that Cleveland's Tom McCraw had blasted a pinch-hit, two-run homer in the ninth inning off Baltimore's Pat Dobson, giving the Indians a 4–3 win and increasing Detroit's lead over the Orioles to 2½ games. The second night back from the All-Star break was not as bright, however, as the Tigers felt the sting of a last-inning defeat. Milwaukee's Tommie Reynolds singled in Dave May in the bottom of the ninth, giving the Brewers the 3–2 victory. Jim Lonborg handcuffed the Tigers, allowing only six hits while defeating them for the second time that season. Gaylord Perry's 17th win kept Detroit's 2½-game margin in tact, however, as Cleveland won in ten innings over Baltimore. On the final day in Milwaukee, Johnny Briggs hit a three-run homer in the first inning off Bill Slayback, giving the Brewers an early 3–0 lead. The Tigers managed to tie it at three on homers by Cash and Kaline, but Joe Lahoud socked a two-run homer off Slayback in the bottom of the third, Ron Perronoski served up a two-run homer to May in the sixth, and Milwaukee was on its way to an 8–3 rout of Detroit and a split in the four-game series. Baltimore managed to shave a game off the lead this time when Brooks Robinson hit a solo home run in the eleventh inning of the Orioles' 4–3 win in Cleveland.

The Tigers returned to Detroit the next day, and in a highly unusual scheduling quirk, started a two-day, three-game series with Boston on a Sunday afternoon. Boston capitalized on a last-minute pitching change in the first game when Seelbach was forced to start in place of an injured Tom Timmerman, and the Red Sox pulled out a 4–3 decision. The Tigers managed a split on the day when Joe Niekro led them to a 7–2 complete-game victory in the nightcap. The hitting hero for the day was Gates Brown, who blasted a home run in each game. With Horton and Kaline struggling with injuries, Brown was again seeing extended duty as a regular in Martin's outfield. "It's been this way with us all year," said Martin afterwards. "The injuries aren't staggered with us — they hit us all at one time. You've got to keep trying to win with what you've got."[2]

As the month of July came to a close, the nation watched as a presidential bid was slowly unraveling. The Democratic nominee, George McGovern, was forced to cancel a scheduled national television appearance due to uncertainty over his vice presidential selection. Thomas Eagleton, who had been McGovern's choice as running mate since the Democratic Convention earlier in the month, had been under constant scrutiny ever since reports had surfaced about his suspect mental health history. The unwanted attention to the matter had resulted in Eagleton's resignation earlier in the day. With the general election less than 100 days away and a fractured Democratic Party split about its choice for the top of the ticket, McGovern's campaign was headed for disaster.

Back in Detroit, the Tigers made a pair of personnel moves prior to their series finale with Boston. They placed Kaline on the 15-day disabled list with his hobbled leg, while also giving veteran reliever Ron Perranoski his release. Their roster spots were filled by pitcher Bill Gilbreth and second baseman John Knox, who were both called up from Toledo. Kaline had been plagued by muscle pulls around his left knee, as well as a bad hamstring that left him unable to run the bases or play in the outfield. Perranoski's release was viewed as an expensive mistake by Martin. The 36-year-old left-hander had been the ace reliever for Martin during his division-winning 1969 season at Minnesota, where Perranoski had recorded nine wins and 31 saves while pitching in 75 games. After another strong campaign in 1970, everything fell apart for Perronoski and the Twins gave him his release. Perranoski was quickly snatched up by Detroit at the request of his former manager. However, despite being viewed in the spring as a likely contributor in the bullpen, he had been used little by Martin, particularly in tight situations. In seventeen games he was 0–1 with an ERA over 7.00, hardly numbers to justify a spot with a contending team's staff, let alone at the princely salary of $65,000, big money for a reliever at that time.[3]

In the Monday night game with the Red Sox, Freehan and Rodriguez each swatted two-run home runs, and Mickey Lolich picked up his 18th win in a 5–2 Tiger victory before 41,431 Family Night fans at Tiger Stadium. With Baltimore dropping both ends of a doubleheader to New York, the win boosted Detroit's lead in the division to 2½ games.

The next day was the dawn of a new month. August brings what is traditionally referred to as the "dog days" of the baseball season, as the long grind begins to take its toll. The excitement of the early games gives way to the seemingly never-ending grind of the long six-month regular-season schedule. Promising starts by the pretenders had faded into the normalization that takes place during the course of a major league schedule. The National League was turning into a two-team race, with the Pittsburgh Pirates and Cincinnati Reds pulling away in their respective divisions and heading on a collision course towards a post-season match-up. The defending world champion Pirates had the best record in baseball (60–35, .632), and now led the N.L.'s Eastern Division by seven games over the Mets and ten games over the Chicago Cubs. The Reds had opened a five-game lead on the surprising Houston Astros and an 8½-game lead over the disappointing Los Angeles Dodgers. The American League West remained the domain of the Oakland A's, who were looking to repeat as champions of that division. At 59–39, the Athletics had a 5½-game bulge over the White Sox and 9½ games over the Twins.

Individually, an old face on a new team in the N.L. had made arguably the biggest impact on the league. The Reds' Joe Morgan had been the catalyst for a startling turnaround for one of 1971's most disappointing teams. The 5'7" second baseman had come over in a seven-player blockbuster deal with Houston during the offseason. The 1970 pennant-winning Cincinnati team had slumped to fourth place in the N.L. West, finishing with a losing record in '71. But with Morgan providing Gold Glove–caliber defense at second base and a dynamic, game-changing presence to the Reds' batting order while hitting out of the second slot, the revitalized Big Red Machine was clicking on all cylinders. Morgan was leading the league in runs scored by a huge margin (84), walks (78), and on-base percentage (.424), and was second in stolen bases (37), all while hitting behind Pete Rose and ahead of Cincy sluggers Bobby Tolan, Johnny Bench, and Tony Perez in the order.

Billy Williams of the Cubs was leading the N.L. in hitting at .346. Houston's Cesar Cedeno (.344) and Atlanta's Ralph Garr (.331) trailed. Nate Colbert of the San Diego Padres was leading the league in home runs (25), with Bench (24), Williams (22), and Pittsburgh's Willie Stargell (22) close behind. Bench and Stargell were the big run producers for their teams and shared the RBI lead with 75 each. Colbert and Williams each had 69. Steve Carlton of the last-place Philadelphia Phillies was leading the senior circuit in wins with 15, with Chicago's veteran Ferguson Jenkins (14) right on his heels.

In the American League the batting marks were much lower, and views of a batting title being won in a fashion similar to Carl Yastrzemski's puny .301 winning percentage in 1968 were being bandied about. Kansas City outfielder Lou Piniella led the league with a .315 average, with Boston's rookie catcher Carlton Fisk trailing at .312. KC's Richie Scheinblum (.311) and Chicago's all-everything Dick Allen (.310) were also in contention for the batting title. Allen was starting to run away with both the home run and RBI races. He led Cash and Reggie Jackson by seven homers, including the major league-tying two inside-the-park homers he had hit the previous day in a game against Minnesota. The two round-trippers legged out by Allen gave him a total of 27 on the season. His RBI total of 77 was well ahead of Jackson (59) and Royals first baseman John Mayberry (56). Lolich was leading the league in wins with 18, just head of Gaylord Perry (17) and Wilbur Wood (16). Lolich's 167 strikeouts were second in the league to California's Nolan Ryan, who was starting to pull away with 181. Joe Coleman and Perry were third with 145 each. Perry also led the league in earned run average at 1.69, with the Yankees' Steve Kline (1.93) and the Orioles' Jim Palmer (1.97) all under two runs per game.

The new month started auspiciously for the Tigers, as they were blasted at home by the last-place Brewers, 9–0, in a rain-shortened game. Milwaukee's Skip Lockwood held Detroit to just one hit on the night, while his teammates knocked out 16 against Tiger pitching in only six innings of play. A more notable evening was being enjoyed in Atlanta by San Diego's Colbert, who pounded five home runs and knocked in 13 runners in a doubleheader sweep of the Braves. The five homers tied a record set previously by Hall of Famer Stan Musial for the most long balls in a twin-bill.

The unexpected thumping by Milwaukee was explained away as "one of those nights" until an even worse dismembering was endured the next evening. Coleman lasted only 2⅓ innings before departing, having given up six earned runs. He was only the first of seven Detroit pitchers that combined to give up a Brewer/Seattle Pilot team record 18 hits, including eight straight in the third inning. The humiliation continued in the final game of the series, when the Tigers were beaten, 6–3, to the jeers of 12,795 fans in Tiger Stadium. The three-game sweep came at the hands of a team that even Milwaukee's slugging first baseman George Scott termed the "laughingstock of baseball."[4] The only consolation was that Baltimore had lost five of six games since the All-Star break and remained two games back of the front-running Tigers. Creeping back into the race, however, were both New York and Boston, who had taken advantage of the slumping teams ahead of them and moved up to within five and 5½ games, respectively, of the division lead.

As the Tigers tucked their tails between their legs and scampered around Lake Erie and over to Cleveland to open a weekend four-game series with the Indians, the focus among much of the country's sports media, let alone Detroit's, had shifted to the Oakland Hills Country Club in the northern suburb of Birmingham, Michigan. "The Monster," as the course was known, was playing host to the PGA Tournament, the last of the four major tournaments for the U.S. PGA. The first day of tournament play on Thursday saw Ray Floyd, Arnold Palmer, Johnny Miller, and Sam Snead all finish within two shots of the lead, with pre-tournament favorites Lee Treviño and Jack Nicklaus lurking not far behind.

The Tigers' fortunes didn't fare much better in the first game against Cleveland. Twenty-four-year-old rookie starter Dick Tidrow locked up with Lolich in a scoreless pitching duel into the bottom of the seventh inning. Then the Tribe's light-hitting shortstop, Frank Duffy, homered off Lolich for the game's only run, and the Tigers suffered their fourth straight loss. The rare home run by Duffy was one of only three he hit that season, and one of only 26 he hit in his nine-year career.

The next day didn't start any better. The Indians took a 2–0 first-inning lead on a double by Graig Nettles that scored Chris Chambliss and Roy Foster. Later in the same inning, with the bases loaded and two outs, Martin felt he couldn't afford to wait for his struggling rookie pitcher, Bill Slayback, to pull out of the jam. Instead, he turned to a newcomer who had just joined the club after being acquired from the National League. Thirty-two-year-old Woodie Fryman entered the game, got out of the inning, and proceeded to pitch six additional scoreless innings in an effort that Martin described as "sensational."[5]

Fryman was a tobacco-chewing, hard-throwing left-hander who challenged hitters with fastballs and hard sliders. He was in his seventh year in the big leagues, having spent most of his career with bad Philadelphia teams, where he compiled a 61–69 career win-loss mark. His record thus far in 1972 had been a less-than-impressive 4–10 with a 4.35 ERA in 120 innings of work. He also had been suffering from elbow problems. The report that Jim Campbell and his major league scouts had received, however, was that Fryman could be effective if used properly, and they were able to purchase his contract for $60,000 in an inter-league waiver deal.

The game remained 2–0 with the Indians leading into the seventh inning on a day when the Tigers had again been unable to solve the mystery of the dipping sinkers served up by Cleveland ace Gaylord Perry. Then the momentum shifted, thanks to another Detroit newcomer. Duke Sims, a veteran left-handed hitting catcher, had been claimed off waivers the previous day from the Dodgers, and then was inserted immediately into the lineup against Perry. Sims proceeded to crush a Perry pitch that finally landed in the barren right field grandstand in Municipal Stadium for the Tigers' first run. Fred Scherman, who had relieved Fryman, gave the run back to Cleveland in the eighth, but Gates Brown and Cash hit back-to-back homers in the ninth inning off Perry to tie the contest. The game stayed that way until the eleventh inning, when Rodriguez doubled and then came home with the winning run on Sims' RBI single.

The 4–3 victory by Detroit on August 5 in Cleveland was significant in that it broke a four-game losing streak. In doing so, the team overcame a two-run deficit to the hottest pitcher in the American League at the time, while

Left-hander Woodie Fryman came over in early August from the last-place Philadelphia Phillies in a deal that provided a tremendous boost to a weary Tigers pitching staff. Over the last two months of the season, Fryman went 10–3 for Detroit with a 2.03 ERA (National Baseball Hall of Fame Library, Cooperstown, New York).

also introducing two key additions that would go on to play prominent roles with the Tigers for the rest of the season. For Fryman and Sims, who were picked up by Detroit within a span of 48 hours of each other, the change of scenery was a welcome change from seasons that were going nowhere elsewhere.

"Leaving a club that didn't think I could hit any more, and right away helping a club that thinks I can," said Sims wistfully about his move to Detroit, after he batted only .192 in 51 games for Los Angeles. "Now you're talking about satisfaction."[6]

"This is a break for me — especially at my age," Fryman said after his Detroit debut. "I know the Tigers are an experienced ball club and they score a lot of runs. I just hope I can help them do what they want to do, and that's win the pennant."[7]

Not to be lost in the relief that permeated the Tiger clubhouse after stopping the four-game slide was the passing of an achievement by shortstop Ed Brinkman. In the ninth inning, his double-play relay was wide of first base that got by Cash for an error. The miscue ended a 72-game errorless streak by Brinkman, setting a major league record for the position. It was also only the fourth error of the season for a player who was in the lineup nearly every inning of every game at the most crucial defensive position on the infield. He also served as the backbone of a team that rarely beat itself.

On Sunday the two teams split a doubleheader, with each team taking a one-run decision. In the first game, the Tigers stranded eleven runners and could only score on a Northrup home run in a 2–1 loss. Coleman was the tough-luck pitcher once again, and saw his record drop to a misleading 12–10. Detroit won the second game, 6–5, on some late heroics by Willie Horton, who hit a two-run shot that overcame a 4–3 deficit. Stanley had two home runs in the game, which was held up by a long rain delay in the seventh inning, much to the chagrin of Billy Martin, whose team led at the time. Meanwhile, back in the Detroit area, Gary Player wrapped up the PGA Tournament, winning by two strokes over both Tommy Aaron and Jim Jamieson. The 35-year-old South African native pocketed $45,000 as the winner's share of the golf season's fourth major.

An off day was spent in New York on Monday, August 7, as the Tigers waited to play a four-game series against the Yankees. On a day when the Democratic Party gained the headlines with party approval for Kennedy family brother-in-law Sargent Shriver as the newest vice presidential selection to go with top man George McGovern, the baseball world looked further upstate from New York City to Cooperstown, where the latest class of the Baseball Hall of Fame was being inducted. Yankee greats Yogi Berra and Lefty Gomez were enshrined, as was modern pitching great Sandy Koufax, 300-game winner Early Wynn, and former Negro League star Buck Leonard.

"Bring on the Tigers" screamed the *New York Post* headlines on Tuesday, as the Yankees eagerly awaited Detroit at Yankee Stadium.[8] Since June 13, the hometown team had been the hottest in the A.L. East, posting a 32–19 record. After dawdling along at or below .500 through most of the first two months of the season, New York was hitting its stride, and the recent slump by Detroit let them back into the divisional race. Outside of their 26-year-old budding superstar Bobby Murcer in center field or their fiery 25-year-old catcher Thurman Munson, the Yankee lineup was rather nondescript, and a far cry from their "Bronx Bombers" title from days gone by. Players like the steady Roy White in left field and Horace Clarke at second base were joined by a plethora of platoon players in manager Ralph Houk's lineup. The starting pitching was solid, led by long-time ace Mel Stottlemyre and fellow starters Fritz Peterson, Steve Kline, and Mike Kekich, while the new man in the bullpen, Sparky Lyle, had solidified the late innings for New York.

In an unusual series format, with the first game played on a Tuesday afternoon, followed by a daytime doubleheader on Wednesday and a night game on Thursday, the Yankees drew first blood with a 4–2 win over Lolich and the Tigers. Detroit had tied the game in its half of the seventh inning, with Rodriguez dropping down a suicide squeeze to drive in the Tigers' second run. Lolich did himself in, however, as in the eighth inning he fumbled a sacrifice bunt attempt for an error and then hit a batter, which led to the game-winning, two-run rally by New York. Lyle pitched the last three innings for the Yankees and allowed only one hit in relief of Peterson while picking up his fourth win. The scoreboard didn't prove any friendlier, as the suddenly hot Boog Powell slammed his fifteenth homer for Baltimore, a three-run shot that upended Milwaukee, 4–2, and brought the Orioles back within a game of Detroit.

It was the Yankees that seemed obsessed with their chances at taking over the division. "We're only two back in the loss column and our guys think they can win the pennant," said Houk after the first game, which brought the Yankees within three games of the Tigers. "At this stage of the season you've got to call us a definite contender," added Murcer, who was the face of the current era of Yankees.[9]

Martin was not as quick to acknowledge New York as a true contender for the crown. "We'll beat 'em the next three games and they'll be right back where they belong," he said after his team had fallen in the first game of the series. "As far as I'm concerned, it's between Baltimore, Boston, and us — and Baltimore is the one we have to worry about."[10]

Martin's decree about taking care of his upstart rival the rest of the series was on its way to being true in the Wednesday afternoon doubleheader. Fryman made his first start for Detroit and tossed a six-hit shutout, as Tiger batters knocked around Stottlemyre in a 6–0 win in the opener. The second game also started promising when Timmerman limited New York to one hit through the first six innings, and Detroit led, 1–0. But in the Yankee seventh inning, with runners in scoring position and a raucous Yankee Stadium crowd of 32,610 rooting them on, New York took the lead on a Celerino Sanchez two-run single. "I've never seen anything like it. They really got us psyched up," said New York first baseman Ron Bloomberg, who scored the go-ahead run on a close play at the plate. "No way was anyone going to stop me at third base. And no way was anyone going to block me at the plate. I'd have sent their man back to the screen if he got in the way."[11]

The crowd continued to roar over the final two innings, chanting "Defense! Defense!" taking a queue from the Madison Square Garden crowds at New York Knicks' games. Lyle came in and set the Tigers down in order, including two by strikeout, in the ninth inning for his 25th save, and the two teams split the twin-bill. When Baltimore blasted Milwaukee, 10–0, later that evening, the divisional race tightened up even more, with Detroit's lead now down to ½ game.

Sparky Lyle came over to New York from Boston in a spring training trade, and then put together one of the greatest seasons ever recorded to that point by a reliever. Lyle went 9–5 with 35 saves and a 1.92 ERA for the Yankees, and had surprising New York in the thick of the divisional race well into September (National Baseball Hall of Fame Library, Cooperstown, New York).

On Thursday night the Tigers arrived at Yankee Stadium already knowing the Orioles had lost to the Brewers that afternoon, 1–0. With a chance to gain a game on its chief rival, Detroit fell by the most frustrating of margins, 1–0, for the sixth time of the season. Coleman's ill fortune continued as he lost again, this time to the league's ERA leader among starting pitchers, Steve Kline, who went the first eight innings to lower his mark to 1.69. Lyle came in again to seal the victory in the ninth. The crowd of 40,145 roared, as he set down the Tigers for his 26th save, and fifth of the week.

"Our big edge is that we've got a pitcher like Lyle," said Houk of his greatest asset in the many close games that were taking place. "I don't see anyone else in the league who has one like him. If he continues to pitch as he has, we could do it."[12]

"We're well on our way," said Lyle, full of confidence as the series concluded. "I think we'll win it now, and if not, we're going to scare the dickens out of a lot of people."[13]

Luckily, Detroit would not see New York on the schedule again for nearly a month. The slump by the Tigers had fortunately come at a time when the Orioles were also struggling. Unfortunately, the losing streaks by the two clubs presumed to be division favorites had coincided with hot streaks by both the Yankees and Red Sox. All four teams were now bunched to within 3½ games of each other, with only eight weeks left in the season. What had shaped up as a two-team race just two weeks earlier had turned into a wild free-for-all between four teams that had played with maddening inconsistency throughout the campaign.

"New York and Boston are up there because Baltimore and us lost so many games these past two weeks," Martin said after he watched his team lose three of the four games in Yankee Stadium.[14]

After scampering out of the Big Apple, the Tigers hooked up again with Cleveland for a four-game weekend series, only this time in Detroit. The first game on Friday night started poorly for the home team when Gates Brown dropped a fly ball with two outs in the first inning. That led to three unearned runs being scored off John Hiller, who was making his first start of the year. In the third inning, the Tigers threatened by loading the bases with no outs, only to see Rodriguez ground to the pitcher, who got the force at the plate, before Brown bounced into an inning-ending double play. After Cleveland tacked on two more runs off Scherman in the eighth inning, the game was effectively over. Mickey Stanley's solo home run in the ninth inning was Detroit's only run in the 5–1 loss. In fact, Stanley's home run was the first run pushed across the plate by the Tigers since the first inning of game two of the doubleheader with New York, some 26 innings earlier. When Bobby Grich homered for the Orioles in the bottom of the ninth inning, allowing Baltimore to defeat Boston, 2–1, the Tigers fell out of first place.

On Saturday the situation turned ever more bleak. Cleveland clobbered Detroit, 6–1, and in the process handed Lolich his third straight loss. The lone run scored by the Tigers fell in line with a troubling trend that saw them score either zero or one run in nine of their previous thirteen games.

"We've just got to wait this thing out," Martin said of his team's recent woes. "And I know that is the hardest thing in the world to do. Nine thousand million [*sic*] people think they got the answer. But they're all as wrong as they can be. If anybody was that smart he would have written a book long ago, and it would have been a best seller. These are human beings. They've got to grind it out themselves. There's only so much a manager can do. I can't swing the bat for them. I don't have any miracle powders in my pocket."[15]

Martin may not have had any miracle powders, but that didn't prevent him from trying other remedies in his bag of tricks to reverse the Tigers' recent slide. He had already tried manning the third-base coaching box for a few innings, standing in for his regular coach, Joe Schultz. He also had substituted Tony Taylor in the first base coach's box, in place of the normal occupant, Dick Tracewski. However, his wildest venture came before the first game of the doubleheader on Sunday, when he wrote out names on strips of paper of the players he wanted in the lineup and then dropped them into his hat. Martin then asked the injured Kaline to pull the names out of the hat one by one. Martin then wrote out his lineup card in the batting order that was drawn. The intent was to loosen the team and remove some of the daily pressure that built on individuals slotted into certain roles and responsibilities in the everyday batting lineup. Cash-1b, Northrup-rf, Horton-lf, Brinkman-ss, Taylor-2b, Sims-c, Stanley-cf, Rodriguez-3b, pitcher (Fryman) was the lineup Kaline drew for the first game of the Sunday doubleheader. The spots that attracted the most winks belonged to Cash, the prototypical cleanup hitter for much of his career, leading off, and then the Punch-and-Judy hitting Brinkman, who was holding down the cleanup spot instead of hitting in the eighth position he held for all but one other game that season.

The unusual method used to fill out his lineup card paid off, as Detroit bested Perry for the second time in a week. Horton crashed a home run in the first inning to get the team on the board against the slick right-hander. Brinkman doubled in the tying run in the sixth inning, and then came around to score the eventual game-winning run on a Taylor single a few moments later. More significant than the role the batting order played in the victory that day was the four-hit, complete-game pitching effort of Fryman, who won his second straight start for his new ball club.

The second game didn't work out quite as well as Timmerman was hammered for five runs in 4⅔ innings, and Martin's more conventional lineup was handcuffed for only two runs in a 9–2 Indians rout. The string of strong starts put together by Timmerman in the season's first half had become a distant memory, as the tall right-hander saw his record fall to 7–10. Stability in the rotation behind Lolich and Coleman was once again in question, as Timmerman joined the likes of Cain, Niekro, and Slayback as pitchers who had gained spots and then fell out of favor.

"We've gotta get pitching," said Martin, still searching for answers. "For the time being it's gonna be Lolich, Coleman, Fryman and 'undecided,' but he'll know he's going to pitch the day before he does pitch."[16]

The split with Cleveland coincided with a New York sweep of Milwaukee, putting the Yankees one percentage point ahead of the Tigers and into second place in the division. Baltimore won its game with Boston that day, 8–2, and led the Yankees and Tigers by 1½ games. "Our fans are getting frustrated, and I don't blame them," lamented Martin about his team's recent troubles and its drop to third place in the division.[17] Elsewhere in the American League, Vida Blue threw a four-hit shutout over the hard-charging White Sox, who had managed to catch the A's in the standings at the top of the West Division. The 3–0 win for Oakland pushed the A's back in front by one game.

Monday, August 14, was an off day for Detroit, but as would become commonplace in the wild divisional race that was the American League East that season, the Tigers were able to gain ground, as both Baltimore and New York lost their games that night. That moved Detroit back into second place in the division and within one game of the Orioles. The positioning was important as they entered a three-week period of games exclusively against teams from the West Division before finishing out the season with a grueling four-week stretch that would be played entirely within their own division. As the team waited to open a home series with the Twins, the Tigers activated Kaline from the disabled list and optioned pitcher Fred Holdsworth to Toledo. The hope was that Kaline, who had been hampered with a series of aggravating injuries throughout the season and had appeared in only 68 of Detroit's 110 games thus far, would be able to contribute as a pinch-hitter or part-time first baseman down the stretch.

In the series opener with Minnesota, Coleman was knocked out of the game during a four-run Twins rally in the fourth inning. But thanks largely to a Stanley three-run homer, the Tigers led, 6–5, with two outs in the top of the ninth inning and Seelbach one strike away from sealing the victory. However, Minnesota's Steve Braun singled on a 3–2 pitch, and then Harmon Killebrew followed with a single of his own. After Twins manager Frank Quilici inserted a pair of pinch-runners, Rich Reese drove in Steve Brye with the tying run. The game then dragged forward until Minnesota was able to scratch across two more runs off Tiger rookie Lerrin LaGrow in the 13th inning to salt away an eventual 7–6 win. After the game, Martin was distraught about the manner in which his team had lost. "It's tough to lose when you haven't been getting runs, and then suddenly you get the runs, and then your pitchers can't hold 'em. We had it won and we lost it."[18]

After a rainout on Wednesday, the Twins and Tigers played a make-up doubleheader on the last scheduled date for Minnesota to be in town that season. With Baltimore having already lost, 6–1, that day to Chicago, the opportunity was there for Detroit to take over first place again. A seven-run second inning off Minnesota's Jim Perry broke open the first game while Woodie Fryman benefited from the generous run support in a 12–2 runaway victory. The second game didn't start out well as the Tigers fell behind, 6–0, and still trailed 6–2 heading into the last inning against Twins starter Dave Goltz. Northrup's home run leading off the bottom of the ninth appeared to be too little, too late; however, after Stanley singled, Sims walked, Kaline, in a pinch-hitting role, singled in Stanley, McAuliffe walked, and then Freehan singled, knocking in Sims and Taylor (running for Kaline). The score was tied. Better yet, Detroit was on the cusp of an improbable comeback victory in their last at-bat and a sweep of the twin-bill with two runners on base and only one out. But Gates Brown bounced into an inning-ending double play, and then Seelbach gave up a run to the Twins in the top of the tenth inning that Detroit was unable to match, leading to a heartbreaking 7–6 loss. The split did pull the Tigers to within ½ game of the front-running Orioles. In the National League that evening, Philadelphia's Steve Carlton won his fifteenth straight decision, and his 20th overall for the season, in a 9–4 decision over the Cincinnati Reds.

Detroit welcomed the California Angels to town next and took a 2–0 victory in the first game, as Lolich's three-hitter bested Nolan Ryan. The Tigers managed only six hits against the Angel flamethrower, but benefited from five bases on balls. When word came through that Baltimore had lost its fourth straight game, this time a 3–1 setback to Minnesota, Detroit had regained first place in the division. New York was two games back after getting shellacked by the last-place Texas Rangers, 11–2, and Boston remained 3½ games behind.

The next night took on a completely different complexion as the Tiger bats erupted. The outcome was decided early, as they scored six runs in the first inning to knock out California lefty Rudy May. Detroit banged out 16 hits off four different Angel pitchers, led by Kaline, who had two hits, including a home run, and three RBIs. Taylor chipped in three hits, and Rodriguez, Stanley, Horton and starting pitcher Tom Timmerman all had two hits in the 10–1 pasting of California.

As the series concluded on Sunday afternoon, rookie Bill Slayback's troubles continued. After being staked to a 2–0 first-inning lead, Slayback gave up the first four runs of what turned into a disastrous nine-run Angel fourth inning. Fred Scherman was equally ineffective, getting battered for five runs in his two-thirds of an inning. The Angels appeared on their way to salvaging a win in the series, holding a commanding 9–2 lead as Detroit came to bat in the sixth inning. Then the improbable happened. The Tigers, who had been struggling at the plate for so much of the season, exploded for eight runs off 14-game winner Clyde Wright. A double by Rodriguez, followed by singles from Kaline, Freehan, Horton, Stanley, Gates Brown, and Taylor, with an error thrown in by Angels shortstop Leo Cardenas, did most of the damage before Rodriguez concluded the rally with his second hit of the inning, a two-run homer. Freehan added an insurance run the next inning with a homer of his own, and for the second time in four days, the Tigers had come back from a huge deficit, only this time winning, as they beat California by the score of 11–9. The three-game sweep of the Angels increased the Tigers' lead to a game and a half, as Baltimore lost again to Minnesota, this time 4–1.

On Monday, August 21, as an uneventful Republican National Convention was opening in Miami, the Oakland A's came into Tiger Stadium for a three-game set between the American League's two division leaders. Billy Martin started Fryman, who had allowed only four runs in 35 innings pitched since coming over to Detroit. However, he gave up a first-inning leadoff double to A's shortstop Campy Campaneris, who then proceeded to steal third base. Campaneris then came home on a single by the A.L.'s leading hitter, Joe Rudi (.320). Rudi advanced on a Sal Bando single, and then both runners came home on a double by Oakland first baseman Mike Epstein. The three-run first inning set the tone in an Oakland 5–1 victory, as Fryman suffered his first defeat with Detroit. The second game of the series began no better, as Rudi delivered a first-inning, two-run homer off Lolich, the first blow in what turned out to be a forgettable night for the Tigers ace, who failed in a bid for his 20th win of the season. Lolich allowed six runs in five innings, as the Tigers fell to the A's, 6–3.

The loss was Detroit's sixth in eight games played against Oakland, and only added to a general dislike the two teams already had for each other. That sentiment was punctuated in the seventh inning with the game already well in hand for the A's. Oakland starting pitcher John "Blue Moon" Odom stood on third base, having swiped the bag just moments earlier, much to the chagrin of the Tiger dugout. Slayback was on the mound for Detroit, having come on in relief of Lolich. The Tiger rookie had already fired a pitch that Campaneris had to duck away from before it ended up at the backstop. Now with Oakland outfielder Angel Mangual at the plate, Slayback uncorked another wild pitch, this time behind the head of the batter. As Odom bolted home to score from third, Slayback headed for the plate in anticipation of a play. Mangual, who had already homered in the game and thought the Detroit pitcher had just thrown at him, attacked Slayback as the pitcher ran forward.

The melee that ensued in front of home plate that evening was more than the typical flaring of tempers and milling of players that most baseball bench-emptying situations turn out to be. Mangual landed a two-handed shot to Slayback up around his neck, and within seconds both combatants were swarmed by players charging from the emptied dugouts on each side of the diamond. Martin, of course, led the charge from the Tiger side, with Horton, Ike Brown, and Duke Sims being some of the more volatile fighters. A's catcher Dave Duncan, Epstein, and coaches Irv Noren and Jerry Adair were in the middle of the fracas on Oakland's side. Blows were exchanged in what was an unusually violent display for a baseball brawl. By the time the umpires were able to restore order and the skirmish had cleared, Epstein was found staggered at the bottom of the pile, last seen exchanging blows with Horton, a former amateur boxer. The 47-year-old Noren left the scene with a bloodied face. As the A's returned to their dugout, the vociferously booing Detroit fans tried to douse them by emptying cups of beer in their direction.[19]

The next night, Martin filled out a lineup card with the names of noted fighters, such as Joe Louis, Sugar Ray Robinson, and Rocky Marciano, and presented it to the umpires as well as Oakland manager Dick Williams at home plate before the game.[20] The move was unusual in that the noted combatant was showing levity towards a rivalry that was growing uglier with each game. The Detroit manager had to feel even better once the game began, as his team jumped on A's left-hander Ken Holtzman for seven second-inning runs, the big blow being a grand slam by Freehan in a 7–5 Tiger win. The victory knocked the A's out of first place, as Chicago defeated New York, 5–2. Dick Allen cranked his 32nd home run and Wilbur Wood picked up his 22nd win to lead the White Sox into first place in the A.L. West by ½ game. Elsewhere, the Orioles beat California, 7–1, with Paul Blair's three-run homer the key hit to back Jim Palmer, who improved his record to 17–6. The win by Baltimore kept the Orioles ½ game behind Detroit in the A.L. East standings in what was shaping up as two unusually close races in the American League.

Most of the country that evening was focused on President Nixon's coronation as the Republican candidate for that fall's election. The president enjoyed a healthy 60 percent approval rating as his first term wound down, and faced little resistance within his own party. The year 1972 had been very eventful and productive for the incumbent. He had taken history-making visits to communist Red China in February and to the Soviet Union in May in hopes of initiating a thaw to the Cold War and attempting to alleviate the smokescreen of support those countries had with North Vietnam. On-and-off peace talks had been conducted throughout the spring and summer with the North Vietnamese government, all while the U.S. had increased air bombing to unprecedented levels. Operation Linebacker, as the stepped up bombing was code-named, was in response to the communist Eastertide Offensive, where 200,000 North Vietnamese troops had invaded previously demilitarized zones and South Vietnamese territory. Despite the scaling back of U.S. combat troop presence in the war, the bombing campaign had invited international condemnation and anti-war protests domestically. With protesters being held at bay outside the convention hall in Miami, the smell of tear gas permeated the building as the president spoke of property tax relief and encouraged his fellow countrymen to join the "new American majority."[21]

As Oakland left town, the Tigers embarked on a nine-game journey that would take them to Minnesota, Anaheim, and Oakland, as part of their second and final West Coast road trip of the season. The trip would also mark the final games played against the opposite division before the Tigers headed into the final four weeks of the season, playing exclusively against divisional foes. After an off day for travel and a rainout in Minneapolis, the Twins and Tigers attempted to play a make-up doubleheader on Saturday. Playing entirely in the rain, Lolich led 1–0 in another attempt at his 20th victory before giving up home runs to Twins catcher Glenn Borgmann and outfielder Bobby Darwin. Through numerous weather delays, the Tigers managed to tie the score and force extra innings before Rodriguez clouted a two-run homer in the eleventh inning to give Detroit the much-needed 5–3 win. Martin used eight Detroit pitchers in the contest to try to secure the victory and keep pace with his competitors in the tantalizingly close division race. Both Baltimore and Boston had taken advantage of Detroit's rainout the previous night by winning their games, which allowed the Orioles to climb into a tie for the top position. Detroit and Baltimore both stood at 65–55, with Boston three games back, New York 3½, and Cleveland still not out of the picture, lurking only seven games behind. The White Sox surprisingly had moved out to a 1½-game lead over Oakland in the West Division.

When the Twins and Tigers were rained out in the second game on Saturday, the two teams pushed the make-up game to Sunday, when they would now play a twin-bill. Detroit made it a big day and a successful start to its long road trip by winning both games in dramatic fashion. In the first game, with the two teams tied at three in the eleventh inning, Horton failed in his attempt to bunt Kaline down to second base, but made up for it later in the at-bat by crashing a game-winning two-run homer off Wayne Granger. The second game was scoreless into the eleventh inning, when Rodriguez connected for a solo blast off Dave LaRoche for the game's only run. Coleman went the distance, allowing only four hits and striking out six in a magnificent performance. Detroit had managed to sweep the three-game series from Minnesota, with all three victories coming in the eleventh inning. The Tigers' Sunday doubleheader win made for an especially successful day when the Orioles lost to Oakland, 2–1, dropping them a game-and-a-half behind Detroit.

On Monday, while the team flew to California to open a series with the Angels, the eyes of the world were on Munich, Germany, where the XX Summer Olympics were underway. The opening of the games, to much pomp and circumstance, had been held with considerable apprehension by much of the world, as a divided Germany hosted the games barely a quarter of a century after the end of World War II. A largely unknown American pre-dental student named Mark Spitz won two gold medals in swimming on the second day of competition, setting world records in the 200-meter butterfly and in anchoring the men's 400-meter relay team. The two early medals were only the beginning for Spitz; within days he would become world-renowned and an American hero.

Detroit arrived in Anaheim with a chance to salvage what had been a disappointing month of August. The team had been unable to carry forward the momentum it had built up prior to the All-Star break, losing 13 of 20 games after play had resumed. However, the team had rebounded since mid-month, winning seven of eleven, including the sweep in Minnesota. Now the Tigers went into Anaheim Stadium to face an Angels team that was mired in fifth place in the A.L. West with a 54–67 record, 17 games behind the front-running Chicago White Sox.

California manager Del Rice was hamstrung with one of the weakest lineups in all of baseball. The squad was primarily made up of players on the downside of their career, most of whom had seen better days with other organizations. Vada Pinson, who was the regular left fielder, was no longer the .300, 20-home run, 20-stolen base player he had been in the preceding decade with Cincinnati. Veteran infielders Leo Cardenas and Ken McMullen had enjoyed their best seasons with other teams. The forgettable triumvirate of Art Kusnyer, Jeff Torborg, and John Stephenson shared the catching position. Center fielder Ken Berry was still a fine hitter and outfielder, and slick-fielding second baseman Sandy Alomar provided a steady glove and speed on the bases. But first baseman Bob Oliver provided the only real power source on the team, and the California attack failed to put fear into the opposition's pitcher on most nights.

What the Angels did possess was one of the better starting pitching rotations in the American League, and when they were on, they could make life miserable for opposing batters. Unfortunately for the pennant-minded Tigers, they found that out only too well the last three days of August. In the first game, with four bottles of champagne on ice ready to celebrate Lolich's 20th victory of the season, it was Angels lefty Rudy May who did the post-game celebrating. May limited Detroit to four hits and struck out nine batters in a convincing 3–1 California victory. The second game was even worse for the Tigers, as righty Andy Messersmith shut down Detroit on only three hits and also struck out nine, as the Angels won that one, 4–1.

In the third game Detroit got a look at the hottest pitcher in the league, the flame-throwing Nolan Ryan. Ryan's season, as well as his career, was taking off like never before. A promising but inconsistent pitcher with the New

York Mets, Ryan had spent four seasons piecing together a 19–24 career record with a very pedestrian 3.53 ERA, while never having logged more than 150 innings in any season for the pitching-rich Mets organization. He had joined the Angels in an off-season trade for washed-up shortstop Jim Fregosi, and was now getting the regular turn in the rotation that he had lacked in New York. With a 100 mile-per-hour fastball, a wicked curve, and the bravado to knock hitters off the plate, Ryan was not a pitcher that batters looked forward to facing. He was just wild enough (he would lead the league by a wide margin that season in walks and wild pitches, and place highly in hit batsmen) to keep any self-preserving hitter in an uncomfortable position at the plate.

On the last night of August, Ryan overwhelmed the Tigers, holding them to only three hits while fanning ten. The 4–0 victory was his third straight complete-game shutout and his ninth whitewashing of an opponent on the season. During the ten-day span that concluded with the Detroit blanking, Ryan had completed three shutout victories in which he allowed a total of 13 hits while striking out 31. With his fifteenth win of the season (15–12), he also increased his league-leading strikeout total to 243, well ahead of Lolich, who was second with 201.

The Tigers headed up the coast to Oakland to conclude their West Coast swing, feeling lucky to finally escape the grasp of the Angels. They had managed only ten hits for the entire three-game series, and didn't even have to face the fourth member of California's quartet of starting pitchers, Clyde Wright, who would go on to win 18 games that year. The sweep at the hands of the Angels left the Tigers with a 67–58 record and in second place, a half-game behind the Orioles, who had snuck past them once again. The losses dropped their final record for the month of August to 12–18, and the whispers became louder from skeptics who doubted that a team with Detroit's age throughout its everyday lineup would be able to stay in the race through the grind of the final five weeks of the season.

The pitching staff was a mess with Lolich, the staff stopper, having lost three straight games and struggling to regain his winning touch. He entered the month of August with a personal mark of 18–6 and ended it 19–11. Fryman, who had pitched so beautifully in his first three starts, had dropped his past two decisions and looked more like the player who had been waived out of the National League a month earlier. Coleman had won his past two starts—his only wins since the All-Star break—but was still only 14–11 for the year. No fourth starter had emerged with any consistency, and the overworked bullpen tandem of Scherman and Seelbach had recently struggled. Guys like Timmerman and Slayback were falling out of favor with a manager who liked to ride the hot hand and didn't entrust quality innings to pitchers he didn't believe could help him win. Timmerman pitched only 23 innings during the month, while Slayback struggled to the tune of an 8.50 ERA for August.

The hitters were faring no better as Martin platooned and mixed and matched his lineup each day, trying to find any combination that would offer at least a lukewarm attack for that date's game. Detroit's team batting average hovered around .230. Freehan remained the most productive batter, hitting .272 at month's end and serving as the Tigers' best hitter in key situations. Kaline had worked his way back into the everyday lineup and had upped his average to .289, but still had disappointing power numbers with only six home runs and 22 RBIs on the season. Tony Taylor was still batting at a respectable .293 but had had seen his average dip below the .300 mark in recent weeks. The other Tiger mainstays were mired in either inconsistent or even disappointing seasons. Cash had managed just three solo home runs since his game-winning effort in Milwaukee on July 27. During the month of August, he had hit only two round-trippers while knocking in only four runs. Northrup's average was up to .263, but with only eight home runs. Horton had a paltry nine homers and 27 RBIs, far below the level of production Detroit fans expected out of their right-handed hitting strongman. Stanley was hitting .251; McAuliffe was at .240. Rodriguez and Brinkman were hitting .224 and .202, respectively. Tom Haller hadn't knocked in a run in nearly two months and was hitting just .207. Haller's role as the backup catcher had largely been taken by the newcomer Sims, who was hitting only .211 since coming to Detroit.

The lack of hitting was exacerbated by a lack of team speed on the base paths. When the home runs weren't flying over the fence with any regularity, Detroit struggled to manufacture runs. The lineup was filled with aging plodders. The stolen base was almost nonexistent. Outside of adept base runners like McAuliffe, Taylor, and Stanley, advancing from first to third on singles and scoring from first on a double were rarities for runners in Detroit uniforms. Martin did what he could to alleviate the station-to-station, one base at a time logistics, which most Tiger rallies seemed to feature. He'd try to advance runners by conventional and unconventional methods. The hit and run, sacrifice bunt, and the squeeze bunt were all favorites of the Detroit manager. He also resorted to unusual tactics, such as having a runner get caught off base behind the play, resulting in a rundown, in order to advance a lead runner elsewhere. None of these were substitutions for exceptional speed and athleticism, traits that were lacking in the lineups the Tigers put on the field each night.

"Too old" is how many neutral observers viewed the team. Others looked at the experience that the core players had accumulated through a decade or more of American League play—the near-miss in '67, the world championship in '68 — as a positive factor that would benefit Detroit in the stretch drive. The NBA championship won by an aging Los Angeles Lakers team earlier that spring and the success enjoyed by Coach George Allen's "Over the Hill Gang" with the Washington Redskins were pointed to as comparable examples of older, veteran teams that recently had great success in other sports.

However, the consensus among most experts was that the Detroit Tigers were in the narrow opening of a rapidly closing window of opportunity. Aging veterans such as Kaline, Cash, Haller, and Taylor, all 35 years of age or older, were entering the stretch run of long, productive careers. This chance to get to another World Series was likely their last. Such household names as Freehan, Lolich, McAuliffe, Northrup, Stanley, Brinkman, Timmerman, Gates Brown, and Ike Brown were all thirty-somethings, the majority of whom were thought to be on the backside of solid careers. With four years having passed since their championship season, Tiger fans understood that the clock was ticking on those old familiar '68 heroes.

The task wouldn't be easy, as the divisional race was turning into a four-team sprint to the finish line. Sub-par play over the five weeks since the All-Star break by the season-long front-runners, Detroit and Baltimore, had allowed otherwise fringe contenders New York and Boston to creep back into the race and claim legitimate stakes in the battle for the division crown. The maddening inconsistency displayed by the four teams through the first five months of the 1972 season left the outcome totally unpredictable as they headed into the last 30 games of the schedule. As the calendar turned to September, Baltimore manager Earl Weaver summed up the current state of the A.L. East, saying, "We've got the pitching, but we've been short of hitting. Detroit's been hitting better lately, but their pitching's been spotty. As a result we let those other two bleeps in there."[22]

American League East Standings through August 31, 1972

	W	*L*	*Pct.*	*GB*
Baltimore Orioles	67	57	.540	—
Detroit Tigers	67	58	.536	½
New York Yankees	66	59	.528	1½
Boston Red Sox	64	58	.525	2
Cleveland Indians	58	66	.468	9
Milwaukee Brewers	49	75	.395	18

VIII

Down to the Wire

Detroit jumped into what promised to be a wild and woolly month of September by making a move of gigantic proportions. Gigantic not so much in the impact it was expected to make on the race for the American League's East Division title, but rather the physical proportions of the Tigers' latest acquisition, Frank Howard, who they purchased in a waiver deal from the Texas Rangers. Standing 6'7" and weighing anywhere from 255 to 280 pounds, Howard was arguably the most physically imposing player in baseball at the time. At age 36, he was no longer the player that had amassed 369 lifetime home runs up to that point, nor the one that had hit 44, 48, and 44 home runs in each of the seasons from 1968 to 1970. It was during that time when he was the most feared slugger in the A.L., playing for the Washington Senators with such nicknames as "the Washington Monument" and "the Capital Punisher."

Rumors linking Howard with Detroit had existed for a couple of years. There was speculation near the end of the 1970 season that Howard would be traded in a straight swap for Denny McLain. Instead, the swindle the Tigers later administered in picking up Coleman, Rodriguez, and Brinkman proved to be a much more lucrative deal from Detroit's standpoint, and in fact was the key move in re-tooling the team for the '72 pennant drive. Now the Tigers had acquired the prodigious slugger for a mere $30,000 and assumed the last month of his reported $120,000 annual salary, as the money-starved Texas Rangers franchise looked to dump any sizeable salary they could.

Howard's offensive numbers had declined some in 1971, the Senators' last season in the nation's capital, and then had completely fallen off after the franchise relocated to Texas. His final numbers with the Rangers included a .244 average, with only nine home runs and 31 RBIs in 95 games. Already one of the most lead-footed runners in baseball, Howard had slowed to the point that he no longer played in the outfield and had been reduced to a platoon role at first base under Ted Williams and the Rangers. However, it was his game-busting potential as a situational player that most interested the Detroit organization, as the Tigers looked for any help that might alleviate the offensive woes that had afflicted the team most of the season. When "Hondo" (as he was commonly called) held a bat with his large muscular body and stared out at the pitcher, he still presented a formidable presence and frightened the opposition each time he came to the plate.

"It works out just right," said manager Billy Martin about his newest piece of the Tiger puzzle, one he planned on using in a platoon situation with the slumping Norm Cash at first base. "I used Al Kaline at first base the same way until Al's leg got strong enough to play the outfield. It's good to have a big guy like Hondo ready to swing the bat."[1]

General manager Jim Campbell's expectations were even more modest when he said, "If Frank can win one game for us, it will be worth the time and money we put into it."[2]

Even though eyes in Detroit focused largely on the Tigers' four-way battle in the A.L. East, the sports pages were filled with a wide array of happenings, many of which had an international flavor. The world chess championship was decided when Russia's Boris Spassky forfeited the 21st game of the match, giving Bobby Fischer his seventh win to go with eleven draws and the necessary 12 points needed to clinch the series match. Things were going much better for the Russians in Montreal, Quebec, where 18,000 stunned onlookers in the Montreal Forum watched as the Soviet Union's Red Army team destroyed an NHL All-Star team, 7–3, in the first of a scheduled eight-game series. It was the first match in a battle for world supremacy in the game of ice hockey. The series provided the first dents in Canada's self-proclaimed dominance of the sport; over the remainder of what turned into a classic series, the Soviet squad proved to be every bit the equal of the team made up of Canada's greatest players.

In Munich, Germany, where the Summer Olympic Games continued, the United States and Soviets were engaged in a tight race for the lead in the overall medal count. The United States team was highlighted by Dave Wottle, who won the gold medal in the 800-meter run in thrilling, come-from-behind fashion. Wottle, while wearing his trademark white golf beret, stayed well back in the pack for the first three-quarters of the race, but then finished with a furious kick to win in the final few meters over the pre-race favorite, the Soviet's Yevgeny Arzhonov. Things didn't go as well for U.S. gold medal favorite Bob Seagram, who was upset by East Germany's Wolfgang Nordwig in the pole vault. Seagram's loss didn't come without controversy, however, as his regular pole was banned as illegal just prior to the event.[3]

Back in the United States, the Tigers opened play in September with a weekend series in Oakland against the A's, who were once again in first place.

In the first game on Friday, September 1, Martin put his new acquisition into the lineup against A's left-handed pitcher Ken Holtzman. With the newly stitched "DETROIT" lettering across the chest of his size 54 gray road jersey (because Detroit had no uniforms that large available, two jerseys and a couple of pairs of size 46 waist pants were included as terms of the trade), Howard batted cleanup and played first base, providing an additional right-handed-hitting threat to the Tiger batting order.[4] He drew a walk in his first plate appearance and later singled, but Holtzman was too much, as Oakland took the opener, 4–1.

The second game of the series on Saturday afternoon appeared to be a dream match-up on paper. Vida Blue and Mickey Lolich, who finished 1–2 in the American League's Cy Young Award voting the previous season, faced each other. The duel was about twelve months too late, however, as Blue had been unable to recover from missing all of spring training and was struggling through a 6–10 season. Lolich, meanwhile, seemed stuck on nineteen wins and struggled during the season's second half. Although neither pitcher lasted past the seventh inning, they both pitched well, and the two teams were still battling as they entered the eleventh inning in a 1–1 deadlock. In the top of the second extra frame, Bill Freehan led off with a tie-breaking homer, and later in the inning Mickey Stanley did the same. Fred Scherman and Chris Zachary finished off Oakland, and Detroit had a hard-fought 3–1 victory.

On Sunday, the season-long pattern of Oakland taking two out of three games from every series between the two teams continued when the A's won the finale, 3–1. Sal Bando homered in the fifth inning to give Oakland the lead, and Catfish Hunter went the distance on the mound, allowing only four hits for his 18th win. With the Detroit loss the A.L. East race tightened even more. While Boston was getting rained out, Wilbur Wood of the White Sox was twirling a 5–0 shutout over New York for his 23rd victory of the season. Meanwhile, the California Angels continued their streak of dominant pitching as Andy Messersmith shut out Baltimore over ten innings in a 1–0 Angels' victory. The day resulted in the top four teams in the division residing within one-half game of each other:

	W	*L*	*Pct.*	*GB*
Baltimore Orioles	68	59	.535	—
Boston Red Sox	66	58	.532	½
Detroit Tigers	68	60	.531	½
New York Yankees	68	60	.531	½

Following the series in Oakland, the Tigers boarded a flight back to Detroit, where they opened a series against the Indians the next evening.

Gaylord Perry was antagonizing the Tiger batters once again, leading 1–0 in the bottom of the sixth when Tony Taylor led off with a double. Taylor was making a rare appearance against a right-handed pitcher, starting at third base in place of the slumping Aurelio Rodriguez. After two were out and Taylor was still standing on second base, Norm Cash was intentionally walked so Perry could face slumping Detroit left fielder Willie Horton. Horton was in the throes of a 5-for-36 stretch, which unfortunately had become all too common within the disappointing season he was having in 1972. A career .275 hitter at that point who had averaged 25 home runs and 84 RBIs over his previous seven seasons, Horton was struggling to stay in the .220s, and had driven in only 29 runs as he faced Perry with two men on and two out. The muscular Horton connected with a Perry pitch, however, that clanked off the screen in deep right field, scoring both Taylor and Cash on the two-run triple. Fryman made the slim lead hold up, as he out-pitched Perry the rest of the way for a much-needed 2–1 Detroit victory. The win allowed the Tigers to gain ground on their competitors. Boston split a doubleheader with Milwaukee, while Baltimore and New York also divided a twin-bill. As a result, Detroit was now tied with Baltimore at 69–60 for the top spot, one-half game ahead of the Red Sox and Yankees.

The topsy-turvy race with the frequent changing of the standings even invited perspective from those not in the race. Cleveland had proven to be an early-season pretender but was not equipped to stay with the lead teams in the division, and was now reduced the role of a spoiler. Indians manager Ken Aspromonte chimed in on the factors he thought would come into play over the final four weeks while a champion was decided. "Baltimore's got the best pitching, I don't think there's much doubt of that. But I just don't know what's happened to the hitting in this league this season. The team that starts hitting is the team that will win the division."[5]

On Tuesday, September 5, the line between the sports world and the ugliness of a planet dotted with pockets of international hatred was blurred as startling and tragic events unfolded in Munich, Germany. An Arab group known as "Black September" broke into the Olympic village and took eleven Israeli athletes hostage in their quarters. Two of the hostages were killed during the initial scuffle, and a tense standoff ensued that kept the rest of the world on edge as they watched television coverage of the confrontation for most of the next 18 hours.

As the Olympic village turned from a symbol of international hope and cooperation to a military police stakeout with snipers and SWAT personnel blending into the landscape, the negotiations dragged on between the terrorists and the rest of the civilized world. Finally the Arab terrorists and their Israeli hostages were transferred by helicopter to the airfield in Furstenfeldbruck, where the group was to be moved by plane to an undetermined Arab country. The airport became the scene of a German paramilitary rescue gone awry. The rescue attempt resulted in panic on both sides before a Palestinian threw a grenade into the helicopter with the surviving hostages aboard. When the smoke from the subsequent blast cleared, all of the Israeli athletes had been killed, as well as all but three of the Arab terrorists. The worst fears of the Olympic games had been realized, with much of the world looking on.[6]

While the Olympic games paused for one day in memoriam for the murdered athletes, the race continued on in the A.L. East. The Red Sox pulled out an excruciating, come-from-behind victory against the last-place Milwaukee Brewers. Trailing 3–1 in the eighth inning against the strong pitching of Brewer right-hander Skip Lockwood, the Bosox rallied on the strength of a three-run home run by outfielder Reggie Smith to win, 5–3. In New York, the Yankees and Orioles continued their series, with the home team pulling out a 7–6 decision. Meanwhile in Detroit, the Tigers wrapped up their brief homestand with a 4–2 win over the Indians. Joe Coleman went the distance for his fifteenth win (15–13). The key hit was provided by Eddie Brinkman, who singled in two runs in the bottom of the fifth inning, wiping out a 2–1 Cleveland lead. The victory put Detroit alone at the top of the division, while Baltimore fell from a first-place tie to fourth place. All four teams were now within the tiny array of .007 percentage points.

Aside from the tight races that were dominating attention in the American League, an interesting development was taking place in the individual statistical races. Chicago's Dick Allen, who was already well out in front in both the home run (32) and RBI (92) categories, lifted his batting average to .317, and now led the race for the A.L. batting championship over Oakland's Joe Rudi (.315) and Minnesota's Rod Carew (.314). With less than a month to play, Allen was threatening to be the first Triple Crown winner in the majors since it was accomplished in back-to-back seasons by Frank Robinson with Baltimore in 1966 and Boston's Carl Yastrzemski in 1967.[7]

As Detroit hit the road again, the Tigers traveled to Baltimore for a crucial three-game series with the Orioles. With New York and Boston also having to be considered as legitimate threats for the division crown, the series was not the top-heavy matchup between two runaway contenders as it looked like it would be six weeks earlier. The feeling still existed among many baseball people, however, that the A.L. East would be represented in the playoffs by one of these two teams. Both squads were made up of proven veteran players, battle tested in races over the past half-decade, with each having been to the top of the mountain in the baseball world.

The Tigers came out in the first game looking like they were determined to end this two-team, season-long battle once and for all. They scored three runs in the first inning off the Orioles' top pitcher, Jim Palmer, and rode that all the way to a 4–3 victory. Mickey Lolich was the recipient of the early run support, and despite lasting only 5⅓ innings, was credited with his long-awaited 20th win of the season. Chuck Seelbach provided the relief, as Detroit's bullpen extended a streak to ten games, covering 35 innings, without allowing a run.

In other action that night, the sizzling Red Sox defeated the Yankees, 2–0, courtesy of a Reggie Smith two-run homer. The win was Boston's tenth in its last twelve games and kept the team within a half-game of the first-place Tigers. New York fell to a game and a half behind Detroit, while Baltimore was now two full games back. In the A.L. West, the A's clobbered the second-place White Sox, 9–1. Oakland was now four games out in front and seemed to be taking command of a division the A's had been heavily favored to win since spring training.

The next day, Lolich celebrated his milestone victory in majestic style. Courtesy of Michigan Senator Robert Griffin, Lolich was the guest of President Nixon at the White House. While kibitzing with the president, Lolich was advised to ask for a 27½ percent raise for the next season and to pitch inside sliders to Yastrzemski. Despite the friendly advice, the Tiger left-hander would not tip his hand as to his voting preference for the upcoming election.[8] The results that evening were not quite as friendly for his teammates, as Baltimore ripped Detroit, 9–0. Mike Cuellar tossed a four-hit shutout, while Billy Martin took a chance on Scherman, normally his left-handed relief specialist, to be the night's starting pitcher. Scherman lasted only three batters (good for two runs) before getting the quick hook. Bill Slayback didn't fare much better, giving up four runs, as the game quickly got out of hand for the Tigers. To make matters worse, Boston hammered New York, 10–4, and moved into the division lead for the first time all season. Tommy Harper and Rico Petrocelli each blasted three-run homers for the Bosox in the rout of their traditional rival.

The final game in Baltimore was a test for Martin's struggling team. With his club having lost ten of fifteen games on the season against its primary rival and in desperate need of a series win, Martin handed the ball to his most consistent starting pitcher over the previous month, Woody Fryman. The Orioles, despite a season-long hitting slump and a team batting average that had hovered in the .220s for most of the year, had stung Tiger pitching for 25 hits over the first two games of the series. Fryman, though, held the Orioles to two hits in a masterpiece performance in which he registered eight strikeouts and dominated the Baltimore lineup in a complete-game effort. Gates Brown provided the only run Fryman needed when he homered in the first inning off Pat Dobson. Brinkman singled in Jim Northrup with an insurance run in the seventh inning, and Detroit captured a crucial 2–0 victory that allowed the Tigers to take the series, two games to one. Further up the coast, the Red Sox defeated New York once again, this time 4–2. Yastrzemski hit a two-run homer, and Boston's new-found pitching ace, Luis Tiant, recorded his seventh straight victory. After the evening's action ended, the Red Sox remained in first place with a half-game lead over the Tigers. Baltimore fell to two and a half games back, and New York was three games out.

The Tiger returned home to open a series with the Yankees in an unusual Saturday night series opener. Because of some bizarre quirks in the scheduling between the two teams that season, Detroit hosted their long-time rival for two separate series in September. The Yankees had hosted the Tigers for a highly unusual five-game series in May and a four-game series in early August. Both of those series featured doubleheaders as part of the original 1972 schedule. New York would now be making their second and third trips to Tiger Stadium, not counting a two-game set that had been canceled during the season's first week because of the players strike.

As the two teams arrived at the stadium for the series opener, they were buoyed by news that the first-place Red Sox had lost earlier in the day, 2–1, in Cleveland on Graig Nettles' tenth-inning home run. Despite having the opportunity to overtake the front-running Red Sox, Detroit couldn't capitalize, as the Yankees ground out a 3–1 win. Coleman was the recipient of poor run support once again while taking the loss. The evening turned out to be doubly frustrating when Baltimore rebounded with a doubleheader sweep of the last-place Brewers. The Orioles' Terry Crowley pulled out the first game with a home run in the bottom of the ninth inning in the 2–1 win. The nightcap proved to be much easier, as Baltimore cruised to an 8–0 throttling of hapless Milwaukee. As the first full week of September ended, the standings at the top of the A.L. East tightened once again:

	W	*L*	*Pct.*	*GB*
Boston Red Sox	71	60	.542	—
Detroit Tigers	72	61	.541	½
Baltimore Orioles	71	63	.530	1½
New York Yankees	70	64	.522	2½

On Sunday afternoon the Tigers were listless for the second straight game, managing only three hits off New York pitcher Mel Stottlemyre in a 5–0 loss. Martin was hesitant to give much credit to the opposing pitcher, and instead described the long-time Yankee ace's effort as "very hittable."[9] The losing pitcher was Lolich, who suffered his 12th loss while seeing his record fall to 3–6 since the All-Star break. As Martin held a closed-door clubhouse meeting with his struggling team, Detroit lost ground to the rest of the division as well. Boston continued its amazing streak, which had now seen the Red Sox go 14–3 over their previous seventeen games, including a doubleheader sweep of Cleveland. The first game had gone into extra innings before rookie Carlton Fisk's 20th home run of the season keyed a four-run Red Sox twelfth in a 5–1 win. John Curtis tossed a 2–0 shutout of the Indians in the second game. Meanwhile, Baltimore rode Jim Palmer's 19th win to a 2–0 whitewashing of Milwaukee.

On Monday, September 11, the Games of the XX Olympiad ended in Munich with a superficial show of cheerfulness. As Israel strafed Arab guerillas in Syria and Lebanon with bomb and rocket attacks under the guise of retaliatory actions for the murder of the eleven Israeli athletes, the closing ceremonies took place at the Olympic stadium. Most of the 80,000 spectators on hand were unaware that Arab terrorists had reportedly stolen a plane, and that intelligence reports indicated it may have been loaded with bombs intended for the stadium. While the ceremonies on the ground proceeded, German fighter planes were ordered to shoot down the unknown plane if it neared Munich. Luckily, the perceived threat appeared to be false, and the stolen plane was never recovered.[10]

Aside from the dark specter that will forever be associated with those games, the 1972 Summer Olympics did provide plenty of drama in the athletic competition that took place. International stars surfaced, with the likes of Mark Spitz, who ended the swimming competition with an Olympic record seven gold medals, setting world record times in each event. Fellow American Frank Shorter became the first U.S. participant in 64 years to win the marathon. The Soviet Union's tiny gymnast, Olga Korbut, gained international fame with her three Olympic golds. Overall the Soviets won the medal count, beating the U.S. in total medals (99 to 94) and in gold medals (50 to 33). The most bitterly contested of the events was the gold medal basketball game, where Russian Aleksandr Belov laid the ball in the basket as time expired, giving the Soviet's a controversial 51–50 win over the United States. The Soviet team had three attempts to complete the winning play, as first an inadvertent horn and then a reset clock were given as reasons by the officials to override the results of the two previously failed attempts with three seconds left in the game.

In Detroit the weather turned dreary, as the Tiger and Yankees slogged through five and a half innings in the rain before umpires made an official game out of New York's abbreviated 4–2 victory. Martin was furious at the decision that was made after an hour-and-forty-three-minute delay, especially in lieu of the impact it had in such a close race. The loss dropped his floundering team into fourth place with just more than three weeks left in the season. Cleveland helped out the teams ahead of them by knocking off first-place Boston, 6–5, while Baltimore rode Boog Powell's three-run homer and Mike Cuellar's 16th win in a 3–2 decision over Milwaukee.

The sweep at the hands of New York looked as possibly the beginning of the end for Detroit. Although they were still only two games out of first place, the Tigers had slipped behind three other teams and had been unable to create any momentum since the beginning of September. With Baltimore coming into town for the final two meetings of the season between the two teams, Martin's club stood at the edge of the proverbial abyss as Detroit entered the last nineteen games on the schedule.

Things didn't start any better against the Orioles, as Paul Blair blasted an early home run in the first game to give them a 1–0 lead. However, when the Tigers came to bat in the third inning, Rodriguez singled and then Brinkman came to the plate and lofted a fly ball that just dropped over the left field screen for a two-run homer, giving Detroit the lead. Brinkman later scored a run on a Dick McAuliffe double in the seventh, but by the ninth inning the Tigers were hanging on to a 3–2 lead when the Orioles loaded the bases with one out. Fryman had given another strong effort through the first 8⅓ innings but was running out of gas when Martin came out to the mound for a visit. Powell, Baltimore's left-handed hitting slugger, came to the plate in a game-deciding situation. Usually this was a situation where Martin would call on Scherman. Scherman, however, had been the starter in the previous night's game with New York and wasn't available, so the call went out to John Hiller instead. Hiller struck out Powell, and then got Blair to ground into a force out to end the game. The 3–2 victory was one of the biggest of the season for the Tigers, and the stars of the night were two unlikely sources in Brinkman and Hiller.

"Well I sure wasn't trying to hit it out," said the Detroit shortstop after the game. "I was just trying to do what I always try to do. I was just trying to get my bat on the ball and put it into play."[11]

When asked about his propensity for coming up with big hits throughout the season despite having an average that had hovered around the .200 mark for several months, he said, "Don't ask me why. I bear down every time I go up there. It just seems that whenever I get a hit it means something. I just want to get a shot at that big paycheck at the end."

For Hiller the win was his first of the season. More remarkable, it was his first victory in almost two years, since before his heart attack. After persevering through such a personal setback, his on-field accomplishment while nailing down the save was kept in perspective. "When I had the heart attack, the doctors told me that I could pitch again. They said it was all up to me. That's all I needed to know. Now I'm just trying to do a job."[12]

With Boston having lost again the previous evening 3–2 to New York, Detroit looked to gain ground on its competitors by sweeping the short series from the Orioles. The evening didn't get off on a good note as they trailed 5–1 heading into the bottom of the fifth inning. The big blow was a grand slam off the bat of the suddenly hot Powell, which came at the expense of Coleman, who was hit for five runs in the first five innings. The Tigers rallied, however, as Howard connected on a sixth-inning, opposite-field blast into the right field lower-deck seats for a three-run homer to get Detroit back within a run. They tied the game later in the same inning when Horton scored all the way from second base on an infield single by Rodriguez, and then took the lead when Mickey Stanley faked a break for the plate from third base, causing Baltimore pitcher Doyle Alexander to commit a balk. Stanley's run turned out to be the game-winner. Scherman pitched four scoreless innings in relief, and the Tigers scored a stunning 6–5 come-from-behind win in the final meeting of the season between the two teams.

"This game tonight makes getting Howard worthwhile," said Martin after the game about the mammoth September acquisition who had just made his first big contribution. "His influence among the other players has been tremendous even if he doesn't hit. He's a very unselfish guy."[13]

While Detroit was celebrating the two-game sweep of Baltimore, Boston was salvaging the final game of its brief two-game series with the Yankees by winning, 7–2. The A.L. East race was now garnering national attention as the races in the National League were all but over. Pittsburgh held an astounding fifteen-game lead over the Chicago Cubs, while Cincinnati was holding steady at a seven-game bulge over the pesky Houston Astros. The A.L. West was still in some doubt, with Oakland only three games up on Chicago. But the White Sox were staggering, and the A's seemed to have settled in again as the dominant team in that division as well as the American League as a whole. With exactly three weeks remaining in the season, the East Division was still very much a four-team race:

	W	*L*	*Pct.*	*GB*
Boston Red Sox	74	62	.544	—
Detroit Tigers	74	64	.536	1
Baltimore Orioles	74	65	.532	1½
New York Yankees	74	65	.532	1½

Detroit enjoyed an off day before going to Milwaukee for a three-game weekend. The last-place Brewers had been a thorn in the Tigers' side all season, taking eight of the twelve games played between the two teams thus far. The first game looked like more of the same as Rick Auerbach scored on a disputed call at first base. Jim Lonborg, who had already defeated the Tigers three times, looked like he might make that single run hold up as he allowed only three Detroit singles through seven scoreless innings. In the eighth inning, however, Duke Sims delivered a key pinch-hit single that scored Northrup with the tying run. Then in the top of the ninth, McAuliffe led off with a walk and was sacrificed to second base on a Stanley bunt. After Gates Brown was intentionally walked, Freehan blasted a drive deep enough into center field to allow McAuliffe to tag up and take third. With two outs and the lead run at third base, Norm Cash, who had slumped miserably since the All-Star break, delivered a single, giving the Tigers their first lead of the game. Scherman, in relief of Lolich, again delivered with a scoreless bottom of the ninth to preserve the win. The victory over Milwaukee was critical; in Boston, Reggie Smith knocked a two-out double in the bottom of the ninth inning that scored Carl Yastrzemski with the winning run over Cleveland, 4–3. Yastrzemski delivered a two-run homer earlier in the game. In New York, Baltimore got a three-run homer off the bat of Boog Powell, and Jim Palmer's strong pitching was enough for his 20th win in a 3–1 Oriole victory over the Yankees.

On Saturday afternoon, Martin went to his bag of tricks to scratch out another win. A hit-and-run maneuver, executed by Rodriguez, moved McAuliffe to third base and set up the first Detroit run. Later in the same inning, Rodriguez was on the front end of a double steal with Gates Brown, although both runners ended up being stranded. In the fourth inning, Stanley led off with a single and then stole second base, where he later scored on Brinkman's single. The two Tiger runs, courtesy of some aggressive running and managing, held up in the 2–1 victory, thanks to another strong effort from Fryman (seventh victory) and scoreless relief from Seelbach.

"I unleashed our secret weapon," Martin said sarcastically after the win about the seldom-used running game he employed with his team that day. "But when you're not getting any runs, you've got to do something. We've been waiting and waiting and waiting. I just couldn't wait any more. We don't have the speed to do this all the time.... I got away with it."[14]

As his team continued to eek out wins against the pesky Brewers, the rest of the division contenders followed suite. Boston blasted Cleveland, 10–0, as Tiant unleashed a three-hit shutout. Yastrzemski knocked in four runs, and rookie Carlton Fisk delivered a two-run homer to lead the thrashing of the Indians. Baltimore got two RBIs each from their old-guard, middle-of-the-lineup icons, Powell and Brooks Robinson, in a 7–3 rout of the slumping Yankees. Mike Cuellar won his 17th game for the Orioles.

With their season series with Baltimore completed and seven big games still to be played with the first-place Red Sox, the Tigers couldn't help but look past the final game in Milwaukee and two in Cleveland before heading to Fenway Park for a showdown with Boston. "The next seven days should tell a helluva lot," forecasted Martin after his team had won the first two games in Milwaukee. "We've got one game left with Milwaukee on Sunday, then three in Cleveland and those four with Boston next weekend. By then I think it's got to be down to two clubs, or maybe one which has pulled away."[15]

After four straight one-run victories, Detroit took a "relaxing" 6–2 decision over the Brewers in the series finale. McAuliffe, who hadn't homered in nearly eight weeks, hit two over the wall at County Stadium while also knocking in four runs to lead the offensive barrage. Sims delivered two RBIs, and Coleman was the rare recipient of the offensive outburst by his teammates and won his 17th game. The margin of victory, which was greater than two runs, was the first such win in nearly a month for Detroit.

The somewhat-surprising sweep against Milwaukee was proving to be even more positive when the scores from the other divisional games filtered in. Gaylord Perry slowed down the Red Sox for his 21st win, 9–2. New York, which appeared to be on the verge of falling back out of the race, scored a crucial 2–1 win against Baltimore, who was primed for the knockout punch. Yankee reliever Sparky Lyle had tied an American League record that day with his 34th save of the season, this time in relief of Fritz Peterson, who gained his sixteenth win. "We had to have this game and I know that was on everyone's minds," said Lyle afterwards about the victory that kept New York's hopes of a return to post-season play alive.[16] With the results from the weekend of September 15–17, 1972, in place, the standings now stood as follows with Boston holding a one percentage point lead over the surging Tigers:

	W	*L*	*Pct.*	*GB*
Boston Red Sox	76	63	.547	—
Detroit Tigers	77	64	.546	—
Baltimore Orioles	76	66	.535	1½
New York Yankees	75	67	.528	2½

Monday, September 18, was an off day for Detroit, but as usual in a season where nobody seemed to want to take command in the A.L. East, not playing oftentimes proved to be beneficial. In Boston, the Orioles knocked off the Red Sox, 5–2, dropping Boston a half-game back of the idle but now first-place Tigers. Picking a winner in the divisional race had become almost impossible because the results of every day or night seemed to reshape opinion as to how it would play out. What was becoming more clear to all of the A.L. East contenders was that the winner of the division race was going to be matched in the upcoming league championship series with the Oakland A's. Their fifth straight win had come on Sunday against Texas, 4–1, behind Catfish Hunter's 20th win, which gave them a commanding five-game lead in the A.L. West.

On that third Monday of September, in Detroit and around the rest of the country, much of the water-cooler talk would have centered on the opening week of the NFL regular season, which kicked off the previous day. While the Tigers took care of business in Milwaukee, 54,418 sweltering fans in Tiger Stadium watched the Lions win their opener, 30–16, over the New York Giants. Quarterback Greg Landry threw three touchdown passes and fullback Steve Owens rumbled for 113 rushing yards in the victory. The NFL's marquee matchup of week one took place in Kansas City, where the Chiefs opened their new Arrowhead Stadium with a rematch of the Christmas Day double-overtime playoff game with the Miami Dolphins from the previous December. The Chiefs were the sexy pick of many analysts to win the AFC and reach the Super Bowl in the new season, but Miami gained what would prove to be its first win in a monumental season, 20–10.[17]

Carrying the momentum of a five-game winning streak that had propelled them into first place, the Tigers headed to Cleveland for a series opening on Tuesday with the fifth-place Indians. There wasn't a more depressing setting in the majors during that era than cavernous Municipal Stadium, where the average attendance in 1972 was just over 8,000 fans per game in a ballpark that held more than 70,000. The mid–September weeknight games drew 5,453 and 3,198 for the pair of dates with Detroit.[18] The setting was perfect for a stumble from a pennant-minded team, and that's exactly what happened on the first night. Detroit dropped both ends of a twi-night doubleheader by 3–2 and 6–4 scores. The first game found Lolich giving up a home run to his pitching counterpart, Steve Dunning, as the Indians jumped out to the lead. Detroit was able to scratch out runs to get within one in the eighth inning, but Ed Farmer came into the game in relief for Cleveland and recorded the last four outs. In the second game, Martin's season-long search for a dependable fourth starting pitcher bit him again, as the Indians jumped out to a 6–0 lead against Hiller, who was then followed by Lerrin LaGrow, Scherman, Niekro, Jim Foor, Tom Timmerman, and Bob Strampe. Detroit was able to chip away at the early deficit and close it to 6–4, but former Tiger Mike Kilkenny, who was pitching for his fourth team of the season, came in and shut them down over the last 1⅓ innings to preserve the doubleheader victory. Fortunately, the double loss was not as costly as it could have been, as Baltimore was rained out in Boston, allowing both teams to gain only one full game on the Tigers (with Boston taking over the top spot once again), while New York fell to Milwaukee, 7–2.

On Wednesday the Tigers and Indians completed their season series, with Detroit scratching and clawing to avoid a costly sweep at the hands of a pronounced spoiler. The Tigers jumped in front in the first inning when Northrup stole second and then scored on a Gates Brown single. Detroit's starting pitcher, Fryman, was throwing like he might make the one run hold up until a drive off the bat of the Indians Chris Chambliss skipped by Sims, who was playing right field, for a two-base error. Later in the inning, Chambliss came in to score the tying run. Sims had been inserted into the outfield by Martin as a means of getting a hot bat into the lineup wherever he could. What could have been an extremely costly miscue was made up for, however, when with the score tied at one in the ninth inning, Sims doubled in the lead run. A few batters later, Fryman helped his cause by singling in two more runs, and then set down the Indians for his eighth win, 4–1.

After salvaging the final game with Cleveland, Detroit had no time to relax. The Tigers immediately headed to Boston for a four-game, first-place showdown with the upstart Red Sox. Beantown was going Sox-crazy, with their fans believing it was 1967 all over again.[19] The night before their team had just completed a doubleheader sweep of the vaunted Orioles, and in one remarkable evening had not only killed off the three-time defending division champions, probably for good, but had also solidified itself as the team with the upper hand in the division race. A seven-run fourth inning, off Oriole ace Jim Palmer nonetheless, had keyed the 9–2 Boston victory in the first game. Then their wildly popular new pitching sensation, Luis Tiant, shut out Baltimore, 4–0, in the nightcap, with the chant of "We're number one!" reverberating around Fenway Park, courtesy of 28,777 screaming followers.

American League East Standings through September 20, 1972

	W	*L*	*Pct.*	*GB*
Boston Red Sox	78	64	.549	—
Detroit Tigers	78	66	.542	1
Baltimore Orioles	77	68	.531	2½
New York Yankees	75	68	.524	3½

Boston's doubleheader win against Baltimore did more damage to the Orioles' chances than the 2½-game deficit in the standings indicated. In doing so the Red Sox had defeated Baltimore's two top pitchers in Palmer and Cuellar, leaving Earl Weaver with a dwindling number of opportunities to use his aces over the remaining two weeks. More importantly, Boston had a four-game edge in the loss column over Baltimore, with the Orioles having only nine games remaining on their schedule. In fact, Boston now enjoyed a two-game edge in the loss column over its nearest rival, Detroit, an important measurement at a point in the season where the Red Sox's competition was being forced to win every game in an effort to gain ground.

The Red Sox's improbable journey to that position had been an amazing story in its own right. They started the season slowly and were eight games under .500 at one point in late June. Between an unpopular strike and the slow start, Boston fans had found reasons to boo the team unmercifully. Attendance at Fenway had dropped off sharply. The team had losing records for each of the first three months of the season, before finding themselves in late June. The turnaround was abrupt, although it took time for most neutral observers to take the team seriously. They won nineteen out of twenty-five games in a stretch from late June to mid–July to get back in position to contend. A 17–12 record in the month of August got them even closer, and then a stunning 14–3 hot streak from the last week in August into mid–September catapulted them into the top spot in the division.

The faces behind the turnaround were a combination of old and new, but each seemed to have mirrored the overall pattern of the ball club that season with a slow start and fast finish. Carl Yastrzemski, the Messiah from 1967 and owner of the $165,000 annual salary, probably best exemplified with his performance the team's turnaround. He started slowly, injured a knee in early May, and then missed a month of action. He didn't get his batting average above .200 until June 16, and didn't connect for his first homer until July 22. "He'd lost his power" was whispered around the league about a player who had been among the most feared in baseball for several years. Yastrzemski started heating up, though, in parallel to the Red Sox's surge in the standings. He moved from left field to first base in mid–August, and then went on a tear, hitting home runs and knocking in runners by the handful. As September began, his play resembled that of the Yaz from five years earlier, the one who had carried a team to a pennant and restored a franchise with superhero actions each game. Heading into the series with Detroit, he had already blasted eight home runs and driven in 24 runs in September.

The biggest addition to the everyday lineup had come with the emergence of a rookie catcher by the name of Carlton "Pudge" Fisk. Fisk was a rookie in years of service only, having been up with Boston for brief appearances in two previous seasons. He had brashness and leadership skills that were uncommon for a first-year player. On the field he was a talented defensive catcher with an extremely strong and accurate throwing arm. But at the plate is where he had separated himself from the incumbents of the previous season, Bob Montgomery and John Stephenson. He was a tall and rangy right-handed hitter, capable of pulling balls off and over the Green Monster in left field. He had kept an average at or above .300 for most of the season (.302 entering the series with Detroit), and since July 1 had banged fifteen home runs, giving him a season total of 22.

Elsewhere, the regular lineup was a curious mix of proven veterans and fuzzy-cheeked rookies. The veteran Rico Petrocelli had shaken off injuries and a hitting slump to hit seven homers and amass 33 RBIs over the previous two months, all while playing a solid third base. Luis Aparicio had missed 44 games with a broken finger but was now back as the everyday shortstop, providing the solid presence a 17-year veteran and nine-time Gold Glove winner brings to the lineup. Right fielder Reggie Smith, one of the kids from the '67 Impossible Dream pennant winners in Boston, was now established as one of the true multi-talented players in the American League, capable of winning a game with his bat, glove, arm, or legs. Smith had homered six times already in September, and had come up with numerous clutch hits during the stretch drive. Tommy Harper had come over in an off-season trade with Milwaukee and provided manager Eddie Kasko with one of the premier leadoff men in baseball, adding speed to a lineup that historically had always been slow.

It was an influx of young players, though, that had given Boston much of its personality that season. Besides Fisk, a number of players were emerging in roles, fresh up from recalls from the Louisville Triple-A affiliate. Ben Oglivie was a 23-year-old Panama-born outfielder who was very raw, but held enormous promise, especially as a left-handed hitter. The future Tiger was breaking in as a platoon player in left field, seeing more time after Yastrzemski's move to first base. The Red Sox acquired veteran right-handed slugger Andy Kosko in August from the California Angels to share left field with Oglivie, but an injury had given that job to another new recall from Louisville, Dwight Evans. Evans was a 20-year-old "can't miss" prospect who had a tremendous throwing arm that would be showcased in the A.L. for nearly two decades. Other players, like the sweet-swinging Cecil Cooper and the brilliant defensive outfielder Rick Miller, were playing lesser roles but had contributed nonetheless.

While Boston's batting lineup was on its way to leading the American League in runs scored and finishing second to Kansas City in overall team batting average, it was the pitching that had always been in question. The team traded its one-time ace Jim Lonborg as part of a blockbuster deal with the Brewers the previous winter. Although pitching well for Milwaukee, Lonborg had never rebounded to the dominant form he had displayed during his brilliant 1967 Cy Young Award–winning season after injuring a knee during the early winter of 1968. Instead, the Red Sox were rebuilding their starting rotation around veterans Marty Pattin, Sonny Siebert, and Ray Culp. Pattin, like the rest of the Sox, had gotten off to a bad start, going 2–8 in his first ten decisions. Since that time, however, he had gone 15–5 and lowered his ERA from 5.06 to a much more respectable 3.24. The 35-year-old Siebert was turning in one of his typically steady seasons, one in which he would end up at 12–12 with a 3.80 ERA. Culp was in his next-to-last season in the big leagues, and was struggling through a 5–8 campaign with an ERA well over 4.00. A pair of rookies, however, were making their marks and picking up much of the slack for Kasko. Left-hander John Curtis and right-hander Lynn McGlothen had combined to start 43 games while going a respectable 19–15 on the season. Overall, Boston's team ERA of 3.54 was the second-highest in the A.L., just barely ahead of the 100-loss Texas Rangers, and nearly half a run more than Detroit's team ERA and over a run worse than league-leading Baltimore. What they lacked through much of the season was a staff ace.

Luis Tiant came off the scrap heap to barely make the Red Sox roster out of spring training in 1972. At midseason he was a long reliever and spot starter, but ended up being the hottest pitcher in the American League over the season's second half, nearly leading Boston to the East Division title. Tiant ended up with a 15–6 record and league-leading 1.91 ERA (National Baseball Hall of Fame Library, Cooperstown, New York).

That player, the savior of the staff, was quickly becoming one of 1972's biggest stories. Luis "Louie" Tiant was enjoying a streak that saw him carving up A.L. hitters in a manner reminiscent of streaks put forth in recent seasons by the likes of Bob Gibson, Don Drysdale, and Denny McLain. Tiant's story again paralleled that of Boston's. He had been a dominant pitcher in the mid to late '60s with the Cleveland Indians, where he put together a 21–9 record in 1968 with a 1.60 ERA, remarkable numbers that were completely overshadowed by the incredible records put forth by McLain and Gibson that season. He lost twenty games pitching on a terrible Indians team that next season, and then suffered through a couple of injury-plagued years before ending up with Minnesota, who then released him during spring training in 1971. Tiant signed on with Atlanta but spent most of the season with the Braves' AAA team in Richmond before being released yet again. With his career prospects withering and few options available, Tiant was picked up by Boston, and after spending time at Louisville, was promoted to the major leagues and went 1–7 with a 4.85 ERA in '71.[20]

Coming off that forgettable season, Tiant's prospects of being part of the 1972 Boston roster were questionable at best. Coming out of spring training, however, he made the pitching-starved Red Sox team as a long reliever and spot starter, the lowest man on the staff. Heading into July he had made 19 appearances, with only three coming in a starting role. His 2–2 win-loss record at that point gave no indication of the type of run he was about to have.

On July 3 he made another of his rare starts and shut down Minnesota with only two runs in a complete-game victory. That performance gained him favor with Kasko, and Tiant continued to do well in a series of irregular starts throughout the rest of the month. By August he was a regular in the rotation, and continued on a streak that found him nearly unhittable. Over a 115-inning stretch, beginning in early July and running up to the Detroit series, he recorded a 1.56 ERA. During that period he shut out six opponents within an eight-game span, including the whitewashing of the Orioles the night before.[21]

The Cuban-born Tiant was one of the most colorful players in the league. He served up a carte du jour of pitches that included tailing fastballs, sliders, curves, screwballs, and an assortment of off-speed pitches, similar to that of National League star Juan Marichal. All were delivered from varying arm angles and from the most unique wind-up in the game. Tiant brought his hands above his head as he started his motion before pivoting on his back leg, corkscrewing around with his back completely exposed to the hitter, while his head fell back until his eyes faced third base, second base, the sky, and points in between. He then uncoiled towards the batter, unleashing pitches from different delivery points, making the ball difficult to pick up for hitters. "El Tiante," as he was affectionately called, could oftentimes be found savoring victories with a fat cigar clenched between his teeth. He also had a physical appearance that suggested he was much older than the 31 years of age he was listed at in the program. Whatever his age, he provided his manager with an almost automatic win every four days through the heated weeks of August and September, as Tiant's 11–3 record heading into the Detroit series attested to.

On Thursday, September 21, the two teams met for the first of seven games they had remaining on the schedule between each other. With Boston holding a slim one-game lead on Detroit (although the Red Sox still held that two-game advantage in the all-important loss column), the divisional race looked like it would be decided in these head-to-head matchups. For the first time, talk about the imbalance in the number of games that would be played by the different teams was coming into focus. Boston was only scheduled to play 155 games, while Detroit was slated for 156. Could the awkward settlement to the two-week strike back in April play a role in determining a pennant?

For the first game in Boston, manager Eddie Kasko had painted himself into a corner with his choice of a starting pitcher. He had pitched his two hottest pitchers, Tiant and Pattin, in the doubleheader sweep of the Orioles the night before, and the steady veteran, Sonny Siebert, was out with an ankle injury. With options limited, Kasko gave the ball to rookie right-hander Mike Garman, a recent call-up from Louisville who would be making his first start of the year for the parent club. The decision proved to be disastrous from Boston's viewpoint.

McAuliffe walked to start the game for Detroit, and then Freehan, placed in an uncustomary second position in Martin's batting order, singled behind him. After Gates Brown hit into a force out at second base, Horton singled in one run followed by Cash, who doubled in another. Kasko quickly replaced his shell-shocked starter by bringing in another rookie, lefty John Curtis. Curtis proceeded to walk Stanley, which loaded the bases, before Brinkman singled to bring in Horton. Cash also tried to score from second on the play but was thrown out at the plate by Dwight Evans. When Brinkman broke for second base on the throw to the plate, Carlton Fisk threw the ball into center field for an error, and Stanley loped in to score. The four runs held up until the third inning, when Cash doubled in another run, and then with the bases loaded, Coleman singled in three runs, with Brinkman scoring all the way from first base. The Tigers had blown the game open, 8–1, within the first three innings. By the time it was over, Detroit had won the all-important first game of the four-game series by a 10–4 margin. They ended up with fourteen hits off four Red Sox pitchers, and moved into a virtual tie with Boston (although they still trailed by a tiny margin in winning percentage, .5455 to .5448).

After the game, the wolves were howling over Kasko's decision to start the rookie Garman in such a crucial game. For Kasko, who was already rumored to be on the hot seat despite his team's second-half rush, the decision came largely by default. "What else could I do? You've got to go with right-handers in this ballpark, and I didn't have anyone else. The kid wasn't nervous. He just couldn't control his fastball. He couldn't get it down."[22]

Elsewhere that night, New York continued their late-season fade by losing again to Milwaukee, 6–4. The Yankees remained 3½ games out, just barely in contention with three teams ahead of them and less than two weeks left to play. Baltimore was rained out in their game and moved back within two games of the lead. In the National League, the Pittsburgh Pirates became the first club in the majors to clinch a playoff spot by downing the New York Mets, 6–2. A five-run third inning ended any suspense in the game and made official what had become a foregone conclusion at least two months earlier; the Pirates would win the N.L. East.

On Friday, the Red Sox faithful showed up at Fenway Park in droves, as the largest crowd of the season — 34,632 — entered the gates to see who would break the virtual tie. Martin, facing a similar situation as Kasko did the night before, started journeyman Chris Zachary in the second game of the series. Boston scratched out single runs in each of the first three innings off Zachary. Yastrzemski scored Harper on a sacrifice fly in the first inning; the pitcher, McGlothen, did the same in the second, scoring Fisk; and Yaz homered in the third, giving the Red Sox the early 3–0 lead. It stayed that way until the sixth inning when with Cash on base, Sims homered for Detroit to cut the Boston lead to one run. Stanley and Rodriguez singled later in that same inning before Brinkman walked to load the bases with one out. Kasko brought in Bob Veale, the veteran left-handed reliever, to pitch, and he struck out Howard, who had been inserted as a pinch-hitter for the pitcher. Tony Taylor, also in a pinch-hitting role, then lined a shot down the third base line that was speared by a diving Rico Petrocelli behind the bag for the final putout of the inning.

In the eighth inning, the Tigers loaded the bases again, this time with nobody out. Brinkman was at bat when he hit a shot to third base that Petrocelli fielded, touched the bag in front of him, and then fired home for the putout by Fisk on Sims, for an extremely rare 5–2 double play. With two outs and the tying run on second base, Northrup hit a looping drive into shallow center field that looked like a sure base hit. Rick Miller, a former standout at Michigan State University and known throughout his major league career as a defensive whiz, raced in and made a sliding catch to end the inning and preserve the lead for Boston. Despite the efforts of a makeshift Detroit pitching lineup that night, where Zachary, Seelbach, and rookie Lerrin LaGrow set down the last seventeen Red Sox hitters in the game, the Tigers could get no closer and dropped a frustrating 3–2 decision.

"I'm convinced we can win by the way we played tonight," Martin said after the game in a surprisingly upbeat demeanor for such a heart-wrenching loss. "We're swinging our bats again. The guys are aggressive up there. We had them in trouble several times and they needed three sensational plays to beat us. We did all the heavy pounding out there. You take Rico Petrocelli's two plays and the catch by the kid in center field and that is the equivalent of seven runs."[23]

Despite the brave face being displayed by Detroit in the post-game clubhouse, the Red Sox's players knew they had scored a big victory that they desperately needed with the pressure mounting daily.

"This is a lot tougher on me than 1967," said Yastrzemski about being "the man" for Boston in another pennant race heading to the final days of the season. "Hell, I was in a groove in '67. I'd go up there and 'bang,' the ball would be out of there. Now it's a struggle. Every day it's a struggle. Every time up. Every pitch. It's a tough thing to live with."[24]

Another vet from the 1967 pennant winners, Petrocelli, talked about the game-changing plays he made at third base that night. "I thought about going to second and try for a triple play, but I thought I'd better get the man at home," he said about Brinkman's ball with the bases loaded and nobody out in the eighth inning. "I didn't know if I could have gotten three on the play." Regarding the ball that was scorched down the line by Taylor two innings earlier, he said, "All I know is that when the ball was hit, I put my glove down and it stuck in it."[25]

Despite the great plays by Petrocelli in the sixth and eighth innings, it still took the sliding catch by Miller to preserve the victory. "I knew Northrup was jammed on the pitch and didn't hit it good," he said. "Luckily, it hung up there and I was able to get it."[26]

With the loss, Detroit was one game back again but did not lose any substantial ground to their competitors in the A.L. East, where New York lost again to Gaylord Perry (22nd win), 4–1, and Baltimore was idle. Back in Motown, the Tigers were given clearance by the commissioner's office to take applications for World Series tickets. Box seats would sell for the handsome price of $15, while reserved seats were put on sale for $10.[27]

After overcoming the sting of the close loss the night before, the Tigers jumped all over the Red Sox on Saturday afternoon. Sonny Siebert was able to take the mound on his gimpy ankle, but was betrayed in the first inning by bad luck and bad defensive play. McAuliffe led off the game by slicing a ball into left field, where Evans, playing his first day game in Fenway Park, lost the ball in the sun before it dropped for a double. Kaline then hit a ball into center field that was misplayed by Harper for a two-base error as McAuliffe came in to score. Siebert walked both Gates Brown and Cash to load the bases before Sims singled in one run and Northrup singled in another. Further damage was avoided when Reggie Smith threw out Cash at the plate while trying to score from second base on Northrup's hit. After Rodriguez walked, Kasko pulled his starting pitcher after one-third of an inning for the second time of the series and brought in Bill Lee. Lee avoided a potential huge frame for Detroit when he induced Brinkman to hit into an inning-ending double play.

The 3–0 lead that Mickey Lolich was handed proved to be the tonic that the struggling pitching ace needed. He cruised to his first win in seventeen days (21–13), allowing just six hits and one run, while striking out six Boston hitters. Kaline and Rodriguez provided late insurance runs with drives over the Green Monster in left field, as Detroit routed Boston, 7–1, to move back into a first-place tie.

"This was the big one," said Martin, barely able to contain the satisfaction that came with guaranteeing at least a split in the road series. "Real big. After the way we lost Friday night, after battling all the way, to come back with a win like this. Now if we win Sunday it'll be a plus on our side."[28]

The first three games of the series had played out according to form, based largely on the pitching matchups for each game. Detroit's number-two starter, Coleman, was able to navigate a victory in the series opener when facing a rookie making his first start. Likewise, Boston had gotten the jump when Martin had been forced to start the little-used Zachary against the Red Sox in the second game. The significance of a struggling Lolich being able to hold serve as the ace of the Tiger staff was crucial, especially with the specter of facing Tiant looming in the series finale.

"It's a whole new game when you've got some runs," Lolich said. "I think I pitched a pretty good ballgame, particularly for this park. For a left-hander to win like this here in Fenway Park, it's pretty tough."[29]

Kaline, whose bat was heating up at an opportune time for the Tigers, commented about Boston's first-inning misplays that had essentially decided the game and the impact they would have on the outcome of the race. "It's going to be pitching and defense. Everyone is tight now and you just can't afford to give up any runs. They're hard enough to get and you can't be giving them away."[30]

With the Red Sox's lead down to the slimmest of margins, .001 (.545–.544), over Detroit, it was apparent the race for the divisional crown was now a two-team affair. Baltimore lost to Milwaukee that day, 2–1, as Lonborg shut down the Orioles. Baltimore remained 2½ games behind the co-leaders, but with only eight games to play. New York won its game with Cleveland, but remained 3½ behind with nine contests left to play. With two and three teams ahead of Baltimore and New York, respectively, and each being at least three games back in the loss column, anything short of winning out the remainder of their schedule (an unlikely prospect for two teams that weren't even ten games over .500) made a division title nearly impossible.

By taking two of the first three games of the series, Detroit was guaranteed to leave Boston no further than one game back nor more than two games behind in the loss column. Detroit had won more total games to date than the Red Sox (80 to 79), but would play one fewer game over the final week and a half of the regular season. It was the loss column, where Boston had dropped one fewer game (66 to 67), that Martin was looking to stay as close as possible since his Tigers would have their opportunity to inflict losses against the Bosox in the season's final series in Detroit.

"This was a big game for us because we would have been three down in the loss column if we'd lost," he said after the Saturday win. Looking ahead to the series finale on Sunday, he said, "We'll be all even with Boston in the loss column and we'll have two more wins. But if we lose, we're still not in bad shape at all."[31]

On Sunday afternoon, the Tigers knew they were facing a mighty task while trying to beat Tiant and take command of the division. As the gate in the Boston bullpen opened just before the game, 34,182 fans rose to their feet and roared as Tiant sauntered to the mound. Detroit countered with a hot pitcher of its own in Fryman, who was 8–2 since joining the team at the beginning of August. The Tigers managed to score a run in the first inning on a Cash sacrifice fly that plated McAuliffe, but the game soon fell apart after that. Fryman walked leadoff man Tommy Harper and then gave up a double to Luis Aparicio. Yastrzemski, who was as hot as anyone in baseball, singled both runners in, and then scored ahead of Reggie Smith, who homered on a "slider that didn't drop," according to Fryman. In the fifth inning, Petrocelli removed all doubt by blasting a three-run homer over the wall in left, and the Red Sox rolled to a 7–2 win. For Tiant, his tenth win since August 1, gave Boston a split in the series to remain one-game ahead in the standings, the same position they had been in three days earlier. The Red Sox now only had to maintain that lead for another week and a half. "I'll have my best men ready for the big games now and that should help," said Eddie Kasko, who wasn't about to get short-changed again with his pitching rotation over the final stretch.[32]

American League East Standings through September 24, 1972

	W	*L*	*Pct.*	*GB*
Boston Red Sox	80	66	.548	—
Detroit Tigers	80	68	.541	1
Baltimore Orioles	78	69	.531	2½
New York Yankees	78	70	.527	3

"Jimmy the Greek" made Boston 2-to-5 favorites to hang on and win the division as the teams took a pause in the high-pressure stakes. Monday, September 25, was an off day for the entire division. Boston would open a two-game home series with Milwaukee on Tuesday, followed by a single make-up game with Kansas City at home before closing the season with three games in

Baltimore and three in Detroit. The Tigers had completed their road schedule for the season and now were off until Wednesday, when New York would come to Tiger Stadium for a two-game set. The Brewers would follow for three games over the weekend before Boston came to town for the season-ending series.

Although closing out the season with games at Tiger Stadium was certainly viewed as a favorable situation, Martin was not convinced that the eight-game homestand to end the campaign was the big advantage it might appear to be. "Last season we were sensational at home. This year we haven't been so hot."[33] Detroit's 38–32 record at home was only marginally better than the 42–36 record the Tigers had compiled on the road. The bigger discrepancy came with Boston, which would be ending its season with a six-game road trip, where the team had been 30–41 on the season. That record was far inferior to Boston's home record. The Red Sox had feasted on opponents in Fenway Park, where they were a sizzling 50–25 (.667).

As play resumed on Tuesday with the rest of the contenders back in action, Detroit sat idle as part of an extremely rare set of back-to-back scheduled days off. "I'd have welcomed one day off," said Martin, complaining about the quirky schedule. "But I would have liked to see the two days staggered — say, one this Monday and one next Monday. That way I could make better use of my pitchers. A club with four starters wouldn't have to worry. But it's a little different with us. I can't understand how they could have ever scheduled it that way."[34]

Despite the unwanted extra rest, Detroit welcomed the results from elsewhere, as the bottom dwellers in the division rose up to help the Tigers' cause. Milwaukee came back from a 4–0 deficit to defeat the Red Sox, 6–4. After Yastrzemski and starting pitcher Marty Pattin connected for two-run homers in the early innings for Boston, the Brewers mounted an unexpected charge, aided by a pair of costly Boston errors, and culminating with former Red Sox first baseman George Scott blasting a two-run homer that gave Milwaukee the lead. In Baltimore, the Indians' Ray Fosse followed Chris Chambliss' two-run homer with a home run of his own, leading Cleveland to a 3–2 victory over the Orioles. The defeat was the sixth for Baltimore in eight meetings with Cleveland since the All-Star break; their inability to handle the Indians was proving to be their undoing.

American League East Standings through September 26, 1972

	W	*L*	*Pct.*	*GB*	*Games Remaining*
Boston Red Sox	80	67	.544	—	8
Detroit Tigers	80	68	.541	½	8

	W	*L*	*Pct.*	*GB*	*Games Remaining*
Baltimore Orioles	78	70	.527	2½	6
New York Yankees	78	70	.527	2½	7

With series remaining against contending rivals New York and Boston sandwiched around a three-game series with last-place Milwaukee, Martin had his pitching set up perfectly. Lolich and Coleman would each work in the two-game set with the Yankees, and then be ready three days later for what was being anticipated as a title-deciding, season-ending series with the Red Sox. The careful planning didn't appear to matter when New York's Johnny Callison crashed a three-run first inning home run in the first game off Coleman. It was quickly apparent that the Tiger right-hander wasn't going to have one of his better games, as he allowed eight of the twelve batters he faced to reach base. Coleman was pulled in the second inning in favor of Scherman, who didn't fare much better. Between the two of them, they allowed five runs in 2⅔ innings of work. Martin used four pitchers before the third inning was completed and seven overall, as Tiger pitchers combined to give up 10 hits and 12 walks. Yet despite the heavy traffic on the bases, 17 Yankee runners were stranded while Tiger pitchers, despite working in and out of trouble all evening, doggedly kept their team within striking distance. Despite the determined effort, however, the Tigers trailed by four runs, 5–1, heading into the bottom of the eighth inning against Yankee starting pitcher Steve Kline.

With the days drawing short and Boston leading on the scoreboard in Milwaukee, Detroit could ill afford to drop the opening game of the series. Hopes were raised only slightly for the 21,850 in attendance when Horton singled to get things started in the home half of the eighth and then came around to score from second on a Kaline single. Sims, however, also followed with a single, and then Howard, in a pinch-hitting role, singled in Kaline. Ike Brown walked to load the bases before Stanley drove in Detroit's third run of the inning with a sacrifice fly. With the Tigers back within one run and runners on first and second, Yankee manager Ralph Houk brought in reliever Sparky Lyle, who proceeded to strike out Rodriguez to end the inning. Lyle had been almost un-hittable against Detroit throughout the season. He pitched seven times against them, winning once and saving five other games, while never allowing a run. He was largely responsible for New York's five-game winning streak against the Tigers, and on a larger scale, had been joined by superb center fielder Bobby Murcer as the catalyst for his team's revival over the season's second half.

Trailing 5–4 as the Tigers came to bat in the bottom of the ninth inning, the thought of Detroit scoring a run off Lyle was almost unthinkable.

Brinkman, however, started the inning with a single. Horton, who had entered the game as part of a double-switch earlier and was hitting ninth in the batting order, also singled to put runners on first and second base. Taylor then batted for McAuliffe and dropped a perfect bunt down the third base line that turned into the inning's third straight single. With barely more than half of the original mid-week crowd still in their seats, screaming wildly, Kaline delivered the tying run with a sacrifice fly to Murcer. That brought up Sims, who because of the injury to Freehan had taken over the full-time catching duties. He was forced into an unenviable lefty versus lefty situation, against a premier pitcher in Lyle and his nasty slider. But Sims laced a ball into the left-center field gap that dropped for a single, and the winning run in the form of pinch-runner Marvin Lane came around to score as Detroit capped an improbable 6–5 comeback victory.

As the Tiger players stormed onto the field to celebrate Sims' hit and the stirring win, Murcer picked the ball up off the turf in deep left-center field and flung it into the stands, a gesture that largely symbolized New York's fallen hopes. Now 3½ games behind the division leader with only six games remaining on their schedule, the Yankees were all but eliminated from the race.

For Detroit the win characterized a team still believing it could win a pennant. Void of the type of superstars who could carry a team on its back, Billy Martin's squad was finding ways to scratch out victories down the stretch. "Another laugher," he said mockingly afterwards about a game in which he used six pinch-hitters, three pinch-runners, and seven pitchers in a desperate attempt to navigate to a victory. "We're never dead. They should know that," he said in a jab towards the fickle fans that left the game early.[35]

Even with the win, Martin's thoughts never ventured far from the task of catching the front-running Red Sox. He had already found a bright spot in the quick exit forced upon his number two starter that evening against New York. "I can change my rotation now. I'll come back with Joe on Saturday, and all I need is a starter on Sunday."[36]

Boston continued to hold its one-half game lead, as the Red Sox finished off Milwaukee, 7–5. Luis Aparicio spearheaded the Sox's attack with three hits, including a two-run triple. With only seven games remaining, both Boston and Detroit were now locked in a struggle to the finish, with each team waiting for the other to blink. "I would like to pick up a game before we go into Detroit," said Red Sox manager Eddie Kasko. "Then we would be a game and a half in front, and they'd have to sweep the three-game series."[37]

At Memorial Stadium in Baltimore that same night, the death watch was in full alert as the Orioles lost for the fifth time in six games, this time in a 3–0 shutout loss to Gaylord Perry and the Indians. Chris Chambliss belted a two-run triple and scored the third run to provide the offense for Cleveland. The Indians all but sealed the fate of the three-time defending American League champions, who were now three and a half games back with five games remaining.

	W	*L*	*Pct.*	*GB*	*Games Remaining*
Boston Red Sox	81	67	.547	—	7
Detroit Tigers	81	68	.544	½	7
Baltimore Orioles	78	71	.523	3½	5
New York Yankees	78	71	.523	3½	6

On September 28 the Tigers concluded their brief two-game series with the Yankees. The game looked in control throughout, as Detroit scratched out a first-inning run on a Horton sacrifice fly, and Lolich shut down New York through the first seven frames. In the eighth, however, with Lolich only five outs away from a desperately needed victory, the Yankees' fine hitting catcher, Thurman Munson, blasted a 400-foot drive for a game-tying home run. Detroit was poised to take the lead again in the bottom of the inning when with runners on first and third and only one out, Lolich missed the pitch on a squeeze play and Northrup was easily tagged out while running in from third base. Instead, New York grabbed the lead when veteran relief pitcher Lindy McDaniel stunned everyone in the ballpark by connecting off Lolich for only the second round-tripper in his 18-year career. Detroit was able to tie the game in the bottom of the ninth when Kaline scored from third after an errant throw from the outfield missed its mark at second base.

With the score tied at 2–2, the game dragged on into extra innings. Lolich continued on the mound for Martin throughout the 3½-hour game until Roy White lofted a drive that clanked off the facing of the upper deck in left field in the top of the twelfth inning. Detroit threatened in the bottom of the inning, but Paul Jata struck out with two runners on base, including Northrup at third, to end the game.

In the Yankee clubhouse after the game, New York players made no secret of their dislike for the Tiger manager and his season-long belittling of their team. "Let's hear it for Billy Martin," some were overheard yelling. "Hey Billy, how'd you like that one?"[38]

"I'm happy to hurt them the way they hurt us," Roy White said in more diplomatic terms about his game-winning homer. "That's what it is all about. If you can't win it yourself, you like to keep others from doing it."[39]

"Our toes are still wiggling," Yankee manager Ralph Houk said of his team's extremely slim, but still mathematically alive, chances in the division race. "This has been a heckuva race. It's the best thing that's happened to our league in years."[40]

In the more-sedate Detroit dressing room, Martin shrugged off the antics by the New York players and instead focused on the missed opportunities of his own team, including those of his pitching ace, losing hurler Mickey Lolich.

"Mickey just missed the ball," he said about the failed bunt attempt in the bottom of the eighth inning that could have scored the potential winning run. "It was a suicide, and on a suicide the runner breaks as soon as the ball is thrown, not after the batter has made contact with the ball. Mickey just bunted through the ball and when you do that, you make everything look like hell. And Mickey's let pitchers hit home runs off him in two of the last three games he's pitched."[41]

The loss to the Yankees was a crushing blow. Detroit now found itself 1½ games behind the front-runners after Boston's 3–1 win over Kansas City in the Red Sox home finale. Rookie starter John Curtis had ground out the complete-game victory in an effort that left his team with "one less game to go," as described afterwards by manager Eddie Kasko. Heading into the final two series of the season, Boston had a margin of error that could be huge with the three season-ending games in Detroit looming. For the Tigers, any margin of error that may have previously existed was gone. The reality was, they would likely need to win out to have any chance of fulfilling their season-long dream of winning the East Division and advancing to post-season play. A loss of any kind would most likely end their playoff hopes. For a Detroit team that had just spent its top two pitchers and had never won more than five straight games all season, the prospect of winning six straight games to end the season was a daunting task indeed.

American League East Standings through September 26, 1972

	W	*L*	*Pct.*	*GB*	*Games Remaining*
Boston Red Sox	82	67	.550	—	6
Detroit Tigers	81	69	.540	1½	6
New York Yankees	79	71	.527	3½	5
Baltimore Orioles	78	71	.523	4	5

IX

Showdown in Motown

The opposition for Detroit heading into the last weekend of the regular season was the last-place Milwaukee Brewers. When looking at the standings, the matchup appeared favorable for the Tigers. Milwaukee's record was the fourth worst in either league, and sitting 20½ games out of first place, the Brewers were just playing out the string. However, the team had played the Tigers tough all season, and despite being swept in the three-game series back in Milwaukee just two weeks earlier, the Brewers still held an 8–7 games edge in the season series with Detroit.

For the Tigers, the goal was to survive through the weekend and give themselves a shot in the final series with Boston. Sitting 1½ games back of the front-running Red Sox, Detroit needed to stay within striking distance and hope to take care of Boston themselves once they got them into Tiger Stadium. The Baltimore Orioles, who were set to host the Red Sox over the weekend, had collapsed down the stretch and couldn't be counted on to help Detroit close the margin. The realistic scenario was the Tigers needed to take care of Milwaukee and then sweep Boston in order to win the A.L. East crown.

In the Friday night game, the Tigers faced one of their season-long nemesis in Brewers starting pitcher Jim Lonborg. The tall right-hander had already beaten them three times thus far, and had pitched well each time. The fact that Lonborg had been pushed back a day in the rotation and would now be facing Detroit instead of Boston the previous day had Billy Martin fuming before the game even started.

"Maybe Crandall knows something about pitching left-handers in Boston," Martin said of Milwaukee manager Del Crandall's unconventional decision to pitch lefty Ken Brett in Fenway Park the previous day instead of sending the right-handed Lonborg on his regular day in the rotation. "I talked to him about it at home plate and he said Brett's had good luck against them. I didn't know left-handers had good luck in Fenway Park."[1]

As it turned out, the move didn't matter to Tiger hitters, who battered

Lonborg like they hadn't all season. After Milwaukee scratched out a run in the first inning, Detroit came back with three in the bottom of the frame. Willie Horton's two-run triple was followed by the first of Jim Northrup's four hits on the evening to drive in the third run. The next inning, Al Kaline and Duke Sims hit back-to-back doubles for another run, and then the Tigers really exploded in the third inning, scoring seven runs while sending eleven batters to the plate. The big blow was Northrup's bases-clearing double that was part of a five-RBI night for the silver-haired center fielder. Detroit pounded out sixteen hits in a 12–5 rout of the Brewers. The runs allowed by Lonborg were the first he had given up in Tiger Stadium all season, covering three previous starts. "We owed him one," said Northrup afterwards. "He's been rough on us this year."[2]

Despite the win, the Tigers could only hold their ground, as in Baltimore, Carl Yastrzemski connected off Oriole ace Jim Palmer in the tenth inning with a high drive that pushed left fielder Don Buford back to the fence in Memorial Stadium. Buford leaped for the ball, but it glanced off his glove and into the Baltimore bullpen, giving Yastrzemski a two-run homer and the winning margin in Boston's 4–2 victory. The home run was Yaz's seventh in the month of September, and officially eliminated the Orioles from the divisional title race. Holding a 1½-game lead with only five games remaining to be played while also slaying the defending champions made Boston the commanding leader to play Oakland the following weekend in the American League Championship Series.

"I wouldn't say we're in the driver's seat," said Red Sox manager Eddie Kasko while downplaying his team's envious position. "But it's nice to get one team out of the race."[3]

News of the game's outcome didn't sit well with Martin, who couldn't resist the chance to return the barbs that had been directed at him, specifically by the Orioles' ace pitcher. "It's too bad Jim Palmer couldn't beat his buddies. When we were in Boston, he said if the Orioles couldn't win it, he didn't want the Tigers to win it."[4]

	W	*L*	*Pct.*	*GB*	*Games Remaining*
Boston Red Sox	83	67	.553	—	5
Detroit Tigers	82	69	.543	1½	5
New York Yankees	79	71	.527	4	5

As baseball struggled to compete with college football for the nation's attention that last day of September, a pair of newsworthy events took place in the waning days of the regular season. In Arlington, Texas Rangers manager Ted Williams resigned his position just prior to watching his team suffer its fifteenth straight loss, this time a 3–1 decision to the White Sox. For Williams, who would rank as one of the all-time great players of the game but with a less-than-stellar managerial career, the season would mark his last in a major league uniform in any official capacity. Elsewhere, a more current great reached a personal milestone that day. Pittsburgh Pirates right fielder Roberto Clemente whacked a fourth-inning double into the left-center field alley at Three Rivers Stadium, giving him his 3000th career hit, a plateau reached previously by only ten other players at that time.

In Detroit the temperature turned unseasonably cold for a Saturday afternoon game, making the weather seem better suited for football than baseball. NBC's *Game of the Week* crew was on hand to broadcast the contest to a national television audience. With only one division title left undecided, Tiger Stadium was the obvious location for the last regular-season broadcast of the season. A win for the Tigers would guarantee themselves the opportunity to play Boston with at least a chance at the title.

Like Friday night's game, the outcome was decided early. Second baseman Dick McAuliffe led off the Detroit first inning with a single. Kaline doubled him to third and both came home on a Norm Cash single, making the score 2–0. Horton followed with a walk before Northrup continued his hot hitting with an RBI single. Before the inning ended, Ed Brinkman provided the big blow, a three-run homer, to put the exclamation point on a six-run first frame.

By the eighth inning, the game had long been decided, but the Tigers pushed across five more runs to make it a complete runaway. The big blows that inning were a two-out double by Tony Taylor and a Kaline two-run homer. Red-hot Duke Sims had barely greeted Kaline as he crossed the plate before he crashed a homer of his own into the right field pavilion. The 13–4 rout of Milwaukee featured a season high for the team in runs and hits (16), as they pummeled the disheartened Brewers into submission. Kaline led the onslaught with four hits in five trips to the plate, part of a hot streak that raised his average to a team-leading .305. Sims, Taylor, and Northrup all contributed at least two hits each for a Detroit attack that had been relentless the past two games.

"I've waited four and a half months for this," said Martin after the game. "I don't think it's come too soon. I think we're just coming into our own."[5]

Joe Coleman rebounded from the disastrous effort in his last start against New York and went eight strong innings for his 19th win of the season. Chuck Seelbach mopped up the last inning in order to save wear on Coleman, who was now perfectly positioned to start what could be the title-deciding season finale with Boston on Wednesday.

"I'm looking forward to that game, I really am," Coleman said later about the possibility of pitching on the final day with post-season stakes on the line. "I just hope we get in a situation where we have a chance to win it all. I'd love to have that opportunity. I always pitched well against Boston. And every year it seems I have one real good game against them — and I haven't had that one outstanding game yet this year. I think next Wednesday may be the day to do it. I've never played on a pennant-winning team before. That's something I've always dreamed about. If it comes down to that, I'd say the heck with twenty wins. That's no time to worry about personal accomplishments."[6]

As soon as Brinkman's first-inning drive landed in the lower left field deck, giving Detroit the commanding lead, it was only natural that all eyes drifted to the huge center field scoreboard and the progress of Boston's game in Baltimore. Yastrzemski again had gotten the Red Sox off to an early lead with a first-inning RBI single. The game remained tight throughout, but another home run by Yastrzemski contributed to the difference in a hard-fought, 3–1 win over the Orioles, keeping Boston's first-place lead at 1½ games.

"We hope to force the Tigers into the situation where they'd have to win all three," said Eddie Kasko about his team's position one day before the Red Sox would travel to Detroit. "I'd rather not have to win two games in their park."[7]

With one more victory, the Boston manager would get his wish. If they rode into Detroit with their current lead, they would force the hometown Bengals to sweep them in the three-game series in order to take the crown. In a season where no East Division team had been dominant, and his team had been as hot as any over the season's final two and a half months, Kasko had to like his chances of winning the one game necessary to ensure themselves a playoff spot opposite Oakland.

"I doubt very much if we can afford to lose another game," said Kaline about the gravity of his team's predicament.[8]

Although neither team was able to gain ground on the other, they were able to make official what had appeared to be the case for the past ten days or more. The race was down to two teams, Boston and Detroit. New York sat idle in the rain at Yankee Stadium, and despite a postponement of its game with Cleveland, was officially eliminated from the race after the Red Sox's win over Baltimore.

	W	*L*	*Pct.*	*GB*	*Games Remaining*
Boston Red Sox	84	67	.556	—	4
Detroit Tigers	83	69	.546	1½	4

Sunday, October 1, dawned cold and rainy in Detroit. A crowd of only 17,429 turned out for the final Sunday of baseball on a dreary day that begged for sitting in front of the television and watching the home team Lions play in Chicago against the Bears. For Martin the dilemma was the same as it had been for much of the season: Who to pitch on a day needing a fourth starter? With Fryman and Coleman having already pitched in the first two games against Milwaukee, and Lolich due to start on Monday night in the series opener against Boston, his choices were limited. Tom Timmerman had pitched well in a starting role for much of the season's first half but had worn down as the innings accumulated and had fallen out of favor. Bill Slayback and Joe Niekro had started with varying degrees of success but with no consistency, and hadn't been shown much trust as the season wound down. Seelbach and Scherman had started games, but were too valuable to Martin as workhorses out of the bullpen to burn up ahead of the series with the Red Sox.

Instead, Martin turned to the mid-season gamble, the player that some in the organization had been hesitant to allow back onto the team. He gave the ball to John Hiller. Hiller started slowly in his unprecedented return from a heart attack, but had steadily gained trust through a string of solid outings in relief. His 2.39 ERA over 23 appearances had provided a boost to a pitching staff in need of a fresh arm at that point of the season.

The gamble seemed to be paying off for Martin, as Hiller set down the Brewers without allowing a run through the first five innings. Unfortunately, the Tigers hadn't fared any better; after scoring 25 runs in the first two games of the series, they had been shut out thus far. In the bottom of the fifth inning, however, Aurelio Rodriguez connected for a three-run homer that broke the scoreless tie and lifted much of the tension from the Tiger dugout. By the eighth inning, with everyone in the ballpark looking ahead to the showdown series with Boston, McAuliffe and Kaline hit back-to-back home runs to increase the margin and provide even more breathing room. Hiller pitched way beyond Martin's wildest dreams while going the distance in a complete-game five-hitter in Detroit's crucial 5–1 victory. The win by Hiller was the first by a Detroit starter not named Lolich, Coleman, or Fryman in more than six weeks, illustrating the ineffectiveness down the stretch of the myriad of pitchers Martin had tried in the fourth spot in the rotation.

"I go at this game with a little different attitude than I used to," Hiller said after the game about the personal significance of his performance. "I guess in terms of importance to the team, this was the biggest game I ever pitched. But for me the biggest thrill was that first time I pitched after I came back."[9]

"At least there'll be no need to watch the scoreboard tomorrow night," said Martin from the manager's tiny office inside the Tiger clubhouse. "We had to win these three against Milwaukee. We couldn't afford to lose even one."[10]

By sweeping the series against the Brewers, the Tigers guaranteed themselves at least a chance to take the division from the front-running Red Sox if they could pull off the series sweep at home. What they did not anticipate going into that final Sunday of the regular season was that they would get help that would make the job more manageable. In Baltimore, the Orioles' Bobby Grich hit a sixth-inning home run off fellow rookie Lynn McGlothen, and Mike Cuellar made it stand up for his 18th win in a 2–1 victory over the Boston Red Sox.

The magnitude of the Boston loss was enormous. Entering the weekend, the two teams had been separated by a game and a half, meaning that if they each held serve, Boston would only have to win one of the three games in Detroit to win the division title. With Detroit pulling off the sweep of a Milwaukee team that had given the Tigers trouble throughout the season, and the Red Sox blinking in the last game against the Orioles, the Tigers had pulled to within one-half game of Boston. In actuality, the half-game margin was meaningless. Whichever team was able to take at least two of the three games would win the title. Because Detroit had played an extra game (and won it) due to the schedule having been resumed following the players strike at the beginning of the season, a half-game difference existed and made the possibility of a tie impossible. The stage was set for a final head-to-head series in an A.L. East race that was destined from early on to come down to the final games.

"This is the way it should be — between them and us," Northrup said of the upcoming showdown with Boston.[11]

"Everyone knows what's riding on this series," said Boston's manager Eddie Kasko after the Sunday game in Baltimore. "They've known it for quite some time now."[12]

	W	*L*	*Pct.*	*GB*	*Games Remaining*
Boston Red Sox	84	68	.553	—	3
Detroit Tigers	84	69	.549	½	3

The city of Detroit was buzzing with baseball fever on Monday, October 2. Long lines snaked out all day from the box office windows at Tiger Stadium, with fans eager to gobble up tickets to the season-ending showdown series. A crowd of 51,518 showed up for the first game, an attendance figure that nearly equaled that of the entire three-day turnout for the just-concluded series with Milwaukee. Lolich would start on the mound for Martin in the all-important first game of the series. A win would propel the Tigers ahead of Boston and leave them needing only one more victory to clinch the division title. A Boston win would leave Detroit in the unenviable position of having to win the final two games of the season. Lolich's pitching counterpart would be rookie left-hander John Curtis, who came into the contest with an 11–7 mark for the season.

In the Red Sox's first inning, Luis Aparicio singled with one out, and then Lolich, pitching carefully to the hot-hitting Carl Yastrzemski, ended up walking him to put two men on base. The Tigers' big left-hander worked out of the jam, however, by striking out in succession right fielder Reggie Smith and third baseman Rico Petrocelli, two other hot bats down the stretch for the Bosox.

In the bottom half of the inning, the Tigers prepared to face the rookie Curtis. Martin had loaded his lineup with his right-handed bats, meaning Tony Taylor, Frank Howard, Willie Horton, and Mickey Stanley found their names on the lineup card, joining Kaline, Rodriguez, and Brinkman. Catcher Duke Sims, still filling in for the injured Bill Freehan, was the only left-handed hitter in the batting order. After Taylor grounded out to the mound to lead things off, Kaline, who Curtis later described as having "the most determined look he'd ever seen," pounded a drive into the left field seats for his third home run in three days, giving Detroit the early 1–0 lead.[13] In the second inning after Boston went down in order, Stanley managed to work his way to second base following a single, but was stranded there when Brinkman popped out to shortstop.

In the Boston third, Curtis struck out to start the inning, but then leadoff man Tommy Harper singled and was sent to third on a single by Aparicio. Yastrzemski then came to the plate and drove a ball over the head of Stanley in center field. The blast scooted past Stanley and rolled into deep center field. Harper scored easily, and Aparicio was being waved around third as well by third base coach Eddie Popovich. However, as Aparicio rounded third, he slipped on the bag and fell down in the grass down the third base line. With the throw from the outfield coming in, Aparicio scrambled back to third base, only to be met by Yastrzemski, who was cruising in with what had looked only seconds earlier like a stand-up triple. When Sims fired the ball from the plate down to Rodriguez at third base, Yastrzemski was tagged for the second out, as he and Aparicio were occupying the same base. When Reggie Smith was called out on strikes just moments later, Lolich had managed to wiggle out of his second jam in three innings, giving up only one run in the process.

Through the top half of the fifth inning, the Red Sox had put runners on base in every inning except the second, but had managed only the single run. Lolich was helping his cause by racking up strikeouts in droves, with ten whiffs already to his credit. Curtis, meanwhile, had retired seven straight Detroit batters before Rodriguez led off the bottom of the fifth with a home run to left field, breaking the 1–1 tie and giving the Tigers the lead again. In the sixth, after Boston had again managed to put a runner on base yet failed to score, with Lolich striking out two more Bosox batters, Detroit added another run. Kaline led off the inning with a single to left field and was sacrificed to second on a bunt by Sims. After Howard grounded out and Horton walked, Rodriguez stepped in the box and lined a Curtis pitch into center field for a hit that scored Kaline, giving the Tigers a 3–1 lead.

With the big Tiger Stadium crowd starting to sense their team was taking control, pinch-hitter Phil Gagliano singled to lead off Boston's seventh inning but advanced no further while Lolich recorded two more strikeouts. Sonny Siebert, who was the third of five pitchers used by manager Eddie Kasko on the night, set down Detroit 1-2-3 in the Tigers' half of the seventh. An inning later, Smith led off with a walk, as Boston started yet another frame with its leadoff man on base. The rally was short lived, however, as Smith was eliminated one out later when the Red Sox's dangerous hitting rookie catcher, Carlton Fisk, grounded into an inning-ending double play, Rodriguez to McAuliffe (who had come into the game for Taylor) to Cash (for Howard).

Before Lolich came out to try to get the final three outs to wrap up the first game, Kaline led off the Tiger eighth with his third hit of the game, a single to left field, and then advanced to third when Fisk made an error on Sims' sacrifice bunt attempt. After Cash struck out against veteran left-hander Bob Veale, and Northrup grounded to third with Kaline being thrown out at the plate, Rodriguez singled for his third run-scoring hit of the game, plating Sims from second base.

The crowd roared on every pitch Lolich threw with a 4–1 lead in the ninth inning. He put them on the edge of their seats, however, by walking a man and hitting another before striking out Harper and inducing Aparicio to fly to left field, with Northrup making the catch to end the game. Lolich's 22nd win of the season, in the most tension-filled game he had pitched in since the seventh game of the 1968 World Series, had been another masterpiece. He allowed six hits and five walks but had been doubly tough with men on base, striking out a season-high fifteen Red Sox batters and stranding ten runners on base. More importantly, his performance lifted the team past Boston in the standings, where the Tigers now led by half a game, and needed only a single victory in the last two contests, to reach their season-long goal of winning the East Division title.

"It really makes up for the game I pitched four days ago," said Lolich, comparing the results with his previous start, four nights earlier against the Yankees. "I pitched pretty well for 12 innings, but I was the loser. That game really upset me a lot."[14]

When asked if he had altered his pitching patterns, Lolich commented on a slight adjustment he had made in pitch selection. "Threw more sliders (instead of curveballs). I decided to go with the slider."

"This is probably the best I've pitched this year," he said. "I had some pretty good stuff. Usually a guy will have a good fastball and good curve, but the slider won't work. Tonight I had all three."

As a heavy throng of media invaded the Detroit clubhouse after the game, many were drawn to the cubicle of the Tigers' veteran symbol, Al Kaline, who was enjoying a renaissance during the month of September with his outstanding play.

"I feel like I just ran in an Olympic race," the veteran outfielder said some twelve weeks away from his 38th birthday, exhausted from the grind and pressure of the season-long pennant chase. "I'm really tired now. But I'll be all right Tuesday night."[15]

Kaline's line in the box score that night was typical of what he had been producing of late, under the most intense pressure — three hits in four at-bats, with the home run and two runs scored. Together with Rodriguez, who had also gone 3-for-4 with a home run, three runs batted in and a run scored, they had been the hitting stars of the pivotal first game of the series.

"For some reason I'm really able to get myself up," he said after the first game of the series. "All of a sudden I'm able to do things I haven't done in years."[16]

In the other clubhouse, the Red Sox tried to take what solace they could in dropping the first game. Manager Eddie Kasko bemoaned the bad luck that had struck his team, and attributed much of the loss to that misfortune rather than to the Tigers.

"Aparicio's slip certainly turned the game around," he said to the gathered reporters about the unusual play that halted whatever momentum Boston would generate on the night. "It would have been 2–1, and we'd have had a runner on third with one out. It would have been an entirely different situation."[17]

Regarding his team's chances of rebounding in the series and playing with their backs against the wall, he said, "We've had some tough ones and we've bounced back before."

"We got rid of their big one," said Kasko, referring to Lolich's status as Detroit's top starter. "And now we have our two big ones left.[18]

"I'm willing to take my chances with Tiant tomorrow, and I like Marty Pattin in the final game against Joe Coleman."[19]

The losing pitcher, John Curtis, may have voiced the thoughts of the rest of the Red Sox's players best when he said, "They've got a lot of momentum going for them now. It's not gonna be an easy chore for us to take it away from them."[20]

	W	*L*	*Pct.*	*GB*	*Games Remaining*
Detroit Tigers	85	69	.552	—	2
Boston Red Sox	84	69	.549	½	2

Tuesday, October 3, was the night Tiger fans had been waiting for all season. With a chance to win the East Division title and move on to post-season play for the first time since the 1968 World Series, an electric atmosphere gripped the city throughout the day. As the 8:00 P.M. game time approached, a capacity crowd of 54,079 packed every seat and corner of Tiger Stadium, ready to roar on every pitch. The pitcher taking the mound against Detroit would be much different on this night, though. Instead of a rookie left-hander, they would be facing the most dominant pitcher in the league over the season's second half in the whirling, twirling Luis Tiant. Tiant was on an 11–1 run since August 1, and seemed to be unbeatable of late, including the dusting of the Tigers he delivered only nine days earlier in Boston. Detroit would counter with Woodie Fryman, the savior to the Tiger pitching staff since his arrival in early August. Fryman entered action that evening with a record of 9–3 as a Tiger, and had been Detroit's top starter over the final two months.

Boston's fine leadoff man Tommy Harper singled to begin the game. He then stole second, and was joined on base by Yastrzemski, who walked with one out. That brought up switch-hitting right fielder Reggie Smith, who batting right-handed grounded a ball up the middle that was fielded neatly by Brinkman, who then flipped it to the second baseman, Dick McAuliffe, for what looked like a possible inning-ending double play. McAuliffe, however, dropped the ball at second base, allowing Yastrzemski to slide in safely. Harper, meanwhile, rounded third base and kept going, scoring from second on the infield error. It was an inauspicious start for a Detroit team that rarely beat itself with errors that season. They hadn't just given away a first-inning run; they had allowed an unearned run in a game where Tiant was the opposing pitcher, and shutouts had become the norm for the Cuban veteran.

Fryman was able to get out of the inning without further damage, thanks largely to a shoestring catch by Kaline, who charged a looping liner into right field off the bat of Fisk. In the Detroit first inning, Kaline singled and Sims walked to put two runners on base with only one out, but Cash and Horton both made outs to end the threat.

Both pitchers settled down in the second inning and again into the third before Fryman led off Detroit's half of the inning with a single and eventually moved to second base. Again the Tigers stranded the runner after Kaline flew out and Sims grounded out. Boston moved runners into scoring position in both the fourth and fifth innings but failed to score. In Detroit's fifth inning, Brinkman led off with an infield single, and after Fryman struck out, McAuliffe walked to move him into scoring position at second base. Tiant then fanned Kaline before Sims hit a hard drive to the opposite field that Dwight Evans chased before slipping on a divot in the left field grass and falling down. As the rookie left fielder and future multiple Gold Glove winner sat in the outfield grass, he was able to reach back and make the catch for the final out. Detroit still trailed, 1–0, as the game moved to the sixth inning.

Reggie Smith walked and stole second base on Sims in the sixth inning but was stranded as Fryman struck out Evans with two outs. In Detroit's sixth, Cash led off with a walk, and then after a lengthy conference between power-hitting fifth hitter Willie Horton and third base coach Joe Schultz, Horton laid down a perfect bunt towards third base for the sacrifice. With Cash at second representing the tying run, Northrup lined a ball between the outfielders in right-center field. The ball hit the turf, allowing Cash to score easily, but Northrup slipped and fell between first and second base and had to retreat, giving up what looked like a sure double. Consecutive ground balls that resulted in force-outs off the bats of Rodriguez and Brinkman ended the inning.

As Martin looked on from the Detroit dugout, Fryman was pitching a great game in his personal duel with Tiant, allowing only two Red Sox hits through the first six innings. A single by Tiant was the only damage in Boston's half of the seventh. After Fryman led off the bottom of the inning with a weak flare to second base, McAuliffe belted a ball into the gap in deep right-center field. The ball bounced against the fence, allowing the Detroit second baseman to cruise into second with an easy double.

The big crowd came to their collective feet and roared as they watched the man resting on one knee in the on-deck circle slowly rise and walk towards home plate. Although slightly built, with his brilliant home white uniform with the big number six seemingly hanging from the back of his 6'1", 185-pound frame, Al Kaline was the man everyone in the ballpark wanted at the plate in that situation. After nearly two decades spent brandishing a reputation as one of the toughest outs in the game, including the preceding two weeks that saw him playing with as fierce a determination as at any time in his career, Kaline was also the most feared Tiger batter to those occupying the dugout on the first base side of the diamond. With first base open, the temptation was there for Boston to walk him. However, with two left-handed hitters following, including the hot-hitting Sims on deck and the always-dangerous Cash after him, the Red Sox elected to pitch to Kaline.

For most of his twenty seasons in a Detroit uniform, Kaline had been the symbol of the Tigers. He was an iconic figure for a conservative organization; steady, consistent, proficient in the fundamentals of the game, all while

Tiger star Al Kaline unleashes his classic swing, shown here in a 1974 action shot. Detroit's 37-year-old veteran star was never better than when he hit .500 over the final weeks of the 1972 season and provided the team with a bundle of clutch hits (National Baseball Hall of Fame Library, Cooperstown, New York).

avoiding excessive attention or controversy. He possessed a classic swing that was both under control and without any wasted effort. Defensively, he had slowed afoot, but he studied hitters and was so fundamentally sound that he was still an asset in right field. Most of his 1972 season had been a washout due to a series of nagging injuries, with the pulled muscles in his left leg being the primary albatross. After a slow start, he gained momentum into May before the injuries shelved him for much of July and August. With the exception of his debut season of 1953, when he appeared in only 30 games, Kaline would log the least number of at-bats in 1972 of any campaign in his career.

By the start of September, however, he was healthy and able to play regularly in the outfield. He appeared in 23 games in September, more than any other month all season, and had now played all three days in October as well. With the team in a pennant race and Martin relying on him more than ever that season, Kaline got hot. His batting average had been a respectable .281 on September 15, but a blazing last two and a half weeks of the season had raised it to a sizzling .313. After spending most of his starts hitting in either the third or fourth positions in the batting order, Kaline had been used in the number-two slot over the last two weeks, and responded with key hits to drive in runs or spark rallies at a breathtaking clip. He hit .436 over 35 at-bats after being moved to the second position, with four home runs, eight runs batted in, and thirteen runs scored. Most importantly, he had come up with clutch hits in key situations, something that he now faced again in a 1–1 tie with the Red Sox and the division title within reach.

Ignoring the pandemonium that accompanied each pitch to Detroit's hottest hitter, Tiant was able to get ahead in the count. Mixing off-speed pitches with hard stuff inside, Tiant worked the count to 1–2. The second strike fooled Kaline badly, with the Tiger veteran only able to flick a weak swing at an outside pitch. The next pitch, however, was just a little better to hit. A mistake. It was the type of pitch Kaline had made a living out of by ripping them into outfields for the past two decades. He sent the ball into left field for a solid single. Dwight Evans fielded the ball cleanly and threw to the plate, but not before the hard-charging McAuliffe was able to cross the dish standing up. When the throw went all the way through the infield, Kaline advanced to second base.

As the waves of noise cascaded around the double-decked stadium, Eddie Kasko walked to the mound and relieved his weathered starter, Tiant. In came Bill Lee, a gangly left-hander who later became as well known for his crazy antics as for his solid big league career. He would face Sims and Cash, both lefties, as the next two batters in Detroit's lineup. Lee sawed off Sims' bat with an inside pitch, but the Tiger catcher was able to muscle a weak grounder towards shortstop. Whether it was the spin of the ball off Sims' bat or the

Dick McAuliffe races home with what proved to be the winning run in Detroit's division-clinching win over Boston on October 3, 1972. The Tigers second baseman doubled, and then scored on a single by Al Kaline in the seventh inning to break a 1–1 tie. Duke Sims (far right) directs McAuliffe, while Luis Tiant (23) backs up catcher Carlton Fisk (27), who is awaiting the throw to the plate. Carl Yastrzemski (8) moves into position to cut the throw off (AP/Wide World Photos).

distraction provided by Kaline, who cut in front of the shortstop position and then hesitated slightly before bolting for third base, the usually sure-handed Aparicio bobbled the ball, and everyone was safe.

What was ruled as an infield hit left Detroit runners on first and third with only one out. Cash, who had slumped terribly over the last two months of the season, squared and dropped a bunt down the third base line on Lee's first pitch as Kaline raced home from third base. The suicide squeeze, the favorite tactic of Martin's, failed when Cash's bunt rolled foul some thirty feet down the line. It missed by inches ending up as an infield hit and another run. On the next pitch, though, Cash topped a ball towards the right side of the Red Sox infield. Yastrzemski, who was holding Sims on the bag at first base, bolted in and fielded the ball near the mound, ready to make a play on Kaline, who was running towards home. As Yastrzemski pulled the ball out of his glove, the ball popped loose and fell to the turf. Detroit had scored another run on the seemingly harmless hit off the bat of Cash, and now led by what appeared to be the colossal margin of two runs, 3–1.

Boston looked to be coming unglued as the Tigers threatened to add on more. Horton struck out for the second out, but then Northrup singled sharply into left field. Cash sped from second base around third and tried to score, but Dwight Evans, showing off the arm that would make him famous throughout a twenty-year career, threw him out at home plate to end the inning.

With Detroit only six outs away from wrapping up the title, the Red Sox shifted into desperation mode. Yastrzemski led off the eighth with a single and then advanced to second on Fryman's wild pitch. After Smith followed with a fly out to Kaline, Petrocelli blasted a ball into deep right field that caused a collective groan and holding of breath from the 54,000-plus in the old ballpark. The drive off Petrocelli's bat looked like a game-tying home run as it soared towards the right field stands. The ball seemed to hang up in the October night air, however, and came down in Kaline's glove while his back brushed against the green fence for the inning's second out.

The two long drives by Smith and Petrocelli gave Martin reason enough to make a pitching change. Fryman's last start of 1972 had been another grinding effort when his new team needed it the most. He pitched 7⅔ innings, allowing only four hits, four walks, five strikeouts, and, most importantly, only one run. Despite battling an arthritic elbow that gave him problems throughout the season, he consistently challenged hitters with fastballs and sliders. Once again he had been a godsend to the Detroit staff as a desperately needed starting pitcher who was able to provide quality innings. As Seelbach came on for his 61st appearance, the fans rose and gave Fryman a thunderous ovation while he walked to the Tigers' dugout. Just moments later, when Fisk's line drive was speared by a diving Rodriguez for the third out, Boston's scoring threat had ended.

The anticipation grew as Detroit batted in the bottom of the eighth inning. Rodriguez and Brinkman both grounded out before a crowd that was getting louder as each minute passed and the realization of a season-long dream drew near. With the Red Sox due to send up two right-handed hitters to start the ninth inning, Martin sent Seelbach to hit for himself before he meekly struck out.

With the big crowd ready to bust loose, Boston came up for their last chance, hoping to extend their season. Evans, who was only weeks removed from his late-season call-up from Louisville, was the first batter. Seelbach fell behind 2–0 before coming back to even the count at 2–2. The crowd roared louder and louder with each pitch, when home plate umpire Nestor Chylak brought up the right hand for strike three to call Evans out.

As confetti started to fall from the upper-deck stands, jam-packed with fans already celebrating, pinch-hitter Cecil Cooper came to the plate to bat for the number-eight hitter, Doug Griffin. Cooper was another young player, just up from Louisville, and a future major league All-Star who would be known best for his years as a run-producing first baseman in the 1980s for the Milwaukee Brewers. Seelbach quickly got ahead of Cooper 1–2 before ringing him up on a called third strike as well.

With the pitcher's spot due in the Red Sox lineup, Eddie Kasko again went to his bench for a pinch-hitter. With bedlam overtaking Tiger Stadium, which had become a snake pit for Boston over the past two nights, it wouldn't have mattered who wandered up those steps from the first base dugout with a bat in his hands. The series had already been decided. Mistakes had undone the Red Sox over the first two games, and the Tigers had jumped all over every miscue, and were now poised to close out the deciding game of the season-long race. Kasko turned to part-time outfielder Ben Oglivie to try to extend the season for the Bosox. The future Tiger was in his first full year in the majors as he headed towards home plate. It was hard to ignore the irony of the situation. With the season on the line, a Detroit team that had been labeled as being too old and filled with players on the downside of their careers was riding a 24-year-old rookie relief pitcher as the Tigers moved to the cusp of a division title four years in waiting. Boston, a team filled with such veterans as Yastrzemski, Aparicio, Petrocelli, Harper and others, had sent 20-year-old Dwight Evans, 22-year-old Cecil Cooper, and 23-year-old Ben Oglivie, all rookies, to the plate in its last-chance at-bat of the season.

As Al Kaline caught Boston pinch-hitter Ben Oglivie's short fly ball to right field, the Tiger dugout readies to erupt following Detroit's 3–1 American League East Division-clinching victory over Boston on October 3. Tiger coach Dick Tracewski (arms spread) and pitching star Mickey Lolich (arms raised) lead the way out of the dugout for what turned into a riotous celebration (AP/Wide World Photos).

The first pitch to Oglivie was a fastball down and in. Ball one. The noise level within the sixty-year-old stadium was attained levels not reached since 1968. On Seelbach's next pitch, Oglivie took a weak swing and lofted a fly ball into shallow right field. Kaline, the symbol of the Tigers and the leader of their late-season surge, raced in under it and raised both hands, removing any doubt as to who would take care of this final out. In a moment best described at the time by *Detroit Free Press* columnist Joe Falls as "willed by the gods," the ball settled into Kaline's glove for the final out.[21] The time in Detroit was 11:13 P.M. The Detroit Tigers were the 1972 East Division champions.

Within seconds the playing field turned into a sea of humanity, as fans dropped over the short barricades down each line and ran towards the infield. In the outfield, the hordes scaled the nine-foot screened fences that surrounded the warning track and raced in as well. The players wanted to celebrate, but quickly turned their thoughts to sheer survival and made a bee-line towards the third base dugout and the sanctity of the tunnel that led to the Tiger clubhouse. Kaline was swarmed by adoring fans. Mickey Stanley, who had come in as a defensive replacement in the top of the eighth inning in center field, and Northrup, who had shifted to left field, also had long runs through the gauntlet of fans tearing across the turf at Tiger Stadium. Long-time Red Sox radio announcer Ned Martin succinctly summarized the scene when he described to his listeners, "This place has gone stark, raving mad!"[22]

Inside the Detroit clubhouse, the scene was only slightly less chaotic, as the team let loose the bottled up emotions that had built over nearly six months of intense pressure, stemming from a pennant chase that had never allowed them to relax. The local television stations in Detroit—WJBK channel 2, WXYZ channel 7, and WKBD channel 4—cut in with live feeds at the conclusion of the game. Neither of the games in the series had been broadcast locally, but the stations aired score updates throughout their regular programming during the evening. Now with the celebration under way inside the Tiger clubhouse, on the field, and all around the ballpark, the local channels were bringing the scene into the homes of fans throughout the metro–Detroit area.

"Battlers ... that's the only word for them," said a jubilant and drained Billy Martin to the reporters that surrounded him about the way his team had fought through every obstacle all season. "These guys really showed me something."[23]

He then turned his praise to the team's catalyst through the pressure-packed games of the past two weeks, Al Kaline. The veteran had gone 22 for his last 44 at-bats, and his play over the final few days amazed many who had written him off because of age and injuries. "He's a great inspiration," said Martin. "He's been just super for us these past few weeks. Go out there and look at him. He sure doesn't look like an old man, does he?"[24]

"There's no happier person in the world," said Fryman, whose season changed dramatically after coming from the last-place Philadelphia Phillies to a division-winning team. "Not only for myself, but for the ball club. They've treated me great here."[25]

"Great" was a word that could be used to describe Fryman's contribution to the Tigers through the stretch run. The 3–1 decision over Boston was his tenth win of the season for Detroit, against only three losses. Without him, it is safe to assume the Tigers would never have been able to hang on over the final two months.

Back outside, bedlam took over in and around Tiger Stadium. Inside, the playing field was littered with fans trampling across the turf, milling in mobs intent on taking with them a piece of the title won by their heroes. For many that meant a chunk of sod, pulled from a field already feeling the effects of the NFL's Lions having played several pre-season and regular-season games there. Dozens of fans recklessly climbed the protective screen that ran from the stands directly behind home plate up to the second deck. Despite the efforts of the stadium security crew on duty, celebration was quickly turning into vandalism of Detroit's baseball temple. Outside, fans took to the streets just outside the stadium, hoisting bottles and stopping traffic. Cars blared their horns in celebration until the gridlock lessened, although nobody seemed particularly hurried to leave the scene.

The Tiger players in the locker room attempted to match the intensity of noise and chaos that was being conducted by their vociferous fans outside. Frank Howard's on-field contributions may have been small down the stretch, but he had provided a great presence in Detroit's dugout with positive encouragement, and now led the team through a sophomoric chant, spelling out "T-I-G-E-R-S" while being the easy target of champagne spray. Beer, water, ice, and shaving cream were the other favorite propellants, and any person with dry clothing, in uniform or not, was a target. Martin was sprawled while fully clothed in a whirlpool full of ice, his hair wet and sticky, plastered with champagne and shaving cream.

As the level of exuberance increased, it provided for embarrassing moments for a pair of Tiger heroes. As Eddie Brinkman, the glue to the Detroit infield all season long, was giving the standard champagne-drenched locker room interview with WXYZ's Dave Diles, he lost track of the fact that his comments were beamed through the live feed being pooled by the three major stations in the Detroit-metro area.

"It's a fantastic feeling, not so much for myself but for the rest of the fucking guys," said Brinkman, to the horror of Diles and the channel 7 crew. Before they recovered from the shock of one F-bomb being delivered over live TV, the Tiger shortstop delivered another zinger that would make his mother blush. "We had to struggle through the whole fucking season ... the whole time."[26]

In another corner of the Detroit clubhouse, Duke Sims, the free-spirited veteran with the sandy-blonde curls who had hit so brilliantly down the stretch in the absence of Bill Freehan at catcher, dropped another line that was unsuitable for innocent ears while talking to radio station WJR's Don Howe: "We could beat the fucking shit out of Cy Young if they threw him up there."[27]

Bill Bonds, the well-known anchorman for WXYZ's news broadcasts, wiggled out of the jaw-dropping statements by Brinkman with an honest summation: "People often ask me if the Channel 7 (remotes) is film or live," he said to his viewing audience. "Well, it's live."[28]

Meanwhile, across the way in the Boston clubhouse, the atmosphere was understandably morose. The distant sound of honking horns from cars outside the stadium broke up the hushed tones being judiciously exchanged in a mostly silent dressing room. Yastrzemski was one of several Red Sox players who openly wept at his locker after having let a race they seemingly controlled only days before slip through their fingers.

"Nobody expected us to be this far," Eddie Kasko said to the writers after having kept the media out of the closed locker room for fifteen minutes. "We can hold our heads up about that. It looks like we just stopped hitting and scoring when they started.[29]

"We knew it was going to be tough," he continued, commenting on the task his young team faced coming into Detroit for the showdown series. "We knew they both had good clubs. We knew we had to score runs and we just haven't been scoring runs. Even winning in Baltimore, we didn't score many runs."

As the exuberance started to wane in Detroit's dressing room, the focus turned for some from the mere division title they had just won to the opportunity that lie immediately ahead.

"I just don't feel like we've won anything," said Freehan, who was still out of action while nursing the broken thumb on his throwing hand. "We've played about 160 games (actually 155 to that point) and we really haven't won anything. We'll probably have the poorest record of any of the four teams left in it. But we're playing as good a brand of baseball as any team. We've got a real chance to win."[30]

Dick McAuliffe also liked the way his team was playing, especially now that the pressure was at its highest point and the games now counted the most. With a core of players who already had a world championship on its resume, he didn't see any reason why they couldn't continue their roll into post-season play.

"We can go all the way," said the fiery Tiger second baseman. "We've got a bunch of veterans and guys who don't quit. We've got the ball club to win it. We've played good pressure baseball for two months. I can't say enough about our pitchers — they kept us in it all the way."[31]

When asked by the media about his feelings on Detroit's chances in a playoff series with the A's, Boston manager Eddie Kasko replied with no shortage of sarcasm, "To tell the truth, I wasn't figuring on that."

	W	*L*	*Pct.*	*GB*	*Games Remaining*
x-Detroit Tigers	86	69	.555	—	1
Boston Red Sox	84	70	.545	1½	1

x-clinched division title

Wednesday, October 4, was an anticlimactic last day of the regular season. A hangover lingered over the stadium as the two teams prepared to play the first, and only, meaningless game of 1972. The day began with Boston conducting a bizarre late-morning press conference, announcing that Kasko would return as the Red Sox manager in 1973 as part of a two-year extension on his contract. Despite his team's second-half surge during the season, there had been much debate among Boston's media and fan base as to whether the 40-year-old manager would be brought back for a fourth season as skipper of the Red Sox.[32]

Meanwhile, Martin, whose team had just won a hard-fought tightly contested divisional race, signed a contract extension of his own, extending his pact through the 1974 season, with a retroactive raise to $65,000 per season. His contract extension, however, was announced only as part of a press release distributed to media members that day.

Neither team was particularly motivated to play that last day, and in reality it was a miracle the game could be played at all. Nearly 30 regular groundskeepers and stadium maintenance crew and 40 temporary hires began work at 3:00 A.M. in an attempt to repair the damage inflicted on the 60-year-old stadium and its field. An estimated 450 square yards of turf was missing or in need of repair, including at least 50 different spots in what had been the infield grass. Work was also being done to replace items taken or damaged during the riot described as a celebration the previous evening. Bases, the pitching rubber, seats, and pieces of the outfield wall padding and screen had been obvious targets of the vandals. Even mundane items, such as light bulbs, had been taken or damaged. Stadium manager Ralph Snyder described the effort required to make such numerous repairs barely twelve hours after the previous night's game had ended as "almost impossible," and gave a forewarning to those within listening distance as to what they could expect for that afternoon's game.

"He will have all his kids out there today," said Snyder, in reference to manager Billy Martin's lineup. "He wouldn't let his regulars play on this field. He'd be afraid they'd get hurt."[33]

Martin did send out a lineup that included McAuliffe, Gates Brown,

Horton, and Brinkman, as well as the starting pitcher, Coleman. All except Brown made early departures, and the Tiger lineup soon included mostly unfamiliar names, such as John Knox, Ike Brown, Tom Slaton, Ike Blessitt, Marvin Lane, Gene Lamont, Paul Jata, and John Gamble. Boston likewise littered its lineup with backups and September call-ups. Regulars Yastrzemski, Smith, Petrocelli, Harper, Aparicio, Fisk, and Griffin never took off their warm-up jackets.

The game did have some meaning for Coleman and Brinkman. Coleman was shooting for his second consecutive 20-win season, but fell behind early and ended up being pulled. Brinkman played the first two innings, and by doing so, became one of just three American League players that year to play in every one of their team's games.

"I wanted to play," Brinkman said after the game. "At least to start, because I had played in every game this year. I didn't have to mention it to Billy; he had me in the starting lineup."[34]

Nearly 22,000 partisans showed up to cheer for the newly crowned A.L. East champions, but for the most part, they sat through what turned into a dull, lackluster affair. A few enthusiastic pleas of "Kaline! Kaline!" were chanted periodically throughout the gray afternoon, but those cries went unanswered, as Martin cleared the bench of his regulars, sending most of them home by the fifth inning to catch up on their rest. Ike Brown's ninth-inning error, while playing third base, prevented the Tigers from tying the major league team record of only 95 miscues in a season. By then, however, the crowd had thinned considerably, and Boston took the meaningless finale, 4–1. Neither Detroit's players nor fans really cared. Their thoughts were on the upcoming playoffs with Oakland that would start on the weekend and a potential World Series appearance, if they could get past the A's.

As the curtain closed on the regular season, the Tigers won the American League's East Division by the smallest margin possible, one-half game; a margin made possible only by the player strike at the beginning of the season and the quirky settlement the players and owners had reached. When the schedule was picked up after the ten-day strike without making up any of the postponed games, Detroit played one more contest (156) than Boston (155). The Tigers made good on that one game and finished with one more victory (86), while each team suffered 70 losses.

The season had been a struggle all the way, with batting slumps, a shortage of pitching depth, and injuries seemingly plaguing the team at every turn. The naysayers had said the team was too old and too slow, and didn't have enough pitching. Yet the Tigers fought their way from behind in a four-way dogfight over the final two months of the season and prevailed. Now they were playing their best baseball at the most clutch time of the season.

"I would have liked to use one set lineup all season," said Martin after his team had finally won out. "And if I had the personnel to do it with, I would have. But if I had played a set lineup all season, we'd have gone down the drain. It was just impossible in our situation. I had to go the way I did because of the age on our ball club. By playing guys off and on, I was able to keep everybody fresh. That's why they're so strong now—when it counts.[35]

"I couldn't do the things I wanted. We didn't have any speed. I couldn't steal. I couldn't hit and run. We had to do other things. Little things. The sacrifice. The squeeze. I needed a third pitcher. Then we got Woodie Fryman. Then I needed a fourth pitcher. It was tough. It was the toughest battle I've ever been in."[36]

1972 Final American League East Standings

	W	*L*	*Pct.*	*GB*	*Games Played*
Detroit Tigers	86	70	.551	—	156
Boston Red Sox	85	70	.548	½	155
Baltimore Orioles	80	74	.519	5	154
New York Yankees	79	76	.510	6½	155
Cleveland Indians	72	84	.462	14	156
Milwaukee Brewers	65	91	.417	21	156

X

California, Here We Come!

Any extended celebrating the Detroit Tigers had in mind was quickly curtailed by the reality of another pressure-packed series of baseball that needed to be won before they could move on to the ultimate goal of reaching the World Series. Less than 48 hours after their dramatic 3–1 division-clinching win over the Boston Red Sox, Tiger players, coaches, management, and staff, and many of their wives were on a flight headed to Oakland, California, where Detroit was set to open the American League Championship Series with the A's.

The League Championship Series, or playoffs, as they were also called, was only in its fourth year of existence, and had provided no real drama in either league over its initial three seasons. Purists considered it an abomination towards a sport that in its first seven decades had rewarded only the best team in each league with post-season play. The heavily favored Baltimore Orioles had made short work of their opposition during the first three American League Championship Series, dispensing with the Minnesota Twins twice and the A's in 1971 without ever really being challenged. The National League had advanced three different teams to the World Series from 1969–71, but no real surprises or even memorable moments had been etched in the baseball conscious during those playoff series either.

The playoff series in 1972 looked to be another matter, however. Both leagues presented intriguing matchups without overpowering favorites. The National League Championship Series featured the teams with the two best records in the majors locking up. The Pittsburgh Pirates and Cincinnati Reds had won 96 and 95 games, respectively, and possessed indisputably the two most intimidating hitting lineups in the game, with stars like Roberto Clemente, Willie Stargell, Manny Sanguillen, Al Oliver, Richie Hebner, Dave Cash, Pete Rose, Joe Morgan, Johnny Bench, Tony Perez, and Bobby Tolan dotting their batting orders. Each of those two teams scored greater than 50 runs more than the American League's highest-scoring team, the Boston Red

Sox. They were the reigning N.L. champions from the previous two seasons, and their clash in the upcoming playoff series was highly anticipated. The winner of the American League series would undoubtedly be the underdog to the N.L. champion in the World Series, but the A.L. playoff held a high level of intrigue as well. The matchup between Oakland and Detroit was a contrast in styles, both on and off the field.

Talent-wise, the Oakland A's were now the class of the American League. They presented the most balanced team in the league, capable of beating their opponents with pitching, defense, power, and speed. Since relocating from Kansas City, where the franchise was perennially mired in the second division, often as a last-place club, the team had been coming on strong. The A's finished above .500 at 82–80 in 1968, their first season in Oakland, with a core of young players playing key roles. The A's then won 88 and 89 games over the next two seasons, finishing second each time to the West Division–winning Minnesota Twins. In 1971, Oakland put it all together, winning 101 games and running away with its division before succumbing to the Orioles in the playoffs. Now winners of 93 games in the strike-shortened 1972 season, the A's had established themselves as the best team in the league during the regular season, and were regarded as a slight favorite over Detroit in the playoffs.

Their starting rotation was outstanding, rivaling Baltimore as the league's best. Each starter brought a different element to the staff, and with two right-handers and two left-handers, manager Dick Williams had a perfect balance to work with. Jim "Catfish" Hunter had established himself as the team's ace. A winner of 21 games that season, he was in the midst of five straight twenty-plus-win seasons. He ate up innings, as top starters were expected to do during that era, pitched with pinpoint control and never seemed to give in to a hitter. Ken Holtzman had come over in an off-season trade with the Chicago Cubs for talented center fielder Rick Monday and solidified the rotation as the No. 2 man. The tall, graceful left-hander was coming off a 19-win season, and oftentimes made it look easy. Comparisons with Sandy Koufax had been whispered during his early years in the National League, a comparison nobody, including Holtzman, was able to stand up to. However, at age 26, he had his best season yet by going 19–11 with Oakland, and appeared ready to assume his place with the great pitchers of the day. John "Blue Moon" Odom was a thin, wispy right-hander who came at hitters with a high leg kick and pitched coming from all arm angles. He wasn't quite the workhorse that Hunter and Holtzman were but still managed to go 15–6 that season. The fourth starter was the defending Cy Young Award winner, Vida Blue. The mercurial Blue had been unable to rebound from missing all of spring training and the first month of the season with his prolonged salary holdout.

The missed time took its toll, and the 23-year-old struggled to approach the form he displayed the previous season when he had taken the game by storm. Nevertheless, the big left-hander still possessed a golden arm capable of slinging balls past hitters while also dazzling them with an outstanding overhand curveball. In a short series where an entire season can be decided by the exploits of a hot pitcher, Blue remained an extremely dangerous commodity.

Dick Williams' bullpen was equally deep and effective, and he didn't hesitate to use the relievers. Rollie Fingers, Bob Locker, Darold Knowles, and Joel Horlen appeared in 65, 56, 54, and 32 games, respectively, in 1972. Fingers had emerged as an elite reliever, capable of stamping out the opposition's rallies in the most pressure-filled situations, while racking up 21 saves. Locker, Knowles, and Horlen were veteran relievers who had many years of pennant-race experience between them, giving a plentitude of options for Oakland to use out of a bullpen that combined for a league-leading 43 saves.

Offensively, the A's offered a diverse lineup with the ability to score runs in different ways. Leadoff hitter Bert "Campy" Campaneris was the Oakland shortstop and the catalyst in the batting order. Although he hit only .240 that season, Campaneris was a smart hitter who got his bat on the ball and put pressure on the defense with his speed. Once on base, he was one of the most disruptive forces in the league. He was among the most accomplished base stealers in the game, adept at reading a pitcher's moves and getting a good jump. Combining speed and quickness with a fearless style, he led the American League that year with 52 steals, and ranked annually among the leading base thieves in the game.

Corner outfielders Joe Rudi and Matty Alou were pure hitters who consistently put the ball in play and proved to be difficult outs. Rudi was one of the most underrated players in the league, an excellent fielder in left field, and among the best all-around hitters in either league. He hit .305 with nineteen home runs and 75 RBIs that season while ranking among the A.L. leaders in doubles and triples. Alou had been a late-season pickup from the St. Louis Cardinals, where he hit .314 and sported a lifetime average of .307 over thirteen National League seasons. The 34-year-old contact hitter was the perfect complement to Campaneris. As the No. 2 batter, Alou was skilled at shooting balls through the holes in an infield preoccupied with holding a runner on base.

The middle of the Oakland order provided outstanding power to the A's attack and helped them lead the A.L. in home runs. Reggie Jackson, Mike Epstein, and Sal Bando were proven run-producers and long ball threats each time they stepped to the plate. Though he had suffered through an off-season by his standards (.265-25-75), Jackson was the main cog in the lineup. However, the 1972 version of the man who would one day have a candy bar named after him was far from being the one-dimensional slugger he became later in his career with the New York Yankees. Instead, at age 26, Jackson was a true five-tool player capable of winning games with his glove (he played primarily in center field that season), his arm (considered among the game's best at that time), and his legs (a fast and aggressive base runner who averaged 18 stolen bases over the first eleven full seasons of his career). It was his bat, though, that gave him his reputation. He had prodigious power, hitting as many as 47 homers back in 1969, and averaged 30 over his five major league seasons. Two of the most well-known feats in his young career to that point involved the Tigers. As a rookie in 1968, Jackson homered twice in a September game against Denny McLain, with the latter going for his 30th win in a game before a national TV audience and much of the nation's sports media in attendance. Then in 1971's All-Star game that was played in Tiger Stadium, Jackson hit a colossal home run that ranks among the all-time tape-measure shots in history. The drive cleared both decks in right-center field and showed no sign of descending when it hit a light transformer on the roof of the stadium. That the titanic blast occurred on one of the game's biggest stages only added to the awe in which many viewed his immense talent.

Mike Epstein arrived to play first base for Oakland after a trade with Washington in 1971. The hulking, left-handed-hitting slugger had been an enigma through most of his career, struggling to stay in the lineup against left-handed pitchers while often playing below the level many thought he was capable of. Despite the "difficult" rap that seemed to have accompanied him from Washington, Epstein was still a legitimate home run threat who connected for 26 round-trippers that season. Sal Bando was the A's captain, a stocky overachieving type at third base who was known for knocking in clutch runs. Bando, like many hitters throughout the league during 1972, suffered through an off-season, hitting only .236 with just fifteen home runs.

The catching duties were owned primarily by Dave Duncan, who broke in with Kansas City when he was only eighteen years old back in 1964. Duncan had some pop in his bat, accounting for nineteen home runs in 1972, but had struggled to keep his batting average much above .200. He shared time late in the season with Gene Tenace, a less-accomplished defensive player behind the plate but one who showed signs of being a dangerous threat with the bat.

The weak spot in the Oakland A's lineup that year was second base. Dick Green had been the regular second baseman for several years, but he suffered a back injury in 1972, which limited him to 26 games. In his place the A's had shuffled in and out of the lineup such journeymen as Tim Cullen, Larry Brown, Ted Kubiak, and Dal Maxvill, none of whom proved satisfactory enough with the bat to keep the job on a regular basis. Late in the season

Oakland manager Dick Williams resorted to the highly unusual strategy of rotating through multiple second basemen in each game, usually pinch-hitting for the position each time one was scheduled to come to the plate. It was not uncommon for the A's to use four different players at the position in one game.

Overall, team athleticism appeared to be decidedly in favor of Oakland. While Campaneris was the only consistent base-stealing threat on either team, the A's had a number of fleet runners on their roster, which allowed Dick Williams to employ an aggressive brand of baseball on the bases. Besides Campaneris, Jackson was an outstanding runner who could tear around the bases with powerful strides, as were Alou, Rudi, and a couple of roadrunners on the Oakland bench in outfielders Angel Mangual and George Hendrick. Even the A's pitchers contributed to the advantage Oakland seemed to have in all-around athletes. All of the starters were quick and agile off the mound, providing the Oakland infield with a capable fielder in the middle of the diamond. Hunter, Holtzman and Odom were also outstanding hitters as pitchers went, capable of helping their own cause by being able to execute a bunt when needed or coming through with a well-timed base hit. Odom's athleticism had been put to further use during the regular season when he was used 28 times in a pinch-running capacity, scoring 16 runs, which was a remarkably high total for a pitcher of that era.

Even more startling than the contrast between the two teams' styles of play was the difference in appearance and decorum of the two franchises. Detroit remained a tradition-rich organization steeped in conservative values, both fiscally and in the on-field product. Lightning-rod-type personalities such as Denny McLain had surfaced occasionally throughout the Tigers' long history, but most had not remained in Detroit for any extended period, especially under the guidance of owner John Fetzer and general manager Jim Campbell. Those two had built an organization based on foot soldiers with solid character that fit the image and toed the company line. Detroit's roster was filled with players from that same mold. They were the types that Fetzer and Campbell wanted wearing the home whites with the old English "D."[1]

Oakland, on the other hand, reflected the flashy, brash breed of team, built with dynamic personalities, none any bigger than their eccentric owner, Charles O. Finley. Finley was an Indiana-based insurance mogul who had built a fortune developing a group policy for those in the medical industry. He had purchased the Kansas City Athletics in 1960, and had almost immediately set his mind on finding a new home for his franchise. In 1968 he moved the team to Oakland, re-branded them as the "A's," and dressed his team in garish uniforms with team colors Kelly green, California gold, and wedding gown white. Finley had a penchant for wanting to modify the game through a number of gimmicks that were not openly accepted by baseball's establishment. Among his ideas that were largely met with disdain was use of an orange baseball instead of the traditional white, abbreviated ball-strike counts, use of designated batters and runners as a regular position in the lineup, ball girls in short shorts retrieving foul balls hit down each baseline, and even a mechanical rabbit he installed behind home plate that popped out of the ground with a new supply of baseballs for the umpire. While still in Kansas City, he had the grounds crew at Municipal Stadium mark out a chalk line in right field that matched the dimensions of Yankee Stadium. Hoping to make a mockery of New York's famous right field short porch at 296 feet, he had his public address announcer point out any fly ball that was caught beyond the chalk line and exclaim, "That would have been a home run in Yankee Stadium."[2]

By the time Finley moved the A's to California, his young team was maturing into a talented contender. The Bay Area fan base didn't seem overly interested, however, as attendance figures had been disappointing in the cold and dark Oakland Coliseum. Playing the role of public relations director as well as being the de facto general manager, Finley tried to drum up interest by making his team even more colorful. He fabricated stories about the origins of the nicknames of "Catfish" and "Blue Moon" for Hunter and Odom, which quickly caught on and were often repeated by the media. He dressed his team in white shoes, and broke out an alternative uniform combination of green, gold, and white that strayed from the traditional home whites and road grays that had predominantly represented baseball's attire for nearly a century. Earlier in the season, Finley orchestrated a promotion where he offered $300 to any Oakland player who grew a mustache before a designated home date. All but one of the players took him up on the promotion, including manager Dick Williams, and soon the A's had as much notoriety over their longish hair and mustaches as they did for their many accomplishments on the field. As the season rolled along, they began to be commonly referred to as the "Swinging A's," a tag that wasn't downplayed within the organization.

The contrast between the two teams couldn't have been any greater. It was the slow, long in the tooth, gray hairs from Detroit, relying on their big-game experience stemming from a host of players who had won a world championship four years earlier, against the young and brash "Swinging A's," oozing with a delicious blend of young, yet experienced, talent. The American League pennant would be decided between the two teams in a best-of-five series, starting with two games in Oakland before shifting to Detroit for game three, and then games four and five, if necessary.

Verbal sparring between the two teams started before the Tigers' flight had landed in Oakland. The focal point was Detroit's Frank Howard. Howard's acquisition from Texas had been completed after the midnight deadline on August 31, making him ineligible for post-season play with the Tigers. His on-field contributions had been minimal down the stretch. He batted .242 in fourteen games, hitting only the one home run against Baltimore. However, his presence in the clubhouse and on the bench had been tremendous. He had a wonderfully positive influence with an uplifting personality that quickly made him a favorite of his new teammates. The Tigers petitioned to have him allowed in uniform during the playoff series, if only to sit on the bench, even though he wouldn't be able to play. American League president Joe Cronin denied the request when Oakland wouldn't agree to it. Word was that Dick Williams was OK with the move, but not Charlie Finley.[3]

"I think it's just chicken soup on Finley's part," said Billy Martin, already fuming about the early slight from his playoff counterpart. "And I'm going to tell him so to his face when I see him. All we asked was that (Howard) be allowed to sit on our bench. What could that hurt? I didn't realize the A's were so afraid of us that they won't let us have an extra man on the bench."[4]

Never one to duck from controversy, Finley fired back through the media when informed of Martin's accusations. "This is just another phony, erroneous story planted by Billy Martin to help his players against the A's. And considering the way the A's kicked the shit out of the Tigers eight times during the regular season, I don't blame him for grasping at straws.

"Number one, we don't give a shit whether Frank Howard plays in the playoffs or not. Number two, we don't give a bleep whether he sits on the Tigers bench or not. And number three, Billy Martin cooked all this up to inspire his players. And I'm certain he's going to need help from every angle to beat the A's."[5]

Adding salt to an already-open wound, when the Tigers checked into their hotel in Oakland, Martin found that his usual suite had already been reserved and wouldn't be available to the Detroit skipper over the weekend. None other than Charlie Finley held the reservation.[6]

It was the upcoming games that would be played on the field — not ineligible bench jockeys or hotel reservations — that would be the topic of conversation on Friday as the teams made final preparations for the first game on Saturday. Conventional thought was that Detroit might be able to ride the momentum of their late-season run and tight margin of victory over Boston into the playoff series and have that propel them into the World Series. Dick Williams, though, didn't agree with that line of thinking.

"If anything the Tigers might have a letdown after the way they had to fight to win their division. Besides, we were in the playoffs last year and that has to help. We're keyed up for this, but we're loose. We know what we have to do. The Tigers have been in a World Series ... but they have never been through a playoff to get there.

"They said we had the momentum in Boston in 1967, too," said Williams, referring to the "Impossible Dream" Red Sox team he had managed five years earlier. That team won the pennant on the last day of the season but then fell in the World Series to the St. Louis Cardinals.[7] "I think we're better prepared, both mentally and physically, than we were a year ago. And having been here once before has to help. The playoffs are a little different from anything else in baseball. Here we're just fighting to get where the money is. There's a tendency to relax more in the playoffs than you might in the Series."[8]

After tasting post-season play for the first time the previous fall, the A's brought a more-focused goal into the playoff series with Detroit. Merely reaching post-season play wouldn't be good enough; performing on the game's biggest stage and advancing to the World Series was now the goal. Oakland superstar Reggie Jackson kept a picture of himself from the previous season as motivation throughout the year, especially now that his team was headed again into the League Championship Series. The picture was of Jackson weeping in the dugout following the A's dismissal by the Orioles in the previous October's ALCS.

"All of this, all of it means nothing," said Jackson, who was still five years away from garnering his "Mr. October" moniker. "All the games we played. Nothing. It begins Saturday. The practice, the preparation, the thinking, the planning — it doesn't mean a thing. Doing it against Milwaukee or Texas or KC doesn't mean a thing. Only Saturday counts, and I've got to do it against Lolich."[9]

For the Tigers, the playoff round was also a new experience. When they ran away with the A.L. pennant in 1968, they advanced directly to the World Series. Now they would have to play a pressure-packed series just for the right to represent the American League in the Fall Classic.

"I don't like the idea of having playoffs to begin with," said Martin, who was making his second appearance as a manager, his first coming with Minnesota during the initial A.L. playoff series in 1969. "It's rough on the players and on the manager to go through a whole season, and win, and then have to win another three out of five to get into the World Series. I think the team that wins in its league should go right into the World Series."[10]

Making the task even more difficult was the fact that the Tigers hadn't played well in their season matchup with Oakland. The A's had taken two out of three in all four series the teams had played during the season, and in several games the West Division champions had made Martin's squad look downright bad.

"They had a five- or six-game lead in their division every time they played us," Martin rationalized to the media that was gathering in Oakland for the start of the playoff series. "And because they are in the other division, those games didn't really mean that much. We could have played them a lot differently if they had been Boston or Baltimore, a team we had to beat to get here. And another thing, every time we faced them our bats were asleep. Now we're swinging the bats real good, and I think they're going to find it's a different story."[11]

The championship series for both leagues began on Saturday, October 7. Harrah's Tahoe listed Oakland and Pittsburgh as 6–5 favorites in their respective playoff series. The early afternoon game was played in Pittsburgh's Three Rivers Stadium, barely two years old at the time, and home to the Pirates, who were hosting the Cincinnati Reds. The Reds struck with a first-inning home run from their sparkplug second baseman, Joe Morgan, but the Pirates came right back with three runs of their own in the bottom of the first frame. Al Oliver and Willie Stargell both contributed first-inning extra-base hits to drive in runs. From there, the pitchers on both teams, Pittsburgh's Steve Blass and Cincinnati's Don Gullett, settled down and the game droned on with all zeroes being posted on the scoreboard, with the only exception being Oliver's two-run home run in the fifth inning, which broke the game open. Blass gave way late to Ramon Hernandez, who closed out the game, and the Pirates took game one of the NLCS by a score of 5–1.

When Detroit opened the American League Championship Series in the late afternoon game that day, the Tigers welcomed a familiar but surprising figure to their dugout. Frank Howard was back in uniform, although not eligible to play, as part of a negotiated agreement with the league president and the Oakland team. The move was not made without the A's combative owner getting in another verbal blast at the man he blamed for the whole situation.

"He was lying when he said we wouldn't let Frank Howard sit on the bench," said Charlie Finley about Martin. "And on top of that, he's a 24-karat kook."[12]

Both managers sent their ace pitchers to start in game one. Martin started 22-game winner Mickey Lolich, while Williams countered with 21-game winner Catfish Hunter. Both teams went down 1, 2, 3 in the first inning, with McAuliffe, Kaline, and Sims failing to hit for the Tigers.

In the second inning, however, Norm Cash, who had slumped horribly over the last two months of the regular season, led off by connecting on a drive to right field that cleared the wall for a home run and an early 1–0 Detroit lead. In the Oakland second inning, Lolich got into his first jam of the game, giving up a single to Jackson and a walk to Epstein sandwiched around a fly out to left field by Bando. Gene Tenace followed by flying out to left, and then Williams, following his standard operating procedure of late, went to his bench and pinch-hit Angel Mangual for starting second baseman Dick Green. Mangual grounded out to Aurelio Rodriguez, and Lolich was out of the inning.

Tiger ace Mickey Lolich poses with Oakland's Jim "Catfish" Hunter before the first game of the 1972 American League playoffs. Lolich, winner of 22 games, and Hunter, winner of 21 that season, hooked up in a pair of classic low-scoring pitchers' duels in the series (AP/Wide World Photos).

In the third inning, Oakland put two men on base again with only one out. After the pitcher, Hunter, grounded out to lead off the inning, Campaneris singled and then scampered around to third base on Matty Alou's hit to right field. Joe Rudi then scored the speedy A's shortstop when he lofted a sacrifice fly to Jim Northrup in center field. Jackson followed with his second hit, moving Alou over to third, before Lolich got Bando to fly out to end the rally and keep the game tied at 1–1.

The middle innings belonged to the pitchers as neither team could push across another run. Detroit appeared helpless at the plate, as Hunter dazzled the Tigers with his full array of pitches and pinpoint control. Fifteen consecutive batters went down against his right-handed slants, with the Tigers unable to hit the ball hard. Oakland threatened in the bottom of the sixth when Jackson reached base on an error by McAuliffe, and then took second base on a sacrifice bunt by Bando, followed by a walk to Epstein. Tenace, who was in the lineup at catcher in place of the slumping Dave Duncan, lined a Lolich pitch directly to Rodriguez, who proceeded to double off Jackson at second base for the third out.

As the Tigers came to the plate in the eighth inning, they had managed only two hits off Hunter and only one base runner, a Cash walk, since the second inning. Ed Brinkman started their first real rally of the game, however, when he doubled to center field to lead off the inning. Lolich batted for himself and was called out on strikes after failing to get a crucial sacrifice bunt attempt down. McAuliffe then flied out, followed by Kaline, who grounded to second base, and the threat was finished. Oakland managed a pair of two-out singles from Bando and Epstein in its half of the inning, but Lolich got Tenace to strike out to end the inning.

With the two teams tied at one run apiece heading into the ninth inning, the tension mounted. Detroit's spirits were lifted when Sims led off the inning with a double. With the left-handed-hitting Cash coming to the plate after having already homered off Hunter earlier in the game, Williams called on his erstwhile pitching phenom, Vida Blue, to come in and face the Tigers' power-hitting first baseman.

With only a five-game series to plan for and a day off scheduled for Monday, Williams only needed three starting pitchers, and had the luxury of moving the previous season's Cy Young Award winner to the bullpen to serve as his primary left-handed relief ace. Hunter, Holtzman, and Odom would take care of the starting assignments, leaving Blue as the odd man out. Additionally, a late-season injury to the A's regular left-handed relief specialist, Darold Knowles, had created a need for a late-inning reliever who threw from that side, making Blue the obvious choice.[13]

With the potential winning run on second and no outs, and Cash facing the fire-balling left-hander in Blue, Martin had his first baseman bunting. He laid one down towards third base that Oakland third sacker Bando fielded and zipped to first base, which was being covered by second baseman Ted Kubiak. Kubiak, however, mishandled the throw, leaving Cash safe and Sims at third base, and the Tigers had their greatest scoring chance of the game, with runners on first and third and nobody out.

Willie Horton was the next batter, and Williams wasn't about to give the right-handed slugger the opportunity to hit off Blue with runners on base. The Oakland manager brought in his relief ace, Rollie Fingers, which triggered a move by his counterpart in the Detroit dugout. Martin sent out Gates Brown to bat for Horton. Fingers proceeded to induce Brown into popping out to Bando in foul territory along the third base line. With one out and runners on the corners, the right-handed Fingers now faced the lefty-hitting Jim Northrup.

With Brown having failed to drive in Sims, Martin was desperate to get the lead run across the plate. He ordered the suicide squeeze. As Fingers went to his motion and brought the ball to the plate, Sims streaked for home as Northrup held out the barrel of his bat to bunt the ball. The attempt failed, however, when the ball was fouled off. With the element of surprise gone, the squeeze was no longer an option. Northrup would have to hit away. He grounded the ball directly to the second baseman, Kubiak, who flipped the ball to the bag at second base, where Campaneris forced Cash and then relayed his throw to Epstein at first for a double play. A golden opportunity had come and gone for a frustrated Tiger team.

Even though he lacked the electric stuff he had in his repertoire against Boston five days earlier, Lolich was pitching another superb game. He set the A's down in order in the bottom of the ninth inning and then watched as Brinkman ripped his second double of the game down the left field line with one out in the tenth. Martin was now faced with a dilemma. With one out, the bunt served no real value. He either had to pinch-hit for Lolich and lose his big-game pitcher in the bottom of the inning, or roll the dice and let the weak-hitting pitcher hit away and hope that either he or McAuliffe following could come up with a clutch hit to score Brinkman. Martin decided to keep Lolich in the game and allowed him to hit. Lolich grounded out, as did McAuliffe, and another scoring chance was missed.

In the bottom of the tenth inning, Lolich again set down Oakland, this time thanks to Jackson hitting into an inning-ending double play. Leading off the eleventh, Kaline, who had been held hitless in four previous at-bats, made solid contact on a low and away pitch from Fingers, and drove it over the wall in left field for a home run. The dramatic homer was his third of the week and fourth in the last five games he had played, and once again it appeared the man who had been a Detroit icon for so many years had provided another clutch hit in what was already a magical autumn for him. After Sims, Cash, and Stanley went down following the homer, Lolich returned to the mound determined to preserve the victory.

Lolich had given up eight hits while striking out only three Oakland batters in the game, but the single run he allowed in ten full innings was more indicative of the toughness he had displayed in grinding his way out of jams and giving his team the chance to win late. The eleventh inning started ominously, however, when Bando singled and Epstein, a notoriously ineffective batter against left-handed pitching, went the opposite way and singled into left field. With two runners on and no outs, Martin relented and went to his bullpen, calling on Chuck Seelbach to come on for a tired Lolich. Blue Moon Odom and Mike Hegan came on as pinch-runners off of Dick Williams' bench, running for Bando and Epstein, respectively. Tenace laid down a bunt, attempting to move the runners up, but Rodriguez made a quick break on the ball, fielded it and fired to Brinkman, who had rotated ahead of the runner to get the force-out at third base. Brinkman then fired to first base, where McAuliffe just missed the tag on Tenace coming across the bag.

When time was called after the play at first base, it appeared Rodriguez's sharp reaction to the Tenace bunt, which nearly resulted in a double play by the Tigers, was the type of defensive play that could nip a promising inning before it could materialize. Oakland still had runners on first and second base, but now there was one out, and the fastest runner, Odom, had been eliminated on the force-out. In addition, the A's were due to send up their eighth and ninth hitters as the next two batters. In the place of Dal Maxvill, who had come on in the tenth inning as the third Oakland second baseman of the game, Williams sent up Gonzalo Marquez as a pinch-hitter. Marquez was a 26-year-old rookie and a native of Venezuela. He had come up to the A's after spending most of the season in the minor leagues and appeared in 23 games, all but two of which were as a pinch-batter. To the surprise of many, he had excelled in that role, hitting .381 in his limited appearances with the big league team.

Now the rookie left-handed hitter settled in to face the Tiger rookie reliever, Seelbach. Seelbach got ahead in the count, 1–2, before Marquez grounded a ball towards the hole between first and second base that found its way through into right field for a hit. Hegan got an excellent jump from second base and rounded third on his way to scoring easily and tying the game. As Kaline charged the ball in right field, Tenace, streaking from first base, rounded the bag at second and headed to third. With no play at the plate, Kaline came up throwing for third base in an attempt to gun down Tenace. The ball came in, on-target, on one skip. Amidst the cloud of dust that kicked up as the ball and a sliding Tenace reached the waiting Rodriguez at the same time, everyone watching anticipated the call from third base umpire Don Denkinger. Instead, the unthinkable happened. The ball skipped by Rodriguez and into the cavernous foul area between the base line and the stands in Oakland's Alameda Coliseum. As Tiger coaches, players, and fans all watched in horror and disbelief, Tenace jumped to his feet and raced home with the winning run.

Tenace's slam dunk, with both feet coming down upon home plate as he was swarmed by his teammates, put the exclamation mark on a dramatic comeback victory by the A's. Detroit's players staggered slowly off the field and into their dugout, not quite sure of what they had just seen. Oakland had defeated the Tigers, 3–2, in eleven innings to take a 1–0 lead in the best-of-five series.

The play was ruled an error by Kaline on the throw. In reality, it was a cruel stroke of bad luck as the ball, despite being on line, simply skipped by Rodriguez while the runner was arriving simultaneously. Both Rodriguez and Brinkman said afterwards that they thought the ball might have glanced off Tenace's hip as he slid into the bag.

"It just jumped up and I couldn't stop it," said Rodriguez in a sullen Tiger clubhouse.[14]

NBC game analyst Tony Kubek, who had shared the broadcast booth that day with play-by-play announcer Curt Gowdy, said after the game that he thought the play was a perfect illustration for a scoring concept being kicked about at that time, the "team error," rather than having it assigned to an individual player.[15]

"I threw the ball where I wanted," Kaline explained. "I had no chance for the man at the plate. I fielded it right, my throw was on line with the bag, but the runner just happened to get there as the ball did. It is just one of those things that happen in this game.... What can you do?"[16]

Frustration was the emotion of the day in the Detroit dressing room. Missed scoring opportunities in the late innings proved as damaging as the final crazy play that followed Marquez's single.

"We should have never played extra innings," said an irritated Martin afterwards. "We should have won it in nine innings. The suicide squeeze beat us."[17]

"I wasn't as strong as I've been," said Lolich about his first post-season start since facing Bob Gibson of the Cardinals in Game Seven of the 1968 World Series. "I had pretty good stuff but my fastball wasn't popping." The big left-hander hardly needed to apologize for his performance. In spite of the fact that he was the losing pitcher in the box score, Lolich pitched ten full innings, allowing only two earned runs. "We've been known to lose that kind before and bounce back."[18]

"This thing is far from over," rationalized Kaline. "We've come back before and I think we can come back again.[19]

"I never went from being a hero to a goat any quicker in my whole life."[20]

"It's all history now," said Martin, trying to move past his team's eleventh-inning collapse in game one. "All I care about is Sunday's game."[21]

* * *

On Sunday, October 8, game two was played in each of the two League Championship Series, sharing the spotlight with the NFL games that were also played that day. The early game was in Pittsburgh again, and the home crowd had barely settled into its seats before the visitors from Cincinnati had put a four-spot on the scoreboard. The first five batters for the Reds collected hits, including two-run doubles by Bobby Tolan and Tony Perez. The Pirates were able to chip away at the lead in the middle innings, scoring single runs in the fourth, fifth, and sixth innings, to close within a run at 4–3. The game stayed that way until Joe Morgan hit his second home run of the series, a solo shot in the eighth inning. That gave reliever Tom Hall more than enough of a cushion as he worked from the fifth inning on and closed out the game for the Reds. Pittsburgh and Cincinnati were now tied in the series at one game apiece, with the series headed to the Queen City.

Back in Oakland, the Tigers were trying to shake off the emotional hangover stemming from the heartbreaking bottom-of-the-eleventh loss on Saturday. For Martin and the rest of the Detroit organization, the pre-game news that greeted them that day could hardly have been any worse. Ed Brinkman, the team's glue throughout the entire season with his spectacular play in the middle of the infield and his clutch play when the team needed it most, would be out of the lineup, possibly for the rest of the series. On his eighth-inning double in game one, he had aggravated a disk in his back, causing his left foot to go numb. Brinkman had played the rest of the game, but was diagnosed later with a pinched nerve in his back, putting him out of Sunday's game.

"Eleven years. I've played eleven years," moaned Brinkman of his untimely injury. "I finally get into the playoffs and something like this has to happen. It's the worst thing that could have possibly happened. I finally get here and I can't play."[22]

For Martin the news was sobering. Since Martin came to Detroit to manage the previous season, Brinkman had been the shortstop in 315 of the 318 games under the manager's direction. The player known as "Steady Eddie" had come to be taken for granted, playing nearly every inning of every game. Martin didn't even carry a backup shortstop on the roster, having used McAuliffe, Rodriguez, and Tony Taylor on the infrequent occasions when Brinkman came off the field.

"It's bad, very bad," said Martin about the unkind hand his team had been dealt when the stakes were at their highest. "But what choice do I have now? I've just got to go with what I've got."[23]

McAuliffe was Martin's choice at shortstop for game two. The twelve-year veteran had started his career at short, playing the position during his first four years as a regular, before shifting to second base in 1967. Taylor would be inserted into the lineup at second base and would hit seventh in the lineup, with Rodriguez sliding down to the number-eight position.

Woodie Fryman was the choice on the mound for Detroit in what amounted to a must-win situation for the Tigers. Fryman had finished a remarkable two-month stint in which he posted a 10–3 win-loss mark with a sterling 2.03 ERA, easily the best of any Tiger during that period. As the game began, however, it became apparent that it was going to be a struggle for Fryman. After Detroit went down quietly in its first at-bat against A's starter John "Blue Moon" Odom, Campaneris started the Oakland half of the inning with a single, and then promptly stole second and third base with relative ease against a Tiger team that quickly appeared to be back on its heels. After Matty Alou failed to drive in Campaneris with a short fly to left field, Rudi delivered the run with a single through a drawn-in Detroit infield.

The A's threatened again in the third inning when Campaneris and Rudi delivered hits, but an Alou force-out and an unsuccessful steal attempt effectively ran Oakland out of the inning before they could do further damage. As the game passed the midway point, a couple of trends had become clear in the contest. Detroit could do nothing against the freewheeling, sidearmed pitches from Odom, managing only three singles through the first five innings. Fryman was laboring on the mound for the Tigers, consistently falling behind batters in the count and barely working his way out of trouble.

In the bottom of the fifth, it all fell apart for Fryman and his teammates. George Hendrick, batting for starting second baseman Dick Green, led off the inning with a single. After an Odom sacrifice bunt, Campaneris singled Hendrick to third with his third hit of the day. Alou then singled, scoring Hendrick, to make the score 2–0, with Campaneris motoring to third. Martin replaced Fryman with Chris Zachary, an infrequently used 28-year-old right-hander, who proceeded to throw back-to-back wild pitches, scoring Campaneris and moving Alou to third, before losing Rudi on a walk. Fred Scherman came on for Zachary to face the left-handed-hitting Jackson, but the Oakland slugger raked a double into left-center field, scoring two more runs. When the inning ended, the A's added four runs on four hits and an error, and now led by what looked like an insurmountable 5–0 score.

Detroit's bats were lifeless as Tiger batters went back to their dugout after a number of mind-dulling and weakly hit ground-ball outs, coming off of the slants of the freewheeling Odom. Only 23 Detroit hitters had come to the plate through the first seven innings, just two over the minimum number. The contest was on the verge of putting most of its late Sunday afternoon, national television audience to sleep on its couch before the fireworks began to burst.

It was no secret that the Detroit and Oakland teams didn't like each other. Besides the cultural differences that existed between the two franchises, there was a whole history of beanballs and fights between the two teams, going back a half-dozen years. The most recent brush had come in the August fight in Tiger Stadium, touched off when Bill Slayback threw a pitch behind Angel Mangual. With the Tigers down and all but out of game two of the series and still bitter over the disheartening loss in the first game, the fuse on the powder keg had just about burned to its end.

The play that set things off would become the single-most remembered play of that series, and arguably the most remembered moment of the Tigers' entire 1972 season. The first batter for Oakland in the bottom of the seventh inning would be Campaneris, the A's shortstop and leadoff hitter who had been a thorn in the side of the Detroit ball club throughout the day. Campaneris was a 30-year-old, Cuban-born player in his ninth season with the franchise. He had homered on the first pitch thrown to him in the major leagues, one of two round-trippers he would hit in his very first game. In 1965 he became the first player in either league's history to play every position within a single regular season nine-inning game, and he even threw ambidextrously while on the pitching mound, switching hands depending on the hitter. However, his legs were what made him a menace throughout the American League. He led the circuit in stolen bases six times, including that season, and was adept at distracting pitchers and infielders with his sizeable leadoffs and daring antics on the bases.

As Campaneris came to bat that inning, he was already three-for-three, had stolen two bases, and scored two runs, serving as the catalyst for the Oakland attack. He was relatively small physically (5'10", 160 pounds), but wore a villainous expression on his face, rarely showing any trace of a smile, while oozing with an intensity he backed up with a fiery temperament. With the exception of the hometown Oakland crowds who adored him, that surface disposition made Campy an unpopular player around the league. It also made him an inviting target.

Campaneris had been a target of knockdown pitches by Martin's staff throughout the season, including earlier in this game. He crouched down in his stance while holding his hands high and leaned out over the plate while awaiting the pitch from 24-year-old right-hander Lerrin LaGrow. LaGrow had been a late-summer call-up from Toledo and had pitched well in sixteen appearances for Detroit, earning a spot on the post-season roster. He was big and strong, 6'5" and 220 pounds, and was a hard thrower.

LaGrow's first pitch of the inning was a fastball down and in. Campaneris tried to skip out of the way, but the ball struck him cleanly on the left ankle. He fell on his backside after spinning around in the batter's box. His right hand never released the bat. Campaneris hesitated only slightly before pushing himself up slowly off the ground. Then, suddenly, he reached back with the bat fully extended in his right arm and flung it at the object of his angry glare. The bat whirled on a horizontal plane, like helicopter blades, no more than five feet off the ground and directly over the head of a startled and ducking LaGrow, before hitting the turf and bouncing wildly behind the mound.

Home plate umpire Nestor Chylak quickly corralled Campaneris before

A's shortstop Bert "Campy" Campaneris rears back to fling his bat at Tigers pitcher Lerrin LaGrow in the seventh inning of game two of the 1972 American League playoffs. Campaneris had been a thorn in the Detroit team's side with his daring on the base paths, and was hit in the ankle with a pitch late in the game on October 8. Looking on are Tiger catcher Duke Sims, umpire Nestor Chylak, and Oakland third base coach Irv Noren (AP/Wide World Photos).

the A's shortstop could spark any more trouble by charging the mound. Chylak then had to change gears and revert to a protective mode, keeping the instigator safe from the charging Tigers. As the Detroit players in the field meandered towards the plate in defense of their stunned pitcher, Martin led a combative charge from the Detroit dugout towards Campaneris. The Tiger manager had to be restrained by three members of the umpiring crew as he tried to get his hands on Campaneris. Remarkably, as both dugouts emptied and the likelihood of a full-scale riot between the two teams reached dangerous levels, the umpires were able to keep the peace. Martin eventually turned his rage towards the umpires once he realized he wasn't going to be able to engage in fisticuffs with Campaneris. Meanwhile, the Tiger players fumed over the actions of the bat-throwing perpetrator.

After a fifteen-minute delay, the game resumed. Campaneris and LaGrow were both ejected by the crew chief, Chylak, "to keep order in the ball park" but the fireworks were over.[24] Neither team managed to put a runner on base over the final two innings, and Oakland closed out the 5–0 victory while taking a commanding 2–0 lead in the best-of-five series. Odom went the distance for Oakland, facing only 29 batters and allowing only three harmless singles to Tiger batters in an outing that manager Dick Williams described as "tremendous."[25]

After the game, the spotlight focused on the ugly incident in the seventh inning that marred an American League playoff game while the entire nation watched on television. As could be expected, Campaneris was being branded as a cowardly rogue in a combustible Detroit locker room.

"I don't know what the idiot was thinking," said an irate Martin. "He may have to talk to his psychiatrist to find out. You can bet your ass I was going out there for him. I'm not going to get after him now, but if there's ever another fight out there, I'm going out there and find him and beat the __ out of him."[26]

"I wanted to get at the gutless __," said utility man Ike Brown, whose brawny body could be counted on to be in the middle of things when the action turned rough. Brown had smashed Campaneris' bat into pieces before throwing it towards the Oakland dugout during the heat of the on-field melee. "If he isn't man enough to fight, he should have just gone to first base and shut up."[27]

In the Oakland clubhouse the A's shortstop was viewed as a victim who had defended himself in the face of a vengeful Detroit manager who wasn't above resorting to beanball tactics.

"I knew when I walk(ed) to the plate that Billy Martin (is) going to throw at me," said Campaneris shortly before being whisked off to nearby Merrit Hospital for x-rays on his ankle. "I tell myself to be ready. But the ball was right at me and I couldn't get out of the way."[28]

Much of the media surmised that LaGrow's pitch was thrown under orders from Martin. It appeared to most to be a desperate measure from a desperate team that had battled all season, only to see a small, skinny leadoff hitter become the symbol of their demise.

"If I did, he wouldn't have hit him on the foot," Martin pleaded afterwards while convincing no one of his innocence. "He would have hit him in the ribs. The one thing I won't allow is for any of my pitchers to throw at a batter's head."[29]

"Hard stuff down," uttered LaGrow when questioned about the pitch that nailed Campaneris on the ankle. "That's the way I always pitch to Campaneris. This one just got away from me. I certainly didn't want to hit him. If he wanted to fight, I don't know why he didn't at least come out to the mound."[30]

"I feel the Detroit pitcher threw at him," said A's left fielder Joe Rudi. "Campy had run the Tigers ragged in the first two games, and when Martin gets his ears pinned down, he's going to do something about it."[31]

"I no try to hit him with the bat," explained Campaneris of his actions, which were already being reviewed for a possible suspension. "If I want to hit him, I throw it more sidearm than overhand. I just want to warn him not to do that again to me."[32]

The possibility of Campaneris being suspended by league president Joe Cronin appeared to be the only mystery remaining in a series that was now decidedly one-sided. Whether the removal of the A's shortstop from the Oakland lineup would make any difference in the outcome of the series was doubtful. Still, it was an action the Tigers manager felt strongly had to be taken.

"He's got to be suspended. That's the dirtiest thing I ever saw in my whole life in baseball. He could have killed my man. Campaneris is as gutless as any player who ever put on a uniform in this game. It was like using a gun and then running away. The next time he'll probably use a knife, or does he fight with his feet?"[33]

Cronin would not be rushed into making a decision, at least before the teams left Oakland. "That's something that doesn't belong in baseball" is all he would say about the incident Sunday evening as the teams boarded flights to head to Detroit.[34]

Whether Campaneris would play or not, the Tigers didn't have time to contemplate the decision. They had come to Oakland looking for at least a split in the two games, but instead were heading home with their backs against the wall, down 2–0 in the series, and facing elimination with their next loss. The euphoria from only five days earlier, when they had clinched the A.L. East title against the Red Sox, was fading quickly. Their top two pitchers from the stretch drive had been beaten, and they had managed only two runs in 21 innings of playoff baseball. Defensively they had not been sharp, and their glue at shortstop, Brinkman, was likely finished for the duration of the series due to a back injury. For Martin and the rest of his Detroit team, what appeared to be a hopeless, uphill climb loomed before them.

XI

"I'm Proud of Every One of You Guys"

As the American League paused with an off day from the hostilities that had taken center stage in its playoff series, the National League continued its series on Monday, October 9, with the action shifting to Cincinnati's Riverfront Stadium for the third game. The hometown Reds got third-inning RBI singles from Darrel Chaney and Bobby Tolan to take an early 2–0 lead. Pirates catcher Manny Sanguillen cut that lead in half when he lofted a home run in the fifth inning off Gary Nolan. Pittsburgh tied the game in the seventh on Rennie Stennett's RBI single, and then Sanguillen knocked in the go-ahead run an inning later. Meanwhile, Cincinnati, whose feared lineup was known as "the Big Red Machine," was being held scoreless since their third-inning tallies, first by starter Bruce Kison and then by reliever Dave Giusti. It was Giusti who closed out the Reds in the ninth inning, giving the Pirates the 3–2 come-from-behind victory, as well as the two games-to-one lead in the playoff series. The win left the defending world champions needing only one more victory to secure a return trip to the World Series.

The locale for the A.L. playoffs shifted to Detroit, but the media remained focused on the Campaneris bat-throwing incident and speculation as to what punishment the league president might be handing down to the parties involved. On Monday, Joe Cronin suspended Campy Campaneris for the remainder of the American League Championship Series and fined him $500, while stating that "such actions cannot and will not be tolerated."[1] If the A's advanced, as it appeared they would at that point, then he would be eligible to play in the World Series. No Detroit players nor manager Billy Martin were reprimanded for the incident.

When asked whether the suspension fit the crime, Martin seemed satisfied with what had been handed down by the A.L. president.

"Tough enough or not tough enough, he's suspended. That's all I care about.[2]

"I hold no grudges, but I'd like to bounce Campaneris about fifteen rows into the bleachers," he added, still irked at the actions of the Oakland shortstop. "He's got to be suspended."[3]

"If the ball was up around his head — where he could get hurt — then I can see why he might be mad. But he gets hit on the foot and throws the bat ... that's a joke."[4]

From Oakland's perspective, the suspension was irrelevant. While the x-rays on Campaneris' ankle had come back negative, the chance of him being able to play in the days following the beaning was doubtful. Considering that speed and quickness were a big part of his game, the LaGrow fastball could not have hit him in a worse spot. By the time word of the suspension was handed down, the A's leadoff hitter was already on his way back to California.

"We decided after we arrived here that Campy's ankle was too bad to let him play in the rest of this series," Oakland manager Dick Williams said to media members gathered around him in Detroit. "He had his foot in ice on the plane trip here and it was puffed up and swollen pretty bad. He would have been unable to play here so we put him on the first plane back to Oakland."[5]

Taking Campaneris' spot at shortstop would be Dal Maxvill, a 33-year-old, eleven-year veteran who had been picked up at the end of August in a deal with the St. Louis Cardinals. He was a good-field, no-hit shortstop who had been acquired primarily to give Oakland an additional option at second base for the stretch run and into post-season play. Maxvill was no stranger to the postseason, having played in 21 career World Series games, including starts in all seven games against Detroit in the 1968 Series.

"There's no pressure on me," he said when asked about the unexpected starting role he would assume on his new team. "I've played enough baseball games the last ten years. This is just another game you'd like to win."[6]

"Another game" is all the A's needed to win in order to make short work of the Tigers in the playoff series. History was against Detroit, as all three previous A.L. Championship Series had ended in three-game sweeps. What little hope remained rested primarily with getting Oakland back into Tiger Stadium, where the familiar surroundings and home crowd might make a difference. Optimists pointed out that the Tigers had been down three games to one to St. Louis in the '68 World Series before storming back to win the Series in seven games. Many of those same players who had been part of that comeback four years earlier still made up the core of the ball club.

Despite his team being in an unenviable 0–2 hole, Martin liked the pitching matchups for the balance of the series, especially considering the Tigers' success that season against Oakland starter Ken Holtzman.

"We've beaten him (Holtzman) every time we've seen him," explained

Martin. "If we win Tuesday, we'll be in good position with Mickey Lolich and Woodie Fryman ready for Wednesday and Thursday."[7]

As the frenzy from game two rescinded and the teams prepared to play game three, the gamesmanship between the two organizations continued. Detroit made a half-hearted request that Frank Howard be ruled eligible to play in consideration of the Brinkman injury. A.L. President Cronin quickly rejected it. What Detroit got instead was an unwanted gift from the Oakland players. The two teams held short workouts at Tiger Stadium during the off day on Monday. As Detroit sauntered out of its dugout and onto the field to take batting practice, the players found a reminder of Sunday's incident in the batting cage. Standing on its end at home plate was a Bert Campaneris model bat, courtesy of the Oakland players who had already exited the field.

Tuesday, October 10, was sunny and pleasant in Detroit for the 1:00 P.M. game. Oakland's players and staff had already checked out of their hotel, with travel bags packed and on the bus as they came to the ballpark.[8] A Tiger Stadium crowd announced at 41,156 showed up, perhaps with some trepidation, as the figure was nearly 15,000 below capacity. That caused embarrassment to locals who prided themselves as citizens of a true "baseball town." The Detroit media had even chided Oakland and its fans over the attendance figures of just 29,566 and 31,068 for the two games at the Coliseum, but was now forced to eat crow over the slight.[9]

With Campaneris missing from the top of the A's lineup, manager Dick Williams shuffled his lineup, inserting Matty Alou as the new leadoff hitter. Alou greeted Tiger starter Joe Coleman with a liner into the right-field corner and managed to beat Al Kaline's throw to second base for a leadoff double. Maxvill, who had been placed in the second slot in the lineup because of his ability to handle the bat and move runners along, worked Coleman for a walk, and the A's had two runners on base with no outs.

Everyone in the ballpark could sense that a key point in the game was already at hand. Detroit could ill afford to fall behind, being down 0–2 in the series, and having scored only two runs in Oakland. Joe Rudi, arguably the toughest hitter in the A's lineup, dug in at the plate. However, in an early sign of what was to portend, Rudi was called out on a sidearmed breaking pitch from Coleman. Reggie Jackson struck out swinging on a full-count pitch, as both runners advanced on a double steal. With two outs and two runners in scoring position, Mike Epstein, the A's big power-hitting first baseman, also struck out swinging. Epstein's strikeout came after being fooled badly and nearly striking out on the previous pitch. Despite the early jam he had gotten himself into, it was readily apparent that Coleman had electric stuff on this day.

After his team failed to hit with any consistency in the first two games, and with a left-hander pitching for Oakland, Billy Martin shook up his batting lineup as well. With the exception of emergency shortstop Dick McAuliffe, Martin threw an all right-handed-hitting lineup at Ken Holtzman. Tony Taylor, who because of the Brinkman injury would now be the starting second baseman, was elevated to the leadoff spot. Mickey Stanley received his first start of the series, playing center field in place of Jim Northrup. The surprise move was the start being given to seldom-used utility man Ike Brown at first base, taking the place of Norm Cash. But the biggest move that many felt might provide a spark was the return to the lineup of Bill Freehan at catcher. Freehan made his first appearance in Detroit's lineup since breaking his thumb several weeks earlier. It was hoped that his presence would bring stability to a team that had struggled defensively through the first two games and to a pitching staff that was in disarray after the bullpen meltdowns in the previous two games.

Detroit attacked the ball aggressively in the first inning but failed to score. Jackson made a couple of nice running catches in center field sandwiched around a Kaline single. Following a scoreless second inning, Oakland threatened again in the third when Alou led off with a single and one out later moved to second base on Rudi's bunt single. Coleman, however, coerced Jackson to ground out and then struck out Epstein for a second time to end the A's scoring opportunity. An inning later, Gene Tenace managed to draw a walk but was thrown out attempting to steal on a strikeout-throw out with pinch-hitter Don Mincher at the plate.

The Tigers finally put together their first scoring threat of the game in the fourth inning. With one out, Kaline walked and then moved to third when Freehan lined a pitch over third base and down the left field line for a double. Willie Horton fell behind in the count but battled back to draw a walk of his own to load the bases with only one out. Stanley batted next, but he flew out to shallow center field. Kaline tagged but bluffed coming in, as Jackson's throw was on target to the plate. With two outs and the bases loaded, the unlikely first baseman, Ike Brown, came to the plate.

Brown was a thirty-year-old veteran who had spent seven years in the minor leagues before finally making the big league roster as a utility player. He appeared in 51 games in 1972 but batted only 84 times, hitting .250. Most of his appearances had come in bit roles — the second games of doubleheaders, mop-up time in one-sided games, or an occasional pinch-hitting opportunity. They certainly had not come in key situations where the season was on the line.

With the tension mounting and an anxious partisan crowd watching, Brown lined a 1–1 pitch up the middle and into center field for a solid single. Kaline and Freehan both came in to score and the Tigers had gotten the key hit they needed to grab the lead, 2–0.

With his teammates having staked him out in front, Coleman struck out the side in the A's fifth inning for his ninth, tenth, and eleventh strikeouts through the first five innings. He was pitching the game of his life. His fastball was electric and his forkball was dancing downward in an utterly unhittable fashion.

The score remained 2–0 for Detroit into the seventh inning, when some shoddy fielding by the Tigers nearly cost them their lead. Gene Tenace reached base leading off the inning when McAuliffe committed a throwing error. The ad-hoc shortstop's miscue appeared to be harmless until two outs later when a miscommunication in the outfield between Stanley and Kaline allowed Matty Alou's routine fly ball to drop in safely. Only some lax base running by Oakland's Mike Hegan, who had reached base on a force-out, kept a run from scoring. With the tying runs on second and third, both because of defensive miscues, Coleman took advantage of an over-eager Dave Duncan, who was pinch-hitting for Maxvill, and recorded a clutch strikeout. In the eighth inning, Rudi led off with a single, but Coleman got the heart of the A's order by retiring Jackson, Epstein, and Bando.

In Detroit's half of the eighth, the Tigers delivered the knockout punch. After a Rodriguez strikeout and Kaline fly out, Freehan connected on a bomb that left little doubt from the time it left his bat. The drive landed well into the lower left field stands, and with the way Coleman was pitching, gave his team a commanding 3–0 lead. Freehan's return to the lineup seemed to be the perfect tonic for the Tigers and gave them the spark they so desperately needed in the do-or-die situation they found themselves in.

Detroit pitcher Joe Coleman (right) is congratulated by catcher Bill Freehan at the conclusion of game three of the 1972 American League playoffs on October 10, 1972. Coleman struck out 14 batters while shutting out Oakland, 3–0, in arguably the best performance of his major league career (AP/Wide World Photos).

Tenace walked, giving Oakland yet another leadoff batter on base as they came up for their final at-bat. Amazingly, the A's would put their leadoff hitter on base in seven of the nine innings that day. However, as had been the pattern all day, they wouldn't be able to capitalize on the scoring opportunity. Tim Cullen grounded to McAuliffe, who forced Tenace at second base for the first out, and then left the rest for Coleman, who finished the day in high style, as he struck out pinch-hitter George Hendrick and then Alou to end the game.

The performance by Coleman is one of the most overlooked pitching feats in Detroit Tigers history. He gave up a very mortal seven hits and three walks on the day, but stranded ten Oakland runners thanks largely to an American League playoffs record-setting 14 strikeouts. The complete-game shutout victory gave life to a team that had been staggered by the bizarre losses out in Oakland, and made a series competitive when most observers had already penciled the A's into the World Series.

"I think I've pitched better on other days, but I don't think I have had a better forkball than I had today," said the 25-year-old Coleman about the biggest win of his career.[10]

"When I got into that jam in the first inning, I had to go to my forkball right away. And when I found out I had a good one it helped my confidence a lot. As it turned out I had an exceptional forkball, but I never know for sure until the game gets going."[11]

The masterpiece performance didn't just impress those in Tiger uniforms. The A's Mike Epstein, who contributed two of the 14 whiffs by Coleman, was blown away by the stuff the Tiger right-hander had that game. "The way he pitched today, he could have beaten any one of the last 15 All-Star teams."[12]

Not to be forgotten was the clutch hit delivered by Detroit's surprise choice at first base, erstwhile utility man Ike Brown. His two-run single was undoubtedly the big blow in the game and lifted a huge burden off the Tigers in a game and series where runs were hard to come by.

"That was the same pitch he struck me out on in the second inning," Brown said about his key single off Holtzman while finding himself in the rare situation of being surrounded by reporters. "And I made up my mind, if he threw it again, I'd be ready.[13]

"It was the biggest hit of my career."[14]

Some wondered whether the pressure would shift from a Detroit team that had crawled back into the series and had history on its side with the comeback from the 3–1 deficit in the '68 World Series still fresh in many people's minds over to the younger and less-proven Athletics team.

"We're OK," A's manager Dick Williams said to the press as he tried to squash those fears. "We could be better if we had won, but we're still up two games to one on them. We're all right.[15]

"We had the opportunities. We had the leadoff man on base seven out of nine innings. But we just couldn't get 'em in."

Not surprisingly, Tiger manager Billy Martin took a very different viewpoint. With the win in game three, he viewed his club as being the superior team in the series and holding several advantages heading into game four.

"Really we should be 2–1 right now instead of 1–2. We had that first game won and we let it get away.[16]

"If we win Wednesday, then I think we will have an edge going for us in that final game. And you couldn't ask for anything any better than having Mickey Lolich going for you in a game as big as the next one will be."

If the Tigers were looking for good omens, one appeared in Cincinnati later that afternoon. The Reds, who had entered the day trailing the Pittsburgh Pirates 2–1 in the series, staved off elimination and forced a final game by routing the visiting Pirates, 7–1. Ross Grimsley shut down the powerful Pittsburgh attack while twirling a sparkling two-hitter for Cincinnati. A Pittsburgh error contributed to the Reds scoring a run in the first inning, and then another miscue led to two more runs in the fourth. Cincinnati continued to tack on runs against four Pirate pitchers, while Grimsley stymied the Bucs in a complete-game performance. The only run he allowed came on a seventh-inning home run off the bat of Roberto Clemente. The win by the Reds evened the series at two games apiece.

* * *

Wednesday, October 11, would prove to be the greatest day of baseball thus far in the short four-year history of major league playoffs. Bitterly fought series in each league saw contests that day provide the drama that had largely been missing in previous seasons. Three of the four teams faced elimination and fought desperately to continue on in post-season play and secure a World Series berth. The National League would play the first-ever fifth and deciding game in a League Championship Series. Up until that year, only one playoff series in either league had gone more than the minimum three games. Only the San Francisco Giants in 1971 had avoided a three-game sweep (they lost in four games to Pittsburgh), as all three previous American League Championship Series had resulted in sweeps by Baltimore. The New York Mets (1969 over the Atlanta Braves) and Cincinnati Reds (1970 over the Pirates) had also won three straight in previous N.L. playoff series.

In Detroit, the Tigers, fresh off their uplifting 3–0 win in game three, were looking to draw even in their series with Oakland. Dark and threatening skies hung over the ballpark and neither team took batting practice while the tarp remained on the infield until game time. The pitching matchup was a repeat of game one, with staff aces Lolich and Hunter dueling again. Dick Williams went with the same lineup he used for game three, while Billy Martin again shuffled his lineup. Freehan had provided a much-needed spark in game three, and he and Lolich had spent the better part of their careers as batterymates. Freehan, therefore, would remain in the lineup as the catcher. However, with the right-hander Hunter back on the mound for the A's, Martin also wanted to keep Duke Sims' left-handed bat in the lineup and decided to gamble and play him in left field, a position he had played only briefly in his career. Sims would replace the slumping Willie Horton, who was 0-for-8 thus far in the series.

The A's probed the weak spot in Martin's defensive alignment right away when Matty Alou led off the Oakland first inning with a solid drive that caused Sims to back up before making a staggering catch in left field. Maxvill and Jackson each singled that inning, but Lolich was able to work his way out of trouble as Bando popped up to end the threat. Sims managed a wrong-field, bloop double in the bottom of the first but was stranded when Freehan popped out. Each team's second baseman, Dick Green for Oakland and Tony Taylor for Detroit, doubled into the alleys in their respective second innings but were stranded by the pitchers batting in the ninth position. The hot-hitting Alou led off the A's third inning with a double into the right-field corner, but Maxvill failed to get a bunt down, and instead popped a ball back to Lolich. Rudi then grounded to Rodriguez, who spotted Alou wandering too far off second base and fired the ball over to Taylor, who applied the tag on the over-eager Oakland runner before Jackson struck out to end the inning.

With both teams having squandered early-inning opportunities, Dick McAuliffe took all of the guesswork out of his next turn at bat by lofting a high drive into right field that just glanced off the upper deck facing above a backtracking Alou. The third-inning leadoff home run gave the Tigers the early lead in a game that promised runs would be at a premium.

After the McAuliffe round-tripper, both pitchers found their grooves and the game settled into the expected battle between two of the winningest hurlers in the majors over the previous two regular seasons. Lolich, who along with Philadelphia's Steve Carlton had accumulated the most wins over the 1971 and 1972 seasons (47), set down thirteen straight Oakland batters following Alou's leadoff double in the third inning. Hunter, whose 42 victories over the preceding two seasons trailed only Lolich, Carlton, and Chicago's Wilbur Wood (44), was only slightly less effective, setting down thirteen of fourteen Detroit batters during one stretch.

Anticipating that the Tigers' lone run might be all it would take to win on the day, Martin substituted defense for offense early. After Sims flied out to end the fifth inning, Mickey Stanley replaced him in the lineup and played center field while Jim Northrup slid over to left field. With Lolich pitching another remarkable post-season game, it appeared the strategy was sound until the seventh inning, when Mike Epstein connected on a pitch that caught too much of the plate. Epstein blasted a laser off the facing of the upper deck in right field to tie the game at 1–1.

The homer by Epstein was Oakland's first in the series and gave life to an A's team that was slowly being smothered by Lolich's effort. Detroit was able to withstand the blow, however, and coming into the bottom of the eighth inning threatened to win the game. McAuliffe again was the spark plug. He led off the inning by drawing a four-pitch walk off Hunter. Kaline, the consummate professional, adept at all aspects of the game, then laid down a neat sacrifice to move the runner up. Stanley, now batting in the third position in the place of Sims, grounded deep into the hole between shortstop and third base. Ted Kubiak, who was the third Oakland shortstop to play that day, fielded the ball in the hole but could not throw out Stanley, who was one of Detroit's faster runners. McAuliffe advanced to third base on the play, giving the Tigers runners on first and third with only one out.

Williams went to his bullpen, bringing in his ace reliever, Rollie Fingers. Fingers was quickly becoming one of the most recognizable figures of the early 1970s A's teams as well as one of their key players. With his tall, slender frame, inky black hair and handlebar mustache, Fingers looked like he was cast as an 1800s bartender in a Dodge City saloon. He was 26 years old that fall and like most of their core players had come up through the Oakland system. He struggled to find a niche as a starting pitcher, but proved to have a rubber arm, pitching both as a reliever and a starter through his first few years in the major leagues. In 1971 he established an identity as a reliable fireman, saving 17 games for the division winners, and then solidified that role in 1972 by making all 65 of his appearances in relief while leading the staff with 21 saves. In an era where short relievers were asked to come in and put out fires instead of just closing out games with a lead, Fingers was becoming known as one of the best. He had worked his way out of a first and third and nobody out situation in the ninth inning of game one, allowing no runs, and was being asked to perform a similar Houdini act by Dick Williams now.

With one out and McAuliffe standing on third while representing the potential winning run, Oakland was highly suspicious of the tactics favored by Billy Martin.[17] The A's called for a pitch-out on Fingers' first delivery to the cleanup hitter, Freehan, who took the pitch for ball one. On the next delivery, however, McAuliffe bolted for the plate as Freehan pivoted to bunt. The suicide squeeze attempt went awry when Freehan missed the pitch with his bunt attempt, leaving McAuliffe exiled between third base and home plate, where he was tagged out moments later by the third baseman Bando. The play nearly triggered another riot between the two teams as McAuliffe attempted to knock the ball from Bando's glove on the tag, a tactic he had tried the previous day against Dick Green. This sent Williams into a tirade,

Detroit's Dick McAuliffe is congratulated as he reaches the dugout following a fourth-inning home run in game four of the American League playoff series with Oakland on October 11, 1972. The 13-year veteran had suffered a poor season offensively in 1972, but responded with several key hits during the stretch drive for the division title as well as in the American League Championship Series with the A's. McAuliffe, who was forced to play shortstop over the final four games of the series, went 2-for-4 on the day with two runs scored (AP/Wide World Photos).

who charged the umpiring crew to protest while looking for an obstruction call. With two outs now and Stanley standing off second base, Fingers could concentrate on putting away the batter. Oakland's ace reliever went to his trademark slider, serving up a repeated dose of sidearm and three-quarters deliveries that put Freehan away swinging.

The missed opportunity for Detroit was repeated again in the bottom of the ninth inning. With two outs and nobody on base, Taylor laced his second double of the game but was stranded. The failure to score Taylor and end the game was doubly costly because after Taylor's double, Oakland elected to intentionally walk the number-eight hitter, Rodriguez, bringing up the ninth position in the batting order, which was Lolich. The decision was a tough one for Martin, who faced the dilemma of removing Lolich from the game and possibly having to go to a bullpen that had been less than trustworthy so far in the series. However, the chance to use a pinch-hitter and end the game right then was too tempting to avoid. Martin elected to use Horton as the batter in place of Lolich. Horton flied out to center field to end the inning.

With Lolich off the mound and the game moving to extra innings, the Tigers could ill afford another poor performance from the bullpen. When Lolich tired in game one with an eleventh-inning lead, Chuck Seelbach had been unable to squelch an Oakland rally, resulting in the A's coming from behind for the victory. In game two, a series of Detroit relievers had been ineffective in the middle innings, turning a still-manageable 2–0 deficit into a lopsided defeat. Now Seelbach got the call from the pen and induced Duncan to ground out to Rodriguez to start the tenth inning. Gonzalo Marquez, who delivered the winning hit in game one, then pinch hit in the pitcher's spot and delivered a sharp single to right field. Alou, the leadoff hitter, came to the plate next. The Detroit outfielders, particularly in left field, had been playing Alou very shallow since he liked to flick balls that way with his inside-out swing. He nearly crashed one over Sims' head out in left to start the ball game, but this time he socked Seelbach's first pitch off the wall in straightaway left field, narrowly missing a home run.

As Northrup rounded up the ball below the 365-foot marker and fired it in to McAuliffe at shortstop, Marquez rounded third and headed home. McAuliffe's relay throw from shallow left field easily beat the runner with a perfect one-hopper to Freehan, who was a couple of steps up the third base line. However, as Freehan turned to make the tag, Marquez barreled into the Tiger catcher, jarring the ball loose. As the ball fell free and both players lay sprawled out in the dirt, Marquez crawled the last couple of feet to touch the plate with the lead run.

A deathly quiet fell over the crowd of 37,615. The A's had taken the lead and were threatening to score again, as Alou had advanced to third on the throw to the plate. While Ted Kubiak prepared to bat, Detroit pulled its infield in, trying to choke off any more runs in hopes of having a chance to stay alive in the series in the bottom of the inning. Seelbach, pitching deliberately, fell behind 3–0 in the count, as the Tigers were wary of Oakland trying a suicide squeeze of its own. Finally, on a 3–1 pitch, Kubiak connected on a soft blooper that fell safely behind Taylor, barely onto the outfield grass behind second base. The nubbed hit over the pulled-in infield had increased Oakland's lead to a seemingly insurmountable 3–1 score. As Seelbach and then John Hiller finally got the last two outs of the inning, the cold day and darkened skies only added to the gloom that was besetting the ballpark. The end of the Tigers' season looked to be only minutes away.

Bob Locker took the mound for Oakland to pitch the tenth inning. The 34-year-old veteran reliever was coming off one of his typical seasons. He had appeared in 56 games, sporting a 6–1 record and saving ten games as part of the league's deepest bullpen. He would face the top of the Detroit batting order, needing only to limit the Tigers to one run or less in order to nail down the A's franchise's first pennant in 41 years. The radio broadcast crew for Oakland had already sent a reporter down to the A's clubhouse in anticipation of the post-game celebration.[18] The A's bench players were all up and on the top steps of their dugout along the first base line, ready to race out onto the field.

However, when McAuliffe greeted Locker's first pitch with a line drive single and then Kaline followed with a ground single of his own, one could sense a huge momentum shift taking place. The crowd came alive after McAuliffe's hit, and then followed with a standing ovation for Kaline as he strode to the plate. When Al's grounder bounced into left field, the stadium shook. The atmosphere within the ballpark was electric.

Whether it was because of Locker's ineffectiveness or perhaps an attempt to quiet the crowd and reverse the momentum, Dick Williams made the decision to replace Locker with Joe Horlen. Horlen was a curious choice for the situation. He was a 35-year-old right-hander who had spent ten seasons as a regular in the Chicago White Sox starting rotation. Now on the downside of his career, he had served primarily as a long reliever on Williams' staff, and had only four career saves.

With the right-hander pitching, Martin went to his bench and brought in Gates Brown to pinch-hit for Stanley. Brown removed all doubts as to whether or not he was up there to bunt when he took a vicious swing on Horlen's first pitch, missing it for strike one. After a ball was thrown, Horlen then delivered a pitch in the dirt that eluded Duncan and went all the way to the backstop, moving the runners to second and third with no outs. The stadium was now in an uproar, as what had looked to be an impossible situation just minutes earlier (scoring at least two runs to tie the game) now looked very possible. The count went full before Brown drew the walk from Horlen to load the bases.

Freehan came to the plate with the bases full and the potential tying and winning runs on base. The Tiger catcher had been one of the team's most clutch hitters all season and had hit a big home run the day before, but had struggled in this game. He had popped out in the first inning with Sims in scoring position, and then missed the squeeze bunt, costing Detroit a run in the eighth inning, before striking out and stranding another runner in the same at-bat. He fell behind 1–2 to Horlen before he hit a hard ground ball straight to Sal Bando at third base. Bando had a split-second decision to make as whether to fire the ball to the plate and get the force-out on McAuliffe or to go for the more conventional "round the horn" double play. With the slow-footed Freehan running, he chose the percentage play, which was to go for the twin killing. If executed properly, his team would have sacrificed a run but would have two outs in the inning and still hold a one-run lead.

Bando's throw was perfect, exactly to where the second baseman should receive it. Second base, however, was a position now being occupied by Gene Tenace, the A's backup catcher throughout most of the regular season. With Brown thundering down the path towards the second base bag, looking to deliver whatever physical punishment was possible to prevent the relay throw to first base, Tenace simply dropped the throw from Bando, leaving all of the runners safe.

Tenace's error would become the most notable play of the game, and a point of contention with purists looking to pick apart Dick Williams' managerial decisions. The season-long strategy of rotating through second basemen each game, often pinch-hitting for them at each plate appearance, had finally come back to haunt him. The suspension of Campaneris had left the middle infield situation in even more of a mess for Oakland. Maxvill, Tim Cullen, and Kubiak had already played shortstop in the game, with the first two having been removed for pinch-batters. Dick Green had started at second base but had been pinch-hit for by Duncan in the seventh inning. Since Duncan was the only other catcher on the post-season roster besides Tenace, Williams did not want to risk a situation that left him without a catcher, so he kept Duncan behind the plate and moved Tenace out to second base, a position he had played twice in the major leagues. Williams had gotten away with the same maneuver in game three for a couple of innings, but now it had bitten him at the most crucial time in game four.

The score was now 3–2 in Oakland's favor, but Detroit still had the bases loaded and nobody out. Norm Cash would be the next hitter. Williams went to the bullpen yet again, bringing in his sixth pitcher of the game, rookie

Dave Hamilton. Hamilton had been a part-time starter throughout the season with modest success (6–6 record) in 25 appearances. He had yet to make an appearance in the playoff series, but with Cash and Northrup due as the next two hitters and the Oakland bullpen depleted, Williams was willing to take his chances with the left-handed pitcher.

Hamilton's first pitch missed the strike zone for a ball before he got Cash on two swinging strikes. His fourth pitch missed to make the count 2–2. From there Cash, who had been platooned frequently throughout his career because of perceived difficulties against left-handed pitchers, dug in for one of the most important at-bats in his career. He battled Hamilton by fouling off three consecutive pitches. He took the eighth pitch of the at-bat, which was called a ball by home plate umpire Don Denkinger to the chagrin of Hamilton, Duncan, and everyone else wearing the green and gold uniforms. As Oakland players fumed over a pitch they felt should have resulted in a strikeout of Cash, third baseman Sal Bando gave the choke sign around his neck in an obvious gesture towards Denkinger. With the crowd on its feet creating a din of even higher levels, Hamilton delivered the payoff pitch — a ball high. Cash had walked, forcing in another run. The game was now tied, 3–3.

With pandemonium sweeping the stadium, Northrup stepped up to the plate with Gates Brown standing on third base as the potential winning run and nobody out. The Oakland infield moved in on the grass, ready to make a play at the plate on a ground ball. The outfielders moved in to choke off any short flies or line drives. The first pitch to Northrup was a ball, too high above the strike zone. With the game having all but slipped through his fingertips, Dick Williams went to the mound to try to settle his young pitcher, hoping for a miraculous escape for his flustered team. A game and a series that seemed to be wrapped up fifteen minutes earlier now looked headed for a decisive fifth game.

Williams had no sooner resumed his place on the steps of the first base dugout when Northrup drove the 1–0 pitch by Hamilton into the air towards right-center field, well over the head of the pulled-in Matty Alou. As Northrup's drive landed on the turf in deep right field, the roar of the crowd exploded into jubilant cries that threatened to shatter glass throughout southeastern Michigan. Gates Brown loped in from third base with the winning run, and the Tigers had escaped with an improbable 4–3 come-from-behind victory to even the series at 2–2.

The Tigers poured out of their dugout and mobbed Brown and Northrup. Meanwhile, many in the Tiger Stadium crowd jumped into the celebration by swarming over the walls down each foul line and scaling the screens on the outfield fences. The scene was a repeat from that of eight days earlier when a similar party took place following the division-clinching victory over Boston. The infield grass was soon littered with fans trampling across the recently repaired sod, causing even more damage to the playing field in what had become a disturbing but common custom for fans celebrating a milestone win.

"You'd think they just won it instead of tied it," cried A's radio network broadcaster Jim Woods as he described the scene. "I've never seen such bedlam in my life."[19]

The Detroit clubhouse was understandably exuberant over the dramatic victory but nonetheless relieved to have survived when it appeared their season was about to come to a close.

"I wasn't feeling very good about things," said Mickey Lolich, who was close to seeing his team drop both games he started despite pitching brilliantly in the series. The Tigers' ace had sported a 1.42 ERA over 19 innings in the playoff.[20]

"I felt like I had been in a serious accident, everyone else got killed, and I somehow got out," explained Freehan in an eerily bizarre analogy.[21]

"We've never quit before and there was no reason to think we were going to quit now," said Northrup in a confident tone after he had escaped the mob scene outside and reached the sanctity of the dressing room. "Not even when they got us down two games and then got those two runs in the tenth inning."[22]

"Everyone was making noise when we came off the field," said Kaline about the game-winning rally in the bottom of the tenth inning. "They kept saying 'Let's give 'em a finish.' But I have to admit it didn't look too good.[23]

"I can't remember anything that's ever been this exciting," he said almost in disbelief.

Always able to find humor in a situation, Norm Cash found time to play with the writers surrounding him. "This has to be more exciting than '68. I knew we had 'em all the way ... like hell! I thought it was all over for us."[24]

"All I was trying to do was get the ball into the air," said Northrup of his game-winning hit. "If anything pleased me, it's that I got it off a left-hander. It's been said that I don't do too well against left-handers."[25]

Imparting a sense of bravado towards October games that were yet to be played, Northrup added, "I may get some bigger ones yet this year."[26]

As could be expected in a downtrodden Oakland clubhouse, the media's questions centered on the unconventional decision to use Tenace at second base and the costly error on the potential double-play ball off the bat of Freehan.

"I thought we should have got the sure one," said Dick Williams, perhaps deflecting criticism on the personnel decisions that had been made and instead questioning the judgment used by the fielder on the play. "If we go home, we get the force there."[27]

"We could have got him at home, but I knew I had him (Brown) at second base," explained Bando. "If we have a second baseman, we might have turned two the way Freehan runs. You're talking about a catcher."[28]

"We lost the ballgame, we didn't get beat," said Reggie Jackson, who hadn't yet garnered his "Mr. October" moniker, but was trying to hold together an A's team that appeared ready to fall apart. "I'm down, I'm sad, I'm embarrassed. I want to go into hibernation."[29]

With the series now tied and one game being all that separated his team from a berth in the World Series starting the upcoming weekend, Detroit manager Billy Martin was confident of his team's chances. He especially liked the pitching matchup that would see his team facing an Oakland pitcher in Blue Moon Odom, who was not highly thought of in the Detroit clubhouse despite the three-hit shutout he had twirled at them only four days earlier.

"It will be Woodie Fryman pitching for us, and Mouthy going for them," chided Martin. "We've got all the exits cut off ... he has to go out there and pitch ... there's no way he can escape. He pitched well against us Sunday, but this is a different ballgame. Things are going to be a little tighter out there Thursday."[30]

The excitement in Tiger Stadium could only be matched by what took place in Cincinnati's Riverfront Stadium that day. The darkened skies that threatened play in Detroit did delay the start of the game further south. When they finally were able to play, the Reds and Pirates battled in a one-game, winner-take-all contest for the National League pennant. Pittsburgh grabbed the early lead with a pair of runs in the second inning, added a single run in the fourth, and then rode the solid pitching of their 19-game winner, Steve Blass, who allowed two runs in his seven innings of work. Heading into the bottom of the ninth inning, the defending champions led, 3–2, and needed only three more outs to secure a repeat World Series berth. On the mound was relief ace Dave Giusti, who had saved 22 games during the season and 78 over the past three. The first batter he faced was the Reds' Mr. Everything, Johnny Bench. After getting ahead of Bench in the count, Giusti served up a 1–2 changeup that Bench blasted over the wall in right field for a game-tying home run. Before the exuberance over Bench's home run had subsided, Cincinnati had strung together consecutive singles by Tony Perez and Denis Menke.

Rookie Pirates manager Bill Virdon pulled his normally reliable reliever and replaced him with game two starter Bob Moose, who had failed to record an out in his lone appearance in the series. Cesar Geronimo flew out, but pinch-runner George Foster was able to tag on the play and move up to third base with the potential winning run. Moose got the weak-hitting Darrel Chaney to pop up for the second out, and needed only one more out to force extra innings. Reds manager Sparky Anderson sent up little-used Hal McRae as a pinch-hitter for Cincinnati pitcher Clay Carroll, setting the scene for one of the most dramatic endings in baseball's post-season history.

Moose's pitch to the right-handed-hitting McRae appeared to be a breaking ball thrown at a three-quarters arm angle that bounced in the vicinity of the left-handed hitter's batter's box. Pirates catcher Manny Sanguillen had no chance to stop the pitch, which caromed wildly back to the grandstands behind the plate. McRae excitedly waved his arms to signal Foster, who was already streaking towards the plate. As McRae leaped up in the air with joy, Foster crossed the plate and was engulfed by the red-jacketed players and coaches from an emptied Reds dugout. The Cincinnati Reds had won the National League pennant for the second time in three years and would host Game 1 of the 1972 World Series.

As the Cincinnati players mobbed each other and fans celebrated the dramatic come-from-behind victory and N.L. pennant, they barely noticed a stunned bunch of Pirates walking dejectedly off the artificial turf and into their dugout. Among those players was the great Pittsburgh right fielder, Roberto Clemente. He was only a small part of the overall scene, little noticed at the time, but it was a moment that would hold greater significance in the months ahead.

* * *

Dawn came grudgingly in the city of Detroit on Thursday, October 12. It was a cold, gray, blustery morning with temperatures that had dipped to near freezing during the night. As the skies lightened ever so slowly, a trail of blankets and sleeping bags outside Tiger Stadium began to stir. Heads and bodies emerged from beneath them. Fans that had spent a chilly overnight vigil were at the front of an ever-lengthening line that formed on the sidewalk outside of the ticket booths, ready to snap up the remaining tickets for the deciding game of the American League championship.

The mood in Detroit had brightened considerably, as the hometown team had fought its way back to even the series since returning from Oakland. The Tigers had limped back into town down two games in the series and staring elimination straight in the face. They appeared old and slow, with the doubts that had existed all season coming into full view against the young and vibrant A's team. However, a return to Tiger Stadium, the insertion of Freehan to the lineup, and a couple of timely hits had changed everything. Now Oakland appeared to be the team that was staggered. With only a one-game, winner-take-all match standing between them and a second World Series appearance in four years, the Tigers were looked upon as even bets or better to complete the playoff comeback. "Jimmy the Greek" Snyder made Detroit an 11–10 favorite for the deciding fifth game.[31] The Tigers had all that experience and the comeback from a three games-to-one deficit in the '68 World Series to fall back on. The A's, although superbly talented, were still the unproven team heading into that day.

Another thing the A's wouldn't have that day was the first-hand support of their suspended shortstop, Bert Campaneris. The Oakland leadoff hitter had returned to Detroit for game five, hoping to be able to sit on the A's bench and at minimum lend moral support. Joe Cronin, who ruled that the suspended player would not be allowed to be in the dugout, quickly rejected that notion. Campaneris then planned on sitting in a box seat accompanied by A's owner Charlie Finley just to the left of the Oakland dugout. The judgment of that idea was brought into question when it was pointed out that Campaneris' safety could be jeopardized while sitting out in the open among the Detroit throng. Instead, it was decided that he would watch the game on television from the comfort of the Oakland clubhouse.[32]

A couple of things became apparent very early as the crowd of 50,276 settled in to their seats. One, the weather was going to play a huge factor in the game, likely keeping it a low-scoring affair. Besides the cold, which made it difficult for hitters to be aggressive at the plate, the wind was blowing straight in over the left-field roof, making it unlikely many balls would reach the seats that day. Secondly, Tiger starter Woodie Fryman was going to be a very different pitcher than what he had been in his game two start in Oakland. He set down the A's in order in the first inning, displaying much better stuff than he had in the earlier game.

In Detroit's half of the first inning, McAuliffe led off with a single into right field, much to the delight of a raucous crowd. Oakland starter Blue Moon Odom managed to strike out Kaline, but was becoming more distracted by the runner at first base. The bold antics of McAuliffe, who hadn't stolen a base all season, served their purpose as Sims drew a walk to put two runners on base. Odom then fell behind the cleanup hitter, Freehan, 1–0, before uncorking a pitch that bounced away from the catcher Tenace for a passed ball. With runners on second and third and only one out, Detroit clearly had the A's starter on the ropes. The game was following the script envisioned by Martin, who didn't believe that Odom would hold up under the pressure of such a big game. Odom, however, got Freehan to ground to shortstop, which scored a run, and then Cash to fly out to right field to end the inning. The Tigers had scored a run but failed to deliver the early knockout blow they were looking for.

The lead was short lived as Oakland came back in the second inning to tie the game without the benefit of a hit. Jackson led off the frame and walked on four pitches. With Bando batting, Jackson stole second base easily before moving to third on a fly out to deep right. Epstein was the next hitter and in a hole with a 1–2 count when Fryman tried to jam him with an inside fastball. The ball clipped Epstein on the right hand, putting A's runners on the corners. Fryman got Tenace on strikes for the second out, and it appeared Detroit might get out of the inning and preserve the lead. Coming to the plate was one of the A's light-hitting second basemen, Dick Green. It was a situation that invited a pinch-hitter and the start of the merry-go-round at second base that had so often been the norm for Oakland. Instead, Dick Williams decided to be daring and sent Epstein running on a 1–1 pitch on the first leg of a double steal. Freehan came up throwing, but the ball seemed to float towards second base, where Taylor cut in front of the bag and made a relay to the plate in an attempt to cut down the streaking Jackson, who was trying to score. The ball arrived chest high to Freehan, who was unable to get the glove down in time to tag out the sliding runner. Jackson and Freehan, both of whom were very large athletes for early '70s baseball at over 200 pounds each, went down in a heap, with Jackson writhing in pain at the conclusion of the play. Oakland's center fielder and all-around best player had severely torn a hamstring muscle and would have to be helped off the field.

Both teams moved runners into scoring position in their next at-bat, but each pitcher continued to show signs of nerves. Odom threw a wild pitch in the Detroit second inning, while Fryman committed a balk in the Oakland third. Neither team was able to push a run across, however, and the game remained tied at 1–1 heading into the fourth inning. There, a play occurred that would be little noted on the national scale but would provide a point of controversy for Tiger players and fans to fume over for decades to come.

George Hendrick, a tall, slender athlete who would go on to stardom in the National League as part of a career that lasted well into the 1980s, had taken over for Jackson in center field, and led off the inning for Oakland. Hendrick hit a ground ball to deep shortstop, a routine play for most major leaguers at the position, but one that McAuliffe needed to hurry on. His throw came in low to first base, but still beat the fleet-footed Hendrick by a step-and-a-half. The first baseman Cash, reaching out to make the play before the ball hit the dirt, appeared to pull his toe off the bag ever so slightly. As the Detroit first baseman went to whip the ball around the infield as part of the game's custom with nobody on base, base umpire John Rice emphatically signaled that the runner was safe.

The call infuriated the Detroit team, particularly Cash, Freehan, and Martin, who had bolted from the dugout. The feeling was that the play was routine enough that the couple of inches that Cash might have gained while pulling his foot had no effect on the outcome. In a game and series that was quickly growing short, where runs were precious and tempers had flared easily, the leadoff runner reaching base on such an innocent play was a dangerous omen.

Williams, playing for any run he could muster, had right-handed-hitting strong-man Bando bunt Hendrick over to second base. Epstein struck out to make two outs, but then Tenace lined a sharp single to left field that was fielded on one hop by Duke Sims, who was playing out for the second consecutive day. The A's third base coach, Irv Noren, didn't hesitate while sending the runner around third, challenging the Tiger catcher-turned-outfielder's throwing arm. Sims seemed to get handcuffed by the ball when he fielded it and was unable to get the ball off quickly. The throw was on target, however, and the ball arrived at the plate at the same time as Hendrick. For the third time in less than 24 hours, Freehan was involved in a close play at home plate with an Oakland runner. For the third time the runner was safe. Hendrick slid in safely, as the ball popped loose from Freehan's glove. The A's had gone ahead, 2–1.

From that point forward, the game turned into a race against time for the Tigers. The outs were ticking down like sand trickling through an hourglass, and Detroit hitters struggled to mount any type of rally. Sixteen straight batters went down at one point against Oakland pitching as the game headed towards its conclusion. Fryman, meanwhile, was putting up a gutsy performance, keeping his team within one run while snuffing out Oakland scoring opportunities in the fifth and seventh innings. In the sixth, Williams went to his bullpen, calling on the disgruntled reigning Cy Young and Most Valuable Player Award winner, Vida Blue. He took over for Odom, who had found his rhythm and battled through the first five innings, giving up only the one first-inning run.

It was Blue, however, who was taking the air out of Detroit's balloon. He had been relegated to the bullpen for the playoff series, a move that didn't agree with the moody 23-year-old who had taken the baseball world by storm the previous season. Blue had been used in three games previously in the series, mostly as a situational left-handed pitcher, and had been very effective each time. Now with the season on the line, he pitched with a fury seemingly born from the frustration of a season that had been polar-opposite from what he had enjoyed in 1971.

Blue set the Tigers down meekly in the sixth, and then struck out the side in the seventh outside of an infield single by Northrup. His fastball was as explosive as it had been all season and his breaking ball was sharp. Detroit hitters were overmatched, unable to get good swings against the Oakland flamethrower. In the eighth inning a flicker of hope appeared when Horton led off in a pinch-hitting role for Fryman and delivered a single into right-center field. McAuliffe then tried to bunt the tying run into scoring position, but Blue showing his superior athleticism, pounced on the ball and fired it to second base to get the force on pinch-runner John Knox. The A's left-hander then deflated the boisterous Tiger Stadium crowd by getting Detroit's most dangerous hitters, Kaline and Sims, on weak pop-ups on the infield. A promising inning had ended.

With only three outs standing between their Tiger heroes and the end of the 1972 baseball season, the fans tried to awaken whatever magic might still exist for a team that had been counted out so many times. When John Hiller set down Oakland in the top of the ninth, the crowd rose to its feet and created a din that shook the stadium. Freehan, Cash, and Northrup were the scheduled batters in the bottom of the ninth inning, and after the previous day's miracle in the bottom of the tenth inning, a comeback from a one-run deficit was certainly possible.

Blue remained on the mound for Oakland, although Williams had his ace reliever, Fingers, warming up in the bullpen, along with the left-handed Ken Holtzman. The first batter, Freehan, fell behind in the count before fouling out to Epstein in front of the A's dugout. One out. Cash was the next batter and delivered a line-drive single into center field. There was still hope. Mickey Stanley came in to pinch-hit for Northrup, as Martin played the right-handed bat against Blue. Stanley hit a ground ball to deep shortstop that Maxvill flipped to Dick Green, who nearly completed the game- and series-ending double play. Stanley just barely managed to beat the relay throw to first base.

With the Tigers down to their last out, the finality of the situation began to sink in for the fifty thousand disappointed partisans, many of which were determined not to go down peacefully. The crowd had been surly all day. The first-inning run scored by McAuliffe was celebrated with a barrage of toilet paper that streamed from the bleachers and across the sky before littering the grass in deep center field. Once Detroit fell behind and the futility of the Tiger efforts against Oakland pitching continued inning after inning, the scene turned ugly. Toilet paper was replaced by firecrackers, smoke bombs, paper cups, ice, and flying discs as the projectiles of choice. Most of it was targeted at A's players standing in the field below the upper-deck bleachers. Anything that could be propelled from the upper-deck stands that might cause a disruption in the disappointing turn of events on the field was sent flying onto the turf. The game was halted repeatedly to allow the grounds crew to pick up the litter in the outfield. The reward for their efforts was to be bombarded even more.

With the Oakland team sensing the elusive victory was within its grasp, the Tiger Stadium crowd reared its ugly head one more time. An overly fueled fan jumped over the fence in the outfield and ran towards the diamond before sliding into second base. Before the Detroit police could cart him off the field, a number of followers made their way onto the field and provided a comical diversion as they tried to elude the billy-clubbed officers. In a day and age when law enforcement was given derogatory names like "fuzz" or "pigs," their forceful arrests of the trespassers were greeted with boos and an even greater barrage of garbage being thrown on the field. Police would arrest or issue tickets to 114 fans during the afternoon.[33]

The frustration was no less for the men in the home white uniforms. The Detroit dugout was filled with anguish-filled faces, agonizing over having come so far, but seemingly falling short. In the Tiger clubhouse the television set reflected the same story. Frank Howard, who had been allowed to serve as the first base coach in the place of Dick Tracewski, had been ejected from the game in the fourth inning after picking up the argument with umpire John Rice about the contested call with Cash pulling his foot. Now he watched from the clubhouse as the remaining outs dwindled until he wasn't able to take it any longer and started hurling stools against lockers while screaming at the television.[34]

Tony Taylor represented Detroit's final hope at the plate. Mickey Stanley, being held closely at first base, represented the tying run. Taylor battled Blue to a 2–2 count and then fouled off several pitches. Finally he connected and drove the ball into center field. The ball was well struck, but would come down well within the range of the lanky Hendrick, who loped back and settled under the drive. He made the catch for the third out. It was 3:28 P.M. and the Detroit Tigers' season had come to an end. The Oakland A's were the American League champions.

As the Oakland players mobbed each other, they were greeted mainly by silence, punctuated only by distant booing. They were soon chased off the field by mobs of fans that had crawled over the walls and tore down the lower center field fence. For the second day in a row, and the third time in a little over a week, the stadium and grounds would fall prey to a destructive band of rogues, only this time they didn't have a celebration to excuse their mischief.

The Detroit players, frustrated and angry, trudged into the clubhouse for the final time of the season. Martin, livid at the situation, ordered the clubhouse cleared of all media and outsiders, as he wanted some time with his team to deal with the demons that accompany such a hard-fought loss. As the clubhouse doors were closing, Martin could be overheard shouting to his players, "I'm proud of every one of you guys. Every one of you'se [*sic*]."[35]

* * *

"We worked hard all year, but came up a little short," Martin surmised once the doors had opened up to reporters in an understandably dejected Tiger dressing room.[36] An interview platform stood quietly in the room, with a big network television camera sitting dark next to it. Cases of champagne were stacked but remained closed. When asked if that was his toughest defeat as a manager, he replied, "That would be an understatement."[37]

"We weren't embarrassed," said Al Kaline defiantly about the battle he and his teammates had given. "In the last three, four weeks of the season, we never gave up."[38]

What Detroit hadn't done was play well enough to win. The Tigers batted only .198 as a team in the series, and scored a scant ten runs over the five games. Four of the runs came on solo home runs. If not for wild streaks by Holtzman in game three, and the Oakland bullpen in the tenth inning of game four, Detroit's offense would have been even more anemic. The pitching had been hot and cold. Lolich was superb in two series starts that are often overlooked on his career resume. He had the poor fortune of not getting a win in the playoff series despite pitching extremely well in both starts, wins that could have cemented his status as one of the great post-season pitchers in baseball history. Coleman was brilliant in game three, the only post-season game of his career. Fryman, plagued by a bad elbow in game two, rebounded to pitch a solid four-hitter over eight innings in game five, but ended up with two of the series losses. The bullpen faltered when it was needed most, after being solid for most of the regular season.

A scene that Tiger fans had difficulty watching: Oakland catcher Gene Tenace and pitcher Vida Blue embrace in celebration, as the A's finish off Detroit in a climactic and tightly contested game five, 2–1. Oakland took the bitterly fought series, three games to two, and advanced to play Cincinnati in the 1972 World Series (AP/Wide World Photos).

In retrospect, however, it was the play in the field that was the team's undoing against Oakland. The Tigers' play was never as sharp, never as mistake-free as it had been during a near-record-setting regular season that saw them commit the second-fewest errors in major league history. The bad-luck bounce on the throw to third in game one that skipped past Rodriguez and allowed the winning run to score was the first of several misplays that would haunt the Tigers in the series. Detroit committed seven errors in the series and probably just as many miscues that weren't ruled as errors but proved just as costly.

In the final loss, two players who had been forced to play out of position were at the center of the defensive failures. Without their glue-man, Eddie Brinkman, at shortstop, McAuliffe was forced to play the position for the final four games, a move that weakened the team at both of the keystone spots. McAuliffe struggled on several long throws from the hole in the series, and one can only assume that the controversial call at first base with Hendrick running might have been a non-issue if Brinkman had been able to make the throw. Instead, the eventual winning run reached base, and Detroit's players put the blame on the call by the umpire, chiding it as ticky-tack or bush league.

"We had him beat by a step and a half," said Cash after the game, referring to Hendrick crossing the bag. "That one wasn't close and we lose the game on a little ol' technicality."[39]

"The umpire knew he blew the play," agreed Howard of the decision by John Rice.[40]

Later in that fourth inning, with two outs and Hendrick at second base, Tenace's single — his only hit of the entire series — might not have scored the runner with the decisive run except for the time it took Sims out in left field to get the ball out of his glove, rear back, and fire towards home plate. A true outfielder playing his natural position might have prevented the run from scoring.

"I thought I could field the ball on the hop, about eye high," explained Sims. "But it skipped on me and I got it at my waist. I had to take the extra time to bring the ball up so I could throw it. Then the throw carried on me more than I thought it would and Bill (Freehan) had to come up to get the throw. I made it tough on him."[41]

"Nobody on our team has got a stronger arm than Duke Sims — nobody who can play left field," said Martin, deflecting any criticism that may have been leveled at his judgment in using a catcher in the outfield in such a crucial situation.[42]

Overall, the tone in the locker room seemed to be reasonably even keel. Some of the players sipped on beer, while a few took solace in the trainer's room, which was off limits to media. They had battled the A's in a hard-fought series filled with hotly contested games, several of which were decided in dramatic fashion. In the end, Oakland found ways to manufacture a run or two, while Detroit's lack of speed had reduced the Tigers to an over-dependence on the long ball. The lights-out pitching of Odom and particularly Blue late was more than they could overcome.

"Vida Blue had good stuff," said Fryman, tipping his hat to the opposition. "They've got a good club and I wish 'em well in Cincinnati."[43]

In the Oakland clubhouse the mood was understandably more upbeat, yet a feeling of relief permeated the room as much as any display of excess exuberance. After climbing steadily in the standings, from a second-division club in Kansas City to a division winner four years later, and having lost in the playoffs in a decisive manner the previous season against the Orioles, the A's knew they had survived against a proud, veteran team that had scrapped with all its might when cornered.

"This was our greatest victory, and it followed our worst loss," said manager Dick Williams, savoring the first American League pennant for the A's franchise since 1931. "It shows what kind of club we are."[44]

For catcher Gene Tenace, whose error on the dropped play at second the previous day had opened the gates for a Detroit victory and cast doubts as to whether the Oakland team would be able to close out the Tigers, vindication came in the form of his game-winning single. "I didn't sleep hardly at all Wednesday night. All I kept thinking about was that 10th inning Wednesday."[45]

All was not happy, though, as the A's dressed and prepared to travel to Cincinnati for the opening of the World Series that was slated to begin in less than 48 hours. Their star slugger, Reggie Jackson, was on crutches in the locker room and looked unlikely to be ready for the opening of the Fall Classic. Elsewhere, the actions of the day's star, Vida Blue, was casting a cloud over what should have been the sunniest moment in the team's young history in Oakland.

"I'm still sour," he said, ready to tell his story to anybody who would listen in the crowded clubhouse. "It doesn't really make up for anything. I just had a golden opportunity to do a job and stand out."[46]

Blue used the opportunity to re-visit the bitter negotiations that had taken place earlier in the spring and the unsatisfactory terms he had been forced to agree to with owner Charlie Finley. The two shared a brief, cold handshake as the otherwise jubilant A's owner paraded about the victorious locker room.

"I got a bum deal in my contract negotiations," Blue said. "I had a bad year but I'm a little happier now. I got a golden chance today and I came through. I respect him (Finley) and I want him to respect me.[47]

"I'm glad to be in the World Series. Let contract negotiations start again."[48]

With a dominant performance in a clutch situation under his belt, Blue used the forum to complain about the uncertain role Williams had relegated him to in the postseason.

"I'm disappointed because I didn't get a chance to start a playoff game. I just wanted to know whether I was going to start, but he (Williams) never told me anything."[49]

Even more bizarre were Blue's comments concerning his supposed best friend on the squad, Odom. The Oakland starting pitcher had obviously suffered through a severe case of nerves at the game's outset before settling down after the first couple of innings. However, the nervous feeling returned, and he complained to Williams following the fifth inning about the difficulty he was having breathing, and that he was also battling nausea. That prompted Williams' switch to Blue, who ended up pitching the final four innings and recorded the save.

"Hey man, why didn't you go nine?" chided Blue towards Odom in front of reporters. After a pause for effect, he then lifted his hand up to his neck, insinuating choking and said, "I know why."[50]

The accusation infuriated Odom, who charged Blue, only to be intercepted by Rudi and others. The scuffle was short-lived, never came to blows, and was quickly smoothed over. However, it was oddly placed in the dressing room of a young team that had just won its first pennant. It certainly wouldn't be the last bit of infighting for a talented group of athletes that would be known in subsequent years for arguing and fighting among themselves, as well as against their celebrated owner, Charles Finley. For the Oakland A's team that boarded the bus outside a quieted Tiger Stadium on a dark and dreary day, the thirty-minute ride to the airport did not appear as if it would be an entirely contented trip. However, they could bask in the accomplishment of the day and look forward to a World Series date with Cincinnati. They might have been disgruntled champions, but they were champions nonetheless.

XII

Extra Innings

The Oakland A's went on to win the 1972 world championship, defeating the Cincinnati Reds in a memorable World Series that saw six of the seven games decided by a single run. The matchup had been playfully dubbed the "Hairs against the Squares," alluding to the contrast between the mustachio-laden "Swinging" A's, and Reds manager Sparky Anderson's clean-cut and straight-laced crew. Gene Tenace, whose only hit in a 1-for-17 performance in the A.L. playoffs against Detroit had driven in the series-winning run, was the World Series hero and named MVP, hitting four home runs and driving in nine Oakland runs. The Series victory was the first of three straight world championships for the A's, baseball's greatest streak since the legendary Yankee teams of the early 1950s. By the time their run ended after a playoff loss to Boston in 1975, the Oakland squad from the early 1970s would be recognized as one of the sport's true dynasties, made up of some of the most talented, colorful, and outspoken players of the second half of the twentieth century.

Reggie Jackson, who wouldn't begin to establish his "Mr. October" persona until the next season's Fall Classic, was unable to play at all in the '72 Series, having severely torn muscles in his left leg while also stretching knee ligaments in the home plate collision with Bill Freehan in Game 5 of the playoffs. Over the next decade and a half, however, Jackson would cement his place in history as one of baseball's all-time big-game players, as well as being arguably the biggest personality in the major leagues over that period.

Campy Campaneris was allowed to play in the World Series by commissioner Bowie Kuhn, although he was still forced to serve a suspension without pay for the first seven games of the 1973 regular season as part of his punishment for the bat-throwing incident against Detroit. Campaneris played all seven games of the 1972 Series against Cincinnati, batting in his customary leadoff slot and playing his usual steady game at shortstop. Throughout the remainder of his career, he would be booed heavily each time he stepped to the plate at Tiger Stadium, a villain forever in the eyes of Tiger fans.

Vida Blue went 0–1 while appearing in four games during the '72 World Series, including one start. He returned to the 20-win plateau in 1973, going 20–9, and won 22 games in 1975 as part of a solid career as an upper-echelon pitcher for the A's, and then later across the bay for the San Francisco Giants. He won nearly 200 games in his career, but never again approached the levels reached during his astonishing 1971 breakout season, which saw him win 24 games with a sub–2.00 ERA and more than 300 strikeouts.

Dick Williams managed the A's to the World Series title again in 1973, but then resigned abruptly, tired of working for the meddling Charles O. Finley. In his three-year term as skipper of the Oakland franchise, Williams' teams won three division titles, averaged more than 96 wins per season, and captured the two world championships. He continued to manage for many more years, including 1984 when his San Diego Padres team faced Detroit in that season's World Series. He was elected to the Baseball Hall of Fame as a manager in 2007.

* * *

Sixteen days after Oakland wrapped up its World Series victory, Richard Nixon was re-elected as president of the United States in a landslide decision over the Democratic nominee, George McGovern. Unimaginable at the time was the prospect of Nixon being forced from office less than two years later, brought down by the seemingly petty break-in and subsequent coverup of the Democratic National Committee's headquarters in the Watergate complex. That curious story first appeared in newspapers in the early summer of 1972 and gained momentum throughout the fall and into the spring of 1973. Over the next twenty-six months, its threads were traced upwards to the highest offices in the executive branch of the government, and a presidency was ultimately toppled.

An end to the Vietnam War, much too late for some and with an unsatisfactory conclusion for others, played out uncomfortably in the months after the 1972 baseball season ended. A cease-fire existed through much of that fall, as peace talks took place between the United States and the North Vietnamese and South Vietnamese governments. A settlement appeared to be in place before the North Vietnamese backed out, triggering eleven days of a massive U.S. air campaign known as the "Christmas bombings" in mid–December. By late January 1973, a peace agreement had been reached as President Nixon declared "peace with honor" to appease his war-weary country. A few months later the last of the United States' troops were removed from Vietnam. Peace would prove elusive in the Southeastern Asian countries, however. Just over a year later, the North Vietnamese were again massing troops with the inevitable invasion of their southern neighboring country a foregone conclusion. On April 30, 1975, the last marines were evacuated from the U.S.

Embassy in Saigon, just hours before the Communist-based North Vietnamese army took over the country.[1]

Hate and violence continued in the wake of the murders of the Israeli athletes at the Olympic Games in Munich. The bodies of the five Palestinian terrorists, who were killed during the failed rescue attempt, were treated to hero's burials upon their return to Libya, much to the dismay of the people of Israel as well as much of the western world. Making matters worse, on October 28, a German Lufthansa passenger flight was hijacked, with the perpetrators demanding, and getting, the release of the three surviving terrorists who had been captured from the Arab group known as "Black September." The Israelis sought revenge through a clandestine operation known as "Wrath of God," which allegedly carried out a series of targeted assassinations over a 20-year period of the planners and financiers of the Olympic terrorist group. The botched handling of the rescue attempt and the subsequent release of the prisoners to the hijackers brought heavy criticism to the West German authorities that were ill prepared to prevent and combat such acts. The horrors of the XX Olympiad became a primary impetus in nations forming sophisticated anti-terrorist units and the development of the type of security that exists with such events today.

In December, the first night time launch took place of a manned flight, and the crew of Apollo 17 headed to the moon for the sixth and final journey of that historic NASA program. Geologist Jack Schmitt became the first scientist to travel in space, and on December 14, after a largely successful mission consisting of three lunar surface excursions, and the collection of over 200 pounds of rocks, commander Eugene Cernan walked up the steps of the lunar module, the last man of the twentieth century to walk on the surface of the moon.[2]

As the fall months of 1972 unfolded, many sports fans cast their attention to the accomplishments of the Miami Dolphins, who were in the process of completing the first undefeated season in NFL history. Overcoming a difficult early-season road schedule and the loss to injury for much of the season of their star quarterback, Bob Griese, the Dolphins leaned on a powerful ground attack and a stifling defense to pull off the monumental task, which was capped off in January 1973, by their 14–7 victory over the Washington Redskins in Super Bowl VII.

* * *

When the post-season awards were handed out for the 1972 season, some of the game's biggest names were honored. Johnny Bench of Cincinnati won the National League Most Valuable Player award. The Reds catcher hit 40 home runs and drove in 125 runs, both major league-leading figures, while continuing to be arguably the greatest defensive presence in either league.

Dick Allen, the much-traveled superstar with the malcontent reputation, had turned on White Sox's fans with his near-Triple Crown performance, hitting .307 with 37 homers and 113 RBIs. Those types of numbers earned him the A.L. MVP award in a landslide vote, taking 21 of the 24 first-place votes cast by the Baseball Writers Association of America.[3]

Steve Carlton, in his first season with the Philadelphia Phillies, put together an amazing 27–10 record with a sparkling 1.98 ERA and 310 strikeouts to run away with the N.L. Cy Young Award. Included that season was a personal 15-game winning streak. What was most astounding about Carlton's record, however, was the fact that he earned 27 victories for a miserable team that won a total of only 59 games all season. Another veteran playing his first season for a new team, Gaylord Perry of Cleveland, won the American League Cy Young Award. Perry edged out Wilbur Wood and Mickey Lolich in a tight decision. Perry started 40 games for Cleveland, finished 29 of them, and put together a 24–16 record with a 1.92 ERA in the hitting-challenged American League of 1972.

The Rookies of the Year were the New York Mets' Jon Matlack, a sharp, left-handed pitcher who won 15 games that season, and Boston's Carlton Fisk, the fine-hitting catcher who was a unanimous A.L. selection. Manager of the Year awards were handed out to Sparky Anderson in the National League and Chuck Tanner, the Chicago White Sox manager, in the American League.

The N.L. batting title went to the Chicago Cubs remarkable left fielder, Billy Williams. The sweet-swinging Williams hit .333 in one of his greatest seasons, finishing second in the MVP voting to Bench, while picking up *The Sporting News* Player of the Year award. He hit 37 home runs, drove in 122 runs, and led the majors with a .606 slugging percentage. Atlanta's Ralph Garr (.325) and Dusty Baker (.321), along with Houston's Cesar Cedeno (.320) and Bob Watson (.312) rounded out the top five batters in the senior circuit. The Padres' Nate Colbert (38 HRs, 111 RBIs) finished second in the home run derby and third in RBIs.

Met superstar Tom Seaver (21), Chicago's Ferguson Jenkins (20), and Los Angeles' Claude Osteen (20) were the only other twenty-game winners in the National League outside of Carlton.

Rod Carew of the Twins won the American League batting title, hitting .318. The batting crown was the second of the future Hall of Famer's career, and the first of four straight and six overall he would win during the 1970s. Kansas City's Lou Piniella hit .312 to place second in the league. Chicago's Dick Allen and Carlos May each hit .308, and the A's Joe Rudi hit .305. Allen led the league in homers and RBIs, outdistancing the Yankees' Bobby Murcer (33) as the only A.L. sluggers topping the thirty mark in round-trippers, while KC's John Mayberry (100) was the only other player to hit the century mark in runs batted in.

Gaylord Perry and the White Sox's Wilbur Wood topped A.L. pitchers in wins with 24 each. Lolich was next with 22, followed by Catfish Hunter, Oriole Jim Palmer, and Chicago's Stan Bahnsen (21 each). Luis Tiant of the Red Sox capped his great comeback season by taking the ERA title (1.91) over Perry (1.92). California's Nolan Ryan struck out 329 batters to easily take that title over Lolich (250) and Perry (234). Joe Coleman finished fifth with 222 whiffs. Collectively, American League pitchers enjoyed a banner year, and the list of notable accomplishments and outstanding seasons by individuals extended well beyond the leaders in the various categories.

More than one thousand fewer runs were scored in the American League in 1972 compared to the previous season.[4] The total was also nearly 800 fewer than what was scored in the National League. The A.L.'s combined ERA of 3.07 was lower by nearly half a run from the National League. That figure was also down nearly three-quarters of a run from 1970, and was approaching the miniscule 1968 "Year of the Pitcher" figure of 2.98. The league batting average was a dismal .239, with home runs also down from preceding seasons and lagging well behind the senior circuit. Those numbers helped cement the notion that despite the World Series crown going to an American League team in the A's, the National League was the superior league, and certainly the more exciting league. They hit more home runs, stole more bases. They had the most exciting players, and played a more aggressive and entertaining game. That thought was supported at the box offices around the leagues, as only three of the twelve A.L. clubs drew even a million customers in 1972, while nine of the twelve N.L. franchises reached that milestone figure. Nothing was more embarrassing to the A.L. than seeing its flagship franchise, the New York Yankees, finish under the one million mark in paid attendance for the first time since World War II, while its cross-town counterpart, the New York Mets, finished with a major league high of more than 2.1 million in home attendance. Overall, eight A.L. teams showed a decrease in attendance from the previous season.[5]

To combat fan apathy that management attributed to decreasing offense in the sport, the American League's owners voted in early December for radical change and incorporated the use of a "designated pinch hitter" (or "DH" as the position would become commonly known as) in the place of the pitcher's slot in the batting lineup. The experimental rule would go into effect for the 1973 season, and would further divide the styles of the two leagues, as the N.L. decided against the change. "We like the game the way it is," explained N.L. president Charles (Chub) Feeney.[6] The Detroit organization, staying true to its conservative views towards any type of change in the game, voted vehemently against the rule change until recognizing they would be out-voted by their A.L. peers, rescinded their position in order to make the passing unanimous.

Every season a batch of talented newcomers are introduced to the major leagues, while some old familiar names are either finally forced out of the game, or in the case of the lucky few, they get to walk away on their own terms. The 1972 season was no exception as two future Hall of Fame players, Mike Schmidt of the Philadelphia Phillies and Rich "Goose" Gossage for the Chicago White Sox, made their major league debuts. Other rookies getting their first exposure at the major league level prior to playing meaningful roles in future years included Buddy Bell, Bob Boone, Al Bumbry, Dwight Evans, Johnny Grubb, Davey Lopes, Lee Lacy, Garry Maddox, Gary Mathews, Doc Medich, Charlie Spikes, Dick Tidrow, and Steve Yeager. Likewise, some well-known and well-accomplished names played their last games in a big league uniform that season. Among them was Bill Mazeroski of the Pittsburgh Pirates, regarded by some as the greatest fielding second baseman in the game's history up to that point and the man who hit arguably the most famous home run in World Series history with his dramatic winning blow in the bottom of the ninth inning of Game 7 of the 1960 Series against New York; Maury Wills, the base-stealer extraordinaire who served as the offensive catalyst for the great pitching-heavy Dodger teams of the 1960s; Hoyt Wilhelm, the knuckleball specialist who pitched more than 1,000 games in relief over his 21-year career; and Wes Parker, the stylish, smooth-fielding and clutch-hitting first baseman for the Dodgers. Other notable names winding up careers that season included Phil Regan, Moe Drabowsky, Donn Clendenon, and Ted Uhlaender.[7]

On September 12, 1972, one other notable player made his last appearance in a major league regular-season game. The Cincinnati Reds were in Atlanta that evening, and the score was tied at four heading into the top of the ninth inning. Braves manager Eddie Mathews pinch-hit for his pitcher in the bottom of the eighth and called on Denny McLain to come on to pitch in the ninth inning. McLain had fared no better with Atlanta than he had in Oakland earlier in the season, nor from what he had done in Washington the previous season. Since his much-ballyhooed National League debut in early July, McLain had scuttled his way to an unremarkable 3–4 record with an unsightly ERA while continuing to suffer from arm miseries. Cesar Geronimo was the first Reds batter he faced that evening. Geronimo blasted McLain's first pitch over the right field wall, giving the Reds a 5–4 lead. Joe Hague followed with a pinch-hit single, and then leadoff man Pete Rose singled to center field, putting two men on base. Mathews had seen enough and quickly called for a new pitcher. McLain had nothing left. He had given up three hits on four pitches. Both of the runners he left on base ended up scoring, and McLain was tagged with the loss.

He wouldn't pitch again that season, finishing with a combined 4–7 record between Oakland and Atlanta with an overall ERA of 6.37. McLain tried again in spring training that next season, but was released by the Braves near the end of camp. Unable to hook on with another big league squad, he tried to resurrect his career in the minor leagues later that summer. The magic in his one-time golden arm was gone, however, and Triple-A batters were feasting on his deliveries just as eagerly as big league hitters had for the past three seasons. The former 31-game winner had pitched his last big league contest at age 28.[8]

Three other baseball personalities, all giants of the game, were taken away that year under tragic circumstances. Gil Hodges, the long-time slugging first baseman for the great Brooklyn Dodger teams of the 1950s and later the manager of the "Miracle" New York Mets, died suddenly of a heart attack on April 2. Hodges had run his New York team through the paces in spring training that year but was stricken just three days into the player walkout while playing golf. His death came just days short of his 48th birthday. Later that year his former teammate, Jackie Robinson, the pioneer who braved unthinkable indignities and abuse in order to become the first black player in the major leagues, passed away on October 24, less than two weeks after throwing out the first pitch of Game 2 of the World Series. Robinson had been suffering from diabetes and heart disease, and his health had deteriorated dramatically in the years leading up to his death at the relatively young age of 53. The ground-breaking accomplishments of Robinson would grow in stature over the years following his death, and today his jersey number 42 is forever retired by all major league teams as a symbol of his impact on the sport and his race.

However, the blow that most shook the baseball world that year wouldn't come until the last day of 1972. On December 23, a massive earthquake struck Nicaragua, leaving a wake of death and destruction in the impoverished country. Roberto Clemente, generally recognized as the greatest Latin player in history and an activist in bettering the lives of people — especially children — from that region of the world, organized a shipment of relief supplies in his home country of Puerto Rico for the emergency effort. Wary of possible corruption in the handling and distribution of the relief supplies once they reached Nicaragua, Clemente decided to accompany the shipment to the disaster-stricken country. An overloaded and under-maintained DC-7 cargo plane, with Clemente aboard, crashed into the sea just moments after its takeoff from San Juan. Clemente's death spurred a swell of posthumous appreciation for a four-time N.L. batting champion, 12-time All-Star, 13-time Gold Glove winner, and MVP of the 1966 National League season and the 1971 World Series. Larger yet was a newfound appreciation of the man and what he represented to the sport, his country, and the human race with his many humanitarian activities. Today, the Roberto Clemente Award is given annually in recognition of the current player who best reflects the contributable and humanitarian qualities of the former Pirates star, and is one of the most esteemed awards in baseball.[9]

Clemente's death on New Year's Eve in 1972 was the final event of a calamitous year in the world of major league baseball. Although the season itself— the games on the field, the events, the numbers posted — would largely slide into history with little note given, the ramifications from that season would echo well into the succeeding decades and the new century.

The hard-fought and bitterly contested playoff series in both the American and National leagues were classics, the first of their kind, and permanently validated a round of post-season play that had previously been viewed as artificial and unnecessary. Today, there is an additional divisional playoff round, ahead of the League Championship Series, and with the exception of a diminishing number of staunch traditionalists, playoff baseball is an accepted part of the sport. Many of the most memorable moments in post-season play over the past 40 years are now associated with playoff games, and not the exclusive hold of the World Series. Additionally, races for division crowns and even wild card slots are viewed in much the same way as pennant chases were during the first six decades of the twentieth century. The wild four-team scramble for the 1972 East Division crown was an early example of those mini-races that have replaced the larger-scale league races that existed previously.

The experimental designated hitter rule, instituted initially on a three-year trial basis by the American League, proved to be successful in increasing offense and was soon an accepted part of baseball in the junior circuit. Initially the position provided a haven for aging stars, such as Kaline, Tony Oliva, Orlando Cepeda, Tommy Davis, and others, who got at-bats in the place of what had been fly-swatting pitchers. Within a matter of years the rule had trickled down to the minor leagues and even amateur baseball. The position evolved to include not only older sluggers but contact hitters and speedsters as well, and players that aren't especially adept with a glove but that have lightning in their bats are sometimes groomed in the minor leagues for the role. The position has permanently changed how the game is played, as the construction of batting orders, the use of pinch-hitters, starting pitchers, relief specialization, and even the makeup of rosters has been impacted by the incorporation of the DH. It has also further divided the differences between the American and National leagues, the tactics they use within their games, and the types of players that are effective in each league. For many years after it was implemented, the merit of the designated hitter rule was debated, as baseball purists tried to make arguments either for or against the rule being used in all of major league baseball. Today that argument has largely subsided, and fans seem to accept and even enjoy in many cases the contrast between the two leagues, a contrast that has lost some of its intrigue in the years since inter-league play became a regular part of each season.

Without a doubt, however, the most lasting legacy from the 1972 season was the impact of the ten-day players strike in early April. The walkout was short lived, and the tangible gains resulting from the settlement were minimal, but the solidarity and resolve showed by the players association proved to be lasting. The action gave leverage to future bargaining efforts by the union and helped give momentum to their craving for an overturning of the reserve clause. Within three years, pitchers Andy Messersmith of the Los Angeles Dodgers and Dave McNally of the Orioles would play out the 1975 seasons without a contract, arguing that the reserve clause could not control them if they didn't have a contract in place. An arbitrator agreed, allowing them to become free agents and opening the door to the long-lusted for player movement.

With the handwriting clearly on the wall, owners were forced to make concessions with the players' union, and in the offseason between the 1976 and 1977 seasons, the first full-fledged free agent class of players peddled themselves on the open market. High-level players found that with teams bidding on their services, they were able to secure salaries on a scale that was oftentimes ten times the rate they had been making. Within a year of the onset of free agency, the average salary in the major leagues jumped from $51,051 in 1976 to more than $76,000, as the pendulum of leverage in contract negotiations began to swing the other direction.[10] Five years later, the first million dollar-per-year salary was awarded, as Nolan Ryan reached what had to have been considered an unthinkable financial plateau less than a decade earlier. By the end of the century the salary structure had been inflated such that individual contracts worth hundreds of millions of dollars were being awarded to the top players, causing most outsiders to shake their heads and complain that ballplayers were overpaid. A sport that had once been ruled by tight-fisted owners who had set rigid rules that prevented the players from establishing a true market value for themselves now found itself largely controlled by one of the most successful and powerful bands of organized labor in the world, the Major League Baseball Players Association.

XIII

End of an Era

Although they failed to make it to the World Series, the 1972 season was a success in every other conceivable way for the Detroit Tigers. Their East Division title broke the three-year stranglehold that had previously been held by the Baltimore Orioles, a team that had begun to appear invincible to the rest of the American League. Spurred by the specter of watching their old, familiar heroes fighting in the thick of a season-long pennant race once again, the fans of Detroit and greater Michigan poured out in droves until a full-season total of 1,892,386 patrons made their way through the turnstiles at Tiger Stadium. That figure was second only to the New York Mets in the majors, and led the American League by nearly half a million fans over the next-highest total, which belonged to the Boston Red Sox, who drew just over 1.4 million fans to Fenway Park. When adding in the 128,000-plus fans that came out for games three, four, and five of the ALCS, Detroit attracted more than two million in home attendance. In a day and age where the team payroll in 1972 came in just slightly higher than $1.05 million, a season's gate of two million provided for a very successful season off the field, as well as on.

Individually, the Tigers probably had a harder time parlaying their division title into big raises that next season. Unlike the leverage held by many Detroit players coming off the 1968 championship season, the statistical accomplishments for 1972 were much more modest. There were no 30-game winners, no World Series MVPs, no 30-home run hitters, no league leaders in runs scored, or grand slam specialists. The biggest beneficiary was probably Billy Martin, who pushed and prodded his aging team through the lingering effects of an unforeseen strike, injuries, batting slumps, and an up-and-down pitching staff. He used dozens of different lineups in order to maximize performance over the 156 games the team played in the regular season, plus another five in the playoffs. Besides that, the fans loved the fire he brought to the ballpark each night and the way the team seemed to respond in tow. The rail-thin, 165-pound Martin was a battler who never backed away from any opponent, making him beloved by a hard-working fan base in a blue-collar city.

As was expected heading into the season, Lolich and Coleman carried the heavy burden for the Detroit pitching staff. They combined to start more than 50 percent of the team's games that season (81), and ate up over 600 innings (43 percent of team total). Their 41 combined wins (Lolich 22–14, Coleman 19–14) represented nearly 43 percent of the Tigers' victory total and made them the second winningest duo in baseball that year, next to Wilbur Wood and Stan Bahnsen for the White Sox (45). Woodie Fryman was a godsend to the pitching staff, arriving in early August in time to make 15 starts and go 10–3 with a 2.05 ERA. Without his contribution, it is unlikely that Detroit would have had the horsepower on the hill to survive those last two months. No other Tiger hurler reached double figures in wins that year. Tom Timmerman faded after a strong start but still posted a respectable 8–10 record with a 2.88 ERA in 34 games. Chuck Seelbach and Fred Scherman pitched in 61 and 57 games, respectively, combining for 16 wins and 26 saves, while giving Martin a pair of viable options coming out of an otherwise spaghetti-thin bullpen.

The offensive stars for Detroit were few and far between. Nearly every position player on the roster contributed at different times, and could be lauded for a big hit in key a moment. However, few had what could even be considered typical seasons, let alone a good one. As a team, the Tigers hit two points below an already extremely low league average, but ranked a respectable third in the A.L. in home runs, and were fifth in runs scored. Norm Cash was the big run producer for the team. He hit 22 home runs to tie for seventh in the league, with most of his power coming before July ended. He led the team with a pedestrian 61 RBIs and batted .259. Cash was one of seven Tigers in double figures in home runs (two others had eight), giving the Detroit club balance in that department, but with no one consistent power source. Mickey Stanley, surprisingly, ranked second on the team in home runs with 14. Bill Freehan and Aurelio Rodriguez knocked in 56 runs apiece to rank second on the team, followed by Stanley with 55 and Ed Brinkman with 49.

Most of the offensive problems during the year occurred on days when the ball wasn't flying over the fence. Al Kaline's strong finish to an injury-plagued season lifted his average to a team-leading .313, but his 278 at-bats were far below the minimum to qualify among the league's leaders. Beyond the numbers, however (he also had 10 HRs and 32 RBIs), Kaline had once again displayed his greatness with superb all-around play during the closing weeks of the pennant race, when at age 37 he performed at the level of a superstar half a decade or more younger. Tony Taylor was the only other Detroit batter to hit over .300, at .303, but he also had limited at-bats (228). Cash, Freehan (.262), and Northrup (.261) were the leaders among the regulars, but the averages of McAuliffe (.240), Rodriguez (.236), Stanley (.234), Horton (.231), Gates Brown (.230), and Brinkman (.203) were dismal, which certainly affected Martin's decisions when he filled out a lineup card before each game.

When the voting for the Tiger of the Year award, handed out by the Detroit chapter of the Baseball Writers Association of America, was announced in the fall of 1972, the winner was a surprise to many, but not to those within the organization. Ed Brinkman, the affable shortstop who had barely managed to get his final batting average above .200, was recognized for his unsung contributions to the team, playing every game of the regular season and providing stability within the league's best infield. Brinkman also had been a much more dangerous hitter than his average indicated, and amongst his 49 RBIs were numerous key moments throughout the season. His absence over the final four games of the ALCS had cemented in everyone's minds the value that Brinkman provided to the Tiger lineup. "There was nobody close to him," added Martin, when asked about the selection.[1]

Brinkman's value to Detroit was also recognized in the American League's MVP voting, where he finished ninth in the overall tally, one position ahead of Lolich, who garnered a rather odd and unexpected first-place vote.[2] Kaline and Freehan were the only other Tigers who received votes, finishing 25th and 26th, respectively, in the balloting. Lolich was a distant third in voting for the A.L. Cy Young Award, and Martin finished third in the A.L. Manager of the Year voting. When the Gold Gloves were handed out for defensive excellence, Brinkman was the clear-cut choice at shortstop, and took home the prize for the only time in his stellar career as a superb middle infielder.

Beyond the individual accomplishments, however, 1972 was collectively an outstanding season for the team, an historic season in franchise annals. It remains nearly 40 years later one of only three seasons since the inception of divisional play that the franchise has captured a title. In a larger sense, however, the season should be remembered as the swan song for a group of athletes who had become iconic figures in the history of the franchise. While players like Brinkman, Rodriguez, Coleman and Fryman made huge contributions that season — and the team almost undoubtedly would not have made their way into post-season play without them — it was Kaline, Cash, Lolich, Freehan, McAuliffe, Horton, Northrup, Stanley and others from the old 1968 gang, several of them in the twilight of their careers, that made the '72 team so wildly popular with the Tiger Stadium fans. They had come up to the majors together and grew up throughout the 1960s before winning a world championship. They transcended the sports page, and their names struck a chord of long-term familiarity with the public that is rare. The success enjoyed by that group of players in 1972 provided a bookend with '68 around an era that validated their places not only in Tiger history, but also in baseball history.

The success of that season did not come without a cost, however. The feeling by many at the time was that Martin had squeezed everything out of the club and a rebuilding job needed to be started before the team got too old. Martin described the season years later as having "caught lightning in a bottle" and argued with Jim Campbell to make trades because "guys were going backwards."[3] Instead, the organization moved forward, convinced they could go even further in 1973 and get into another World Series with the core of players that existed. If anything, they made moves that made the team even older. After a rather stand-pat offseason, a spring training deal netted them 36-year-old pitcher Jim Perry from Minnesota, giving them what they hoped would be the long-desired fourth starter they had been lacking for several years. They also added Rich Reese, a 31-year-old left-handed first baseman-outfielder who was coming off two straight poor seasons, to fortify the bench.

For the most part, however, it was the same group of players who had battled to within one run of making the World Series in 1972 that made up the '73 roster. Bad omens surfaced early when Martin walked out of spring training only days before the regular campaign was set to open, upset over Campbell's intervention on a disciplinary issue with Horton. The issue was quickly smoothed over, and Martin was back in camp within 24 hours, but the tone was set for a manager and an organization that appeared to be out of step with one another. The A.L. East race was tight once again throughout the spring and into mid-summer, with five teams competing for the top spot in what was shaping up as another mediocre division. The Tigers battled through injuries and slumps much like the previous season, and Martin platooned everywhere except at short and third with Brinkman and Rodriguez and center field, where Stanley was playing every day. Detroit managed to hold its own into early August, and even held first place by a slim margin, before a disastrous four-city road trip left them six games out and slipping fast. The bubble had burst. Age and injuries caught up with the Tigers all at once, and the team tailed off dramatically.

The pitching, which had been such a pleasant surprise the previous season, declined considerably as the 1973 season wore on. Lolich made his usual 40-plus starts and pitched more than 300 innings yet again, but saw his ERA increase by nearly a run and a half to 3.82, and his record slid to a less-than-ace-like 16–15. Fryman reverted to his pre–Tiger form and struggled to a miserable 6–13 mark with a whopping 5.36 ERA. Scherman, Seelbach, and

Slayback battled injuries and weren't able to provide the help that they had earlier. Perry did give the team a much-needed 200 quality innings, but managed only a mediocre 14–13 record. The headliners on the staff that season were Coleman and Hiller. Buoyed perhaps by his spectacular 14-strikeout outing against Oakland in the ALCS, Coleman had the finest season of his career in 1973, winning 23 games. Hiller, in his first full season since returning from his heart attack, became a workhorse in Martin's bullpen. He pitched in a league-high 65 games, logged 125 innings, and saved a record 38 games, while limiting opponents with his miniscule 1.44 ERA. Without the yeoman effort of Hiller, who served as a one-man bullpen at times, the collapse of the pitching staff might have been even more pronounced. Making matters more difficult on the mound was the decline in the defensive ability of the team, as batted balls that might have been fielded the previous season began to find holes or drop in. A team already lacking in foot speed and athleticism had grown yet another year older.

Offensively, Detroit got big seasons from Horton and Northrup, who each rebounded to hit over .300, but there were too many falloffs elsewhere to make up for a pitching staff that allowed 160 more runs to be scored against them than it had in the previous season. Freehan floundered miserably, hitting only .234, and the power expected out of the catching position between he and Sims never materialized, as they combined for only 14 homers. The duo of Gates Brown and Frank Howard, platooning exclusively at the new designated hitter position, didn't produce as hoped, and tied up a slot that was seemingly well suited for an ever-increasing number of players on the Tiger roster. Cash started quickly again, but by season's end his power numbers diminished even further, and the 38-year-old first baseman ended up with 19 round-trippers and only 40 RBIs. Kaline produced similar overall numbers (.255-10-45), but was never able to recreate the magic he possessed over those final weeks in '72. In an offensively rejuvenated 1973 season that saw runs scored in the American League increase by nearly 30 percent, the Detroit lineup was too reliant on dwindling numbers from the likes of Stanley (.244), Sims (.242), Brinkman (.237), Brown (.236), Freehan, Taylor (.229), and Rodriguez (.229). Detroit finished tenth in the twelve-team league in batting, and dropped to ninth in runs scored. The Tigers became even more dependent on the long ball to generate runs, and the lack of team speed and ability to manufacture runs (they finished last in the majors once again in stolen bases) finally caught up with them.

By the beginning of September, Detroit had fallen 7½ games behind the division-leading Orioles and was fading fast. The team was effectively out of the race. With post-season hopes all but vanished, and Martin and Campbell feuding constantly, the organization shocked the baseball world and fired its manager with 19 games remaining in what had turned into a bitterly disappointing season. At the time of his firing, Martin was serving the last day of a three-game suspension handed out by A.L. president Joe Cronin for ordering his pitchers (namely Coleman and Scherman) to throw spitballs in a series against Cleveland. Martin had finally decided to conduct vigilante justice in the face of the league office over its reluctance to take any disciplinary measures against the Tribe's Gaylord Perry. When Martin bragged about his actions while serving the suspension, it was more than the organization was willing to tolerate.

A conservative franchise that served as model citizens within the structure of major league baseball was not destined for a long-term marriage with a maverick manager that shot from the hip. Citing "a breakdown in company policy matters," Campbell released Martin on September 2 with more than a year remaining on his contract.[4] The next day coaches Art Fowler and Charlie Silvera, both brought to Detroit by Martin, were let go as well, as Campbell created further distance from what had become an embarrassment to the franchise. Besides the one-day "quitting" by Martin in spring training, there had been an ugly, early-morning argument outside of a Lakeland bar between the Tiger manager and minor league prospect Ike Blessitt. Managers didn't typically get in fights with minor league players. He frequently lashed out at the directors of Detroit's minor league farm system for being unfruitful, and criticized prospects recommended to him as not being the solutions to replenish his aging roster. He traveled separate from the team on occasion, and showed up later than the players at times, leaving the clubhouse on edge as they waited for a lineup to be posted. His drinking and off-field behavior was frequently a source of distraction. Flaws that had been overlooked while the team was contending had become impossible for the organization to tolerate further. Publicly blasting the league office and baseball commissioner and taking matters into his own hands concerning the spitball allegations with Perry would serve as the final straw for his days managing the Tigers.

"If I had to do it all over again, I wouldn't do anything differently," said Martin, defiant to the end.

"This team was at its lowest ebb, lower than it had ever been in history, after all that business with Denny McLain. The powers that be felt they needed me then. And didn't I give them a winner? Did I, or did I not, do the job for them?"[5]

"From foul line to foul line, Billy has done a good job," said Campbell, preferring to leave unsaid the litany of off-field problems that ultimately decided Billy Martin's fate in Detroit.[6]

The firing of Martin was extremely unpopular with Detroit fans, but proved to be only the first in a series of events that would dampen the enthusiasm and familiarity that had been generated between the players and fans over the previous decade. The Tigers finished a distant third in 1973, twelve games behind Baltimore, which returned to its familiar top spot in the A.L. East.

By 1974 the situation turned even worse. Ralph Houk, the former long-time Yankee manager, was brought in to manage a Tiger team in the midst of an identity crisis. Changes were underway as old favorites were either disappearing or showing up in unfamiliar places on the diamond. McAuliffe had been jettisoned to the Red Sox and Taylor released over the offseason, freeing up second base for a journeyman infielder named Gary Sutherland. A career backup named Jerry Moses had taken over at catcher, with Freehan becoming the primary first baseman. Kaline, his athletic skills having eroded to the point that he was no longer capable of playing effectively in the field, had been made the full-time DH. By late spring the team had dropped to the cellar with little hope of recovery. The inevitable point had been reached where a team that had grown old all at once had to be broken up. The result was a disjointed and unsightly roster. The Detroit Tigers had become baseball's version of Frankenstein's monster, wearing the old English "D."

Cash, who had been benched early in the 1974 season, was unceremoniously released in August. Within 24 hours of that painful move, Northrup was peddled to Montreal for money and a player to be named later. Brinkman's consecutive games streak that exceeded two full seasons ended so the organization could get a look at a hotshot shortstop prospect named Tom Veryzer. Stanley broke his hand while getting hit by a pitch, and was replaced for the rest of the season by a fleet, talented but raw outfielder named Ron LeFlore, who was less than two years removed from serving a prison term at Jackson State Penitentiary. An era in Tiger history, filled with familiar names, exciting personalities, unforgettable moments, and as much heartbreak as glory, was over.

The result was a last-place A.L. East finish in 1974, followed by a major league-worst 57–102 mark in 1975. Tiger Stadium became the stomping grounds for nondescript players with unfamiliar names, such as Meyer, Roberts, Ruhle, Lemanczyk, Bare, Scrivener, and Pierce. The meteoric appearance of a pitcher named Mark "the Bird" Fidrych, who brought an energetic personality and crazy antics to the game in 1976, would provide much-needed excitement to the club and help mask a third straight losing season. It would be two more seasons following that, however, before the franchise would get to the plus side of .500 again, and another half-decade from there to return to post-season play, when finally the Detroit fans had a new batch of heroes to cheer for with names like Trammell, Whitaker, Gibson, Parrish, and Morris, and a world championship in 1984.

For Tiger followers, the demise of their old heroes was difficult to watch at times. Most had come up to the majors in the mid–1960s, felt the sting of a near-miss in 1967, and tasted the champagne a year later. From there they became mainstays, providing fans with some of the most recognizable personalities and memorable moments in the club's history. Their breakup was inevitable, however, and not without a dose of cold treatment in some cases, and a degree of bitterness being displayed in return. Some departed gracefully on their own terms, while others were sentenced to serve out the remainder of their careers in unfamiliar uniforms.

Following his firing in Detroit, Billy Martin was quickly snatched up by the Texas Rangers, where he became the architect of a remarkable turnaround for what had been one of the worst franchises in baseball. He guided Texas to a second-place finish in the A.L. West in 1974, and had Rangers fans excited about the team for the first time. As was quickly becoming a pattern, however, the good times didn't last, and Martin was fired the following season. He resurfaced from there as manager of the New York Yankees.

It was as manager of the Yankees that Martin gained his greatest fame, had his greatest success, yet also saw his reputation tarnished forever. During his time in New York he won two pennants and a World Series, but eventually became the butt of jokes due to a comic-like relationship with New York owner George Steinbrenner. In Martin's first full season with the Yankees, he led the storied franchise to its first pennant in more than a decade before getting swept in the World Series by Sparky Anderson's Big Red Machine. In 1977, Martin took New York all the way as the Yankees beat the Dodgers to take the world championship despite a season-long contentious public battle between Martin, Steinbrenner, and their prized free-agent acquisition, Reggie Jackson.

In 1978 the melodrama between Martin and Steinbrenner escalated even further. Following Steinbrenner's acquisition of more high-priced talent for the defending world champions, New York struggled over the season's first half, and fell well behind the front-running Boston Red Sox, who appeared to be running away with the A.L. East. Martin was fired 94 games into the season, but then only days later was introduced during an old-timers game at Yankee Stadium as "the next manager of the Yankees." Martin was targeted for a return to pinstripes in 1980, however, Steinbrenner decided to bring him back earlier than planned, during the 1979 season. Martin managed the final 96 games of a difficult season that saw the Yankees fall to fourth place and struggle to overcome the in-season death of their captain, Thurman Munson, in a crash of his private plane.

In 1980, Martin left the Yankees and "Billy Ball" surfaced in Oakland, where he rejuvenated a franchise that had been stripped through free agency of its great stars from the early '70s and lost 108 games in 1979. He led the A's to an 83–79 mark in 1980 behind an aggressive style of play exemplified by his young leadoff hitter, Rickey Henderson, who accounted for 100 of the team's 175 stolen bases, and a talented young pitching staff. Oakland was one of the better teams in baseball during the split-season, strike-interrupted 1981 campaign before being eliminated during the A.L. playoffs, but plummeted all the way to fifth place in the division in 1982. Martin was blamed for ruining through over-use the arms of a quartet of young starters on the A's staff and was fired yet again.

Martin returned to manage New York in 1983, 1985, and 1988, guiding talented Yankee teams that always finished well above .500, but were never able to regain the top spot in baseball's toughest division during that era. The failure to return to post-season play, a series of embarrassing off-the-field incidents, and continuous verbal sparring with Steinbrenner left Martin's job security in a tenuous state at all times. The public feuding between the two took on a comical element, and speculation about Martin's fate began almost as soon as he was hired each time. Yet despite the humiliation and the repeated firings, he returned each time to the job he loved. Martin had become baseball's tragic figure.

Detroit fans regularly cheered Martin each time he returned to Tiger Stadium despite the fact he was wearing the colors of the opposing team. They remembered the fire he brought to the Tigers during his short stay in Detroit, and he remained a favorite of the people. While at the helm of New York in 1983, and in a delicious twist of baseball fate, Martin could look down his bench and find Bert Campaneris in Yankee pinstripes. The 41-year-old Campaneris, who Martin had tried so desperately to get at after the bat-throwing incident in the playoff series with Oakland more than a decade earlier, was playing out his final season in the major leagues and ably served Martin as a utility player for the Yankees, hitting .322 in 60 games.

To the shock of many but the surprise of few, the end for Martin came tragically. He had been hired for a sixth stint as Yankee manager and was looking forward to the 1990 season when he was killed in a single-vehicle crash on Christmas Day, 1989. He was the passenger in a pickup truck driven by a friend. They both had been drinking. Martin was 61 years old. He is buried in the same cemetery as Babe Ruth, Cemetery of the Gate of Heaven in Hawthorne, New York. The marker on his grave has the inscription, "I may not have been the greatest player to wear the Yankee uniform, but I was the proudest."

Al Kaline finished up a 22-year career in a Detroit uniform in 1974, playing 146 games in the designated hitter role. One of the premier defensive players in the American League throughout the previous two decades, he never played an inning in the field that final season. He stroked a double off Dave McNally in Baltimore for his 3,000th hit late in the year, and finished with a career total of 3,007. The career Tiger holds almost every offensive record in the franchise's history that is not held by Ty Cobb. He was a first-ballot Hall of Fame inductee in 1980, went on to a long and successful career as an analyst on the Tigers' local TV broadcasts, remains the elder statesman of the Detroit Tigers, and in many ways is still the face of the organization.

Mickey Lolich suffered through 21- and 18-loss seasons his last two years in Detroit before being traded to the New York Mets for outfielder Rusty Staub in December 1975. He finished his career working out of the bullpen in 1979 with the San Diego Padres, a 217-game winner with 2,832 strikeouts. His strikeout total is the highest for any left-hander in American League history, and is third overall among lefties, behind only Steve Carlton and Randy Johnson. He remains the last pitcher to have three complete game victories in a single World Series. Outside of Kaline, Lolich probably had the greatest case for Hall of Fame consideration of any other player from the Tiger teams of that era. However, he never received more than 25 percent of the vote while he was still eligible through the baseball writers, and would have to be elected by the veterans committee if he was to ever make Cooperstown.

Norm Cash left Detroit bitter over his release in 1974, vowing to land a job with another team. He never played again. At the time his career ended, Cash had the fourth-highest home run total among left-handed batters in American League history, behind only legendary players Babe Ruth, Ted Williams, and Lou Gehrig. He is second on the Tigers career home run list with 373, behind only Kaline's 399. After he was done, Cash remained a popular figure in Detroit, playing briefly for a professional slow-pitch softball team in the area, and then working as a color commentator on cable broadcasts of Tiger games before suffering a stroke while in his late 40s. Cash died tragically in 1986, drowning off a dock on Beaver Island in Lake Michigan.

Bill Freehan remained with the Tigers throughout the rest of his baseball career, and is recognized as arguably the greatest catcher in Detroit history. He retired after the 1976 season, having served primarily as a catcher again over his final two campaigns. After his playing days ended, Freehan became a successful businessman in the Detroit area before going back to serve as the head baseball coach at the University of Michigan in the late 1990s. Freehan's 11 All-Star appearances are believed to be the most of any eligible player not currently in the Baseball Hall of Fame.[7]

Ed Brinkman underwent back surgery following the 1972 playoffs but returned to give Detroit two more seasons of excellent defensive play at shortstop. He was sent to St. Louis as part of a three-way trade in December of 1974 that netted the Tigers Nate Colbert, who had been a prodigious slugger in the National League with San Diego. The trade ended up being one of the biggest busts in team history, as Colbert would last only a couple of months in Detroit, his career on a sharp decline mainly due to failing eyesight. Brinkman would play only that one last season in 1975, after having bounced from St. Louis to Texas to the New York Yankees. His career batting average was .224. He remained in baseball long after his playing career ended, serving as a coach and scout with various organizations. Brinkman passed away in the fall of 2008 after battling lung cancer.

Jim Northrup threatened to retire after being sold to Montreal in August of 1974. He ended up reporting to the Expos, but was soon traded to Baltimore, where he spent a final season playing in 1975. Years later, he would recall that the short time he spent playing with the Orioles was under the "best manager I ever played for" in Earl Weaver. Northrup never made an All-Star team but enjoyed a solid and productive 11-year career nonetheless, hitting .267 with 153 home runs.

Following his career-high 23-win season in 1973, Joe Coleman's career declined rapidly. A winner of 105 games in his career by age 26, Coleman added only 37 more before he was through. He lost 18 games on the horrible 1975 squad and was traded to the National League midway through the next season. He bounced around with four other teams over the next three seasons, finishing his career in 1979 at the early age of 32. Coleman remained in uniform as a pitching coach in various organizations through the 2008 season.

Dick McAuliffe wrapped up an often-overlooked 14-year Tiger career following a 1973 campaign that saw him tie a career high in batting with a .274 mark. The under-appreciated infielder had been one of the premier leadoff hitters in the American League during the late 1960s and early '70s, and the offensive catalyst in Detroit's lineup. He scored 70 or more runs in a season six times during a period in baseball history when pitching dominated and low-scoring games were the norm. McAuliffe spent the 1974 season as a utility infielder for Boston, and then managed a Red Sox farm team in 1975 before getting a late-season call-up himself, where he played the last seven games of his career for the eventual pennant winners.

Aurelio Rodriguez remained in a Tiger uniform throughout the 1970s. He was one of the few recognizable names to Detroit fans through the difficult transition years in the middle of the decade. His flashy glove and rocket arm were a constant at the hot corner, but unfortunately so was his mediocre bat and .237 career average. By the time Sparky Anderson took over as the Detroit manager in 1979, the organization was tiring of Rodriguez's flaws at the plate while also recognizing his decreasing range at third base. He was sold to San Diego following that season, and then bounced between several teams for four more seasons, wrapping up a 17-year major league career in 1983.

The broken hand suffered by Mickey Stanley in 1974 effectively ended his days as the regular center fielder in the Tiger lineup. The speedy Ron LeFlore was the face of the rebuilding effort in Detroit, and to best utilize his greatest asset, LeFlore was placed in the leadoff position in the batting order and asked to patrol the spacious center field area of Tiger Stadium. Stanley would play four more seasons with the club, serving as a super-sub of sorts, capable of playing almost anywhere in the outfield or infield. He even played three games at shortstop in 1977, revisiting the position that gave him his greatest notoriety nearly a decade earlier, when Mayo Smith played him there in the World Series.

Willie Horton was one of the few members of the '72 Tiger team that still had some of his best seasons ahead of him. He enjoyed a bit of a renaissance in 1973 under Martin, hitting .316 with 17 home runs. In '74 he was off to a tremendous start, batting .298 and ranking among the league leaders with 15 homers and 47 runs batted in nearing the mid-point of the season when he was sidelined for the year with a knee injury. He returned the next season as one of the only bright lights in the 102-loss disaster, playing exclusively as the DH, where he hit 25 home runs and knocked in 92 runs. After Horton's injury-plagued season in 1976, the organization wanted to make room for its highly touted prospect, Steve Kemp, a hard-hitting outfielder that had played collegiate ball at USC. Horton was traded to the Texas Rangers one game into the 1977 season for reliever Steve Foucault. In 1979 as a member of the Seattle Mariners, Horton had one of his greatest seasons at age 36 (.279-29-106) before finishing his career a year later.

John Hiller pitched until age 37, completing an unprecedented comeback for a professional athlete after returning from the heart attack he suffered nearly a decade earlier. Almost as remarkable as his recovery from the physical ailment was the metamorphosis of Hiller as a pitcher. He went from being an expendable swingman on the pitching staff prior to his heart attack to becoming arguably the greatest relief pitcher in Detroit history. Like other relief specialists of his era, such as Sparky Lyle and Rollie Fingers, Hiller was a true "fireman," called upon in the most dire game situations, with men on base and the game on the line. He didn't rack up a slew of saves under today's closer situations (pitching only the last inning, and starting with nobody on base), but instead often worked two, three, or even four innings at times. Hiller followed his breakout 38-save 1973 season by winning an almost unbelievable 17 games in relief in 1974. Throughout the rest of the 1970s, Hiller remained one of the most reliable short relievers in the game. He retired during the 1980 season with 72 of his 87 career wins coming in relief while setting the Tiger career record at the time for saves with 125.

Gates Brown played in a career-high 125 games in 1973, the first season of the designated hitter, a role he was seemingly born for. The reprieve in his career was short-lived, however. The next season Kaline was moved to the position on a full-time basis, and the year after that, Horton inherited the role, regulating Brown to the pinch-hitting duty he would always be best known for. Brown played through 1975 and later was a hitting coach on Sparky Anderson's staff, including the 1984 championship team.

Tony Taylor, Tom Haller, Duke Sims, Woodie Fryman, and Frank Howard all made key contributions that pushed the Tigers over the hump in 1972. They were all in the twilight of their careers when they came to Detroit, and their moments of glory in Tiger uniforms were fleeting. Taylor was released with little fanfare after the '73 season, having spent nearly three years in Detroit. Haller was traded after the playoff series to Philadelphia, but decided to retire from the game instead. Sims was never able to harness the lightning his bat produced after coming over to Detroit, when he batted .316 and was the most dangerous left-handed hitter in the lineup; he was sold to the New York Yankees late in the 1973 season. Howard shared time with Brown in the inaugural summer of the DH but was released at the conclusion of the season. Fryman lasted two more seasons with Detroit but never pitched with any consistency or effectiveness, posting losing seasons in both '73 and '74 with a combined ERA of more than five. Surprisingly, Fryman was able to carve out a niche in the National League again after leaving Detroit and pitched as a reliever most effectively for the Montreal Expos. He even received a chance to appear in the postseason again, pitching for the Expos nearly a decade later in the expanded playoffs of 1981.

For the rest of the members of the '72 team, their exits from the Detroit organization came with little notice, and most drifted towards baseball obscurity. Tom Timmerman, winner of eight games that season, was traded to Cleveland midway through 1973 and was out of the major leagues for good a little more than a year after that. Chuck Seelbach and Bill Slayback, rookies who had provided such an unexpected boost to the pitching staff of the division champions, suffered career-damaging arm injuries in '73 that they were never able to fully recover from. Both made their final appearances in 1974 at the age of 26. Fred Scherman was traded to Houston after the 1973 season, and finished out his career with three nondescript seasons in the National League. Lerrin LaGrow suffered through a 19-loss season as a starter with the Tigers in 1974 and lost 14 more in 1975 before becoming a successful relief pitcher. He was traded by Detroit in 1976, and eventually landed with the Chicago White Sox, for whom he saved 41 games over the 1977 and 1978 seasons. He finished his career in 1980 after bouncing around the National League his last couple of seasons.

* * *

What did it all mean? In reality, the players, coaches, broadcasters, and writers that covered the team at the time recall few details of the 1972 season. Reaching back across nearly 40 years, the events of that season are mostly hazy shadows cast in the long-overlooked attics of their minds. The events are drowned out by the constant reminders they receive from fans and media of the 1968 championship summer that has been so thoroughly documented and is held onto so tightly by Detroiters. Most of the memories that do exist from 1972 revolve around Martin — a figure that conjures mixed feelings from those that played under him. Respect is grudgingly paid to him for the turnaround of the team while he was in Detroit, yet that respect is difficult for some to separate from the dulled bitterness still felt over other aspects of Martin's tenure. His abrasive handling of some players, the reckless use of the pitching staff that may have cost more than one Tiger hurler a career, the drinking binges, his late arrivals before games, and assorted other off-the-field issues marred his image within the clubhouse. Regardless of any personal feelings, there is no disputing the impact he had as the face of the ball club during that period.

"Billy could get a team's attention," said 24-year Tiger first base coach Dick Tracewski, who served as a first-year coach under Martin that season. "It was short lived, however, like a sparkler. He could take (a team) further than they had the ability to go."[8]

Players like Jim Northrup thought Martin's antics provided ammunition to other clubs around the league as much or more than they did to inspire the Tigers. "He was always giving other teams something to go for."[9]

Most of the moments remembered today from that season stem from the playoff series with Oakland. Most recall the play at third in game one that ended with Kaline's unfortunate throwing error. The bat-throwing incident with Campaneris is arguably the most famous play of the series and is often recalled. Some still bring up the call at first base by umpire John Rice in the decisive fifth game, which eventually resulted in George Hendrick scoring the winning run for the A's. For some the anguish of that bitter playoff loss subsided long ago. For others it remains a painful memory, a reminder of how close that Tiger team was to another World Series appearance.

"We were a better team than Oakland," said Tracewski decades later. "We would have beaten them. Kaline had the runner thrown out by half the base path (referring to the throw that eluded Rodriguez and resulted in the extra-inning loss in game one), scoring the tying and winning run."[10]

"Shoulda, coulda, woulda," lamented Northrup in a 2008 interview. "We didn't get very many breaks."

One thing that surely won't be forgotten by the players who lived through it is the groundbreaking step they took in collective bargaining that spring.

While it may have been a minor victory in the concessions they gained for their pension fund, the player walkout that cancelled the first ten days of the regular season had long-lasting implications.

"(Marvin Miller) told us how we were being manipulated," recalled Northrup of the patriotic stance players took in the spring of 1972. "We were all in the same predicament as far as making money. There was no going anywhere. It was a battle, and now everything has changed. When I first came up, I made $6,000. We were the ones that made it happen. They didn't believe we'd strike. That was a pivotal year."[11]

In hindsight, the 1972 season was the last hurrah for a group of players that had gained almost legendary status within Detroit and the state of Michigan, primarily off their membership on the 1968 championship team. Their popularity was more than just the result of a World Series victory, however. They largely defined an entire era, a more innocent time remembered fondly by generations old enough to recall the 1960s and early '70s.

"It was a different era and those guys were around a long time," said former Tiger television broadcaster Larry Osterman decades later. "There was an opportunity to establish a relationship with fans."[12]

"The fans realized that we were true ballplayers and that we gave everything we had," said Northrup. "They knew it. Detroit was a great place to play ball back then."[13]

"It started at about '67 and lasted into the 1970s," explained Hall of Fame radio broadcaster Ernie Harwell. "The Tigers had reached their peak and after '72 had stopped and were headed back toward mediocrity. They didn't build the farm system and it wasn't until years later that they were able to head towards the top again."[14]

"I think people, fans, liked the way baseball used to be," said Freehan in a 2004 interview.[15]

Even within the domain of the dugout and the clubhouse, where only those that wore a uniform would truly know, that era and the players that belonged to it is still recalled as a special time.

"It was a hell of a ball club," reminisced Tracewski fondly. "Loaded with talent. Old, but loaded from stem to stern with talent. Getting a little long in the tooth they might say."[16]

If anything, the long-time Tiger coach, who served under managers Billy Martin, Ralph Houk, Les Moss, and Sparky Anderson, looks back at those years with a tinge of frustration, born out of missed opportunities for a team as talented as the Detroit roster was during that period.

"I'm upset that we didn't win more than we did," he explained. "It was a crime. Between '67 and '72 we should have won more."[17]

"If you saw one Detroit Tiger, you saw 25 Detroit Tigers," commented

Freehan about the closeness that existed with that particular group of players. "After a ballgame, we'd all be in the same restaurant, or bar, or back at the (hotel) suite or something like that. If somebody won the card game on the plane going out to Los Angeles, that guy upgraded to a suite. Instead of going down to the bar after a game, everybody would bring a beer or a cocktail and come back to the suite.

"If you've got a group of guys who work with each other and keep each other up and focused on where you want to be — we had that kind of camaraderie."[18]

Perhaps Northrup summed it up best when he explained that they were the lucky ones, the players who donned the uniform and got to play the game they loved with a group of guys that were more than just teammates. They also played in a city, and during an era, where Detroit worshipped its baseball team.

"Bill Freehan was my best friend," he said. "Al Kaline was next to my locker for ten years. We just had good people and the fans knew it and respected us for it. I was fortunate to be born to play the game. I was fortunate to be thrown in with those guys. They were genuine good guys. I was lucky."[19]

Appendix

1972 Final Standings

American League

Eastern Division	*W*	*L*	*Pct.*	*GB*
Detroit Tigers	86	70	.551	—
Boston Red Sox	85	70	.548	½
Baltimore Orioles	80	74	.519	5
New York Yankees	79	76	.510	6½
Cleveland Indians	72	84	.462	14
Milwaukee Brewers	65	91	.417	22

Western Division	*W*	*L*	*Pct.*	*GB*
Oakland A's	93	62	.600	—
Chicago White Sox	87	67	.565	5½
Minnesota Twins	77	77	.500	15½
Kansas City Royals	76	78	.494	16½
California Angels	75	80	.484	18
Texas Rangers	54	100	.351	38½

National League

Eastern Division	*W*	*L*	*Pct.*	*GB*
Pittsburgh Pirates	96	59	.619	—
Chicago Cubs	85	70	.548	11
New York Mets	83	73	.532	13½
St. Louis Cardinals	75	81	.481	21½
Montreal Expos	70	86	.449	26½
Philadelphia Phillies	59	97	.378	37½

Western Division	*W*	*L*	*Pct.*	*GB*
Cincinnati Reds	95	59	.617	—
Houston Astros	84	69	.549	10½
Los Angeles Dodgers	85	70	.548	10½
Atlanta Braves	70	84	.455	25
San Francisco Giants	69	86	.445	26½
San Diego Padres	58	95	.379	36½

AL Playoffs: Oakland defeated Detroit, 3 games to 2
NL Playoffs: Cincinnati defeated Pittsburgh, 3 games to 2
World Series: Oakland defeated Cincinnati, 4 games to 3

1972 Detroit Tigers — Individual Batting Statistics

Batting Statistics	*G*	*AB*	*R*	*H*	*2B*	*3B*	*HR*	*RBI*	*BB*	*SO*	*SB*	*AVG*
Aurelio Rodriguez, 3B	153	601	65	142	23	5	13	56	28	104	2	.236
Ed Brinkman, ss	156	516	42	105	19	1	6	49	38	51	0	.203
Norm Cash, 1B	137	440	51	114	16	0	22	61	50	64	0	.259
Mickey Stanley, cf	142	435	45	102	16	6	14	55	29	49	1	.234
Jim Northrup, of	134	426	40	111	15	2	8	42	38	47	4	.261
Dick McAuliffe, 2B	122	408	47	98	16	3	8	30	59	59	0	.240
Bill Freehan, c	111	374	51	98	18	2	10	56	48	51	0	.262
Willie Horton, lf	108	333	44	77	9	5	11	36	27	47	0	.231
Al Kaline, rf	106	278	46	87	11	2	10	32	28	33	1	.313
Gates Brown, lf	103	252	33	58	5	0	10	31	26	28	3	.230
Tony Taylor, if	78	228	33	69	12	4	1	20	14	34	5	.303
Tom Haller, c	59	121	7	25	5	2	2	13	15	14	0	.207
Duke Sims, c	38	98	11	31	4	0	4	19	19	18	0	.316
Mickey Lolich, p	41	89	3	6	0	0	0	0	20	39	0	.067
Ike Brown, if-of	51	84	12	21	3	0	2	10	17	23	1	.250
Joe Coleman, p	40	82	5	9	0	0	0	5	5	30	0	.110
Paul Jata, if-of	32	74	8	17	2	0	0	3	7	14	0	.230
Tom Timmerman, p	35	44	3	6	0	0	0	1	3	25	0	.136
Woodie Fryman, p	16	40	0	5	0	0	0	3	0	7	0	.125
Frank Howard, if-of	14	33	1	8	1	0	1	7	4	8	0	.242
Bill Slayback, p	23	23	1	4	0	0	0	0	0	6	0	.174
Fred Scherman, p	57	22	1	2	0	0	0	0	1	8	0	.091
Chuck Seelbach, p	61	21	1	3	2	0	0	0	4	11	0	.143
John Knox, if	14	13	1	1	1	0	0	0	1	2	0	.077
Joe Niekro, p	18	12	2	3	1	0	0	1	1	4	0	.250
Wayne Comer, of	27	9	1	1	0	0	0	1	0	0	0	.111
Dalton Jones, if	7	7	0	0	0	0	0	0	0	0	0	.000
Les Cain, p	5	7	0	1	0	0	0	0	0	2	0	.143
Marvin Lane, of	8	6	2	0	0	0	0	0	0	0	0	.000
Ike Blessitt, of	4	5	0	0	0	0	0	0	0	0	0	.000
John Hiller, p	24	4	0	0	0	0	0	0	0	3	0	.000
John Gamble, if	6	3	0	0	0	0	0	0	0	0	0	.000

Batting Statistics	*G*	*AB*	*R*	*H*	*2B*	*3B*	*HR*	*RBI*	*BB*	*SO*	*SB*	*AVG*
Fred Holdsworth, p	2	3	1	1	0	0	0	0	0	1	0	.333
Joe Staton, if	6	2	1	0	0	0	0	0	0	1	0	.000
Chris Zachary, p	25	2	0	1	0	0	0	0	1	1	0	.500
Phil Meeler, p	7	2	0	0	0	0	0	0	0	2	0	.000
Ron Perranoski, p	17	1	0	0	0	0	0	0	0	0	0	.000
Bill Gilbreth, p	2	1	0	0	0	0	0	0	0	0	0	.000
Gene Lamont, c	1	0	0	0	0	0	0	0	0	0	0	.000

1972 Detroit Tigers — Individual Pitching Statistics

Pitching Statistics	*G*	*W*	*L*	*SV*	*ERA*	*GS*	*CG*	*IP*	*H*	*BB*	*SO*	*HR*
Mickey Lolich	41	22	14	0	2.50	41	23	327	282	74	250	29
Joe Coleman	40	19	14	0	2.80	39	9	280	216	110	222	23
Tom Timmerman	34	8	10	0	2.89	25	3	150	121	41	88	12
Woodie Fryman	16	10	3	0	2.06	14	6	114	93	31	72	6
Chuck Seelbach	61	9	8	14	2.89	3	0	112	96	39	76	6
Fred Scherman	57	7	3	12	3.64	3	0	94	91	53	53	5
Bill Slayback	23	5	6	0	3.20	13	3	82	74	25	65	4
Joe Niekro	18	3	2	1	3.83	7	1	47	62	8	24	3
John Hiller	24	1	2	3	2.03	3	1	44	39	13	26	4
Chris Zachary	25	1	1	1	1.41	1	0	38	27	15	21	2
Lerrin LaGrow	16	0	1	2	1.32	0	0	27	22	6	9	0
Les Cain	5	0	3	0	3.80	5	0	24	18	16	16	2
Ron Perranoski	17	0	1	0	7.71	0	0	19	23	8	10	2
Phil Meeler	7	0	1	0	4.32	0	0	8	10	7	5	0
Fred Holdsworth	2	0	1	0	12.86	2	0	7	13	2	5	0
Bill Gilbreth	2	0	0	0	16.20	0	0	5	10	4	2	1
Bob Strampe	7	0	0	0	11.57	0	0	5	6	7	4	0
Jim Foor	7	1	0	0	14.73	0	0	4	6	6	2	1
Mike Kilkenny	1	0	0	0	9.00	0	0	1	1	0	0	1
Don Leshnock	1	0	0	0	0.00	0	0	1	2	0	2	0

Chapter Notes

Introduction

1. Frank Newport, "History Shows Presidential Job Approval Ratings Can Plummet Rapidly," Gallup News Service, February 11, 1998.

2. The History Place, "The Vietnam War: The Bitter End 1969–1975," http://www.historyplace.com/unitedstates/vietnam/index-1969.html.

3. "How Tigers Finished, Season-by-Season," Detroit Tigers 1972 Official Program and Scorebook.

Chapter I

1. Wikipedia, "Al Kaline," http://en.wikipedia.org/wiki/Al_Kaline.

2. George Cantor, *The Tigers of '68* (Dallas, TX: Taylor, 1997), 166–168.

3. *Detroit Tigers: 1969 Official Yearbook* (Birmingham, MI: Averill Press, 1969), Biographical, Statistical Information about Players on 1969 Spring Roster.

4. Cantor, *The Tigers of '68*, 54.

5. Cantor, *The Tigers of '68*, 53.

6. Cantor, *The Tigers of '68*, 9.

7. Wikipedia, "1968 Detroit Tigers Season," http://en.wikipedia.org/wiki/1968_Detroit_Tigers_season.

8. Retrosheet, http://www.retrosheet.org.

9. Joe Falls, *Detroit Tigers* (New York: Macmillan, 1975), 35–39.

10. Cantor, *The Tigers of '68*, 212.

11. Joe Falls, "How Billy Martin Says He'll Handle Denny," *Detroit Free Press*, October 4, 1970, 6-C.

12. Billy Martin and Peter Golenbock, *Number 1* (New York: Dell, 1980), 52.

13. *Ibid.*, 199.

14. *Ibid.*, 267–270.

15. *Ibid.*, 272–274.

16. Joe Falls, "Martin: A Man Who Means Business," *Detroit Free Press*, October 3, 1970, 1-B.

17. Martin and Golenbock, *Number 1*, 279.

18. *Sporting News*, October 17, 1970.

19. Joe Falls, "May End McLain Suspension," *Detroit Free Press*, October 9, 1970, 1-D.

20. "Reaction of Short and Williams," *Sporting News*, October 24, 1970.

21. *Sporting News*, January 1972.

22. *Sporting News*, January 1972.

Chapter II

1. *Sporting News*, January 29, 1972.

2. Joe Falls, "Tigers Can Beat Out the Orioles If We Start Healthy — Billy Martin," *Detroit Free Press*, February 27, 1972, 4-D.

3. Martin and Golenbock, *Number 1*, 282.

4. *Sporting News*, January 29, 1972.

5. Martin and Golenbock, *Number 1*, 28–29.

6. Jim Hawkins, "Lolich Asking 3-Year Contract — Tigers Say 'No,'" *Detroit Free Press*, February 16, 1972, 1-D.

7. *Sporting News*, March 18, 1972.

8. *Ibid.*

9. Dick Tracewski interview, January 12, 2009.

10. *Sporting News*, February 5, 1972.

11. *Ibid.*
12. Jim Hawkins, "Slim Les Cain Shocks Tigers," *Detroit Free Press*, February 22, 1972, 1-D.
13. Martin and Golenbock, *Number 1*, 282.
14. *Sporting News*, March 4, 1972.
15. *Sporting News*, December 4, 1971.
16. Jim Hawkins, "Young Pitchers Excite Tigers," *Detroit Free Press*, March 4, 1972, 1-C.
17. Jim Hawkins, "Match '71 Record? Mick Says 'No Way,'" *Detroit Free Press*, March 2, 1972, 1-D.
18. Jim Hawkins, "Tigers Use (Bleeps)—Bouton's on Blink," *Detroit Free Press*, March 15, 1972, 1-D.
19. *Sporting News*, April 8, 1972.
20. *Sporting News*, April 22, 1972.
21. Jim Hawkins, "Tigers Lose, Fear Strike," *Detroit Free Press*, March 30, 1972, 1-D.

Chapter III

1. *Sporting News*, April 15, 1972.
2. Dallas' Love Field was the airport that President Kennedy flew into on November 22, 1963, and is also where following Kennedy's assassination earlier that day, Lyndon B. Johnson was sworn in as president aboard Air Force One.
3. *Sporting News*, April 15, 1972.
4. *Ibid.*
5. Jim Hawkins, "Tigers Close Down Camp," *Detroit Free Press*, April 2, 1972, 1-C.
6. "Big League Ballplayers Call Strike," *Detroit Free Press*, April 1, 1972, 1-A.
7. Jim Hawkins, "Tiger GM, Billy Bitter over Strike," *Detroit Free Press*, April 1, 1972, 1-B.
8. Hawkins, "Tigers Close Down Camp," *Detroit Free Press*, 1-C.
9. Hawkins, "Tiger GM, Billy Bitter," *Detroit Free Press*, 1-B.
10. *Sporting News*, April 15, 1972.
11. *Ibid.*
12. *Ibid.*
13. *Ibid.*
14. *Ibid.*
15. *Sporting News*, April 22, 1972.
16. *Ibid.*
17. *Ibid.*
18. *Ibid.*
19. *Sporting News*, April 29, 1972.

Chapter IV

1. Jim Hawkins, "Strike Changes Billy—Optimist to Pessimist," *Detroit Free Press*, April 11, 1972, 3-D.
2. Jim Hawkins, "Play Ball," *Detroit Free Press*, April 15, 1972, 1-C.
3. Jim Hawkins, "Kasko on 1st Inning: 'Let Him Get Away,'" *Detroit Free Press*, April 16, 1972, 1-D.
4. Jim Hawkins, "Bring on Those Birds! Tigers Higher Than Kite," *Detroit Free Press*, April 18, 1972, 1-D.
5. *Sporting News*, May 6, 1972.
6. Joe Falls, "Tiger Veterans Bubble Confidence After Big Victory," *Detroit Free Press*, April 19, 1972, 1-D.
7. Falls, "Tiger Veterans Bubble Confidence," *Detroit Free Press*, 1-D.
8. Jim Hawkins, "Weaver Picks Orioles Again," *Detroit Free Press*, April 19, 1972, 4-D.
9. Jim Hawkins, "Rocky Debut for Cain, It's Brewers, 3–0," *Detroit Free Press*, April 24, 1972, 1-D.
10. Jim Hawkins, "Brewer Manager Impressed by Tigers' Bench Strength," *Detroit Free Press*, April 24, 1972, 2-D.
11. Jim Hawkins, "Game Called Off … And Are Tigers Hot About It!," *Detroit Free Press*, April 25, 1972, 1-D.
12. Charlie Vincent, "We're Putting It All Together Now—Freehan," *Detroit Free Press*, April 30, 1972, 1-E.
13. Jim Hawkins, "Freehan's Bat Booms … Lolich Wins No. 6," *Detroit Free Press*, May 14, 1972, 1-D.
14. Joe Falls, "'What's All Concern About?'—Weaver," *Detroit Free Press*, May 16, 1972, 1-D.
15. Curt Sylvester, "'Hope Cuellar Pitches as Well as Jim,'" *Detroit Free Press*, May 16, 1972, 1-D.
16. Jack Saylor, "Perry's Slippery … Cain's Off Target … And Billy's Mad!," *Detroit Free Press*, May 20, 1972, 1-D.
17. Charlie Vincent, "Some Bunt! Stanley's Triple Fools Everybody," *Detroit Free Press*, May 22, 1972, 2D.
18. Curt Sylvester, "Push Leads to Fight, but Nobody's Mad," *Detroit Free Press*, May 26, 1972, 5-D.
19. Jim Hawkins, "Lowly Brewers Surprise Lolich, 2–0," *Detroit Free Press*, May 26, 1972, 1-D.
20. Jim Hawkins, "Cain in Pain, Seelbach

Rescues Tigers," *Detroit Free Press*, May 29, 1972, 1-C.

Chapter V

1. *Sporting News*, June 1972. All trends and figures for batting, pitching, and attendance were taken from June editions of *The Sporting News*.
2. Joe Falls, "The Game Is 'Fun Again'—New Tiger Starter Gates," *Detroit Free Press*, June 4, 1972, 1F.
3. Jim Hawkins, "Tigers Zoom 3 Games Up on Birds!" *Detroit Free Press*, June 5, 1972, 1-D.
4. Curt Sylvester, "3-Hitter? Angels' Ryan Not Satisfied," *Detroit Free Press*, June 8, 1972, 1-D.
5. Charlie Vincent, "Willie or Jim for Jim Perry? Tigers Say 'No,'" *Detroit Free Press*, June 10, 1972, 1-D.
6. Jim Hawkins, "A's Even Beat the Mick," *Detroit Free Press*, June 11, 1972, 1-D.
7. *Ibid.*
8. Jim Hawkins, "Martin, Mick Deny Throwing at A's," *Detroit Free Press*, June 11, 1972, 2-D.
9. Jim Hawkins, "Freehan's Clutch Plays Chill A's," *Detroit Free Press*, June 12, 1972, 1-D.
10. *Ibid.*
11. Jim Hawkins, "Tigers Bid for Bosman of Rangers," *Detroit Free Press*, June 13, 1972, 1-D.
12. David Cooper and Julie Morris, "High Court Blocks Stadium," *Detroit Free Press*, June 17, 1972, 1A.
13. Jim Hawkins, "Martin Puts the Needle to Orioles," *Detroit Free Press*, June 19, 1972, 4-D.
14. *Detroit Free Press*, June 19, 1972, 1-A.
15. "Flood Loses Case Against Baseball," *Detroit Free Press*, June 20, 1972, 1-C.
16. *Ibid.*
17. Joe Falls, "B. Robby: Who's Old!" *Detroit Free Press*, June 26, 1972, 1-D
18. Roger Angell, *Five Seasons* (New York: Popular Library, 1978), 33.
19. Falls, "B. Robby," *Detroit Free Press*, 1-D.
20. Jackie Lapin, "Surprised We're Still Close—Birds' McNally," *Detroit Free Press*, July 1, 1972, 2-B.
21. Joe Falls, "McNally 'Didn't Have a Thing' After His Back Popped," *Detroit Free Press*, June 25, 1972, 1-F.
22. Jim Hawkins, "New Tigers 'Slays' NY in Debut, 4–3," *Detroit Free Press*, June 27, 1972, 1-D.
23. Curt Sylvester, "Martin Gives Dobson Extra Push," *Detroit Free Press*, July 1, 1972, 1-B.
24. Charlie Vincent, "'It Was Jump Then or Never'—Jim," *Detroit Free Press*, July 2, 1972, 1-D.
25. *Detroit Free Press*, July 4, 1972.

Chapter VI

1. Retrosheet, http://www.retrosheet.org.
2. *Ibid.*
3. "Ballpark Tour — Former Ballparks of Kansas City," http://www.ballparktour.com/Former_Kansas_City.html.
4. Jim Hawkins, "Tigers Give Up ... Cain Off to Minors," *Detroit Free Press*, July 8, 1972, 1-C.
5. Cantor, *The Tigers of '68*, 116.
6. Jim Hawkins, "'This Is What I Want'—Hiller," *Detroit Free Press*, July 9, 1972, 1-D.
7. Jackie Lapin, "Baltimore No Longer to Be Feared — Ted," *Detroit Free Press*, July 11, 1972, 1-C.
8. Jim Hawkins, "Timmerman Ends His Pitching Slump — Tigers Win, 5–3," *Detroit Free Press*, July 16, 1972, 1-D.
9. "Concession Prices," Detroit Tigers 1972 Official Program and Scorebook.
10. "Tigers Hold Line on Easy-to-Buy Tickets," Detroit Tigers 1972 Official Program and Scorebook.
11. "Remember These Special Dates at Tiger Stadium," Detroit Tigers 1972 Official Program and Scorebook.
12. Jim Hawkins, "No Fuss This Time: Cash Named to Stars," *Detroit Free Press*, July 21, 1972, 1-D.
13. Jim Hawkins, "Slaybacks Wins, 5–1–13 Strikeouts Best for Tiger This Year," *Detroit Free Press*, July 21, 1972, D-1.
14. *Sporting News*, August 5, 1972.
15. Pitchers' hitting statistics compiled from Retrosheet.
16. *Sporting News*, August 5, 1972.
17. *Ibid.*
18. Wikipedia, "Ed Brinkman," http://en.wikipedia.org/wiki/Ed_Brinkman.
19. *Sporting News*, August 5, 1972.

Chapter VII

1. Jim Hawkins, "Tigers Win 2 ... Lead by 2?," *Detroit Free Press*, July 28, 1972, 1-D.
2. Jim Hawkins, "Pain in Side Idles Timmerman," *Detroit Free Press*, July 31, 1972, 4-D.
3. Jim Hawkins, "Martin Gives Up on His Buddy Perranoski," *Detroit Free Press*, August 1, 1972, 2-D.
4. Jim Hawkins, "Brewers Do It ... Sweep Tigers, 6–3," *Detroit Free Press*, August 4, 1972, 1-D.
5. Jim Hawkins, "Tigers' New 'Duke' Slaps Indians, 4–3," *Detroit Free Press*, August 6, 1972, 1-C.
6. *Ibid.*, 2-C.
7. Jim Hawkins, "Tigers Get Pitching Help, Buy Fryman from Phils," *Detroit Free Press*, August 3, 1972, 5D.
8. Joe Falls, "'8-Year Itch' Hits The Bigtown," *Detroit Free Press*, August 8, 1972, 1-D.
9. Jim Hawkins, "Yanks in Race, Too! Beat Mick, 4–2," *Detroit Free Press*, August 9, 1972, 1-D.
10. *Ibid.*
11. Joe Falls, "Noisy Yank Fans Deserve Assist for Win," *Detroit Free Press*, August 10, 1972, 1-D.
12. Joe Falls, "Lyle Has Yankees Thinking of Flag," *Detroit Free Press*, August 11, 1972, 1-D.
13. *Ibid.*
14. Jim Hawkins, "Yanks Tighten Race ... Beat Tigers, 1–0," *Detroit Free Press*, August 11, 1972, 1-D.
15. Jim Hawkins, "Indians Slip Lolich Another 'Mickey,' 6–1," *Detroit Free Press*, August 13, 1972, 1-D.
16. Charlie Vincent, "'Undecided' Joins Tiger Staff Again," *Detroit Free Press*, August 14, 1972, 5-D.
17. Jim Hawkins, "Still Falling ... Tigers in 3rd Place," *Detroit Free Press*, August 14, 1972, 1-D.
18. Curt Sylvester, "All Is Quiet in Tiger Den," *Detroit Free Press*, August 16, 1972, 1-D.
19. Bruce Markusen, "The Baseball Guru — Oakland A's Diary — Archive," http://baseballguru.com/markusen, August 22.
20. Jim Hawkins, "Whammo! Freehan's Slam Wins, 7–5," *Detroit Free Press*, August 24, 1972, 1-D.
21. William Montalbano, "Nixon Vows Tax Relief, Woos Dems," *Detroit Free Press*, August 24, 1972, 1A.
22. Jim Hawkins, "Why Orioles Just One of Gang Now," *Detroit Free Press*, August 28, 1972, 1-C.

Chapter VIII

1. *Sporting News*, September 16, 1972.
2. *Ibid.*
3. Wikipedia, "1972 Summer Olympics," http://en.wikipedia.org/wiki/1972_Summer_Olympics.
4. *Sporting News*, September 16, 1972.
5. Charlie Vincent, "Hitting Will Decide AL East, Aspromonte Says," *Detroit Free Press*, September 5, 1972, 3-D.
6. Wikipedia, "Munich Massacre," http://en.wik/org/wikipedia/munich_massacre.
7. Retrosheet, http://www.retrosheet.org.
8. Jim Hawkins, "Lolich Drops By the White House to Say Hi to President Nixon," *Detroit Free Press*, September 8, 1972, 3-D.
9. Joe Falls, "Is There a Cure for Tiger Bats?" *Detroit Free Press*, September 11, 1972, 1-D.
10. Wikipedia, "1972 Summer Olympics," http://en.wikipedia.org/wiki/1972_Summer_Olympics.
11. Joe Falls, "'Babe' Brinkman Belts One — And Music Fills the Air," *Detroit Free Press*, September 11, 1972, 1-D.
12. *Ibid.*
13. Charlie Vincent, "'I Just Hope I Can Help Them Win It' — Howard," *Detroit Free Press*, September 14, 1972, 1-D.
14. Jim Hawkins, "Tigers, Bosox, O's All Win," *Detroit Free Press*, September 17, 1972, 1-C.
15. *Ibid.*
16. "Yankees Win 'Must' Game," *Detroit Free Press*, September 18, 1972, 1-D.
17. The Kansas City Chiefs were picked by *Cord Sportfacts Pro Football Guide 1972*, among others, to be in the Super Bowl for the 1972 season. *Cord Sportfacts Pro Football Guide 1972* (New York: Cord, 1972).
18. "1972 Cleveland Indians Batting, Pitching, & Fielding Statistics," Baseball-Reference.com, http://www.baseball-reference.com/teams/CLE/1972.shtml.
19. Angell, *Five Seasons*, 43.

20. *Sporting News*, September 1972.
21. Compiled from Retrosheet.org.
22. Joe Falls, "Eddie Kasko Defends His Pitcher Pick," *Detroit Free Press*, September 22, 1972, 1-D.
23. Joe Falls, "Calm Billy Takes Loss in Stride," *Detroit Free Press*, September 23, 1972, 3-D.
24. Joe Falls, "Pennant Pressure Is Yaz's Burden," *Detroit Free Press*, September 23, 1972, 1-D.
25. Jim Hawkins, "Highway Robbery! Bosox 3, Tigers 2," *Detroit Free Press*, September 23, 1972, 1-D.
26. *Ibid.*, 3-D.
27. "It's World Series Ticket Time!" *Detroit Free Press*, September 24, 1972, F-1.
28. Jim Hawkins, "Tiger Bats 'Blind' Bosox ... Lolich Coasts Home, 7–1," *Detroit Free Press*, September 24, 1972, 1-F.
29. *Ibid.*, 7-F.
30. Joe Falls, "World's Rosy Again! Tigers Hitting," *Detroit Free Press*, September 24, 1972, 7-F.
31. Hawkins, "Tiger Bats," *Detroit Free Press*, September 24, 1972, 1-F.
32. Joe Falls, "No Fast Ball, Tiant 'Beat Them with My Head,'" *Detroit Free Press*, September 25, 1972, 4-D.
33. Jim Hawkins, "Tigers Get a Breather for Stretch Run," *Detroit Free Press*, September 26, 1972, 1-D.
34. *Ibid.*
35. Joe Falls, "Excited? 'You Bet!' Says Stunned Billy," *Detroit Free Press*, September 28, 1972, 1-D.
36. *Ibid.*, 5-D.
37. "Bosox Trim Brewers, 7–5," *Detroit Free Press*, September 28, 1972, 1-D.
38. Joe Falls, "The Yankees' Toes 'Are Still Wiggling,'" *Detroit Free Press*, September 29, 1972, 7-D.
39. *Ibid.*
40. *Ibid.*
41. Charlie Vincent, "Martin Blames Lolich," *Detroit Free Press*, September 29, 1972, 1-D.

Chapter IX

1. Joe Falls, "Win Won't Satisfy Billy ... He's Boiling at Everybody!," *Detroit Free Press*, September 30, 1972, 1-D.
2. *Ibid.*, 3-D.
3. Charlie Vincent, "Bosox Eliminate Orioles," *Detroit Free Press*, September 30, 1972, 1-D.
4. Falls, "Win Won't Satisfy," *Detroit Free Press*, 1-D.
5. Jim Hawkins, "Tigers Win ... So Do Bosox," *Detroit Free Press*, October 1, 1972, 1-E.
6. Jim Hawkins, "Coleman Gets a Chance to Win It All for Tigers," *Detroit Free Press*, October 1, 1972, 5-E.
7. Charlie Vincent, "Yaz Sparks Boston, 3–1," *Detroit Free Press*, October 1, 1972, 1-E.
8. Hawkins, "Tigers Win," The *Detroit Free Press*, 1-E.
9. Jim Hawkins, "Hiller Beat Heart Attack ... Nothing Can Rile Him Now," *Detroit Free Press*, October 2, 1972, 1-D.
10. Jim Hawkins, "It's Best of 3 for All the Marbles!," *Detroit Free Press*, October 2, 1972, 1-D.
11. Joe Falls, "Tiger Pennant Hopes Zoom; Big Series Starts Tonight," The *Detroit Free Press*, October 2, 1972, 1-A.
12. Charlie Vincent, "Thank You, Birds! Red Sox Lose, 2–1," *Detroit Free Press*, October 2, 1972, 1D.
13. "Kaline's Eyes Give Curtis Hint of Trouble," *Boston Globe*, October 3, 1972, 55.
14. Curt Sylvester, "'Best I've Pitched This Year'—Lolich," *Detroit Free Press*, October 3, 1972, 1-D.
15. Joe Falls, "Al Kaline, You're Just Too Much!," *Detroit Free Press*, October 3, 1972, 1-D.
16. "Kaline's Eyes," *Boston Globe*, October 3, 1972, 55.
17. Charlie Vincent, "'I Hit Grass and I Fell,' Looie Moans," *Detroit Free Press*, October 3, 1972, 1D.
18. Harold Kaese, "Red Sox Hoping for One Big, Last Rebound," *Boston Globe*, October 3, 1972, 1.
19. Cliff Keane, "Lolich Was Early, Gave Self 'Good Fight Talk,'" *Boston Globe*, October 3, 1972, 52.
20. Vincent, "I Hit Grass," *Detroit Free Press*, 2-D.
21. Falls, *Detroit Tigers*, 94.
22. Boston Red Sox's Radio Broadcast of October 3, 1972, Danrick Enterprises L.L.C.
23. Joe Falls, "Tigers Do It—Fans Go Wild," *Detroit Free Press*, October 4, 1972, 1-A.
24. Falls, "Al Kaline, You're Just," *Detroit Free Press*, October 3, 1972, 1-D.
25. Curt Sylvester and Jack Saylor, "'Hey,

Gimme a Tiger!,'" *Detroit Free Press*, October 4, 1972, 1-D.

26. Larry Osterman interview, November 1, 2008.

27. James Harper, "Curses! Tigers Tongues Get Twisted," *Detroit Free Press*, October 5, 1972, 1-A.

28. Bettelou Peterson, "What TV Is All About: On the Spot for Tiger Joy," *Detroit Free Press*, October 5, 1972, 8-C.

29. Charlie Vincent, "Only Honking Horns Broke the Silence in Bosox Dressing Room," *Detroit Free Press*, October 4, 1972, 2-D.

30. Sylvester and Saylor, "Hey, Gimme," *Detroit Free Press*, 3-D.

31. *Ibid.*

32. Angell, *Five Seasons*, 43.

33. William Schmidt and Louis Heldman, "Baseball Fever Rages — Everyone's a Fan," *Detroit Free Press*, October 5, 1972, 3-A.

34. Curt Sylvester, "Super Fielding Brinkman Sets 2 Major League Marks," *Detroit Free Press*, October 5, 1972, 2-D.

35. Jim Hawkins, "Martin's Juggling Saved the Tigers," *Detroit Free Press*, October 7, 1972, 5-D.

36. Falls, "Tigers Do It," *Detroit Free Press*, October 4, 1972, 8-A.

Chapter X

1. Cantor, *The Tigers of '68*, 168.

2. Wikipedia, "Charlie Finley," http://en.wikipedia.org/wiki/Charlie_Finley.

3. Jim Hawkins, "A's Boot Frank Off Tiger Bench," *Detroit Free Press*, October 6, 1972, 1-D.

4. *Ibid.*

5. Jim Hawkins, "A's Finley Calls Billy a 'Liar,'" *Detroit Free Press*, October 7, 1972, 1-D.

6. Hawkins, "A's Boot Frank," *Detroit Free Press*, October 6, 1972, 1-D.

7. Jim Hawkins, "A's Boast ... But Tigers Say They'll Show 'Em," *Detroit Free Press*, October 6, 1972, 1-D.

8. Jim Hawkins, "Here We Go Again! Mick vs. A's," *Detroit Free Press*, October 7, 1972, 1-D.

9. Joe Falls, "Reggie Dedicated to Be the Best," *Detroit Free Press*, October 7, 1972, 1-D.

10. Hawkins, "Here We Go Again," *Detroit Free Press*, October 7, 1972, 5-D

11. Hawkins, "A's Boast," *Detroit Free Press*, October 6, 1972, 6-D.

12. Hawkins, "A's Finley Calls," *Detroit Free Press*, October 7, 1972, 5-D.

13. Bruce Markusen, "The Baseball Guru — Oakland A's Diary — Archive," http://baseballguru.com/markusen/oakplayoffs.html.

14. Joe Falls, "Seelback 'Made the Right Play' on Throw — Billy Martin," *Detroit Free Press*, October 8, 1972, 5-E.

15. NBC Broadcast of Game Two between Detroit and Oakland, October 8, 1972.

16. Joe Falls, "Misfired Squeeze Beat Us — Billy," *Detroit Free Press*, October 8, 1972, 5-E.

17. *Ibid.*

18. Falls, "Seelback Made," *Detroit Free Press* , October 8, 1972, 5-E.

19. *Ibid.*

20. Jim Hawkins, "Oops! Error Beats Tigers," *Detroit Free Press*, October 8, 1972, 1-E.

21. Falls, "Seelback Made," *Detroit Free Press* , October 8, 1972, 5-E.

22. Jim Hawkins, "Numb Foot Idles Eddie Brinkman," *Detroit Free Press*, October 9, 1972, 2-D.

23. *Ibid.*

24. Joe Falls, "A's Star Hurls Bat at Tiger Pitcher," *Detroit Free Press*, October 9, 1972, 2-A.

25. *Sporting News*, October 17, 1972.

26. Falls, "A's Star Hurls Bat," *Detroit Free Press*, October 9, 1972, 1-A.

27. *Ibid.*, 2-A.

28. *Sporting News*, October 17, 1972.

29. Falls, "A's Star Hurls Bat," *Detroit Free Press*, October 9, 1972, 2-A.

30. Jim Hawkins, "Tigers Have Backs to Wall Now...," *Detroit Free Press*, October 9, 1972, 1-D.

31. Bruce Markusen, "The Baseball Guru — Oakland A's Diary — Archive," http://baseballguru.com/markusen/oakplayoffs.html.

32. *Sporting News*, October 17, 1972.

33. Falls, "A's Star Hurls Bat," *Detroit Free Press*, October 9, 1972, 1-A.

34. *Ibid.*

Chapter XI

1. Howard Erickson, "A's Beat Cronin to Punch ... Campy Is Long-Gone!," *Detroit Free Press*, October 10, 1972, 1-C.

2. Curt Sylvester, "Campy Suspension 'Sufficient'—Billy," *Detroit Free Press*, October 10, 1972, 1C.

3. *Sporting News*, October 21, 1972.

4. Sylvester, "Campy Suspension," *Detroit Free Press*, October 10, 1972, 1-C.

5. Erickson, "A's Beat Cronin," *Detroit Free Press*, 6-C.

6. "'There's No Pressure'—Maxvill," *Detroit Free Press*, October 10, 1972, 6-C.

7. Sylvester, "Campy Suspension," *Detroit Free Press*, October 10, 1972, 6-C.

8. Jim Neubacher, "A's Ready for Big Exodus; Tigers Send 'Em Unpacking," *Detroit Free Press*, October 11, 1972, 1-A.

9. Joe Falls, "Oakland Crowds: So-So," *Detroit Free Press*, October 10, 1972, 1-C.

10. Curt Sylvester, "Joe's Forkball Did It," *Detroit Free Press*, October 11, 1972, 1-D.

11. Jim Hawkins, "That's Better! Tigers, 3–0," *Detroit Free Press*, October 11, 1972, 1-D.

12. Sylvester, "Joe's Forkball," *Detroit Free Press*, October 11, 1972, 1-D.

13. Hawkins, "That's Better!" The *Detroit Free Press*, October 11, 1972, 1-D.

14. Joe Falls, "Long Time Coming ... Hero's Role for Ike," *Detroit Free Press*, October 11, 1972, 1-D.

15. Curt Sylvester, "A's Not Scared by Lolich...," *Detroit Free Press*, October 11, 1972, 4-D.

16. Hawkins, "That's Better!," *Detroit Free Press*, October 11, 1972, 4-D.

17. Oakland A's Radio Broadcast of Game Four, October 11, 1972, Danrick Enterprises, L.L.C.

18. A's Radio Broadcast, October 11, 1972.

19. A's Radio Broadcast, October 11, 1972.

20. Joe Falls, "'Let's Give 'Em a Finish!' Tigers Cried," *Detroit Free Press*, October 12, 1972, 9-D.

21. Jim Hawkins, "Blue Moon Has Billy Red Hot," *Detroit Free Press*, October 12, 1972, 9-D.

22. Falls, "'Let's Give 'Em a Finish!'" *Detroit Free Press*, 1-D.

23. *Ibid.*

24. *Ibid.*, 9-D.

25. *Ibid.*, 1-D.

26. Jim Hawkins, "Miracles Do Happen, Tigers!" *Detroit Free Press*, October 12, 1972, 1-D.

27. Curt Sylvester, "'Crushed' Is the Word for Once-Confident A's Now," *Detroit Free Press*, October 12, 1972, 5-D.

28. *Ibid.*

29. *Ibid.*

30. Hawkins, "Blue Moon," *Detroit Free Press*, October 12, 1972, 9-D.

31. "Tigers Favored, 11–10," *Detroit Free Press*, October 12, 1972, 1-D.

32. Oakland A's Radio Broadcast of Game Five, October 12, 1972.

33. *Sporting News*, October 22, 1972.

34. Larry Osterman interview, November 1, 2008.

35. *Ibid.*

36. *Sporting News*, October 22, 1972.

37. Jim Hawkins, "Blue Moon, Vida Blue Hurl A's into Series," *Detroit Free Press*, October 13, 1972, 1-D.

38. *Sporting News*, October 22, 1972.

39. Charlie Vincent, "Cash Howard Blast Umpire's Call," *Detroit Free Press*, October 13, 1972, 1-D.

40. *Sporting News*, October 22, 1972.

41. Charlie Vincent, "The Champagne Was There but Tigers Just Drank Beer," *Detroit Free Press*, October 13, 1972, 6-D.

42. Hawkins, "Blue Moon, Vida Blue," *Detroit Free Press*, October 13, 1972, 1-D

43. Vincent, "The Champagne," The *Detroit Free Press*, October 13, 1972, 6-D.

44. *Sporting News*, October 22, 1972.

45. Hawkins, "Blue Moon, Vida Blue," *Detroit Free Press*, October 13, 1972, 6-D.

46. Curt Sylvester, "'I'm Still Sour' About Finley—Vida," *Detroit Free Press*, October 13, 1972, 1-D.

47. *Sporting News*, October 22, 1972.

48. Sylvester, "'I'm Still Sour,'" *Detroit Free Press*, October 13, 1972, 6-D.

49. *Sporting News*, October 22, 1972.

50. *Ibid.*

Chapter XII

1. The History Place, "The Vietnam War: The Bitter End 1969–1975," http://www.historyplace.com/unitedstates/vietnam/index-1969.html.

2. Wikipedia, "Apollo 17," http://en.wikipedia.org/wiki/Apollo_17.

3. "MVPs," *Street and Smith's 1973 Baseball Yearbook.*

4. Joseph L. Reichler, *The Baseball Encyclopedia* (New York: Macmillan, 1985).

5. *Street and Smith's 1973 Baseball Yearbook*, 25–26

6. *Ibid.*, 45.

7. Retrosheet, http://www.retrosheet.org.

8. Denny McLain and Eli Zaret, *I Told You I Wasn't Perfect* (Chicago: Triumph, 2007).

9. Circumstances surrounding Clemente's death; David Maraniss, *Clemente* (New York: Simon & Schuster, 2006), 287–354.

10. "Free Agency Brought Big Changes," *USA Today*, December 22, 2000, http://www.usatoday.com/sports/comment/colbod.htm.

Chapter XIII

1. *Sporting News*, November 1972.

2. "MVPs," *Street and Smith's 1973 Baseball Yearbook*.

3. Martin and Golenbock, *Number 1*, 286.

4. *Sporting News*, September 22, 1973.

5. *Ibid.*

6. *Ibid.*

7. Wikipedia, "Bill Freehan," http://en.wikipedia.org/wiki/Bill_Freehan.

8. Dick Tracewski interview, January 12, 2009.

9. Jim Northrup interview, November 20, 2008.

10. Tracewski interview.

11. Northrup interview.

12. Osterman interview.

13. Northrup interview.

14. Ernie Harwell interview, October 14, 2008.

15. Andy Sneddon, "Former Tiger Bill Freehan Longs for the Good Old Days," *Petoskey News-Review*, January 5, 2005.

16. Tracewski interview.

17. Tracewski interview.

18. Sneddon, "Former Tiger Bill Freehan," *Petoskey News-Review*, January 5, 2005.

19. Northrup interview.

Bibliography

Books

Angell, Roger. *Five Seasons*. New York, NY: Popular Library, 1978.

Cantor, George. *The Tigers of '68*. Dallas, TX: Taylor, 1997.

Cord Sportfacts Pro Football Guide 1972. New York: Cord, 1972.

Falls, Joe. *Baseball's Great Teams: Detroit Tigers*. New York: Macmillan, 1975.

Marannis, David. *Clemente*. New York: Simon & Schuster, 2006.

Markusen, Bruce. "Oakland A's Diary-Archive," (http://baseballguru.com/markusen).

Martin, Billy, and Peter Golenbock. *Number 1*. New York: Dell, 1980.

McLain, Denny, and Eli Zaret. *I Told You I Wasn't Perfect*. Chicago: Triumph, 2007.

Newport, Frank. "History Shows Presidential Job Approval Ratings Can Plummet Rapidly," *Gallup News Service*, 11 February 1998.

Reichler, Joseph L., editor. *The Baseball Encyclopedia*. New York: Macmillan, 1985.

Sneddon, Andy. "Former Tiger Bill Freehan Longs for the Good Old Days." *Petoskey News-Review*, 5 January 2005.

Interviews

Harwell, Ernie. Phone interview with author. 14 October 2008.

Northrup, Jim. Phone interview by author. 20 October 2008

Osterman, Larry. Phone interview by author. 2 November 2008.

Tracewski, Richard. Phone interview by author. 12 January 2009.

Newspapers and Magazines

Boston Globe

Detroit Free Press

"Free Agency Brought Big Changes." *USA Today*. 22 December 2000.

The Sporting News

Websites

Baseball-reference.com

Ballparktour.com

Historyplace.com

Musicoutfitters.com

Retrosheet.org

Wikipedia.org

Other

Andre, Sam E., editor. *Street and Smith's Official Yearbook*. New York: Conde Nast, 1973.

Boston Red Sox Radio Broadcast of 3 October 1972. West Paterson, NJ: Danrick Enterprises. Audio cassette.

Detroit Tigers 1969 Official Yearbook.

Detroit Tigers 1972 Official Program and Scorebook.

Oakland Athletics Radio Broadcasts of 10, 11, and 12 October 1972. West Paterson, NJ: Danrick Enterprises. Audio cassette.

Index